Cisco LAN Switching Fundamentals

David Barnes, CCIE No. 6563
Basir Sakandar, CCIE No. 6040

Cisco Press

Cisco Press
800 East 96th Street
Indianapolis, IN 46240 USA

Cisco LAN Switching Fundamentals

David Barnes
Basir Sakandar

Copyright © 2005 Cisco Systems, Inc.

Published by:
Cisco Press
800 East 96th Street
Indianapolis, IN 46240 USA

Printed in the United States of America 2 3 4 5 6 7 8 9 0

Second Printing September 2005

Library of Congress Cataloging-in-Publication Number: 2002100685

ISBN: 1-58705-089-7

Trademark Acknowledgments

All terms mentioned in this book that are known to be trademarks or service marks have been appropriately capitalized. Cisco Press or Cisco Systems, Inc., cannot attest to the accuracy of this information. Use of a term in this book should not be regarded as affecting the validity of any trademark or service mark.

Warning and Disclaimer

This book is designed to provide information about Cisco LAN switching. Every effort has been made to make this book as complete and as accurate as possible, but no warranty or fitness is implied.

The information is provided on an "as is" basis. The author, Cisco Press, and Cisco Systems, Inc., shall have neither liability nor responsibility to any person or entity with respect to any loss or damages arising from the information contained in this book or from the use of the discs or programs that may accompany it.

The opinions expressed in this book belong to the author and are not necessarily those of Cisco Systems, Inc.

Corporate and Government Sales

Cisco Press offers excellent discounts on this book when ordered in quantity for bulk purchases or special sales. For more information, please contact:

U.S. Corporate and Government Sales   1-800-382-3419   corpsales@pearsontechgroup.com

For sales outside of the U.S. please contact: international@pearsoned.com

Feedback Information

At Cisco Press, our goal is to create in-depth technical books of the highest quality and value. Each book is crafted with care and precision, undergoing rigorous development that involves the unique expertise of members from the professional technical community.

Readers' feedback is a natural continuation of this process. If you have any comments regarding how we could improve the quality of this book, or otherwise alter it to better suit your needs, you can contact us through e-mail at feedback@ciscopress.com. Please make sure to include the book title and ISBN in your message.

We greatly appreciate your assistance.

Publisher	John Wait
Editor-in-Chief	John Kane
Executive Editor	Brett Bartow
Cisco Representative	Anthony Wolfenden
Cisco Press Program Manager	Nannette M. Noble
Production Manager	Patrick Kanouse
Development Editor	Dayna Isley
Project Editor	San Dee Phillips
Copy Editor	Katherin Bidwell
Contributing Author	John Tiso
Technical Editors	Richard Froom and Geoff Tagg
Team Coordinator	Tammi Barnett
Cover Designer	Louisa Adair
Composition	Octal Publishing, Inc.
Indexer	Brad Herriman

CISCO SYSTEMS

Corporate Headquarters
Cisco Systems, Inc.
170 West Tasman Drive
San Jose, CA 95134-1706
USA
www.cisco.com
Tel: 408 526-4000
      800 553-NETS (6387)
Fax: 408 526-4100

European Headquarters
Cisco Systems International BV
Haarlerbergpark
Haarlerbergweg 13-19
1101 CH Amsterdam
The Netherlands
www-europe.cisco.com
Tel: 31 0 20 357 1000
Fax: 31 0 20 357 1100

Americas Headquarters
Cisco Systems, Inc.
170 West Tasman Drive
San Jose, CA 95134-1706
USA
www.cisco.com
Tel: 408 526-7660
Fax: 408 527-0883

Asia Pacific Headquarters
Cisco Systems, Inc.
Capital Tower
168 Robinson Road
#22-01 to #29-01
Singapore 068912
www.cisco.com
Tel: +65 6317 7777
Fax: +65 6317 7799

Cisco Systems has more than 200 offices in the following countries and regions. Addresses, phone numbers, and fax numbers are listed on the
Cisco.com Web site at www.cisco.com/go/offices.

Argentina • Australia • Austria • Belgium • Brazil • Bulgaria • Canada • Chile • China PRC • Colombia • Costa Rica • Croatia • Czech Republic
Denmark • Dubai, UAE • Finland • France • Germany • Greece • Hong Kong SAR • Hungary • India • Indonesia • Ireland • Israel • Italy
Japan • Korea • Luxembourg • Malaysia • Mexico • The Netherlands • New Zealand • Norway • Peru • Philippines • Poland • Portugal
Puerto Rico • Romania • Russia • Saudi Arabia • Scotland • Singapore • Slovakia • Slovenia • South Africa • Spain • Sweden
Switzerland • Taiwan • Thailand • Turkey • Ukraine • United Kingdom • United States • Venezuela • Vietnam • Zimbabwe

About the Authors

David Barnes is a senior manager for Cisco Advanced Services based in Richardson, Texas. He is CCIE No. 6563, MCSE+I, Master CNE, and a Certified Technical Trainer. David manages the Advanced Services team, which is responsible for providing technical expertise on all Cisco routing and switching products to many of the largest Cisco customers. He began his career at Cisco Systems, Inc., as a network consulting engineer specializing in LAN Switching in 1999. In the 10 years before he joined Cisco, David designed, implemented, and managed networks for numerous Fortune 500 companies.

Basir Sakandar, CCIE No. 6040, has dual certifications in Routing and Switching and in Security. He received his undergraduate degree from University of Southern California (USC) in 1997. His current role at Cisco Systems is an advanced services engineer out of Richardson, Texas, office. He has helped with design and implementation of various technologies for Fortune 100 companies.

Contributing Author

John Tiso, CCIE No. 5162, is a senior consultant for Networked Information Systems (NIS), a Cisco Systems Gold Partner in Woburn, Massachusetts. John has a bachelor of science degree from Adelphi University and a variety of industry certifications. John has been published in several industry trade journals and has been a technical editor for Cisco Press and McGraw-Hill for many years. John can be reached at johnt@jtiso.com.

About the Technical Reviewers

Richard Froom, CCIE No. 5102, is a technical leader for the Storage Area Network (SAN) team of the Internet Switching Business Unit—Financial Test Lab at Cisco Systems. Richard has been with Cisco for six years, previously serving as a support engineer troubleshooting customers' networks and a technical leader dealing with Cisco Catalyst products. Richard, being involved with Catalyst product field trials, has been crucial in driving troubleshooting capabilities of Catalyst products and software. He has also contributed substantially to the Cisco.com LAN Technologies Technical Tips and has written white papers dealing with 802.3 auto-negotiation and Hot Standby Router Protocol (HSRP). Richard is currently testing Cisco SAN solutions. Richard is also the coauthor of *CCNP Self-Study: Building Cisco Multilayer Switched Networks (BCMSN)*, Second Edition (ISBN 1-58705-150-8), and *Cisco Catalyst QoS: Quality of Service in Campus Networks* (ISBN 1-58705-120-6) from Cisco Press. He attended Clemson University where he completed his bachelor of science in computer engineering.

Geoff Tagg runs a networking consultancy in the UK, where he has more than 20 years experience of working with companies ranging from small local businesses to large multinationals. Prior to that, he had 15 years experience of systems programming on a variety of mainframe and minicomputers. Geoff's specialty is Internet Protocol (IP) networking over a range of LAN and WAN technologies, including Ethernet, Frame Relay, ATM, and ISDN. Geoff lives in Oxford, England, with his wife Christine and family and is a visiting professor at nearby Oxford Brookes University.

Dedications

David Barnes: For Papa

Basir Sakandar: To my mom and to my wonderful nephews and niece

Acknowledgments

David Barnes: I would like to thank my father for bringing home a computer in 1985 instead of a drum set. While I sometimes still dream of being a rock star, I am glad I am in what I believe is an exciting and ever-changing industry, and I am fortunate to work for the best company in the world—Cisco Systems. Thanks goes to John Tiso for his ideas and for getting this started, Richard and Geoff for their efforts to make this a better book, and Brett Bartow and Dayna Isley at Cisco Press for all of their assistance on this project.

Basir Sakandar: I would like to thank everyone who participated in developing this book.

Contents at a Glance

Table of Contents

Icons Used in This Book

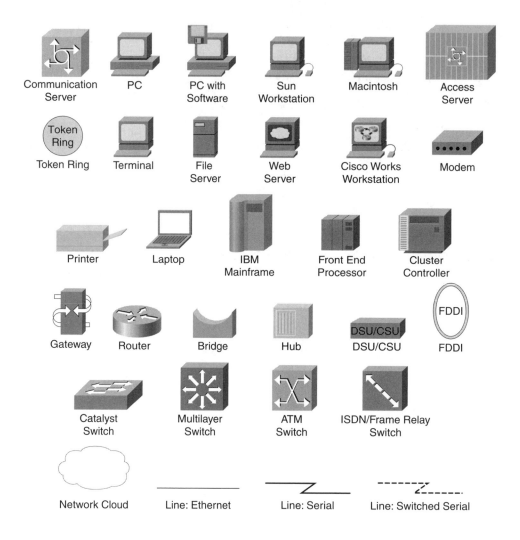

Command Syntax Conventions

The conventions used to present command syntax in this book are the same conventions used in the *Cisco IOS Command Reference*, as follows:

- **Boldface** indicates commands and keywords that are entered literally as shown. In examples (not syntax), boldface indicates user input (for example, a **show** command).

- *Italics* indicates arguments for which you supply values.

- Square brackets ([and]) indicate optional elements.

- Braces ({ and }) contain a choice of required keywords.

- Vertical bars (|) separate alternative, mutually exclusive elements.

- Braces and vertical bars within square brackets—for example, [x {y | z}]—indicate a required choice within an optional element. You do not need to enter what is in the brackets, but if you do, you have some required choices in the braces.

Introduction

Even as Cisco continues to expand its line of products into areas such as IP telephony, content networking, and security, its LAN switching products continue to account for more than half of the company's overall product sales. Because switching devices are considered by many to be the "plumbing" of every campus networking environment, LAN switching is an area of networking that virtually all network engineers need to understand, at least at a fundamental level. It is for this reason we set out to write the *Cisco LAN Switching Fundamentals* book for Cisco Press. Although a wide variety of books exists on traditional routing topics, we saw a need to write a book for those who might have had their hands on a router before, but did not have as much exposure to Cisco LAN switching products.

Goals and Objectives

Cisco LAN Switching Fundamentals will give you exposure to real-world networking and Catalyst switching best practices. Our desire is to provide much more than simply an overview of the various switch architectures, protocols, and features they support. As a result, we kept a few key objectives in mind when writing the book, including the following:

- Provide background on how the architecture and features of Cisco Catalyst switches evolved since their introduction

- Give enough depth of information for an engineer to become functional in each technology in a relatively short period of time

- Offer enough information on the range of LAN switching topics to serve as a reference for everyday use

Who Should Read This Book?

Cisco LAN Switching Fundamentals is intended for beginning and intermediate engineers looking to understand the architecture, configuration, and operation of Cisco Catalyst switches. You will learn about a wide range of topics including quality of service (QoS), multicast, spanning tree, and native and hybrid software. Many design and configuration examples are provided on a wide range of topics that will hopefully make the book a good reference, and a useful read for those wishing to master the fundamentals of LAN switching.

How This Book Is Organized

Cisco LAN Switching Fundamentals is made up of 12 chapters and 1 appendix, as follows:

- **Chapter 1, "LAN Switching Foundation Technologies"**—Chapter 1 creates the building blocks for the rest of the book. It is essential to have an understanding of the basics before tackling the more rigorous topics such as RSTP, QoS, multicast, configuration, and troubleshooting. Chapter 1 discusses the details of various Ethernet technologies and physical and data link layer protocols. Topics of discussion range from introducing Ethernet 10BASE-T to Gigabit Ethernet, and moving on from Transparent Bridging to Spanning Tree.

- **Chapter 2, "LAN Switch Architecture"** — Chapter 2 is dedicated to understanding switching modes, switching paths, and architectures common to many vendor's switches, not only Cisco. This chapter familiarizes you with the some of the challenges of various hardware implementations and their effects on the network. This chapter is a must read before delving into Chapter 3.

- **Chapter 3, "Catalyst Switching Architecture"** — Many of the newest Cisco switching platforms are discussed here in detail. Topics of discussion include the newest Catalyst 6000/6500, 4500, 3750 platforms and even the legacy Catalyst 5000/5500 platforms. There have been great improvements since the popular Catalyst 5000 product line. You will become intimately familiar with the architectures of these platforms.

- **Chapter 4, "Layer 2 Fundamentals"** — Chapter 4 introduces the concept behind virtual LANs (VLANs), types of trunks, VLAN Trunking Protocol (VTP), and private VLANs. This chapter introduces some very important best practices that have been gathered through experience of both authors and the Cisco community. This chapter clears up some confusion regarding VLAN designs, VTP misconfiguration, manual versus VTP pruning, and the significant role of private VLANs.

- **Chapter 5, "Using Catalyst Software"** — This chapter discusses issues such as the difference between native and hybrid code for the Catalyst 6000 product line, hybrid's equivalent command in native code, and the processes in migrating from one code to the other. This chapter also discusses software for the Catalyst 3750 and 4500.

- **Chapter 6, "Understanding Multilayer Switching"** — Multilayer Switching (MLS) is still a source of confusion for many beginner and intermediate engineers. This chapter takes you step by step through the MLS process and discusses the various hardware components involved in making MLS work. This chapter also serves as a good reference.

- **Chapter 7, "Configuring Switches"** — This chapter shows you how to configure Catalyst switches. This chapter provides many examples to familiarize you with the hardware. Configuration examples such as trunking, SNMP, and many others are given through this chapter.

- **Chapter 8, "Understanding Quality of Service on Catalyst 6500"** — In recent years, QoS has become more prominent in the enterprise network. QoS deployment is still in its infancy stage. The exception is with companies who have deployed Voice over IP (VoIP). In VoIP networks, QoS implementation is critical. This chapter introduces the fundamentals of QoS on the Catalyst switches. This chapter takes you through each crucial step as the packet enters a port, and how the packet travels in the switch, and eventually, out of an egress port.

- **Chapter 9, "Implementing Multicast on Catalyst Switches"** — Multicast is another important topic in this book. In this chapter, you are given ample examples and detailed explanations of the more popular multicast features and protocols supported on the Catalyst switches. Some of the more important topics that are introduced are Protocol Independent Multicast (PIM), Internet Group Management Protocol (IGMP) snooping, and Cisco Group Management Protocol (CGMP). This chapter also walks you through how the switch handles and forwards multicast traffic.

- **Chapter 10, "Implementing and Tuning Spanning Tree"** — This chapter describes data link layer features that are available on the Catalyst switches. Features such as BPDU Guard, BPDU Filter, Root Guard, Loop Guard, and so on are discussed. This chapter also covers Rapid Spanning Tree

Protocol (RSTP) and Multiple Spanning Tree (MST). Enterprise companies are currently looking closely at RSTP. Situations exist where spanning tree is necessary because of business or design requirements. RSTP can provide a robust solution in comparison to the legacy Spanning Tree Protocol (STP).

- **Chapter 11, "Design and Implementation Best Practices"**—This chapter focuses entirely on best practices for design and configuration. You are taken through a variety of design options with the goal of providing a stable and available network and avoiding common design pitfalls. The intent of this chapter is to put in practice the theory and practical knowledge gained from the previous chapters.

- **Chapter 12, "Troubleshooting the LAN Switching Configuration"**—This chapter delineates some of the more common steps necessary in troubleshooting Catalyst switches. This chapter introduces common problems that the Cisco Technical Assistance Center (TAC) receives and provides solutions. The strength of this chapter is that it offers you the tools necessary to effectively deal with network problems when they arise.

- **Appendix A, "Catalyst 6500 Series Software Conversion"**—This appendix walks through the options for converting from hybrid software to native software and back again for the Catalyst 6500 series. The appendix begins with an overview of the automated tool for hybrid software to native software conversion, and follows up with the step-by-step manual conversion process using a Supervisor 720. Because no automated tool exists for native software to hybrid software conversion, the appendix shows the step-by-step manual process for converting from native software to hybrid software.

This chapter covers the following topics:

- OSI model
- Ethernet
- Transparent bridging
- Broadcasts and multicasts
- Spanning Tree Protocol

CHAPTER 1

LAN Switching Foundation Technologies

Anyone responsible for implementing and supporting local-area networks (LANs) is increasingly challenged with understanding the fundamental concepts behind Ethernet switching. Almost all new local-area networking infrastructure is based on some type of Ethernet (10 Mbps/100 Mbps/1000 Mbps). It is also worth noting that newer Ethernet implementations include support for the 10 Gbps rate. This book focuses on the concepts, architecture, configuration, and troubleshooting of Cisco Ethernet switches.

Virtually every discussion of networking begins with at least a mention of the Open System Interconnection (OSI) reference model, and for good reason. The OSI model serves as a useful framework for classifying the characteristics and operation of networking devices into seven categories, or layers. While a detailed examination of the OSI model is beyond the scope of this book, a brief overview is useful in understanding the operation of Ethernet switching.

After learning the basic concepts of the OSI model, this chapter moves on to introduce the fundamentals of Ethernet, transparent bridging, and the Spanning Tree Protocol.

OSI Model

The application of a layered framework to networking allows individual layers to be modified, without affecting the layers above or below. The OSI model can be thought of as the networking community's application of the concept of interchangeable parts.

Figure 1-1 illustrates the seven layers of the OSI model. Each layer is tasked with specific functions that allow for the eventual communication of network devices. Note that the model is divided into upper layers and lower layers, which are described in the next sections.

Figure 1-1   *OSI Layers*

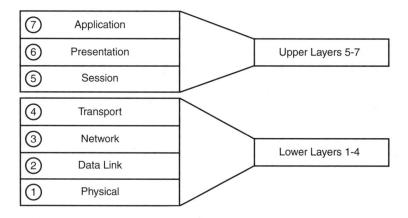

OSI Upper Layers

The upper OSI layers provide application level support such as the user interface, data formatting, and communication sessions. The upper layers are as follows:

- **Application**—The layer where applications and users interface with the network. Examples include web browsers, electronic mail, or a word processing program.

- **Presentation**—The layer that controls format translation and provides data encryption and compression. Examples include ASCII and JPEG.

- Session—The layer responsible for establishing, maintaining, and terminating sessions between presentation layer entities. Protocols that fall at this layer include NetBIOS and RPC.

OSI Lower Layers

The lower OSI layers define how data moves through the network. Because Ethernet itself and the switching of Ethernet frames are classified in the lower OSI layers, most of the discussion in this book focuses on the lower layers. The lower layers of the OSI model are as follows:

- **Transport**—The layer responsible for error detection and correction, flow control, and data sequencing; also determines the size of the packet. Examples include Transmission Control Protocol (TCP) and User Datagram Protocol (UDP).

- **Network**—The layer responsible for the delivery of data packets. Network layer provides logical addressing and path determination. Examples include Internet Protocol (IP) and Internetwork Packet Exchange (IPX).

- **Data Link**—The layer responsible for access to media, hardware addressing, error detection, flow control, and encapsulation of data into frames. The two major components to Data Link layer are Logical Link Control (LLC) and Media Access Control (MAC). LLC handles error detection and flow control. MAC is responsible for communicating with the adapter card, and the type of media used. Examples include IEEE 802.3 CSMA/CD, 802.12 Demand Priority, and 802.5. Bridges and LAN switches also operate at this layer.

- **Physical**—The layer responsible for defining the electrical properties and physical transmission system. The physical layer is responsible in transmitting and receiving data. Examples include any type of cabling, hubs, repeaters, and fiber optics.

Introducing Ethernet

Ethernet's origins begin with the Aloha Radio System, a packet satellite system developed at the University of Hawaii. Beginning in the late 1960s, the Aloha Radio System was designed to facilitate communication between the university's IBM mainframe, located on the island of Oahu, with card readers located among different islands and ships at sea. Work on the Aloha Radio System proved to be the foundation for most modern packet broadcast systems including Ethernet.

Ethernet as it is known today took shape in the 1970s as a research project at Xerox's Palo Alto Research Center. Ethernet was eventually standardized by Digital, Intel, and Xerox in 1979, and harmonized with the international standard, IEEE 802.3, in 1982.

Modern LAN switched networks are based on the theory and operation of Ethernet. This section discusses the basic theory and operation of Ethernet. The initial version of Ethernet operated with a speed of 3 Mbps and used an algorithm called *carrier sense multiple access collision detect (CSMA/CD)* protocol to determine when a device could use the network. Ethernet is currently available in 10 Mbps, 100 Mbps, 1000 Mbps (1 Gbps), and 10000 Mbps (10 Gbps).

Types of Ethernet

As mentioned earlier, Ethernet provides various data rates with different physical layouts. A variety of Ethernet types have come and gone over the years, such as the following:

- 10BASE5 (Thicknet)
- 10BASE2 (Thinnet)
- 10BASE-FL
- 10BASE-T

In the mid 1990s, 100BASE-T (unshielded twisted-pair [UTP]) and 100BASE-FX (using fiber) were ubiquitous in the enterprise network, and they still are. Since the start of the millennium, enterprise networks have actively implemented Gigabit Ethernet, 1000BASE-T, in their network. The push for today is 10 Gbps in the core of the enterprise network.

Transmission Media

The more common transmission media are twisted pair and fiber optics. Coaxial cable is mentioned in this section for historical purpose. Categories defined under twisted pair support transmission over various distances and data rates. The most common UTP cable in the enterprise network is Category 5, which supports 100 Mbps and 1000 Mbps rates.

Ethernet over Twisted-Pair Cabling

Ethernet technology standards are the responsibility of the IEEE 802.3 working group. This group is responsible for evaluating and eventually approving Ethernet specifications as new Ethernet technologies are developed such as Gigabit and 10Gigabit Ethernet. Although this group defines the standards for Ethernet, it looks to other established standards organizations to define the specifications for physical cabling and connectors. These organizations include the American National Standards Institute (ANSI), Engineering Industry Association (EIA), and Telecommunications Industry Association (TIA). The TIA/EIA published specifications for twisted-pair cabling are found in the TIA/EIA-568-B specification document.

The more common forms of cabling are unshielded twisted-pair (UTP) and optical fiber. Twisted pair cable comes in a variety of forms. The most common categories in today's networks are the following:

- Category 3
- Category 5
- Category 5E
- Category 6

The categories represent the certification of the radio frequency capability of the cabling.

Category 3 was initially designed as voice grade cable and is capable of handling transmissions using up to 16 MHz. Category 5 is capable of handling transmissions up to 100 MHz. Category 5E is an improved version of Category 5; while still limited to 100 MHz, Category 5E defines performance parameters sufficient to support 1000BASE-T operation.

Category 6 provides the best possible performance specification for UTP cabling. Category 6 specifies much stricter requirements for cabling than Category 5 and 5E. The frequency range of Category 6 extends to 250 MHz, in contrast to Category 5 and 5E's 100 MHz. While new cabling installations typically install Category 5E or 6 cabling, Category 5 cabling can be utilized for 1000BASE-T applications. With few exceptions, if 100 Mbps Ethernet is operating without issues up to 100 meters on a Category 5 cable plant, 1000BASE-T will operate as well.

Although 10 Mbps and 100 Mbps Ethernet often use two pairs (pins 1, 2, 3, and 6) of twisted-pair cabling, Gigabit Ethernet over twisted pair uses all four pairs of wiring in the twisted-pair cable.

Even if the actual twisted pair is rated a specific category, it does not imply that a cabling infrastructure properly supports the category specification end-to-end. Installation and accessories (such as patch panels and wall plates) must meet the standard as well. Cable plants should be certified from end-to-end. When installing a cabling infrastructure, the installer should be able to use specialized equipment to verify the specifications of the cabling system from end-to-end.

Ethernet over Fiber Optics

Two major types of fiber used in Ethernet networks are multimode and single mode. Multimode fiber (MMF) is used for short haul applications (up to 2000 m). Examples include campus or building networks. MMF is usually driven by LED or low-power laser-based equipment. Single mode fiber (SMF) is used for longer haul applications (up to 10 km) and the equipment is laser based. SMF is generally used in metropolitan-area networks or carrier networks.

Table 1-1 compares Ethernet types over different transmission media.

Table 1-1   *Comparisons of Ethernet over Various Transmission Media*

Ethernet Type	Media Type	Distance Limitations (meters)	Speed (megabits)	Data Encoding
10BASE-T	UTP Category 3 or better	100	10	Manchester
10BASE-FX – MMF	MMF	2000	10	Manchester
100BASE-TX	UTP Category 5 or better	100	100	4B/5B
100BASE-FX – MMF	MMF	2000	100	4B/5B
100BASE-FX – SMF	SMF	10000	100	4B/5B
1000BASE-SX	MMF	2000	1000	8B/10B
1000BASE-LX	SMF	5000[*]	1000	8B/10B
1000BASE-T	UTP Category 5 or better	100	1000	PAM 5x5

[*]   The Cisco implementation of 1000BASE-LX doubles this distance over the standard to 10,000 meters.

Ethernet over Coax Cabling

The use of coax cable for LANs is virtually nonexistent. One might run into it in an old abandoned building. Ethernet's eventual support of twisted pair cabling in a star topology virtually ended the use of coaxial cabling for Ethernet. Keep in mind that coax cable was not cheap either. Two major types of coax were used: thinnet (also called cheapernet) and thicknet. Thinnet uses 50 ohm coaxi cable (RG-58 A/U) with a maximum length of 185 meters when used for Ethernet. This cable is thinner and more flexible than thicknet, which is also 50 ohm coax cable. It is packaged and insulated differently than thinnet. It requires a specialized tool, a vampire tap, to pierce into and has a maximum length of 500 meters for Ethernet. The vampire tap was used to pierce the outer shielding of the cable, creating an electrical connection between the device and the shared media. Traditionally, thicknet was used as a backbone technology because of its additional shielding. Both thinnet and thicknet are virtually extinct in production networks today.

Ethernet Cross-Over Cabling

Network devices can be categorized as either data circuit equipment (DCE) or data termi-nating equipment (DTE). DCE equipment connects to DTE equipment, similar to the male and female end of a garden hose. DCE equipment usually is a type of concentrator or repeater, like a hub. DTE equipment is usually equipment that generates traffic, like a workstation or host.

Sometimes, it is necessary to connect like equipment. Connecting like devices can be accomplished by altering the twisted-pair media, and taking transmit and receive wires and reversing them. This is commonly called a "cross-over" cable. Figure 1-2 shows an RJ-45 connector with its pinouts. Pins 4, 5, 7, and 8 are not used.

The pinouts are a bit different in a Gigabit scenario because all the pins are used. In addition to the pinouts for 10 Mbps/100 Mbps aforementioned, two additional changes are neces-sary: pin 4 to 7, and 5 to 8.

Figure 1-2   *Crossover Pinouts*

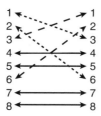

A crossover cable can link DCE to DCE, and DTE to DTE. The exception to connecting like devices is that some devices are manufactured to be connected together. An example would be that some hubs and switches have an uplink or Media Dependent Interface (MDI) port. There is typically a selector that allows the user to toggle between MDI and MDI-X (X for crossover), with MDI-X intentionally reversing the pin out of transmit and receive similar to a crossover cable. A setting of MDI-X allows two DCE devices, such as two hubs or switches, to connect to each other using a typical straight through wired twisted-pair cable.

Ethernet Topology

Ethernet is defined at the data link layer of the OSI model and uses what is commonly referred to as a bus topology. A bus topology consists of devices strung together in series with each device connecting to a long cable or bus. Many devices can tap into the bus and begin communication with all other devices on that cable segment. This means that all the network devices are attached to a single wire and are all peers, sharing the same media.

Bus topology has two very glaring faults. First, if there were a break in the main cable, the entire network would go down. Second, it was hard to troubleshoot. It took time to find out where the cable was cut off. The star topology has been deployed for a long time now and is the standard in the LAN environment. Star topologies link nodes directly to a central point. The central point is either a hub or a LAN switch. Ethernet hubs are multiport repeaters, meaning they repeat the signal out each port except the source port.

The advantages of a physical star topology network are reliability and serviceability. If a point-to-point segment has a break, in the star topology, it will affect only the node on that link. Other nodes on the network continue to operate as if that connection were nonexistent. Ethernet hubs and LAN switches act as the repeaters that centralize the twisted-pair media. Twisted-pair media can also be used to join like devices. Following the OSI model and the concept of interchangeable parts, even Token Ring, which is a logical ring, can use a physical star topology with twisted pair.

Ethernet Logical Addressing

In Ethernet, LAN devices must have a unique identifier on that specific domain. LAN devices use a Media Access Control (MAC) address for such purpose. MAC addresses are also referred to as *hardware addresses* or *burned-in addresses* because they are usually programmed into the Ethernet adapter by the manufacturer of the hardware.

The format of a MAC address is a 48-bit hexadecimal address. Because hexadecimal uses the digits 0-9 and the letters a-f (for numbers 10-15), this yields a 12-digit address. MAC addresses are represented in any one of four formats. All the formats properly identify a MAC address and differ only in the field separators, as follows:

- Dashes between each two characters: 00-01-03-23-31-DD
- Colons instead of dashes between each two characters: 00:01:03:23:31:DD
- Periods between each fourth character: 0001.0323.31DD
- The digits without dashes, periods, or colons: 0001032331DD

Cisco routers typically use the 0001.0323.31DD formatting, while Cisco switches running Catalyst Operation System (Catalyst OS) images use 00:01:03:23:31:DD to represent the same address.

CSMA/CD Operation

Ethernet operates using CSMA/CD. By definition, CSMA/CD is half-duplex communication. Half duplex implies that only one device on the Ethernet LAN "talks" at a time, and devices connected to the same Ethernet network are considered to be part of the same collision domain. Devices sending traffic in the same collision domain have the potential of their packets colliding with each other when two devices attempt to transmit at the same time. The logical definition of this range of devices is called a *domain*, hence the term *collision domain*.

The old style telephone party line example best illustrates the concept of a collision domain, as shown in Figure 1-3.

Figure 1-3 *Telephone Party Line*

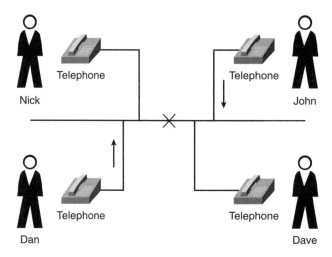

Table 1-2 lists each party line operation and compares it to Ethernet.

Table 1-2   *Comparing Party Line and Ethernet Operations*

Step	Telephone Party Line Operation	Ethernet Operation
1	I pick up the phone. Is anyone talking?	The LAN device listens to the Ethernet network to sense the carrier signal on the network.
2	If no one is speaking, I can start talking. I'll keep listening to make sure no one speaks at the same time as me.	If the LAN device does not detect a carrier signal on the network, it can begin transmitting. The LAN device listens to the carrier signal on the network and matches it to the output.
3	If I can't hear myself speak, I'll assume someone is trying to speak at the same time.	If there is a discrepancy between input and output, another LAN device has transmitted. This is a collision.
4	I'll then yell out to tell the other person to stop talking.	The LAN device sends out a jamming signal to alert the other LAN devices that there has been a collision.
5	I will then wait a random amount of time to start my conversation again.	The LAN device waits a random amount of time to start transmitting again. This is called the *backoff* algorithm. If multiple attempts to transmit fail, the backoff algorithm increases the amount of time waited.

In a party line, people occasionally speak over each other. When the party line is loaded with more callers, the more often people attempt to speak at the same time. It is the same with Ethernet collisions. Because users share Ethernet bandwidth and are part of the same collision domain, it is often referred to as *shared media* or *shared Ethernet*. (See Figure 1-4.) The efficiency of shared Ethernet is proportional to the number of devices attempting to communicate at the same time. As more devices are added, the efficiency decreases.

Figure 1-4   *Shared Ethernet Segment*

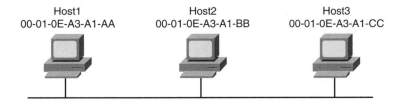

Host1
00-01-0E-A3-A1-AA

Host2
00-01-0E-A3-A1-BB

Host3
00-01-0E-A3-A1-CC

The algorithm in CSMA/CD used after a collision is Truncated Binary Exponential Backoff algorithm. When a collision occurs, the device must wait a random number of slot times before attempting to retransmit the packet. The slot time is contingent upon the speed of the link. For instance, slot time will be different for 10 Mbps Ethernet versus 100 Mbps Ethernet. Table 1-3 shows an example for a 10 Mbps Ethernet link. Cisco switches uses a more aggressive Max Wait Time than what is illustrated in this example. The purpose of the example is to give you a feel for how Truncated Binary Exponential Backoff works.

Table 1-3   *CSMA/CD Collision Backoff Ranges*

Retry	Range	Max Number	Max Wait Time
1st	0-1	$(2^1)-1$	51.2us
2nd	0-3	$(2^2)-1$	153.6us
3rd	0-7	$(2^3)-1$	358.4us
4th	0-15	$(2^4)-1$	768.0us
5th	0-31	$(2^5)-1$	1587.2us
6th	0-63	$(2^6)-1$	3225.6us
7th	0-127	$(2^7)-1$	6502.4us
8th	0-255	$(2^8)-1$	13056.0us
9th	0-511	$(2^9)-1$	26163.2us
$10^{th} - 15^{th}$	0-1023	$(2^{10})-1$	52377.6us

Cisco switches monitor various collision counters, as follows:

- Single
- Multiple
- Late
- Excessive

Of the four types, be wary of late and excessive collisions. Late collisions occur when two devices send data at the same time. Unlike single and multiple collisions, late collisions cause packets to be lost. Late collisions are usually indicative of the cable exceeding IEEE specifications. Cascading hubs (connecting two or more hubs to each other) can also cause the length of the collision domain to increase above specification. You can use a Time Delay Reflectometer (TDR) to detect cable fault and whether the cable is within the IEEE standard. Other factors that cause late collisions include mismatched duplex settings and bad transceivers. Example 1-1 shows the output from a switch that has detected a late collision on one of its ports.

Example 1-1   *Late Collision Error Messages*

```
%LANCE-5-LATECOLL: Unit [DEC], late collision error
%PQUICC-5-LATECOLL: Unit [DEC], late collision error
```

The slot time, 51.2 microseconds, used to detect and report collisions is based on the round trip time between the furthest points on the Ethernet link. The value is calculated by taking the smallest Ethernet frame size of 64 bytes and multiplying it by 8 bits, which gives 512 bits. This number is then multiplied by .1 microseconds. The farthest distance between the end points of the cable should be reached within half of this slot time, 25.6 microseconds.

Excessive collisions typically occur when too much traffic is on the wire or too many devices are in the collision domain. After the fifteenth retransmission plus the original attempt, the excessive collisions counter increments, and the packet gets dropped. In this case, too many devices are competing for the wire. In addition, duplex mismatches can also cause the problem. A syslog message is generated by the switch, as depicted in Example 1-2, when excessive collision occurs on the port.

Example 1-2   *Excessive Collisions Error Message*

```
%PQUICC-5-COLL: Unit [DEC], excessive collisions. Retry limit [DEC] exceeded
```

On the switch, the **show port** *mod/port* command provides information about collisions, multiple collisions, and so on. Example 1-3 is an excerpt from the **show port** command that is useful. This example was taken from a switch that was running Catalyst OS software.

Example 1-3   *Sample of* **show port** *Command*

```
Switch1 (enable) show port 10/3

Port  Single-Col Multi-Coll Late-Coll  Excess-Col Carri-Sen Runts     Giants
----- ---------- ---------- ---------- ---------- --------- --------- ---------
10/3          37          3         24          0         0         0         0
```

Full-Duplex Ethernet

In the party line scenario, congestion occurs when more than two people attempt to talk at the same time. When only two people are talking, or only two devices, virtually all the bandwidth is available. In cases where only two devices need to communicate, Ethernet can be configured to operate in full-duplex mode as opposed to the normal half-duplex operation. Full-duplex operation allows a network device to "talk" or transmit and "listen" or receive at the same time. (See Figure 1-5.)

Figure 1-5 *Full-Duplex Directly Connected Hosts*

Because Ethernet is based on CSMA/CD, full-duplex devices either need to be directly connected to each other or be connected to a device that allows full-duplex operation (such as a LAN switch). Ethernet hubs do not allow full-duplex operation, as they are only physical layer (Layer 1) signal repeaters for the logical bus (Layer 2). Ethernet still operates as a logical bus under full duplex.

Autonegotiation

Autonegotiation is a mechanism that allows two devices at either end to negotiate speed and duplex settings at physical layer. The benefits of autonegotiation include minimal configuration and operability between dissimilar Ethernet technologies.

In today's networks, 10BASE-T and 100BASE-T are ubiquitous. Newer Cisco modules such as the WS-X6548-GE-TX have ports capable of 10/100/1000BASE-T. Most existing network interface cards (NICs) operate at 10/100 speeds, with newer NICs offering 10/100/1000BASE-T operation. NICs capable of autonegotiating speed and duplex are beneficial because more and more users are becoming mobile. One day, a user might be connected to the office Catalyst switch at 100 Mbps, and the next day, a remote site that supports only 10 Mbps. The primary objective is to ensure that the user not only has easy access to the network but also has network reliability. If the user's laptop NIC is hard coded at 100BASE-T full duplex, the user connectivity might be impacted because the two switches might have different types of modules that operate at different speeds. For instance, the module in the office building is WS-X5225 (24 port 10/100BASE-TX), and the remote site has WS-X5013 (24 port 10BASE-T). In this case, because the switches are set by default to autonegotiate, a user with a NIC hard coded to 100BASE-T full duplex will not get any connectivity. Setting up autonegotiation on both the switch and laptop gets rid of this problem. The user no longer has to worry about the laptop NIC settings because the NIC automatically negotiates the proper physical layer configuration with the end device to which it connects.

The actual mechanics behind autonegotiation are straightforward, as depicted in Figure 1-6. Autonegotiation attempts to match speed and duplex mode at the highest priority with its link partner. Since the introduction of 1000BASE-T, the priorities have been readjusted. Table 1-4 describes each priority level.

Figure 1-6   *Ethernet Autonegotiation*

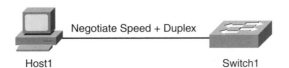

Host1   Switch1

Table 1-4   *Autonegotiation Priority Levels*

Priority	Ethernet Specification	Type of Duplex
1	1000BASE-T	Full duplex
2	1000BASE-T	Half duplex
3	100BASE-T2	Full duplex
4	100BASE-TX	Full duplex
5	100BASE-T2	Half duplex
6	100BASE-T4	---
7	100BASE-TX	Half duplex
8	10BASE-T	Full duplex
9	10BASE-T	Half duplex

The 10BASE-T specification does not include autonegotiation between devices. Auto-negotiation was first introduced in IEEE 802.3u Fast Ethernet specification as an optional parameter. In a 10BASE-T environment, a single pulse, called the Normal Link Pulse (NLP), is sent every 16 ms (±8 ms) on an idle link. The NLP performs a link integrity test for 10BASE-T. When no traffic is on the link, the 10BASE-T device generates a NLP on the wire to keep the link from going down. The 10BASE-T device stops generating pulses when it receives data packets. A link failure occurs under conditions when the 10BASE-T device does not receive NLPs or a single data packet within a specified time slot.

As mentioned earlier, the IEEE 802.3u specification has an optional programmable field for autonegotiation. Within autonegotiation, there are various other optional operations, such as Remote Fault Indication and Next Page Function. Remote Fault Indication detects and informs the link partner of physical layer errors. The Next Page Function provides more verbose information about the negotiation process. One of the more appealing features of autonegotiation is compatibility with dissimilar Ethernet technologies. For example, Fast Ethernet is backward-compatible with 10BASE-T through a Parallel Detection mechanism. Essentially, the Fast Ethernet switches to NLP to communicate with a 10BASE-T device. Parallel Detection is when only one of the two link partners is capable of autonegotiation.

Fast Ethernet uses the same pulse structure as 10BASE-T. In 10BASE-T, there is only a single pulse every 16 ms, whereas in Fast Ethernet, there are bursts of pulses in intervals of 16 (±8) ms. In these pulses, or groups of pulses, the capability of the device is encoded in a 16-bit word called a Link Code Word (LCW), also known as Fast Link Pulse (FLP). The length of the burst is approximately 2 ms.

NOTE   Fast Ethernet vendors used their discretion whether to add autonegotiation capabilities to their devices. As a result, Fast Ethernet NICs without autonegotiation capabilities were once found in the marketplace.

Gigabit Ethernet implementation requires that all IEEE 802.3z compliant devices have autonegotiation capability. Autonegotiation can, however, be disabled through a software feature. From the actual hardware perspective, the 802.3z specification requires autonegotiation capabilities on the device. On Cisco Catalyst switches, autonegotiation can be disabled with the following command. Note that this command must be configured on both link partners:

```
set port negotiation <mod/port> enable | disable
```

The parameters that 802.3z devices negotiate are

- Duplex setting
- Flow control
- Remote fault information

Although duplex setting can be negotiated, Cisco switches operate Gigabit Ethernet in full-duplex mode only. With the introduction of the newer 1000/100/10 blades, a port can operate at various speeds and duplex settings. However, it is unlikely that Cisco will support Gigabit half duplex in any point-to-point configurations with even the aforementioned blades. Use the **show port capabilities** command that is available in Catalyst OS to view the features supported by the line module, as shown in Example 1-4.

Example 1-4   *Output from* **show port capabilities** *Command*

```
Switch1 (enable) show port capabilities 1/1
Model             WS-X6K-SUP2-2GE
Port              1/1
Type              1000BaseSX
Speed             1000
Duplex            full
```

Flow control is an optional feature that is part of the 802.3x specification. The concept behind flow control is to help reduce the burden on the port that is overwhelmed with traffic. It does this by creating back-pressure on the network. If the volume of traffic is such that a port runs out of buffers, it drops subsequent packets. The flow control mechanism simply tells the transmitter to back off for a period of time by sending an Ethernet Pause Frame (MAC address of 01-80-c2-00-00-01) to the transmitter. The transmitter receives this frame and buffers the outgoing packets in its output buffer queue. This mechanism provides needed time for the receiver to clear the packets that are in its input queue. The obvious advantage is that packets are not dropped. The negative aspect to this process is latency. Certain multicast, voice, and video traffic are sensitive to latency on the network. It is recommended that flow control should be implemented with care. Typically, this feature is implemented as a quick fix. Not all Cisco switches support this feature.

```
set port flowcontrol <mod/port>
```

Remote fault information detects and advertises physical layer problems such as excessive noise, wrong cable types, bad hardware, and so on to the remote peer. The switch is programmed to take a proactive approach when excessive physical layer problems exist. A port that is generating errors can potentially disrupt a network. For instance, it can cause spanning-tree problems and traffic black holing, and drain system resources. As a result, the switch error disables the port.

Looking at some examples will solidify the concept and function of autonegotiation. In Figure 1-7, Host1 and the hub are link partners over a 10BASE-T connection. 10BASE-T has no knowledge of autonegotiation, and therefore, the devices must statically be configured. NLPs are sent by both devices when they come online. In this example, these devices operate over a 10BASE-T half-duplex connection.

Figure 1-7   *10BASE-T Autonegotiation*

Figure 1-8 shows a straight 100BASE-T connection with both devices enabled for autonegotiation. FLP bursts are sent to advertise the device's capabilities and negotiate a maximum highest bandwidth connection. The highest connection negotiated is priority 4, which is 100BASE-TX full duplex.

Figure 1-8 *100BASE-T Autonegotiation*

The following is the command that configures a switch to autonegotiate a port:

```
set port speed <mod/port> auto
```

In Figure 1-9, Host1 has a 10BASE-T card. The switch has a capability to operate in both 10BASE-T and 100BASE-T mode. The 10/100 modules are common in a switching environment. Cisco has various 10/100 modules with various features and functionalities. In this example, there is a mismatch between the pulses sent by the Host1 and the switch. Because Host1 has a 10BASE-T card, it can send only NLPs. Initially, when the switch comes online, it generates only FLP bursts. When the switch detects NLPs from its link partner, it ceases to generate FLP bursts and switches to NLP. Depending on the static configuration on Host1, the switch chooses that priority. In this instance, the connection is 10BASE-T operating at half duplex.

Figure 1-9 *10/100BASE-T Autonegotiation*

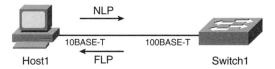

The finer points of autonegotiation have been discussed; however, some drawbacks need to be discussed. Numerous network problems resulted when the autonegotiation feature was first deployed. The issues ranged from degradation in performance to connectivity loss. The cause of some of these problems included advanced software features that came with the NIC, vendors not fully conforming to 802.3u standard, and buggy code. These days, now that manufacturers have resolved these issues, misconfiguration is the biggest remaining problem. Table 1-5 and Table 1-6 show various consequences from misconfigurations. For instance, a duplex mismatch can degrade performance on the wire and potentially cause packet loss.

Network engineers still have heated discussions about whether to enable autonegotiation in the network. As mentioned earlier, autonegotiation is a big advantage for mobile users. A user should not have to worry about configuring his laptop every time he goes to a different location.

Table 1-5   *Autonegotiation Configurations for 10/100 Ethernet*

Configuration NIC (Speed/Duplex)	Configuration Switch (Speed/Duplex)	Resulting NIC Speed/Duplex	Resulting Catalyst Speed/Duplex	Comments
AUTO	AUTO	100 Mbps, Full duplex	100 Mbps, Full duplex	Assuming maximum capability of Catalyst switch and NIC is 100 full duplex.
100 Mbps, Full duplex	AUTO	100 Mbps, Full duplex	100 Mbps, Half duplex	Duplex mismatch.
AUTO	100 Mbps, Full duplex	100 Mbps, Half duplex	100 Mbps, Full duplex	Duplex mismatch.
100 Mbps, Full duplex	100 Mbps, Full duplex	100 Mbps, Full duplex	100 Mbps, Full duplex	Correct manual configuration.
100 Mbps, Half duplex	AUTO	100 Mbps, Half duplex	100 Mbps, Half duplex	Link is established, but switch does not see any autonegotiation information from NIC and defaults to half duplex.
10 Mbps, Half duplex	AUTO	10 Mbps, Half duplex	10 Mbps, Half duplex	Link is established, but switch will not see FLP and will default to 10 Mbps half duplex.
10 Mbps, Half duplex	100 Mbps, Half duplex	No Link	No Link	Neither side will establish link because of speed mismatch.
AUTO	100 Mbps, Half duplex	10 Mbps, Half duplex	10 Mbps, Half duplex	Link is established, but NIC will not see FLP and default to 10 Mbps half duplex.

Table 1-6   *Autonegotiations Configurations for Gigabit Ethernet*

Switch Port Gigabit	Autonegotiation Setting	NIC Gigabit Autonegotiation Setting	Switch Link/NIC Link
Enabled	Enabled	Up	Up
Disabled	Disabled	Up	Up
Enabled	Disabled	Down	Up
Disabled	Enabled	Up	Down

The rule of thumb is to enable autonegotiation on access ports that connect to users. Mission-critical devices should be statically configured to protect the network from possible outages and performance hits. Therefore, connections between routers and switches, or servers and switches should be hard coded with the appropriate speed and duplex settings.

Transparent Bridging

The inability to allow more than one device to transmit simultaneously presents a major challenge when attempting to connect dozens or hundreds of users together through Ethernet.

Transparent bridging is the augmentation of Ethernet allowing partial segmentation of the network into two or more collision domains. The IEEE-defined transparent bridging is an industry standard in 802.1D. Transparent bridges improve network performance by allowing devices in the same segmented collision domain to communicate without that traffic unnecessarily being forwarded to the other collision domain.

Transparent bridges are the predominant bridge type for Ethernet, and it is important to understand Ethernet switches essentially act as multiport transparent bridges.

Figure 1-10 shows a transparent bridge supporting Ethernet segments or collision domains. If Host1 and Host2 are talking to each other, their conversation will use bandwidth only on their side of the bridge. This allows Host4 and Host5 to also hold a conversation. If all devices were in the same collision domain, only one conversation would be possible.

However, if Host1 wants to talk to Host4, as shown in Figure 1-11, the bandwidth will be utilized on both sides of the bridge, allowing only the one conversation.

How does the transparent bridge determine which users are connected to which side of the bridge? Well, transparent bridging has a little more "under the hood" than the example illustrates. The 802.1D specification for transparent bridging defines five unique processes as part of transparent bridging:

- Learning
- Flooding
- Filtering
- Forwarding
- Aging

Figure 1-10 *Host1 to Host2 and Host4 to Host5*

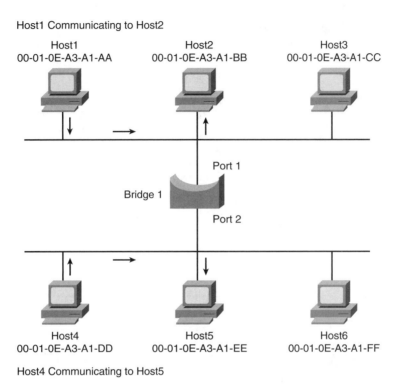

The following sections describe each of these processes in more detail.

Learning

Learning is the process of obtaining the MAC address of devices. When a bridge is first turned on, it has no entries in its bridge table. As traffic passes through the bridge, the sender's MAC addresses are stored in a table along with the associated port on which the traffic was received. This table is often called a *bridge table*, *MAC table*, or *content addressable memory (CAM) table*.

Table 1-7 shows a listing of all the devices on the sample network in Figure 1-10 and Figure 1-11.

Figure 1-11 *Host1 to Host4*

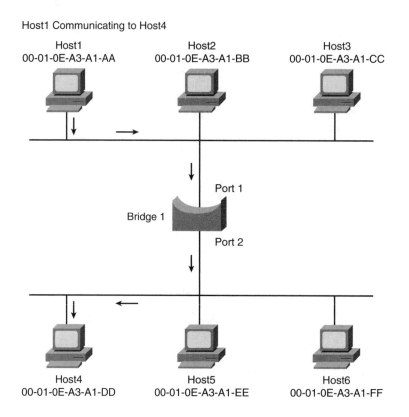

Table 1-7 *Sample Bridge Table*

Hosts	Port 1	Port 2
Host1/ 00-01-0E-A3-A1-AA	X	
Host2/ 00-01-0E-A3-A1-BB	X	
Host3/ 00-01-0E-A3-A1-CC	X	
Host4/ 00-01-0E-A3-A1-DD		X
Host5/ 00-01-0E-A3-A1-EE		X
Host6/ 00-01-0E-A3-A1-FF		X

Flooding

When a bridge does not have an entry in its bridge table for a specific address, it must transparently pass the traffic through all its ports except the source port. This is known as *flooding*. The source port is not "flooded" because the original traffic came in on this port and already exists on that segment. Flooding allows the bridge to learn, as well as stay transparent to the rest of the network, because no traffic is lost while the bridge is learning. Figure 1-12 shows how the bridge forwards the traffic on all its ports.

Figure 1-12 *Bridge1 Floods Traffic*

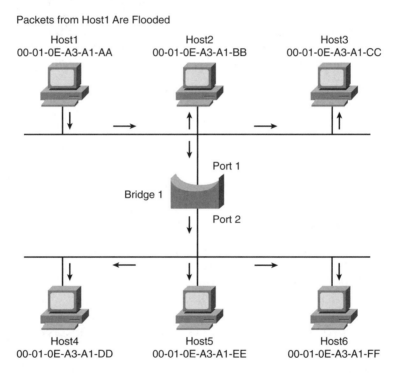

Packets from Host1 Are Flooded

Host1
00-01-0E-A3-A1-AA

Host2
00-01-0E-A3-A1-BB

Host3
00-01-0E-A3-A1-CC

Port 1

Bridge 1

Port 2

Host4
00-01-0E-A3-A1-DD

Host5
00-01-0E-A3-A1-EE

Host6
00-01-0E-A3-A1-FF

Filtering

After the bridge learns the MAC address and associated port of the devices to which it is connected, the benefits of transparent bridging can be seen by way of filtering. Filtering occurs when the source and destination are on the same side (same bridge port) of the bridge. In Figure 1-10, filtering occurs each time Host1 and Host2 talk, as well as when Host4 and Host5 talk.

Forwarding

Forwarding is simply passing traffic from a known device located on one bridge port to another known device located on a different bridge port. Again, referring back to Figure 1-11, after the initial devices were learned, forwarding occurs when Host1 and Host4 talk.

Aging

In addition to the MAC address and the associated port, a bridge also records the time that the device was learned. Aging of learned MAC addresses allows the bridge to adapt to moves, adds, and changes of devices to the network. After a device is learned, the bridge starts an aging timer. Each time the bridge forwards or filters a frame from a device, it restarts that device's timer. If the bridge doesn't hear from a device in a preset period of time, the aging timer expires and the bridge removes the device from its table.

Aging ensures that the bridge tracks only active systems, and ensures that the MAC address table does not consume too much system memory.

Broadcasts and Multicasts

With Ethernet, broadcasts are specialized frames that are destined for all devices on an Ethernet network. Broadcasts use a MAC address of FF-FF-FF-FF-FF-FF. This is a special MAC address because it is the highest number allowed in the 48-bit schema of MAC addresses. In binary, all 48 bits are set to 1.

Multicasts are specialized broadcasts. Multicasts are used by higher layer protocols to direct traffic to more than one select destination, rather than a broadcast, which is sent to all destinations. Application layer multicasts start with 01-00-5E prefix. The rest of the digits are assigned by the application layer protocol handling the multicast. However, other Layer 2-only multicast addresses do not have the prefix of 01-00-5E; for example, STP with MAC address of 01-00-0c-cc-cc-cd. For the most part, Ethernet networks treat multicasts like broadcasts by default. Several higher layer protocols, such as IGMP (Internet Group Messaging Protocol), can be used by switches to differentiate the traffic and forward only multicast out specific ports.

Introducing Spanning Tree Protocol

As with traditional shared Ethernet, transparent bridges inherently lack the capability to provide redundancy. The Spanning Tree Protocol (STP) inserts a mechanism into the Ethernet transparent bridge environment to dynamically discover the network topology and ensure only one path through the network. Without STP, there is no way to make a transparent bridge environment redundant. STP also protects a network against accidental miscablings because it prevents unwanted bridging loops in the transparent bridging environment. A bridge loop is similar to a wrestling match. At first, everything appears orderly, but pandemonium soon ensues. The normal referee and rules do not work. The pandemonium does not stop until someone comes in and shuts the match down. Bridge loops in Ethernet and transparent bridging also cause pandemonium. Figure 1-13 shows a bridge loop in Ethernet.

Figure 1-13 *Bridging Loop*

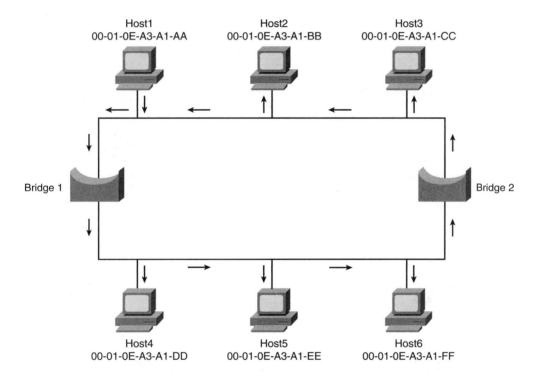

In this basic example, there are redundant links without STP. This creates a bridged loop. In this case, the redundant links cause the Ethernet data frame to have more than one path. Because the bridges are transparent, a copy of the data frame is sent across both paths. Bridge1 and Bridge2 both receive a copy of the data frame that was sent by the other. Then, each bridge sees alternating data frames, assumes that the source host is on the wrong side of the bridge, and updates the bridge table. The data frames then start to be recopied on each side of the bridge again and again. Think about how many data frames are needed for a simple e-mail message. With this bridging loop, the frames would be copied over and over again until they timed out. However, because the upper layer protocols are generating many requests, the process keeps happening. The entire network gets overwhelmed and legitimate traffic cannot pass.

Figure 1-14 revisits the example again, this time adding STP, which blocks one of the redundant links, eliminating the bridging loop. If the first link or Bridge1 were to fail, STP would re-examine the network and enable the shutdown connection. This is how STP provides redundancy in a transparent bridging environment.

NOTE   Be aware that the spanning-tree algorithm is implemented in other media types such as Token Ring. STP has a different purpose and function in Token Ring than in Ethernet because bridging loops can be desirable in Token Ring.

Figure 1-14 *Spanning Tree Blocking*

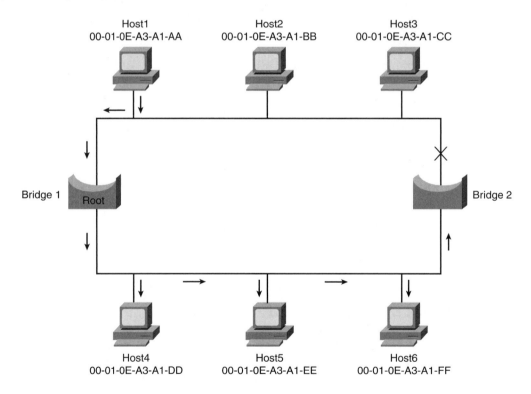

Spanning Tree Operations

STP operation for each bridge can be broken down into three main steps:

- Root bridge selection
- Calculation of the shortest path to the root bridge
- Type of role an active port plays in STP

The main information to be concerned with is the Root ID (bridge that the transmitting bridge thinks is the root), Bridge ID, and cost (which is the cost to the root bridge). The STP topology is considered converged after a root bridge has been selected and each bridge has selected its root port, designated bridge, and which ports will participate in the STP topology. STP uses these configuration messages (BPDUs) as it transitions port states to achieve convergence.

Spanning tree elects one bridge on the LAN to be the master bridge. This bridge is called the *root bridge*. The root bridge is special because all the path calculation through the network is based on the root. The bridge is elected based on the Bridge ID (BID), which is comprised of a 2-byte Priority field plus a 6-byte MAC address. In spanning tree, lower BID values are preferred. In a default configuration, the Priority field is set at 32768. Because the default Priority field is the same for all the bridges, the root selection is based on the lowest MAC address. One method of selecting a specific bridge to be the root is to manually alter the Priority field to a lower value. Regardless of what the MAC address is, the Priority field decides what bridge is going to be the root, assuming that all bridges do not have the same priority value. For the remainder of this chapter, the figures depict a switch, which at its fundamental level is a glorified bridge. (See Figure 1-15.)

Figure 1-15 *Switch1 Becomes Root*

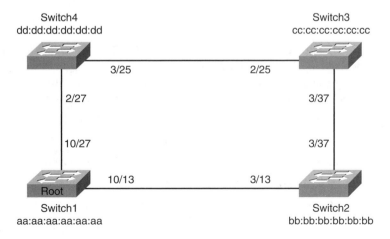

Switch1 has the lowest MAC address of aa:aa:aa:aa:aa:aa.

Each bridge calculates all the paths from itself to the root. It then selects the shortest path. The next-hop bridge toward the root is the designated bridge. The port that leads to the designated bridge is selected to be the root port because it is closest from this bridge to the root bridge. The metric that STP uses for this determination is cost, which is based on the interface speed. Table 1-8 compares bandwidth to STP interface costs.

Table 1-8   *Spanning Tree Interface Costs*

Bandwidth	Cost
4 Mbps	250
10 Mbps	100
16 Mbps	62
45 Mbps	39
100 Mbps	19
155 Mbps	14
622 Mbps	6
1 Gbps	4
10 Gbps	2

As shown in Figure 1-16, Switch3 has two paths to the root. To prevent a loop on the network, it must decide to block one of its ports. The algorithm used to make the decision is based on three choices:

- Lowest path cost to the root
- Lowest sender BID
- Lowest port ID

In this example, the lowest path cost to the root will decide which port will be forwarding and which one will be blocking. Because the cost is less through Switch2 path, 38, Switch3 will be forwarding out of this port and blocking on the other. This behavior of blocking a port allows the spanning tree to be loop free and provide redundancy should one of the ports go down.

Each active port can have a specific role to play in the spanning-tree algorithm:

- **Designated Port (DP)**—The port responsible for sending BPDUs on the segment
- **Non-Designated Port (N-DP)**—Does not send BPDUs on the segment
- **Root Port (RP)**—The closest port to the root

STP sends configuration messages out every port of the bridge. These messages are called bridge protocol data units (BPDUs). BPDUs contain the appropriate information for STP configuration. The Type field for BPDU message is 0x00, and it uses the multicast MAC address 01-80-C2-00-00-00. The BPDU packet is shown in Figure 1-17.

Figure 1-16 *Converged Spanning-Tree Topology*

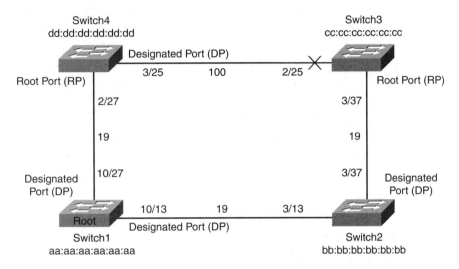

Switch1 has the lowest MAC address of aa:aa:aa:aa:aa:aa.

Figure 1-17 *Bridge Protocol Data Unit Format*

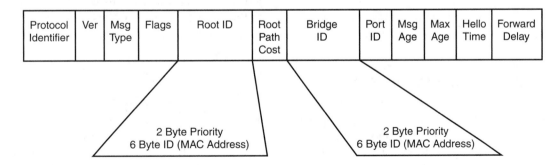

Spanning Tree Port Transitions and Timers

Part of the STP algorithm and process of building a loop-free network, as well as reconfig-uration on a topology change, is to cycle the bridge ports through several states, as follows:

- **Blocking**—A port is placed in blocking mode upon startup and when STP determines it is a suboptimal path to the root bridge. Blocked ports do not forward traffic.

- **Listening**—When a port is transitioned from blocking to listening, it starts to listen for other bridges. It does not send out configuration messages, learn MAC addresses, or forward traffic.

- **Learning**—The bridge continues to listen for other bridges; however, it can now also learn MAC addresses of network devices.

- **Forwarding**—This is normal operation. Data and configuration messages are passed through the port.

STP uses timers to determine how long to transition ports. STP also uses timers to deter-mine the health of neighbor bridges and how long to cache MAC addresses in the bridge table.

The explanation of the timers is as follows:

- **Hello timer**—2 seconds. This timer is used to determine how often root bridge sends configuration BPDUs.

- **Maximum Age (Max Age)**—20 seconds. This timer tells the bridge how long to keep ports in the blocking state before listening.

- **Forward Delay (Fwd Delay)**—15 seconds. This timer determines how long to stay in the listening state before learning, and the learning state before forwarding.

The STP timers can be tuned based on network size. These parameters are designed to give STP ample opportunity to ensure a loop-free topology. Mistuning these parameters can cause serious network instability. Tuning these parameters will be discussed in Chapter 10, "Implementing and Tuning Spanning Tree." When a bridge sees BPDUs with a better path to the root, it recalculates STP. This allows ports to transition when appropriate.

Topology Changes in STP

The other type of STP BPDU that needs to be discussed is Topology Change Notification (TCN). TCN BPDU is generated when a bridge discovers a change in topology, usually because of a link failure, bridge failure, or a port transitioning to forwarding state. The TCN BPDU is set to 0x80 in the Type field and is subsequently forwarded on the root port toward the root bridge. The upstream bridge responds back with acknowledgment of the BPDU in the form of Topology Change Acknowledgment (TCA). The least significant bit is for TCN, and the most significant bit is for TCA in the Flag field.

Figure 1-18 shows the flow of topology change BPDUs. The bridge sends this message to its designated bridge. Remember, the designated bridge is a particular bridge's closest neighbor to the root (or the root, if it is directly connected). The designated bridge acknowledges the topology change back to the sending neighbor and sends the message to its designated bridge. This process repeats until the root bridge gets the message. The root learns about the topology changes in the network in this way.

Figure 1-18   *Topology Change Because of a Link Failure*

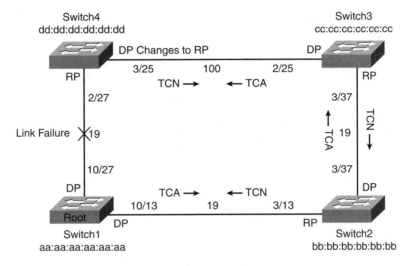

Switch1 has the lowest MAC address of aa:aa:aa:aa:aa:aa.

By default, bridges keep MAC addresses in the bridge table for 5 minutes. When a topology change occurs, the bridge temporarily lowers this timer to the same as the forward delay timer (default: 15 seconds). This allows the STP network to react to changes in topology by having the bridges quickly relearn the MAC address changes that occur when links change state. Without this, network devices could be unreachable for up to 5 minutes while the bridge ages the MAC address out. This is typically called a *black hole* because data is forwarded toward a bridge that no longer can reach the network device. Topology change BPDUs are a mechanism to overcome this. A common misconception is that topology change BPDUs cause STP to recalculate. The purpose of topology change BPDUs is to avoid black holes and allow the bridges to have up-to-date bridge tables. STP recalculations only occur only when the bridge sees BPDUs with better paths through the bridged network or when the bridge no longer receives configuration BPDUs from the root bridge.

This section offers a simple introduction to spanning tree. Later chapters include examples of the complexities of spanning tree and the various enhancement features available.

Summary

Unlike Token Ring and FDDI, which for the most part are defunct, Ethernet technology is alive and very well. 10 Gigabit Ethernet has been introduced and is being deployed in the cores of large networks. It is important to have a solid understanding of some of the basic principles involved with this technology.

This chapter explored numerous Ethernet technologies and architectures. It investigated the importance and functions of CSMA/CD used in shared medium. The chapter also discussed autonegotiation and its specific components as well as the importance of where autonegotiation should be implemented and on which devices.

Transparent bridging solves the issue of too many collisions on a LAN segment by breaking the segment into two or more, with fewer devices to compete for the access on each segment. The limitations of transparent bridging in reference to loops and the repercussions involved were also discussed. Along with redundancy comes some of the potential problems of bridging. Spanning tree ensures a loop-free topology on the network. The chapter also included some of the rudimentary components of spanning tree, such as packet types, timers, and types of decision processes involved.

This chapter covers the following topics:

- Receiving data—switching modes
- Switching data
- Buffering data
- Oversubscribing the switch fabric
- Congestion and head-of-line blocking
- Forwarding data

LAN Switch Architecture

Chapter 2 introduces many of the concepts behind LAN switching common to all switch vendors. The chapter begins by looking at how data are received by a switch, followed by mechanisms used to switch data as efficiently as possible, and concludes with forwarding data toward their destinations. These concepts are not specific to Cisco and are valid when examining the capabilities of any LAN switch.

Receiving Data—Switching Modes

The first step in LAN switching is receiving the frame or packet, depending on the capabilities of the switch, from the transmitting device or host. Switches making forwarding decisions only at Layer 2 of the OSI model refer to data as frames, while switches making forwarding decisions at Layer 3 and above refer to data as packets. This chapter's examination of switching begins from a Layer 2 point of view. Depending on the model, varying amounts of each frame are stored and examined before being switched.

Three types of switching modes have been supported on Catalyst switches:

- Cut through
- Fragment free
- Store and forward

These three switching modes differ in how much of the frame is received and examined by the switch before a forwarding decision is made. The next sections describe each mode in detail.

Cut-Through Mode

Switches operating in cut-through mode receive and examine only the first 6 bytes of a frame. These first 6 bytes represent the destination MAC address of the frame, which is sufficient information to make a forwarding decision. Although cut-through switching offers the least latency when transmitting frames, it is susceptible to transmitting fragments created via Ethernet collisions, runts (frames less than 64 bytes), or damaged frames.

Fragment-Free Mode

Switches operating in fragment-free mode receive and examine the first 64 bytes of frame. Fragment free is referred to as "fast forward" mode in some Cisco Catalyst documentation. Why examine 64 bytes? In a properly designed Ethernet network, collision fragments must be detected in the first 64 bytes.

Store-and-Forward Mode

Switches operating in store-and-forward mode receive and examine the entire frame, resulting in the most error-free type of switching.

As switches utilizing faster processor and application-specific integrated circuits (ASICs) were introduced, the need to support cut-through and fragment-free switching was no longer necessary. As a result, all new Cisco Catalyst switches utilize store-and-forward switching.

Figure 2-1 compares each of the switching modes.

Figure 2-1 *Switching Modes*

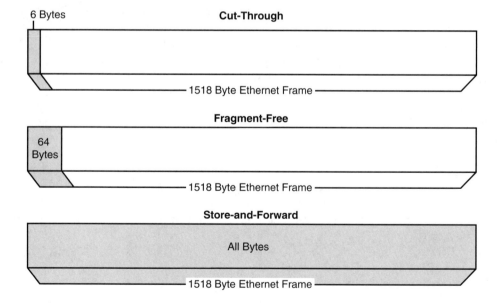

Switching Data

Regardless of how many bytes of each frame are examined by the switch, the frame must eventually be switched from the input or ingress port to one or more output or egress ports. A *switch fabric* is a general term for the communication channels used by the switch to transport frames, carry forwarding decision information, and relay management information throughout the switch. A comparison could be made between the switching fabric in a Catalyst switch and a transmission on an automobile. In an automobile, the transmission is responsible for relaying power from the engine to the wheels of the car. In a Catalyst switch, the switch fabric is responsible for relaying frames from an input or ingress port to one or more output or egress ports. Regardless of model, whenever a new switching platform is introduced, the documentation will generally refer to the "transmission" as the switching fabric.

Although a variety of techniques have been used to implement switching fabrics on Cisco Catalyst platforms, two major architectures of switch fabrics are common:

- Shared bus
- Crossbar

Shared Bus Switching

In a shared bus architecture, all line modules in the switch share one data path. A central arbiter determines how and when to grant requests for access to the bus from each line card. Various methods of achieving fairness can be used by the arbiter depending on the configuration of the switch. A shared bus architecture is much like multiple lines at an airport ticket counter, with only one ticketing agent processing customers at any given time.

Figure 2-2 illustrates a round-robin servicing of frames as they enter a switch. Round-robin is the simplest method of servicing frames in the order in which they are received. Current Catalyst switching platforms such as the Catalyst 6500 support a variety of quality of service (QoS) features to provide priority service to specified traffic flows. Chapter 8, "Understanding Quality of Service on Catalyst 6500," will provide more information on this topic.

Figure 2-2   *Round-Robin Service Order*

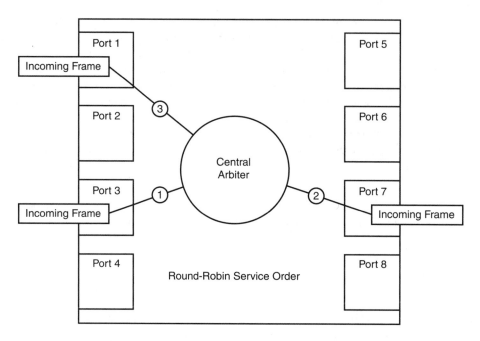

The following list and Figure 2-3 illustrate the basic concept of moving frames from the received port or ingress, to the transmit port(s) or egress using a shared bus architecture:

1 **Frame received from Host1**—The ingress port on the switch receives the entire frame from Host1 and stores it in a receive buffer. The port checks the frame's Frame Check Sequence (FCS) for errors. If the frame is defective (runt, fragment, invalid CRC, or Giant), the port discards the frame and increments the appropriate counter.

2 **Requesting access to the data bus**—A header containing information necessary to make a forwarding decision is added to the frame. The line card then requests access or permission to transmit the frame onto the data bus.

3 **Frame transmitted onto the data bus**—After the central arbiter grants access, the frame is transmitted onto the data bus.

4 **Frame is received by all ports**—In a shared bus architecture, every frame transmitted is received by all ports simultaneously. In addition, the frame is received by the hardware necessary to make a forwarding decision.

5 **Switch determines which port(s) should transmit the frame**—The information added to the frame in step 2 is used to determine which ports should transmit the frame. In some cases, frames with either an unknown destination MAC address or a broadcast frame, the switch will transmit the frame out all ports except the one on which the frame was received.

6 **Port(s) instructed to transmit, remaining ports discard the frame**—Based on the decision in step 5, a certain port or ports is told to transmit the frame while the rest are told to discard or flush the frame.

7 **Egress port transmits the frame to Host2**—In this example, it is assumed that the location of Host2 is known to the switch and only the port connecting to Host2 transmits the frame.

Figure 2-3 *Frame Flow in a Shared Bus*

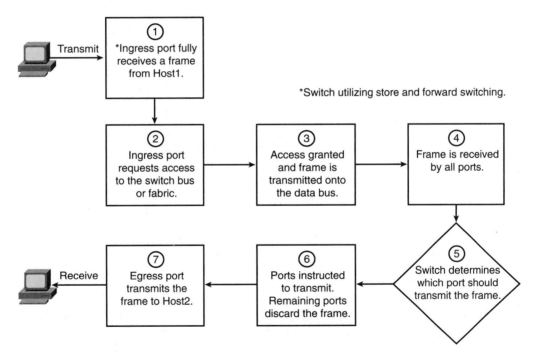

One advantage of a shared bus architecture is every port except the ingress port receives a copy of the frame automatically, easily enabling multicast and broadcast traffic without the need to replicate the frames for each port. This example is greatly simplified and will be discussed in detail for Catalyst platforms that utilize a shared bus architecture in Chapter 3, "Catalyst Switching Architecture."

Crossbar Switching

In the shared bus architecture example, the speed of the shared data bus determines much of the overall traffic handling capacity of the switch. Because the bus is shared, line cards must wait their turns to communicate, and this limits overall bandwidth.

A solution to the limitations imposed by the shared bus architecture is the implementation of a crossbar switch fabric, as shown in Figure 2-4. The term *crossbar* means different things on different switch platforms, but essentially indicates multiple data channels or paths between line cards that can be used simultaneously.

Figure 2-4   *Crossbar Switch Fabric*

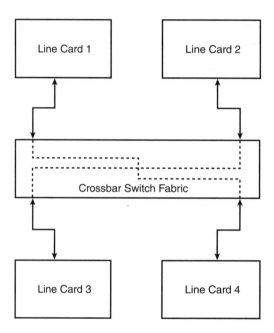

In the case of the Cisco Catalyst 5500 series, one of the first crossbar architectures advertised by Cisco, three individual 1.2-Gbps data buses are implemented. Newer Catalyst 5500 series line cards have the necessary connector pins to connect to all three buses simultaneously, taking advantage of 3.6 Gbps of aggregate bandwidth. Legacy line cards from the Catalyst 5000 are still compatible with the Catalyst 5500 series by connecting to only one of the three data buses. Access to all three buses is required by Gigabit Ethernet cards on the Catalyst 5500 platform.

A crossbar fabric on the Catalyst 6500 series is enabled with the Switch Fabric Module (SFM) and Switch Fabric Module 2 (SFM2). The SFM provides 128 Gbps of bandwidth

(256 Gbps full duplex) to line cards via 16 individual 8-Gbps connections to the crossbar switch fabric. The SFM2 was introduced to support the Catalyst 6513 13-slot chassis and includes architecture optimizations over the SFM.

Buffering Data

Frames must wait their turn for the central arbiter before being transmitted in shared bus architectures. Frames can also potentially be delayed when congestion occurs in a crossbar switch fabric. As a result, frames must be buffered until transmitted. Without an effective buffering scheme, frames are more likely to be dropped anytime traffic oversubscription or congestion occurs.

Buffers get used when more traffic is forwarded to a port than it can transmit. Reasons for this include the following:

- Speed mismatch between ingress and egress ports
- Multiple input ports feeding a single output port
- Half-duplex collisions on an output port
- A combination of all the above

To prevent frames from being dropped, two common types of memory management are used with Catalyst switches:

- Port buffered memory
- Shared memory

Port Buffered Memory

Switches utilizing port buffered memory, such as the Catalyst 5000, provide each Ethernet port with a certain amount of high-speed memory to buffer frames until transmitted. A disadvantage of port buffered memory is the dropping of frames when a port runs out of buffers. One method of maximizing the benefits of buffers is the use of flexible buffer sizes. Catalyst 5000 Ethernet line card port buffer memory is flexible and can create frame buffers for any frame size, making the most of the available buffer memory. Catalyst 5000 Ethernet cards that use the SAINT ASIC contain 192 KB of buffer memory per port, 24 kbps for receive or input buffers, and 168 KB for transmit or output buffers.

Using the 168 KB of transmit buffers, each port can create as many as 2500 64-byte buffers. With most of the buffers in use as an output queue, the Catalyst 5000 family has eliminated head-of-line blocking issues. (You learn more about head-of-line blocking later in this chapter in the section "Congestion and Head-of-Line Blocking.") In normal operations, the input queue is never used for more than one frame, because the switching bus runs at a high speed.

Figure 2-5 illustrates port buffered memory.

Figure 2-5 *Port Buffered Memory*

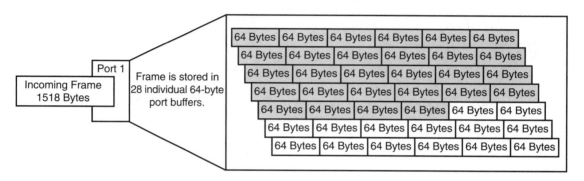

Shared Memory

Some of the earliest Cisco switches use a shared memory design for port buffering. Switches using a shared memory architecture provide all ports access to that memory at the same time in the form of shared frame or packet buffers. All ingress frames are stored in a shared memory "pool" until the egress ports are ready to transmit. Switches dynamically allocate the shared memory in the form of buffers, accommodating ports with high amounts of ingress traffic, without allocating unnecessary buffers for idle ports.

The Catalyst 1200 series switch is an early example of a shared memory switch. The Catalyst 1200 supports both Ethernet and FDDI and has 4 MB of shared packet dynamic random-access memory (DRAM). Packets are handled first in, first out (FIFO).

More recent examples of switches using shared memory architectures are the Catalyst 4000 and 4500 series switches. The Catalyst 4000 with a Supervisor I utilizes 8 MB of Static RAM (SRAM) as dynamic frame buffers. All frames are switched using a central processor or ASIC and are stored in packet buffers until switched. The Catalyst 4000 Supervisor I can create approximately 4000 shared packet buffers. The Catalyst 4500 Supervisor IV, for example, utilizes 16 MB of SRAM for packet buffers. Shared memory buffer sizes may vary depending on the platform, but are most often allocated in increments ranging from 64 to 256 bytes. Figure 2-6 illustrates how incoming frames are stored in 64-byte increments in shared memory until switched by the switching engine.

Figure 2-6   *Shared Memory Architecture*

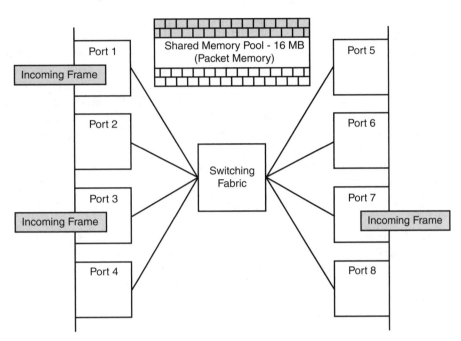

Oversubscribing the Switch Fabric

Switch manufacturers use the term *non-blocking* to indicate that some or all the switched ports have connections to the switch fabric equal to their line speed. For example, an 8-port Gigabit Ethernet module would require 8 Gb of bandwidth into the switch fabric for the ports to be considered non-blocking. All but the highest end switching platforms and configurations have the potential of oversubscribing access to the switching fabric.

Depending on the application, oversubscribing ports may or may not be an issue. For example, a 10/100/1000 48-port Gigabit Ethernet module with all ports running at 1 Gbps would require 48 Gbps of bandwidth into the switch fabric. If many or all ports were connected to high-speed file servers capable of generating consistent streams of traffic, this one-line module could outstrip the bandwidth of the entire switching fabric. If the module is connected entirely to end-user workstations with lower bandwidth requirements, a card that oversubscribes the switch fabric may not significantly impact performance.

Cisco offers both non-blocking and blocking configurations on various platforms, depending on bandwidth requirements. Check the specifications of each platform and the available line cards to determine the aggregate bandwidth of the connection into the switch fabric.

Congestion and Head-of-Line Blocking

Head-of-line blocking occurs whenever traffic waiting to be transmitted prevents or blocks traffic destined elsewhere from being transmitted. Head-of-line blocking occurs most often when multiple high-speed data sources are sending to the same destination. In the earlier shared bus example, the central arbiter used the round-robin service approach to moving traffic from one line card to another. Ports on each line card request access to transmit via a local arbiter. In turn, each line card's local arbiter waits its turn for the central arbiter to grant access to the switching bus. Once access is granted to the transmitting line card, the central arbiter has to wait for the receiving line card to fully receive the frames before servicing the next request in line. The situation is not much different than needing to make a simple deposit at a bank having one teller and many lines, while the person being helped is conducting a complex transaction.

In Figure 2-7, a congestion scenario is created using a traffic generator. Port 1 on the traffic generator is connected to Port 1 on the switch, generating traffic at a 50 percent rate, destined for both Ports 3 and 4. Port 2 on the traffic generator is connected to Port 2 on the switch, generating traffic at a 100 percent rate, destined for only Port 4. This situation creates congestion for traffic destined to be forwarded by Port 4 on the switch because traffic equal to 150 percent of the forwarding capabilities of that port is being sent. Without proper buffering and forwarding algorithms, traffic destined to be transmitted by Port 3 on the switch may have to wait until the congestion on Port 4 clears.

Figure 2-7   *Head-of-Line Blocking*

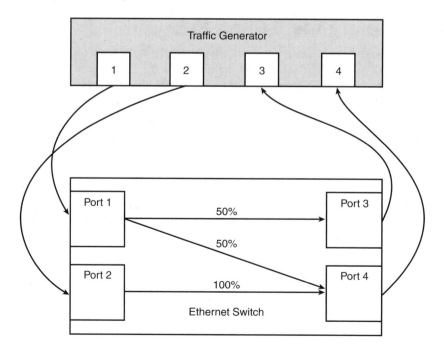

Head-of-line blocking can also be experienced with crossbar switch fabrics because many, if not all, line cards have high-speed connections into the switch fabric. Multiple line cards may attempt to create a connection to a line card that is already busy and must wait for the receiving line card to become free before transmitting. In this case, data destined for a different line card that is not busy is blocked by the frames at the head of the line.

Catalyst switches use a number of techniques to prevent head-of-line blocking; one important example is the use of per port buffering. Each port maintains a small ingress buffer and a larger egress buffer. Larger output buffers (64 Kb to 512 k shared) allow frames to be queued for transmit during periods of congestion. During normal operations, only a small input queue is necessary because the switching bus is servicing frames at a very high speed. In addition to queuing during congestion, many models of Catalyst switches are capable of separating frames into different input and output queues, providing preferential treatment or priority queuing for sensitive traffic such as voice. Chapter 8 will discuss queuing in greater detail.

Forwarding Data

Regardless of the type of switch fabric, a decision on which ports should forward a frame and which should flush or discard the frame must occur. This decision can be made using only the information found at Layer 2 (source/destination MAC address), or on other factors such as Layer 3 (IP) and Layer 4 (Port). Each switching platform supports various types of ASICs responsible for making the intelligent switching decisions. Each Catalyst switch creates a header or label for each packet, and forwarding decisions are based on this header or label. Chapter 3 will include a more detailed discussion of how various platforms make forwarding decisions and ultimately forward data.

Summary

Although a wide variety of different approaches exist to optimize the switching of data, many of the core concepts are closely related. The Cisco Catalyst line of switches focuses on the use of shared bus, crossbar switching, and combinations of the two depending on the platform to achieve very high-speed switching solutions. High-speed switching ASICs use shared and per port buffers to reduce congestion and prevent head-of-line blocking.

This chapter covers the following topics:

- Catalyst 5000/5500 (Project Synergy)
- Catalyst 6000/6500 (Constellation, Constellation+, and Constellation II)
- Catalyst 4500 (Galaxy 3 and 4) Components and Architecture
- Catalyst 3750 (Lord of the Rings) Components and Architecture
- Comparing the architectures

Catalyst Switching Architectures

Chapter 3 introduces the architectures behind Cisco LAN switching, ranging from the first Catalyst switches to the most recent introductions from Cisco into the switching market. Describing the history and evolution of Cisco Catalyst switches is not unlike describing the history and evolution of the automobile. Most discussions of the automobile begin with the Model "A" or Model "T" Ford. This chapter begins with a discussion of the first Catalyst 5000/5500 series switch architectures, followed by detailed examinations of each of the three most popular Cisco switching platforms: Catalyst 6000/6500, 4500, and 3750. Because many of the concepts behind the technologies in the Cisco latest switching platforms originated in the Catalyst 5000 series, a baseline understanding of switching architecture can be achieved by reading the Catalyst 5000/5500 architectures section of this chapter. Readers already familiar with these fundamental concepts may choose to move directly to the sections covering the latest architectural advances in the 6000/6500, 4500, and 3750 series of switches.

In the Beginning—Catalyst 5000/5500 (Project Synergy)

The origins of Cisco's best-selling LAN switching products took shape in 1994 as a project code named Synergy. The goal of project Synergy was to provide dedicated switching (with optional multilayer switching and routing) for 10 and 100 Mbps Ethernet and Token Ring workgroups to Fiber Distributed Data Interface (FDDI), 100 Mbps Ethernet, and Asynchronous Transfer Mode (ATM) backbones. The network world has come to recognize the results of project Synergy as the Catalyst 5000 switch.

The Catalyst 5000 switch introduced a five-slot chassis with one slot reserved for a supervisor module, hot swappable line modules, redundant power supplies, redundant fans, and a 1.2-Gbps backplane bus.

Since the introduction of the original Catalyst 5000 and resulting line of Catalyst switches, Cisco developed substantial improvements in switching architecture, all geared toward processing ever-increasing amounts of traffic. In addition to increased traffic-processing capabilities, switches are now able to make more intelligent traffic forwarding decisions using information found at OSI Layer 3 (Network) and Layer 4 (Transport).

A short time after the introduction of the Catalyst 5000 switch, Cisco introduced additional models including the Catalyst 5500 series. Catalyst 5500 series switches offer an aggregate switching bandwidth of 3.6 Gbps by implementing three individual 1.2-Gbps buses.

Catalyst 5000/5500 Switch Components

Every Catalyst switch is made up of essentially the same general components:

- Chassis
- Power and cooling
- Supervisor module(s)
- Line module(s)

Most Catalyst switches are modular and allow user replacement of each component listed previously, but some are fixed in configuration. Nonetheless, even fixed configuration switches contain the same basic functionality.

In the next section, the Catalyst 5000/5500 family of switches is used to examine the common components of a switch.

Chassis

The switch chassis is the physical housing for all switching modules, power supplies, and cooling equipment. The chassis provides the electrical connections between the Supervisor module and all other modules or line cards as well as the system clock, which is used for bus timing, and connections to the power supplies. After a supervisor module and line modules are inserted into a chassis, the communication paths are enabled. Figure 3-1 is an example of a fully populated Catalyst 5000 switch.

Figure 3-1   *Fully Populated Catalyst 5000 Switch*

Following the introduction of the Catalyst 5000, four additional Catalyst 5000 and 5500 series chassis were introduced, as described in Table 3-1.

Table 3-1   *Catalyst 5000/5500 Models*

Model	Description
5000	Catalyst 5000 Series 5-slot chassis
5002	Catalyst 5000 Series 2-slot chassis
5505	Catalyst 5500 Series 5-slot chassis
5509	Catalyst 5500 Series 9-slot chassis
5500	Catalyst 5500 Series 13-slot chassis

Power and Cooling

Every switch will have one or more power supplies and fans for power and cooling. All but the least expensive Catalyst switches, fixed configuration or modular, offer some type of power supply redundancy.

The original Catalyst 5000 has two power supply bays and supports load sharing between the two power supplies when both are installed. If only one power supply is powered-on on the Catalyst 5000, the system status LED on the Supervisor will glow red instead of green. Over the years, customers have opened numerous trouble tickets to determine why the system status LED on their Supervisor was red when the root cause was simply a single active power supply. A complete list of supervisor system LED statuses is available in the Catalyst 5000/5500 series documentation at cisco.com.

Supervisor Module

The Supervisor module contains the "brains" of the switch. The Catalyst 5000 introduced a Supervisor I containing a number of subcomponents including the following:

- **Network Management Processor (NMP)**—The NMP handles administrative functions such as calculating spanning tree(s), virtual terminal sessions, Simple Network Management Protocol (SNMP), and synchronization of secondary supervisor modules.

- **Master Communications Processor (MCP)**—The MCP communicates statistical and Remote Monitoring (RMON) information to and from the Local Communications Processor (LCP) on each line module via the Serial Communications Protocol (SCP).

- **Nonvolatile random-access memory (NVRAM)**—NVRAM is used to store the configuration of the switch.

- **Dynamic random-access memory (DRAM)**—DRAM is used as working memory by the operating system.

- **Flash memory**—Flash memory is used to store the switch operating system and can be used to store backup configurations.

- **Content-Addressable Memory (CAM)**—CAM is used to store the table of learned MAC addresses, port, and VLAN information; commonly referred to as the *CAM table*.

In addition, the Supervisor I contains highly specialized application-specific integrated circuits (ASICs) including the following:

- **Enhanced Address Recognition Logic Version (EARL)**—The EARL ASIC creates and updates the table of MAC addresses to port mappings stored in CAM.

- **Synergy Advanced Interface Network Termination (SAINT)**—The SAINT ASIC provides the 10/100 Mb Ethernet controller powering the Supervisor's Ethernet uplink ports. The Supervisor utilizes one SAINT ASIC per uplink port.

- **Synergy Advanced Multipurpose Bus Arbiter (SAMBA)**—The SAMBA ASIC handles central arbitration and access to the data bus.

NOTE   It is important to understand the version and functionality of the EARL ASIC on each Supervisor. As newer Catalyst switches were introduced, the EARL evolved with new capabilities, and is commonly referred to in architectural discussions. Documentation of Catalyst switching architecture and Supervisors often includes references to the version of EARL implemented. Understanding the different versions of EARLs can help quickly determine the forward intelligence of a supervisor module. The next section of this chapter describes EARL functionality in detail.

Figure 3-2 is a picture of the original Supervisor I for the Catalyst 5000 series switch.

Since the introduction of the Catalyst 5000 series and the Supervisor I, four additional Supervisor modules have been introduced. A description of each supervisor and its capabilities follows:

- **Supervisor I**—The Supervisor I is capable of Layer 2 switching only and is not upgradable to Multilayer Switching (MLS). Chapter 6, "Understanding Multilayer Switching," describes MLS in detail. The Supervisor I does not support any redundancy using a second standby supervisor and is not compatible with the 5500 series. The Supervisor I includes two Fast Ethernet uplink ports with a variety of support for different media types.

- **Supervisor II**—The Supervisor II is also a Layer 2-only switching engine and introduces support for redundancy with an optional second supervisor. The Supervisor II also includes two Fast Ethernet uplink ports with a variety of support for different media types.

- **Supervisor IIG**—The Supervisor IIG includes an integrated NetFlow Feature Card (NFFC) and supports the addition of an optional Route Switch Feature Card (RSFC). The RSFC is essentially an NPE-200 (see the 7200 Router Platform at www.cisco.com) on a daughterboard. A Supervisor IIG with its built-in NFFC and optional RSFC card enables MLS. In addition, the "G" in the Supervisor IIG signifies support for modular Fast Ethernet and Gigabit Ethernet uplink ports.

- **Supervisor III**—The Supervisor III includes support for an integrated NFFC but does not support the addition of an RSFC. When installed in a Catalyst 5500 series switch, the Supervisor III enables the 3.6-Gbps crossbar switch fabric. The Supervisor III also includes support for modular Gigabit Ethernet uplink ports similar in configuration to the now standard Gigabit Interface Connector (GBIC).

- **Supervisor IIIG**—The Supervisor IIIG includes an integrated NFFC and supports the addition of an RSFC. When installed in a Catalyst 5500 series switch, the Supervisor IIIG enables the 3.6-Gbps crossbar switch fabric and includes support for standard GBIC uplink modules. Figure 3-3 is an example of the Supervisor IIIG module.

Figure 3-2   *Catalyst 5000 Supervisor I Module*

Figure 3-3 *Catalyst 5xxx Supervisor IIIG Module*

EARL Functionality

The Catalyst 5000 EARL is a single ASIC integrated into the Supervisor itself, but later platforms such as the 6500 use multiple ASICs on daughterboards to provide EARL functionality, each responsible for a specific task such as Layer 3 lookup, access control list (ACL) matching, or quality of service (QoS). As platforms have evolved, many versions of the EARL have been introduced. These are discussed in more detail later in this section.

As mentioned in the previous section, the EARL creates and maintains the forwarding tables stored in CAM. The EARL also conducts the lookup operations for each frame received by the switch and determines which ports should forward and which should discard or flush. In its most basic form, the EARL ASIC(s) accomplishes this task by examining the header information from each frame to determine if an entry already exists in the CAM table for the destination address of the frame. If an entry exists, the EARL rewrites the frame and sends it to the line modules, which contain ports that must forward the frame.

EARL version 1 on the Catalyst 5000 created forwarding tables that consisted of the MAC address of individual network devices, the VLAN ID associated with each MAC address, and an index value. The VLAN ID is a 16-bit field, 10 of which are used today. Using 10 bits, the Catalyst 5000 supports up to 1024 individual virtual LANs (VLANs). Additional bits in the EARL tables include the following:

- **An aging bit**—The aging bit is used for aging addresses.
- **A trap bit**—The trap bit is used to indicate an exception, typically that an address should be blocked or filtered.
- **A static bit**—The static bit is used to support static or manually entered addresses.
- **A valid bit**—The valid bit is used so that aged-out addresses are not used.

With the introduction of the EARL2 on the NFFC, the supervisor is capable of examining and acting on Layer 3 IP packet information. After an initial routing decision is made by either an internal (RSM or RSFC) or external router, the EARL2 can rewrite subsequent similar packets based on that information, without sending the packet to the route processor for a routing decision.

In addition, some newer line modules on the Catalyst 5500 are equipped with specialized ASICs capable of what is termed *in-line rewrite*, allowing them to rewrite Layer 3 based on information provided by the EARL. Line modules capable of in-line rewrites are able to rewrite Layer 3 without the help of the supervisor.

Because the EARL is responsible for creating and maintaining the CAM table, all forwarding stops anytime a Supervisor is reset or removed. In switches that support redundancy using dual supervisors, high-availability software features synchronize one or more forwarding tables between the EARLs on each Supervisor, allowing forwarding to continue after a brief, or sometimes not so brief, pause, depending on the platform. Chapter 11, "Design and Implementation Best Practices," discusses high availability using redundant supervisor on various platforms in detail.

CAM and TCAM

The terms CAM and ternary CAM (TCAM) have become almost interchangable with today's switches because all the switching architectures discussed in this chapter are capable of making switching decisions using Layer 3 and Layer 4 information, along with ACLs and QoS parameters. As described earlier in the section "Supervisor Module," a CAM stores the table of learned MAC addresses, ports, and VLAN information. This information is found at Layer 2 and is the basic information every switch needs to function.

The TCAM gets its name from the system of storing 0s, 1s, and *s (* = Don't Care) used to match patterns of entries in the tables. Because this CAM stores three values, the term *ternary* (meaning having three elements) describes this type of CAM. Depending on the platform, various ASICs program and process TCAM entries for functions such as ACLs and QoS in hardware. Both the CAM and TCAM information is processed in parallel during a lookup, resulting in wire-speed processing of packets by the switch.

Catalyst 5000/5500 EARL Versions

Knowing the version of EARL in use helps determine the forwarding intelligence of each platform. Table 3-2 shows existing EARL versions and their forwarding capabilities.

Table 3-2   *Catalyst 5000/5500 EARL Versions*

Supervisor Part Number	Supervisor Model	EARL Version Subtype
WS-X5005	Supervisor I	EARL1
WS-X5006	Supervisor I	EARL1
WS-X5009	Supervisor I	EARL1
WS-X5505	Supervisor II	EARL1+
WS-X5506	Supervisor II	EARL1+
WS-X5509	Supervisor II	EARL1+
WS-X5530-E1	Supervisor III	EARL1++
WS-X5530-E2	Supervisor III NFFC	EARL2 (NFFC)
WS-X5530-E2A	Supervisor III NFFC-A	EARL2 (NFFC)
WS-X5530-E3	Supervisor III NFFC II	EARL3 (NFFC II)
WS-X5530-E3A	Supervisor III NFFC II-A	EARL3 (NFFC II)
WS-X5534	Supervisor III F	EARL1++
WS-X5540	Supervisor II G	EARL 3 (NFFC II)
WS-X5550	Supervisor III G	EARL3 (NFFC II)

Switch Bandwidth

Switch bandwidth can be calculated by multiplying the width of the data bus times the clock speed. In project Synergy, each Catalyst 5000 data bus is 48 bits wide and operates at a speed of 25 MHz. The resulting calculation $(48 * 25,000,000) = 1,200,000,000$ or 1.2 Gigabits per second (Gbps).

With faster processors, greatly improved switch fabrics, and distributed forwarding capabilities, newer Catalyst platforms such as the Catalyst 3750, 4500, and 6500 can achieve data transfer ranging from 32 Gbps to 720 Gbps.

In addition to raw bandwidth, a commonly advertised performance number is the maximum packets per second that can be forwarded by the central switch processors. For example, the Catalyst 6000 with a Supervisor I advertises 32 Gbps of switch bandwidth and is capable of forwarding 15 million packets per second (Mpps).

Line Modules

The first Ethernet line modules introduced along with project Synergy (Catalyst 5000) included the following:

- 12-port, 10/100 Mbps autonegotiation Ethernet/Fast Ethernet with RJ-45 connectors for unshielded twisted-pair (UTP) Category 5 cable

- 24-port, 10 Mbps Ethernet with two RJ-21 Amphenol connectors

- 12-port, 10 Mbps 10BASE-FL with ST fiber connectors

- 48-port, 10 Mbps group switched Ethernet with four RJ-21 Amphenol connectors (4 switched ports, 12 shared ports per switched port)

- 12-port, 100 Mbps 100BASE-FX with SC fiber connectors

- 24-port, 100 Mbps Fast Ethernet with RJ-45 connectors for UTP Category 5 cable (3 switched ports, 8 shared ports per switched port)

- 24-port, 10 Mbps Ethernet with RJ-45 connectors for UTP Category 5 cable

These first modules were limited to 10 and 100 Mbps Ethernet, and introduced many years prior to Gigabit Ethernet becoming a standard.

Each Ethernet line module consists of specialized ASICs providing the module's forwarding capabilities. In the case of the 12-port, 10/100 Mbps Ethernet/Fast Ethernet module, one SAINT ASIC is required for each 10/100 Mbps port on the module.

Since the introduction of the Catalyst 5000, many additional line modules or modules have been introduced. A complete list can be obtained at the Cisco Systems website at Cisco.com. Figure 3-4 shows one of the first 10/100 Ethernet Switching modules.

Figure 3-4   *Catalyst 5xxx 16 Port 10/100 Ethernet Switching Module*

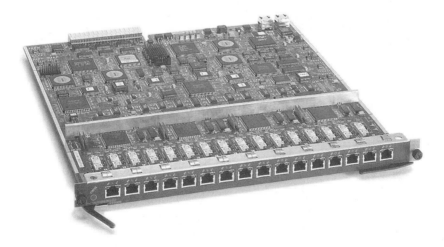

Catalyst 5000/5500 Architectures

As previously discussed in this chapter, the Catalyst 5000 line of switches uses a shared bus architecture to transport incoming frames from source to destination. The Catalyst 5000 uses a total of three buses to move data, communicate configuration and network management information, and determine which ports should forward or discard frames.

The following describes the bus types on the Catalyst 5000 series:

- **Switching or data bus (dBus)**—The dBus is used to switch frames between line cards. The data bus is 48 bits wide and operates at 25 MHz, yielding 1.2 Gbps of bus bandwidth.

- **Management bus (mBus)**—The mBus carries configuration information from the NMP to each module and statistical information from each module to the NMP, using the Serial Communication Protocol (SCP).

- **Results/index bus (rBus)**—The rBus carries port-select information from the central EARL ASIC to the ports. This information determines which ports forward the packet and which flush it from the buffer.

The Catalyst 5500 series implements these same three buses, plus two additional data buses, each providing 1.2 Gbps of bandwidth, yielding 3.6 Gbps of total bus bandwidth. To maintain backward compatibility with the Catalyst 5000 line cards, the chassis of the 5500 series were designed so that newer line cards connected to all three buses, while still allowing older Catalyst 5000 line cards to connect to a single bus. Figure 3-5 illustrates the types of the connections on the Catalyst 5500 backplane.

The Catalyst 5500 introduced a 5-Gbps Asynchronous Transfer Mode (ATM) cell switch bus for use with an optional ATM switch processor based on Cisco Lightstream 1010 technology. As with all Catalyst switches, Slot 1 is reserved for a Supervisor module. Switching modules installed in Slots 1–5 connect to all three 1.2-Gbps buses providing 3.6 Gbps of total bandwidth.

While Gigabit Ethernet modules are available for the Catalyst 5000 and 5500 series, certain restrictions apply to where they can be installed to provide enough bandwidth to enable all the ports. Gigabit Ethernet modules should be installed in slots with connections to all three 1.2-Gbps buses. Slot 13 is reserved for the ATM switch processor (ASP). A detailed discussion of the ATM switching capabilities on the Catalyst 5500 is beyond the scope of this book. More information on Catalyst 5500 ATM switching capabilities is available on the Cisco website at Cisco.com.

Figure 3-5   *Catalyst 5500 Backplane Connections*

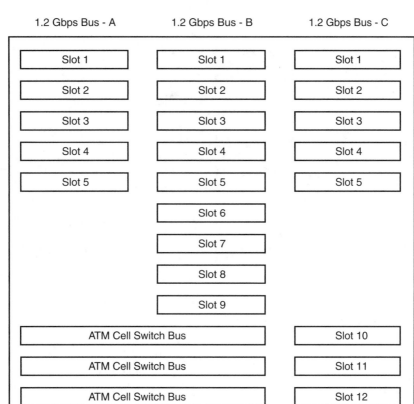

Catalyst 5500 Backplane

Data Flow on the Catalyst 5000

Figure 3-6 describes the path a frame takes from the time it is received on an input port on the WS-X5224, to the time it is transmitted out the egress port on another WS-X5224, using the central rewrite function on the EARL on the Supervisor. This is a high-level overview, focusing on the major steps of forwarding a frame.

Figure 3-6   *Data Flow on the Catalyst 5000*

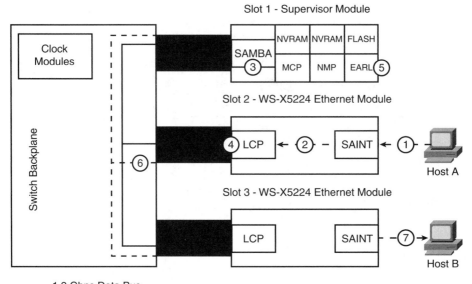

The following list corresponds to the process illustrated in Figure 3-6:

1   Host A transmits an Ethernet frame destined for Host B. When the frame arrives on an input or ingress port on Slot 2, it is fully stored in input buffers and a Frame Check Sequence (FCS) is run on the frame to determine if the frame is "good." If the frame passes the FCS, a 15-byte header is added to the frame containing the port number and VLAN.

2   The ingress port then requests access to the data bus through the local arbiter on the line card.

3   The line card's local arbiter then requests access to the data bus through the central arbiter (SAMBA).

4   After the line card's local arbiter is granted access to the switching bus by the central arbiter on the Supervisor, the frame is transmitted onto the switching bus where all line cards receive it, including the Supervisor.

5   Because the EARL is on the Supervisor, it gets a copy of the frame and goes to work. The EARL inspects the destination address, source address, and VLAN ID of the packet. The MAC address and VLAN ID are then put through a hash function, resulting in a 15-bit address. This 15-bit address gets compared to the forwarding

information in the CAM table. When the 15-bit hash matches an existing entry in the CAM table, the EARL uses what is called Local Target Logic (LTL) and Color Blocking Logic (CBL) to determine which line cards should forward the frame. VLAN numbers were originally referred to by "colors" as an easy way to identify different VLANs.

6   The resulting information is sent via the rBus to each line card.

7   LTL on each line card then determines which ports are to forward the frame. The Ethernet port connected to Host B on Slot 3 transmits the frame to Host B. All other ports on all other line cards simply discard the frame.

If a frame has a broadcast address or does not match an existing entry in the CAM table, the MAC address along with the VLAN ID are sent on the rBus to flood out all ports that belong to that VLAN, excluding the port on which the frame was received.

Catalyst 6000/6500 (Constellation, Constellation+, and Constellation II)

The Catalyst 6000, codename Constellation, was introduced in 1999 and represented a leap forward in switching technology. The Catalyst 6000 increased Ethernet switching bandwidth from 3.6 Gbps to 32 Gbps.

Approximately one year after the introduction of the Catalyst 6000, Cisco introduced the Catalyst 6500 series switches, codename Constellation+. The Catalyst 6500 introduced support for an eventual crossbar switch fabric while providing backward compatibility for modules designed for the 32-Gbps shared bus of the Catalyst 6000. The implementation of support for backward compatibility on the Catalyst 6500 is not much different than the method used on the Catalyst 5500. Both platforms introduced new connections to higher speed crossbar fabrics while providing connections to the legacy shared buses. The 6500 Constellation+ chassis has the electrical connections to support a crossbar switch fabric, but, in 2002, the Switch Fabric Module (SFM) introduced the Constellation II architecture and enabled the 256-Gbps crossbar switch fabric for the Catalyst 6500 platform. The next section discusses each of the Supervisor and Switch Fabric options for these platforms in detail.

Catalyst 6000/6500 Components

Much like the Catalyst 5000/5500 series switches, the Catalyst 6000/6500 is a modular switching platform made up of chassis, supervisors, line modules, and power supply options. The next sections describe each of these Catalyst 6000/6500 components.

Chassis

A wide range of chassis choices are available for the Catalyst 6000/6500. It is important to understand the differences in the various chassis beyond just the number of slots. Table 3-3 describes each Catalyst 6000/6500 chassis model.

Table 3-3   *Catalyst 6000/6500 Models*

Model	Description	Backplane Connections
WS-C6006	Catalyst 6000 Series 6-slot chassis	32-Gbps shared bus only
WS-C6009	Catalyst 6000 Series 9-slot chassis	32-Gbps shared bus only
WS-C6503	Catalyst 6500 Series 3-slot chassis	32-Gbps shared bus and 256 Gbps crossbar fabric
WS-C6506	Catalyst 6500 Series 6-slot chassis	32-Gbps shared bus and 256 Gbps crossbar fabric
WS-C6509	Catalyst 6500 Series 9-slot chassis	32-Gbps shared bus and 256-Gbps crossbar fabric
WS-C6509-NEB	Catalyst 6500 Series 9-slot chassis, NEBS[*] compliant vertical slots	32-Gbps shared bus and 256-Gbps crossbar fabric
WS-C6513	Catalyst 6500 Series 13-slot chassis	32-Gbps shared bus and 256-Gbps crossbar fabric[**]

[*]   Network Equipment Building Standards (NEBS) is the conformance requirement intended to regulate the quality and reliability of telecom equipment. NEBS was introduced by Bellcore (now Telcordia Technologies), an extension of the seven regional Bell Operating companies (RBOCs).

[**]   Requires a Switch Fabric 2 module.

The original Catalyst 6000 series chassis, no longer sold, does not support the crossbar fabric enabled by the SFMs or Supervisor 720. In addition, the SFM and Supervisor 720 can only be installed in designated slots on the Catalyst 6500 series chassis.

Supervisors and Switch Fabrics

Since the introduction of the Catalyst 6000 series switches and the Supervisor I for the Catalyst 6000, three additional Supervisor modules and two SFMs have been introduced:

- **Supervisor I**—The original Supervisor I was introduced with the Catalyst 6000 and implements a shared 32-Gbps bus architecture. It includes two Gigabit Ethernet uplink ports using GBIC connectors and is capable of only Layer 2 switching. The Supervisor I is capable of integrated routing with the optional Multilayer Switch Feature Card version 1 (MSFC1) daughterboard. The MSFC1 is an NPE-200 routing processor not unlike the RSFC for the Catalyst 5500. The Supervisor I does not include a Policy Feature Card (PFC), does not support the MSFC version 2 (MSFC2), and cannot be used with either SFM.

- **Supervisor IA**—In addition to the features of the Supervisor I, the Supervisor IA introduced the PFC, a daughterboard with ASICs enabling multilayer switching, and QoS features at hardware speeds. The PFC on the 6000/6500 is responsible for the same functionality as the EARL on the Catalyst 5000. The Supervisor IA also supports the MSFC2 daughterboard, which is approximately three times faster than the original MSFC at switching packets in software.

- **Supervisor II**—The Supervisor II supports both connections to the 32-Gbps shared bus on the Catalyst 6000/6500 and a connection to the optional crossbar switch fabric enabled via either the Switch Fabric or Switch Fabric II modules. In addition, the Supervisor II includes the PFC version 2 enabling multilayer switching implementing Cisco Express Forwarding (CEF) in hardware. Chapter 6 discusses both MLS and CEF in detail.

- **Switch Fabric Module (SFM)**—The SFM enables a 256-Gbps crossbar switch fabric on the 6500 series switches and is not supported in the Catalyst 6000 chassis. The SFM provides 8 Gbps of bandwidth for each line via direct connections into the switch fabric. The switch fabric contains small input buffers and slightly larger output buffers for each line card connection. The switch fabric utilizes what is termed a "three times overspeed" method of switching frames in and out of the fabric at 24 Gbps. Because frames are being switched between line cards at a much faster rate than they are being sent to the switch fabric, the SFM creates a non-blocking switch fabric with almost all traffic patterns.

- **Switch Fabric Module II**—The SFM version II implemented some internal enhancements over the original SFM including high- and low-priority traffic queues into the switch fabric for each line card, increased available bandwidth from 8 Gbps to 16 Gbps for each line card, and support for the 6513 13-slot chassis.

- **Supervisor 720**—A big breakthrough with the Supervisor 720 is the integration of a 720-Gbps switch fabric into the Supervisor itself, freeing a slot normally taken by a separate SFM. The Supervisor 720 includes a new PFC version 3, a new MSFC version 3 (MSFC3), two fiber Gigabit Ethernet uplink ports, and one 10/100/1000 Ethernet RJ-45 uplink port. The Supervisor 720 cannot be used with either the Switch Fabric or Switch Fabric II modules. Figure 3-7 shows a Supervisor 720 module.

Knowing the version of EARL in use helps determine the forwarding intelligence of each platform. Table 3-4 shows the existing EARL versions. With the introduction of the Catalyst 6000/6500 series switches, EARL functionality is delivered via either a Constellation Advanced Forwarding Engine (CAFE) or a Policy Feature Card (PFC). As of the Supervisor 1A, the PFC replaced the CAFE for all future supervisors. Unlike the Catalyst 5000/5000, Catalyst 6000/6500 documentation rarely refers to an EARL.

Figure 3-7 *Catalyst 6500 Supervisor 720*

Table 3-4 *Catalyst 6000/6500 EARL Versions*

Part Number	Model	EARL Version
WS-X6K-SUP1-2GE	Supervisor I	EARL4 (CAFE2)
WS-X6K-SUP1A-PFC	Supervisor IA	EARL5 (PFC1)
WS-X6K-S2-PFC2	Supervisor II	EARL6 (PFC2)
WS-SUP720	Supervisor 720	EARL7 (PFC3)

Line Modules

Dozens of line cards are available for the Catalyst 6500 platform, ranging from the 24-port WS-X6024-10FL-MT 10 Mb Ethernet multimode fiber-optic module to the 1-port WS-X6502-10GE 10 Gb single-mode fiber-optic module.

Along with the introduction of the SFMs and the Supervisor 720, new switching modules have been introduced to support the higher bandwidth connections into the switch fabrics.

Catalyst 6000/6500 series line cards can be grouped into three major categories:

- **Classic**—Classic line cards have connections only into the 32-Gbps shared bus of the Catalyst 6000 and 6500 series switches.

- **Fabric enabled**—Fabric-enabled line cards have a connection into the legacy 32-Gbps shared bus and a single 8-Gbps connection into the crossbar switch fabric.

- **Fabric only**—Fabric-only line cards do not have a connection into the legacy 32-Gbps shared bus but have two 8-Gbps connections into the crossbar switch fabric.

Distributed switching or forwarding capabilities are possible on some modules via optional Distributed Forward Cards (DFCs). The DFCs are daughterboards that are installable on either fabric-enabled or fabric-only line cards such as the WS-X6516 and the WS-X6816.

Although 256 Gbps of switch bandwidth is available via the SFM and as much as 720 Gbps is available via the Supervisor 720, the Ethernet line cards must rely upon the central switch processors (EARL) in the form of the PFC to make the forwarding decision for each frame or packet. This centralized switching model limits the amount of traffic that can be switched to the processing capabilities of the PFC and the optional routing engine (MSFC). For example, a Catalyst 6500 with a Supervisor II and optional Switch Fabric offers 256 Gbps of switch bandwidth but the PFC2 and MSFC2 on the Supervisor are only capable of forwarding 15 Mpps. The DFCs are essentially a PFC2 and MSFC2 on a daughterboard, capable of making all the same forwarding decisions of the Supervisor at the same speeds. A fabric-enabled line card such as the WS-X6516 with the optional DFC can forward 15 Mpps in addition to the Supervisor's 15 Mpps.

A complete list of available line cards for the Catalyst 6500 can be found by searching the Cisco Systems website at Cisco.com.

Power and Cooling

The type and voltage of power supply is sometimes overlooked. Newer Catalyst switches, especially the 6500 series, offer a range of power supplies with varying power ratings. Depending on the number and type of line cards installed, higher voltage power supplies may be necessary, especially if Ethernet cards with in-line power capabilities are installed. In-line power cards are used to power devices such as IP phones.

For example, Cisco Catalyst 6500 series switch power supplies are available in five power ratings:

- 950W AC input (Cisco Catalyst 6503 chassis)
- 1000W AC input
- 1300W AC and DC input
- 2500W AC and DC input
- 4000W AC input

Consult the documentation for the Catalyst 6000/6500 at the Cisco Systems website for detailed power supply specifications and requirements.

In addition to power supplies, fan trays should be considered when configuring a Catalyst switch. Available with the Catalyst 6500 are different models depending on the number of slots in the chassis, and two speeds of fan trays: normal and high speed. Fan tray model and speed are important because a high speed fan tray is required to support the new Supervisor 720 for the Catalyst 6500 series switches.

Catalyst 6000/6500 Architectures

The Catalyst 6000/6500 series switching platforms represent a great leap forward in switching capabilities compared to the Catalyst 5000/5500. This section introduces new terminology specific to the architecture of the Catalyst 6000/6500 and examines data flow used when a SFM is present.

Shared Bus

Much like the Catalyst 5000 series, the Catalyst 6000/6500 series backplane implements an EARL data bus (dBus), an EARL results bus (rBus), and a control bus referred to as the Ethernet Out of Band Channel (EOBC). The EARL designation to describe the buses in this section denotes that the data buses are connected to the EARL switching ASICs on the Supervisor.

- **EARL Switching or Data Bus (dBus)**—The dBus is used to switch frames between line cards. The dBus is 256 bits wide and operates at 62.5 MHz, yielding 16 Gbps of bus bandwidth (32 Gbps full duplex).

- **Ethernet Out of Band Channel (EOBC)**—The EOBC is a control bus that carries configuration information from the Network Management Processor (NMP) to each module and statistical information from each module to the NMP. On the Catalyst 6000/6500, the out of band communications channel runs at 100 Mbps half duplex. The EOBC on the Catalyst 6000/6500 serves the same basic purpose as the management bus (mBus) on the Catalyst 5000.

- **EARL Results/Index Bus (rBus)**—The rBus carries port-select information from the central EARL ASICs to the ports. This information determines which ports forward the packet and which flush it from the buffer.

The process of switching a frame at Layer 2 on a Catalyst 6000/6500 using a shared bus is not much different than on the Catalyst 5000/5500. Greater differences between the platforms are encountered when doing more intelligent switching using information contained in the dBus header. Chapter 6 discusses these differences.

Crossbar Switch Fabrics

Crossbar switch fabrics on the Catalyst 6500 are enabled via the SFM version I or II, or the Supervisor 720.

With the Catalyst 6509, for example, the SFM provides a 16-Gbps (32-Gbps full duplex) connection to each line card. As mentioned previously in the "Supervisors and Switch Fabrics" section, the SFMII is required to support the Catalyst 6513 but because of the number of slots (13), only 8 Gbps is delivered to the first 7 usable slots, and 16 Gbps is provided to the last 5 slots.

*   Figure 3-8 illustrates the connections from the switch fabric to each module on a Catalyst 6509 switch.

Figure 3-8   *Crossbar Switch Fabric on the Catalyst 6509*

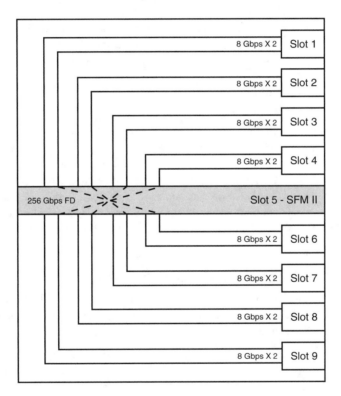

The crossbar switch fabric creates multiple high-speed simultaneous connections between modules.

Catalyst 6500 Switching Modes

All forwarding decisions for all line cards on a Catalyst 6500 utilizing the Supervisor IA are made by the central EARL ASICs on the supervisor (PFC1 or PFC2). This switching mode is called *flow through*, and in this configuration, each packet is fully transmitted onto the shared bus. This configuration limits the aggregate forwarding capabilities to a maximum of 15 Mpps.

With the introduction of new Supervisors, SFMs, and fabric-enabled line cards, new switching modes enable only a portion of the packet to be transmitted, resulting in higher switching performance.

If the Catalyst 6500 is fabric enabled but contains a mix of classic line cards and fabric-enabled line cards, the switch operates in a mode called *truncated*. In truncated mode, the classic line cards transmit the entire frame onto the backplane, while fabric-enabled line cards transmit a 96-byte frame (32-byte header + 64-byte data). Because the classic line cards are transmitting full frames, performance in truncated mode is still limited to 15 Mpps.

A Catalyst 6500 utilizing the Supervisor II and SFM, along with fabric-enabled line cards, allows the transmission of only a small header (32 bytes) and subset of the data packet (32 bytes) across the backplane. The resulting 64-byte "compact" frame contains all the information the EARL ASICs on the Supervisor need to make a forwarding decision. This switching mode is called *compact* and is only enabled when all line cards installed in the switch are fabric enabled. A switch running in compact mode can transmit up to 30 Mpps, twice the speed of a switch operating in flow-through or truncated modes.

Data Flow on the Catalyst 6500 Switch Fabric

Because the high-level operation of the classic shared bus on the Catalyst 6500 and the shared bus on the Catalyst 5000 is similar in many ways, the Catalyst 6500 data flow example uses the optional SFM and fabric-enabled line cards.

Figure 3-9 illustrates at a high level the transmission of a unicast packet from Host1 connected to a Gigabit port on Slot 2 to Host2 connected to a Gigabit port on Slot 3. In the figure, only key ASICs are listed on the supervisor and their locations on the supervisor are not "anatomically correct."

Figure 3-9   *Data Flow on the Catalyst 6500 Fabric Enabled*

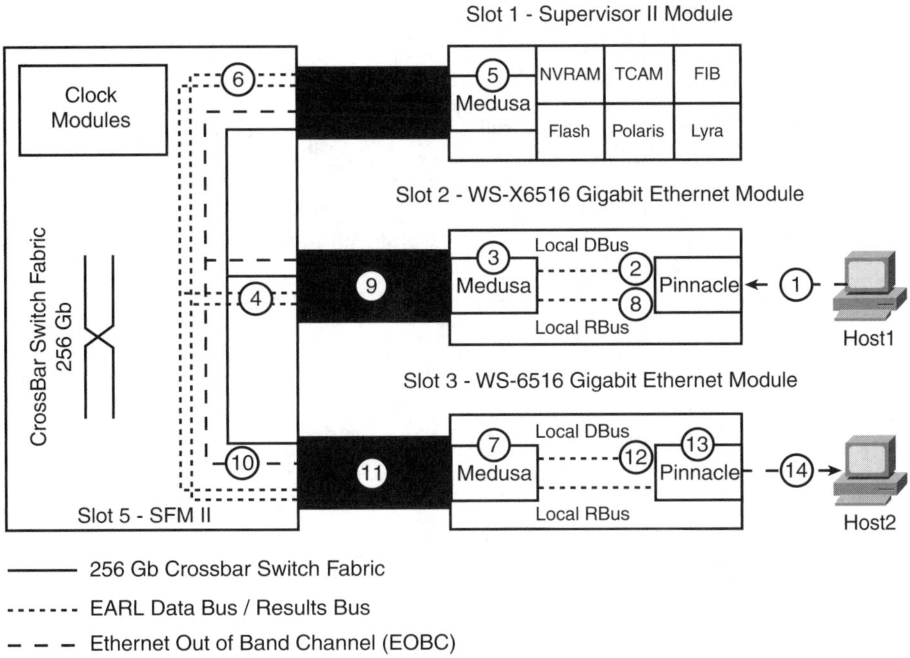

——— 256 Gb Crossbar Switch Fabric

------- EARL Data Bus / Results Bus

— — — Ethernet Out of Band Channel (EOBC)

The two WS-X6516 line cards used in Figure 3-9 differ from classic line cards because in addition to their connection to the classic 32-Gbps shared bus, they are fabric enabled via an 8-Gbps connection to the switch fabric. The Medusa ASIC connects the line card to both the classic shared bus and the switch fabric. The data flow example demonstrates how packets that are capable of being hardware switched are handled.

The following explanation corresponds to the data flow shown in Figure 3-9:

1   The Pinnacle ASIC on Slot 2 sends the frame onto that line card's local data bus (LC-dBus). The line card has a LC-dBus because it is fabric enabled.

2   The Medusa ASIC and all other Pinnacle ASICs on Slot 2 store the entire data frame.

3   Because this card is fabric enabled, a 64-byte header is created (Compact Mode). The Medusa in Slot 2 forwards the header to the central EARL data bus (E-dBus).

4 The Medusa and Forwarding Engine (PFC2) on the Supervisor store the header.

5 The forwarding engines examine the header and then send the forwarding decision onto the central EARL result bus (E-rBus).

6 The Medusa ASICs on all line cards see the result, including Slot 3.

7 The Medusa on Slot 2 forwards the result from the forwarding engine to its local result bus (LC-rBus); all other Medusas (Slot 3) will drop the header.

8 The Fabric Port of Exit (FPOE) is stored in the result received from the Supervisor Forwarding Engine, and this FPOE is placed in a header that is used to determine where the Switch Fabric sends the frame. The Medusa in Slot 2 will forward the header and the entire data frame to the Switch Fabric.

9 The Switch Fabric receives the frame and, based on the FPOE, knows to send it to Slot 3.

10 The Medusa in Slot 3 receives the frame from the Switch Fabric.

11 The Medusa in Slot 3 forwards the frame to the line card's LC-dBus.

12 All Gigabit ports on Slot 3 receive the frame.

13 The Medusa on Slot 3 generates the forwarding result onto the local results bus (LC-rBus).

14 Local Target Logic (LTL) selects a port on the Pinnacle ASIC connected to Host2 to forward the frame; all other ports on the line card will drop the frame.

Catalyst 4500 (Galaxy 3 and Galaxy 4) Components and Architectures

Because the Catalyst 4500 is a modular switching platform, it is comprised of chassis, supervisor, line module, and power supply options. Although Cisco positions the Catalyst 4500 series as a high-density closet switching solution, it is sometimes used as a distribution or server switch.

Chassis

All the Catalyst 4500 series chassis are offspring of a project codenamed Galaxy, with the 4507 classified as codename Galaxy 3 and 4510 as Galaxy 4. Table 3-5 lists the currently available chassis in the Catalyst 4500 series product line.

Figure 3-10 shows the 4503, 4506, and 4507R chassis in the Catalyst 4500 series product line.

Table 3-5   *Catalyst 4500 Models*

Model	Description
4503	Catalyst 4500 Series 3-slot chassis
4506	Catalyst 4500 Series 6-slot chassis
4507R[*]	Catalyst 4500 Series 7-slot chassis
4510R[**]	Catalyst 4500 Series 10-slot chassis

[*]   Supports redundant Supervisor modules

[**]   Requires a Supervisor V

Figure 3-10   *Catalyst 4500 Series Switches*

Supervisors and Switch Fabrics

The Catalyst 4500 series switches support five different Supervisor modules. With the Catalyst 4500 series, the capacity of the switch fabric is determined by the Supervisor installed. Unlike other Catalyst platforms such as the Catalyst 6500 that use per port buffers and are capable of distributing forwarding intelligence to the line modules, all forwarding decisions and packet buffering are handled by the Supervisor. The five Catalyst 4500 Supervisor modules are

- **Supervisor II**—The Supervisor II enables a 64-Gbps switch fabric when installed in a 6-slot chassis, and is capable of handling only Layer 2 forwarding decisions. Using 64-byte packets, the Supervisor II can process a maximum of 18 million packets at Layer 2. All packets are processed by the supervisor and buffered using 8 MB of shared packet buffers. The Supervisor II includes two Gigabit Ethernet uplink ports using GBIC connectors.

The Supervisor II supports an optional Layer 3 services module (WS-X4232-L3) that is capable of processing around 6 Mpps at Layer 3. The Supervisor II utilizes three central forwarding ASICs that Cisco has dubbed the "K1," named after the "Kirky Architectural Specification." Each of the three K1 ASICs supports twelve 1-Gbps full-duplex connections for a total of 24 Gbps (full duplex) per ASIC. Each of the three K1 ASICs are responsible for handling one third of the ports on each line card, and are interconnected via 1-Gbps links. Because of these 1-Gbps interconnections, a bottleneck is created when traffic needs to move from ports serviced by one K1 to ports serviced by another K1 on the supervisor.

- **Supervisor III**—The Supervisor III enables a 64-Gbps switch fabric when installed in a 6-slot chassis, and uses the next generation K2 ASIC capable of Layer 2, Layer 3, and Layer 4 packet processing. The Supervisor III is capable of advanced Layer 3 features including OSPF, EIGRP, and BGP. The K2 ASIC utilizes an entirely different architecture from the K1 by dividing packet handling functions into packet processing and fast forwarding. The packet processing engine (PPE) is responsible for receiving, storing, and transmitting all packets. The fast forwarding engine (FFE) is responsible for performing Layer 2, Layer 3, and Layer 4 lookups and processing ACLs and QoS decisions. Because only one K2 ASIC is used, the Supervisor III does not suffer from the same performance limitations as the Supervisor II.

- **Supervisor II+**—The Supervisor II+ enables a 64-Gbps switch fabric when installed in a 6-slot chassis, and uses the same K2 ASIC as the Supervisor III and IV. The Supervisor II+ is capable of Layer 2, Layer 3, and Layer 4 packet processing like the Supervisor III and IV, but is capable of only basic Layer 3 features such as RIPv1/v2. Because the Supervisor II+ cannot run OSFP, EIGRP, and BGP, it is positioned by Cisco as a wiring closet solution. The Supervisor II+ can provide redundancy when two are installed in the Catalyst 4507R.

- **Supervisor IV**—The Supervisor IV enables a 64-Gbps switch fabric when installed in a 6-slot chassis, and uses the same K2 ASIC as the Supervisor II+ and III. The Supervisor also offers redundancy by implementing dual Supervisors in the Catalyst 4507R. In addition to Supervisor redundancy, the Supervisor IV offers NetFlow support via an optional daughterboard. The Supervisor IV supports the enhanced Layer 3 routing features as the Supervisor III.

- **Supervisor V**—The Supervisor V enables a 96-Gbps switch fabric when installed in a 10-slot chassis, and uses the same K2 ASIC as the Supervisor II+, III, and IV. The Supervisor V provides improved support for as many as 48 wire-speed Gigabit Ethernet ports and is backward compatible with the Catalyst 4006 and all Catalyst 4500 series chassis. The 4510 chassis requires a Supervisor V for operation, and when installed in redundant mode, all four Gigabit Ethernet uplinks are active.

Figure 3-11 shows the Supervisor V for the Catalyst 4500 series switches.

Figure 3-11 *Supervisor V for Catalyst 4500 Series*

Line Modules

A wide variety of line modules are available for the Catalyst 4500 platform because legacy Catalyst 4000 line modules are compatible with the 4500 series platforms. The Catalyst 4500 supports various densities of 10/100 and Gigabit Ethernet, with future support planned for 10 Gigabit Ethernet.

Catalyst 4000/4500 series line cards are considered to be *functionally transparent*, meaning they do not contain local packet forwarding or processing capabilities, and are essentially only interfaces to the ASICs on the Supervisors. This is in contrast to the local forwarding and buffering capabilities of Catalyst 6500 line modules.

Each Catalyst 4000/4500 line module uses what is called *stub ASICs*. The stub ASICs have the simple responsibility of splitting the six 1-Gbps connections from the Supervisor into the proper speed and bandwidth for each port on the line module.

A complete list of available line cards for the Catalyst 4500 can be found by searching the Cisco Systems website at Cisco.com.

Power and Cooling

The Cisco Catalyst 4500 Series internal power supplies are available in four power ratings:

- 1000W AC input (data only)
- 1300W AC input (data and in-line power)
- 1400W DC input (data and in-line power)
- 2800W AC input (data and in-line power)

Figure 3-12 shows an example of the 2800W AC power supply for the Catalyst 4500 series switches.

Figure 3-12 *Catalyst 4500 Power Supplies*

The Catalyst 4500 series power supplies differ from other Catalyst platforms by coupling what are essentially two power systems into one power supply. The 1300W and 2800W power supplies divide their total power capabilities between data and in-line power for devices such as IP phones or wireless access points. Each Catalyst 4500 chassis supports up to two power supplies running in either redundant or combined power mode:

- **Redundant mode**—In redundant mode, both power supplies are on line, with each power supply providing half the power to the system. In this mode, the switch manages power so that should one power supply fail completely, the other is providing enough power for the system to continue uninterrupted operation. In this mode, total power to the system does not exceed the capabilities of one power supply.

- **Combined mode**—In combined mode, the Supervisor combines the power from both power supplies to provide more power than is available from a single power supply. In combined mode, a single power supply failure could cause interruption of power to some in-line powered devices if the total power used by the system exceeds the capabilities of a single power supply.

Power supplies installed in pairs must be identical types when the system is powered on, but individual power supplies can be upgraded but not downgraded during switch operation. A system error message will be reported when upgrading power supplies during live operation. Some configurations of line modules and in-line powered devices may exceed the capabilities of the internal power supplies. In these situations, as many as two external 220VAC power shelves can be added to provide additional power.

Unlike the Catalyst 6500 series, the Catalyst 4500 series only supports one type of internal fan tray. Each fan in the tray is independent and the system can cool properly with only one fan operating. Should a fan fail, an error message is generated to inform the user of the failure.

Data Flow on the Catalyst 4500

Figure 3-13 illustrates at a high level the transmission of a unicast packet from Host1 connected to a Gigabit port on Module 3 to Host2 connected to a 10/100/1000 port on Module 4. Again, only key ASICs are listed on the supervisor and line modules; their locations are not necessarily "anatomically correct."

The WS-X4306-GB six-port Gigabit line module is used in Slot 3 and the WS-X4448-GB-RJ 48-port 10/100/1000 line module is used in Slot 4. Because the K1 architecture is not being carried forward into new Catalyst 4500 series products, the data flow example demonstrates the K2 architecture of the Supervisor II+, III, and IV. The data flow example assumes hardware switched packets.

Figure 3-13 *Data Flow on the Catalyst 4500*

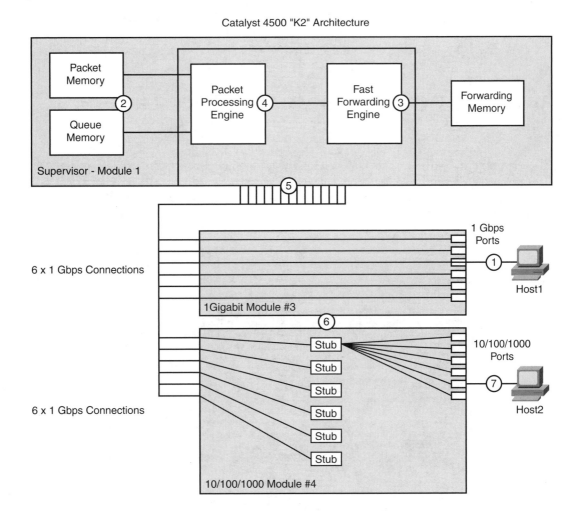

The following explanation corresponds to the data flow shown in Figure 3-13:

1 Host1 transmits a packet. Packet is received by Module 3 and transmitted onto the backplane to the Supervisor.

2 The packet is stored in buffer memory (256-byte buffers) and the PPE builds a lookup descriptor for the FFE.

3 The lookup descriptor is sent to the FFE. The FFE performs Layer 2 and Layer 3 lookups along with any ACL or QoS processing.

4 A packet transmit descriptor is created by the FFE as a result of the lookups and sent back to the PPE.

5 The PPE rewrites the packet and transmits it to Module 4.

6 The stub ASIC on Module 4 utilizes round-robin scheduling to determine when to transmit the packet.

7 The packet is transmitted to Host2.

Catalyst 3750 (Lord of the Rings) Components and Architecture

One of the newest members of the Catalyst family of switches is the 3750 series, codename Lord of the Rings. The 3750 series is made up of fixed-configuration switches allowing expansion through the interconnection or "stacking" of additional switches into what Cisco terms a *cluster* rather than through the addition of line modules as with the Catalyst 5000 and 6500 series.

The Catalyst 3750 series offers four models pictured in Figure 3-14 and explained in Table 3-6.

Figure 3-14 *Catalyst 3750 Models*

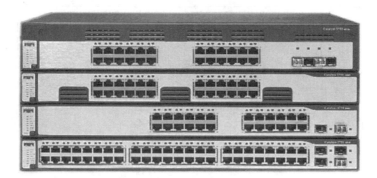

Table 3-6   *Catalyst 3750 Models*

Model	Ports	Modular Uplinks
WS-C3750-24	24 10/100 Ethernet	2 SFP[*]
WS-C3750-48	48 10/100 Ethernet	4 SFP
WS-C3750G-24T	24 10/100/1000 Ethernet	None
WS-C3750G-24TS	24 10/100/1000 Ethernet	4 SFP

[*]   Small Form Factor Pluggable

The Catalyst 3750 series switches use Small Form Factor Pluggable (SFP) uplink ports, which take up less than half the space of a traditional Gigabit Interface Connector (GBIC). The SFPs offer Gigabit Ethernet uplinks using either single or multimode fiber optics. Figure 3-15 shows a SFP and GBIC in a side-by-side comparison.

Figure 3-15 *SFP and GBIC*

Power and Cooling

The Catalyst 3750 series is a fixed-configuration platform and utilizes an integrated power and cooling system. The only option for power and cooling in the Catalyst 3750 series is the RPS 675, which is a separate power supply module using the same form factor as the switches. The RPS 675 provides redundant power for as many as six switches, providing immediate failover should one internal power supply failure occur.

Stackwise Architecture

Cisco introduced the Stackwise architecture with the Catalyst 3750 series. Stackwise allows the connecting of up to nine Catalyst 3750 series switches via 68-pin Stackwise cables. The logical connections between switches form the common switching fabric and allow the stack to be managed using a single master switch.

The Stackwise architecture differs from other Catalyst architectures in a number of ways. When two or more switches are connected via Stackwise cables, a switch fabric consisting of dual counter-rotating rings is formed, with each ring providing 16 Gbps of bandwidth, resulting in 32 Gbps of total bandwidth. Each ring carries data and is self healing via a loopback protection mechanism that is enabled should a Stackwise cable or individual switch fail.

Figure 3-16 shows an example of the switch fabric formed using the counter-rotating rings when connecting three switches.

Figure 3-16 *Functioning 3750 Switch Fabric*

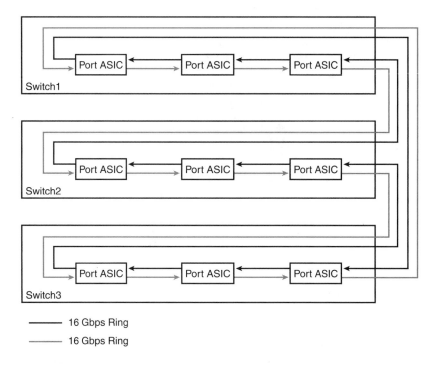

Should a link between switches fail, the switches loop back the connection at the point of failure to heal the break. This mechanism will look familiar to anyone with Fiber Distributed Data Interface (FDDI) implementation experience. Figure 3-17 illustrates the locations of loopbacks when a link fails between Switch1 and Switch2.

Figure 3-17 *Link Failure Between Switch1 and Switch2*

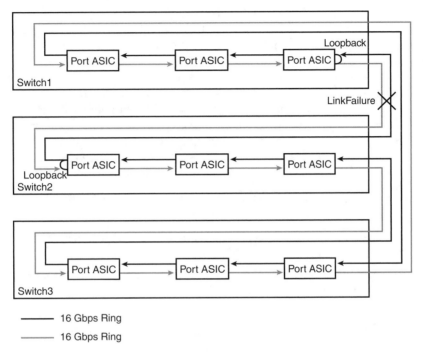

- ———— 16 Gbps Ring
- ———— 16 Gbps Ring

Figure 3-18 illustrates locations of the loopbacks when Switch2 fails completely.

Figure 3-18 *Complete Failure of Switch2*

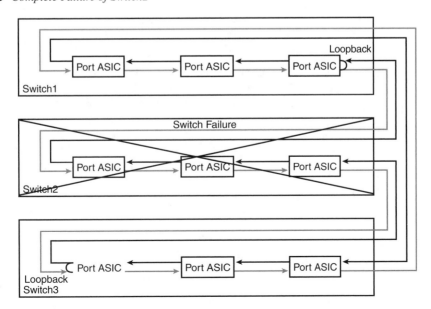

Data Flow on the Catalyst 3750

As described earlier in this chapter, the Catalyst 5000 and 6500 series grant bus access to individual line modules. In contrast to the bus architecture of the Catalyst 6500 using a round-robin mechanism to grant access to the shared bus, the Catalyst 3750 series uses a shared token on each ring to determine the order in which port ASICs may transmit data onto the ring. Unlike the centralized intelligence in the Supervisor and shared memory architecture of the Catalyst 4500 series, the Catalyst 3750 distributes the forwarding intelligence and packet buffers onto the port ASICs illustrated in Figure 3-19. The port ASIC is responsible for analyzing the packet, creating a 24-byte header containing the necessary information to make a forwarding decision, and transmitting the header along with the packet onto the ring or fabric. The data flow example in Figure 3-19 demonstrates how packets that are capable of being hardware switched are handled.

The following corresponds to the data flow shown in Figure 3-19:

1 Host1 is connected to a port on the front of Switch1. The port on Switch1 is connected to a port ASIC on the switch. Host1 transmits a packet to the ingress port on Switch1, destined for Host2 on Switch3.

2 The port ASIC has intelligence built-in to examine the packet and create the 24-byte header containing the necessary information to make a forward decision.

3 Each port ASIC has a connection to both rings. The port ASIC will choose a ring for transmission based on the first shared token to arrive. If a shared token arrives on both rings simultaneously, the port ASIC transmits on the least recently used ring. The port ASIC selects a ring and transmits the 24-byte header and the packet data onto a ring.

4 The destination port ASIC copies the 24-byte header and the packet data from the ring. The header and data are stored in packet buffer memory contained on the port ASIC.

5 The port ASIC transmits the packet through the egress port on the front of Switch3 to Host2.

6 The header and packet data continue around the ring until reaching the ingress port ASIC on Switch1. The port ASIC on Switch1 removes the header and data from the ring.

Figure 3-19 *Data Flow on the Catalyst 3750*

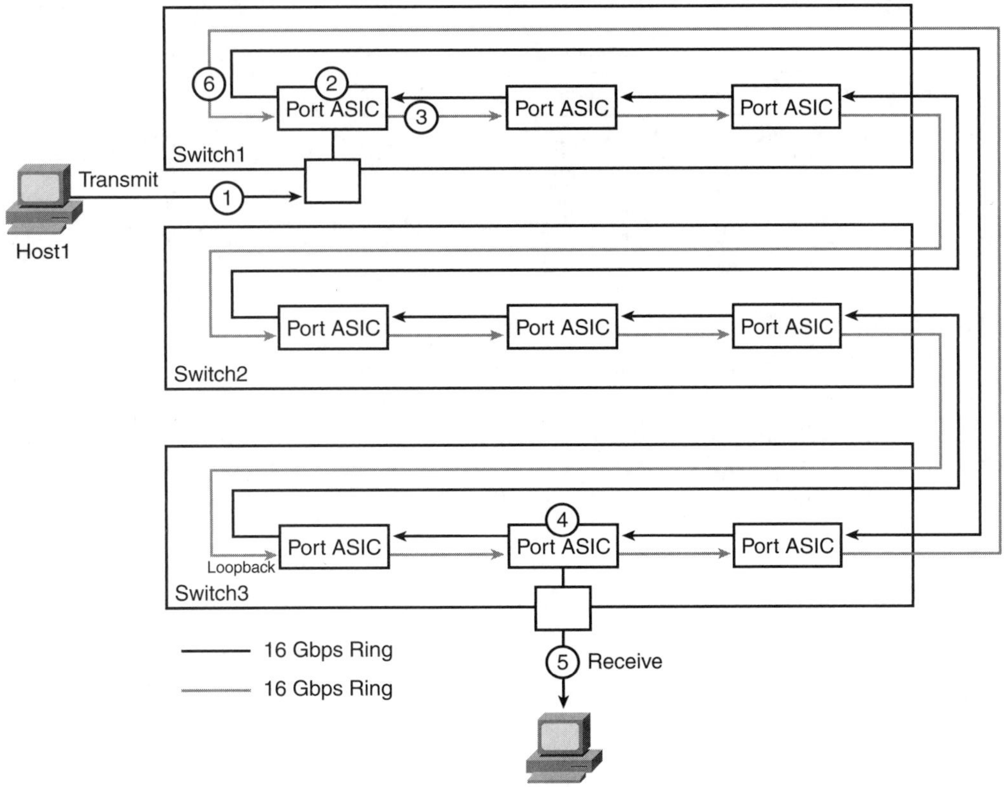

Comparing the Architectures

Table 3-7 provides a brief comparison of the major features of each of the architectures presented in this chapter.

Table 3-7 *Comparison of the Catalyst Architectures*

Catalyst Platform	Form Factor	Switch Fabric	Fabric Bandwidth
5000	Modular	Shared bus	1.2 Gbps
5500	Modular	Crossbar	3.6 Gbps

continues

Table 3-7   *Comparison of the Catalyst Architectures (Continued)*

Catalyst Platform	Form Factor	Switch Fabric	Fabric Bandwidth
6000	Modular	Shared bus	32 Gbps
6500 with SFM	Modular	Crossbar	256 Gbps
6500 with Supervisor 720	Modular	Crossbar	360 Gbps (720 full duplex)
4500	Modular	Centralized	64 Gbps
3750	Fixed-Stackable	Dual Ring	32 Gbps

Summary

The goal of each of the switch architectures presented in this chapter is to move data from source to destination as quickly as possible. Each of the switching architectures implement common features to accomplish this goal, such as high-speed ASICs and switch fabrics, creating very small headers for each packet containing the necessary information, and using a scheduling mechanism when transmitting traffic.

This chapter covers the following topics:

- Understanding legacy LAN segment
- Introducing virtual LANs
- Trunking methods
- VLAN Trunking Protocol
- Configuring VTP/VLAN/Trunk
- VLAN pruning
- EtherChannel
- Understanding VLAN 1
- Private VLANs

CHAPTER 4

Layer 2 Fundamentals

This chapter explores the intricacies of virtual LAN (VLAN) design and implementation. Prior to the almost universal adoption of IP as the Layer 3 method of communication, most applications were written to rely upon Layer 2-protocols for communication. As a result, users needing to share applications and information needed to be on the same Layer 2 network. Despite the potential shortcomings of Layer 2-only designs, they are still commonly found in production networks. This chapter will also bring to light some of the negative aspects of a Layer 2 network, and why it is generally accepted to move off such infrastructure. It is difficult to replace existing Layer 2 networks because it takes time and manpower. In a lot of cases, the existing Layer 2 hardware is also replaced because, more than likely, the equipment is old. Therefore, the potential monetary cost of moving away from a Layer 2 network can be significant. These factors contribute to the continued existence of Layer 2-only networks.

Understanding Legacy LAN Segment

In a VLAN environment, a user can be situated physically anywhere in the network, and still be part of a group of users that have the same requirements such as IP addressing and specific network privileges. In legacy networks, hosts with similar network requirements had to be on the same LAN segment. On the other hand, VLANs are logical and not bound to any physical location.

In legacy networks, users connected to a hub, which may have been connected to some kind of bridge or router if wide-area connectivity was required (see Figure 4-1). Multiple hubs were interconnected to allow more users on the same segment.

This type of network enabled a department with a large number of users to remain part of the same segment. This setup was easy for a network engineer to implement, because generally one network configuration was supported for that department. For example, the department likely had local file servers on the same Layer 2 segment allowing most, if not all, traffic to stay local.

Figure 4-1   *Multiple Hubs Connected to a Router or Bridge*

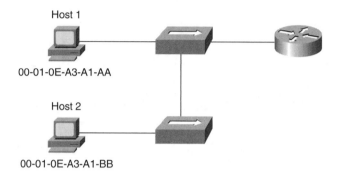

Cascading hubs allow more users to be on the same segment at the cost of causing more contention among hosts trying to access the network. A bigger collision domain translates to more packet collisions on the network, and, therefore, more retransmissions and possible packet drops. By cascading multiple hubs, the possibility of exceeding the cabling requirements of IEEE 802.3 standard exists, which translates to late collisions, causing packet loss. A defective network interface card (NIC) that "jabbers" can cause severe performance issues on this type of network because it continuously sends garbled data, ignoring the carrier sense multiple access collision detect (CSMA/CD) rule that you learned about in Chapter 1, "LAN Switching Foundation Technologies."

Introducing Virtual LANs

With the advent of VLANs, the same users in the legacy example are no longer restricted by physical cabling to be on the same logical segment or have the same access and privileges on the network. VLAN implementation makes the network more flexible as shown in Figure 4-2. Notice that one of the ports off Switch3 is crossed out in the drawing. Spanning tree has put that specific port into blocking state to prevent loops in the network as discussed in "Introducing Spanning Tree Protocol" section of Chapter 1.

In the legacy network, when a host moved to a different location on another router port, the IP address of the host had to be changed. Possible network changes were necessary to accommodate the user; for example, a change in a router access list allowing the user access back to a department server. The main point is that it was not easy to move users in the network without some type of change in the network or host. In an environment that supports VLANs, such network changes are not necessary because of flat Layer 2 network infrastructure. If Host1 in Figure 4-2 is moved to Building B, there is no need to change the configuration of the user's machine or the network. The user simply plugs the host into the jack and is ready to go.

Figure 4-2   *Users Located in Multiple Buildings*

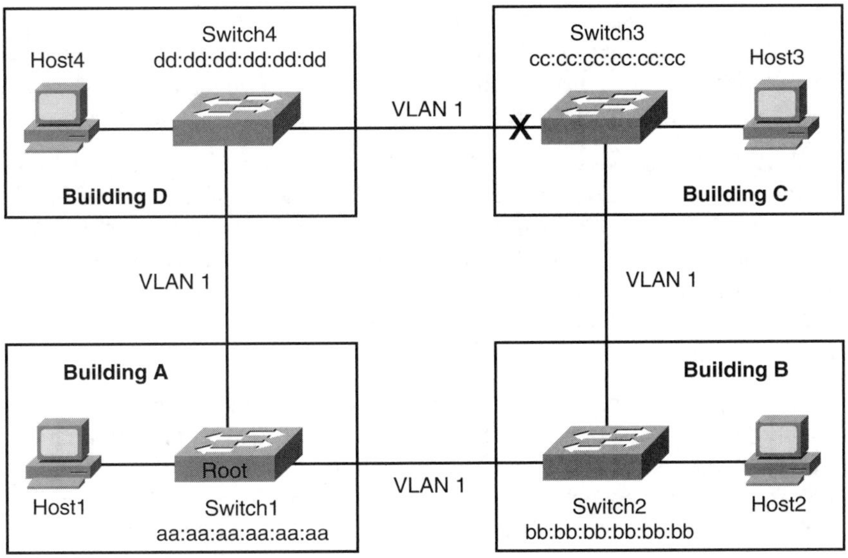

NOTE   Keep in mind that the discussion thus far has been strictly focused on Layer 2, where a single VLAN is extended to multiple switches and with one instance of spanning tree.

Initially, there was big push to extend VLANs across the network. In fact, most universities implemented this technology because the implementation was relatively simple, and many applications at the time had a requirement to be on the same Layer 2 network because of their communications protocols. Network engineers simply configured a VLAN with a large IP range. They pushed security and other network policies on these VLANs on the fly. This was great in saving time and money.

The risks associated with such an implementation were quickly noticed. Extending VLANs has a dark side, enlarging the broadcast domain. If a single host sends out a broadcast message, every machine on that VLAN, regardless of the number of buildings and switches involved, receives that broadcast message. The result is excessive traffic on the network. The greater penalty is a *broadcast storm*, occurring when a host sends an incorrect broadcast message that is received by all hosts on that VLAN, and all those hosts broadcast as well. This process can eventually bring a flat Layer 2 network to its knees.

Spanning trees can also bring the network down when VLANs are extended across the switched network. Too much traffic on the network or some partial or complete hardware failure can cause a spanning-tree outage. In a spanning-tree outage, spanning tree is unable to calculate a loop-free topology correctly, and a loop occurs in the network. Similar to the example of a loop in transparent bridging, traffic exponentially increases causing a network meltdown until the loop is broken, many times requiring manual intervention.

A VLAN is tagged with a user-defined number to differentiate it from another VLAN. For instance, users on VLAN 4 are members of the same subnet and are on the same broadcast domain, whereas VLAN 5 has its own users and broadcast domain. Typically an enterprise switch has no more than 30 VLANs configured on a switch. Depending on the trunking mechanism used, the number of VLANs configured on a switch can be as high as 4096 minus some reserved VLANS. The "Trunking Methods" section later in this chapter discusses trunking further.

Table 4-1 provides the valid range of VLANs that can be configured on a switch. The Catalyst 5500 switch does not support the extended VLANs that fall in the 1025–4096 range. The trunking mechanism used might limit the number of VLANs available for use. For example, Inter-Switch Link (ISL) does not support extended VLAN range. The "VLAN Trunking Protocol" section later in this chapter will discuss VTP further.

Table 4-1   *Valid VLAN Ranges*

VLANs	Range	Usage	Propagated by VTP (Y/N)
0 and 4095	Reserved range	For system use only. You cannot see or use these VLANs.	N/A
1	Normal range	Cisco default. You can use this VLAN but you cannot delete it.	Yes
2–1000	Normal range	Used for Ethernet VLANs. You can create, use, and delete these VLANs.	Yes
1001	Normal range	You cannot create or use this VLAN. May be available in the future.	Yes
1002–1005	Reserved range	Cisco defaults for FDDI and Token Ring. Not supported on Catalyst 6000 family switches. You cannot delete these VLANs.	N/A
1006–1009	Reserved range	Cisco defaults. Not currently used but might be used for defaults in the future. Nonreserved VLANs may be mapped to these reserved VLANs when necessary.	N/A

Table 4-1 *Valid VLAN Ranges (Continued)*

VLANs	Range	Usage	Propagated by VTP (Y/N)
1010-1024	Reserved range	These VLANs might not be seen, but can be mapped to nonreserved VLANs when necessary.	N/A
1025-4094	Extended range	For Ethernet VLANs only. These may be created, used, and deleted with the following exception: FlexWAN modules and routed ports automatically allocate a sequential block of internal VLANs starting at VLAN 1025. If the devices are used, the required number of VLANs must be allowed for.	No

Trunking Methods

The examples so far in this chapter demonstrate one VLAN spanning multiple switches. In the real world, typically, a great number of VLANs are configured, which are extended to multiple switches. Figure 4-3 shows two VLANs in the switched network. Each VLAN has its own STP-topology, IP range, and network requirements.

Figure 4-3 *Multiple Switches with Two VLANs*

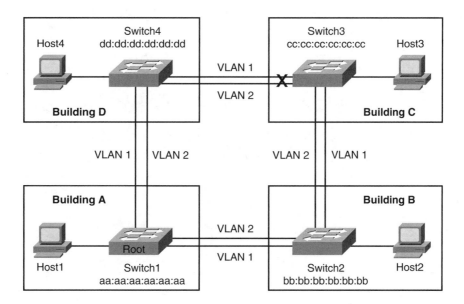

Now imagine a third VLAN is added, which requires another physical link between the switches. Because it may not be efficient to continue to add links as the number of VLANs grows, the solution is *trunking*. A trunk can be configured between two or more switches, between a router and a switch, or between a switch and a host such as a server. Check the hardware to find out what type of trunking capabilities a device has, if any. This section will primarily concentrate on trunking between Cisco switches.

A trunk multiplexes multiple VLANs over a single physical connection. This kind of multiplexing is conceptually similar to the way many television signals are multiplexed onto the airwaves using different frequencies. In this analogy, each VLAN acts like a different television station, while sharing the same physical wire.

Cisco supports only two types of trunks using Fast, Gigabit, and 10 Gigabit Ethernet ports: Cisco Inter-Switch Link Protocol (ISL) and IEEE 802.1Q. The Dynamic Trunking Protocol (DTP) allows a port to negotiate which method to use for trunking. DTP will first attempt to form an ISL trunk if both switches support it; if not, DTP will attempt IEEE 802.1Q. DTP uses the address 01-00-0C-CC-CC-CC with a SNAP value of 0x2004. DTP sends messages every 1 second, and after formation of the trunk, every 30 seconds. The ports negotiating the trunk will not participate in spanning tree until the negotiation is complete. Recently, IEEE 802.1Q is being implemented in networks because it is an IEEE standard, whereas ISL is proprietary to Cisco. Many Cisco routers and some older Cisco Catalyst switches do not support dynamic trunking. In these cases, a static configuration is required. Figure 4-4 shows two VLANs 1 and 2 running over the same cable because of the use of trunking, whereas before, an extra connection was required between the switches in the diagram as depicted in Figure 4-3.

Figure 4-4 *Trunks Used Between Switches*

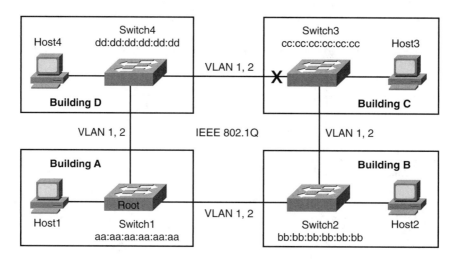

Trunking is an integral part of networking, and it is worth going over Cisco ISL and IEEE 802.1Q methods in detail. This section will also provide some best practices that will help with properly configuring the switches.

Inter-Switch Link Protocol

ISL encapsulates the Ethernet frame with a 26-byte header and a 4-byte frame check sequence (FCS) for a total of 30 bytes of overhead. ISL requires a minimum Fast Ethernet connection between the two devices. The 15-bit VLAN field in the ISL header allows for the multiplexing of the VLANs on a single wire. ISL supports up to 1024 VLANs because Cisco switches use the lower 10 bits of the 15-bit field. The range of ISL packet sizes is 94 bytes (64-byte minimum Ethernet frame + 30-byte ISL overhead) to 1548 bytes (1518-byte maximum Ethernet frame + 30-byte ISL overhead). Each VLAN will have its own spanning-tree topology in an ISL trunking configuration. For instance, if there are two VLANS configured on an ISL trunk, each VLAN will have its own root and spanning-tree topology layout.

The following describes the fields of the ISL encapsulation frame shown in Figure 4-5:

- **DA**—The destination address uses the multicast MAC address 01-00-0C-00-00-00.
- **Type**—The type of frame encapsulated: Ethernet (0000), Token Ring (0001), FDDI (0010), and ATM (0011).
- **User**—This field is used as an extension for the technologies covered under the Type field. The User field can also be used to define priority of the frame. The default value is 0000 for Ethernet with low-priority traffic.
- **SA**—Source address of the switch transmitting the ISL frame.
- **Len**—The length of the packet.
- **AAAA03**—Standard SNAP 802.2 LLC header. This value is constant.
- **HSA**—High bits of SA.
- **VLAN**—VLAN ID.
- **BPDU**—STP bridge protocol data unit/Cisco Discovery Protocol (BPDU/CDP) for control traffic.
- **Index**—The port index of the source of the packet.
- **Res**—Reserved field for additional information, for instance, Token Ring or FDDI Frame Check Sequence field. For Ethernet, this field should be zero.
- **Encap Frame**—The actual Ethernet frame.
- **ISL CRC**—Four-byte check on the ISL packet to ensure it is not corrupted.

Figure 4-5 *Frame Using ISL Encapsulation*

Bits	40	4	4	48	16	24	24	15	1	16	16	Various	32
Frame Field	DA	Type	User	SA	Len	AAAA03	HSA	VLAN	BPDU	Index	Res	Encap Frame	FCS

IEEE 802.1Q

While ISL encapsulates an Ethernet frame with a 30-byte header, IEEE 802.1Q simply adds an additional 4-byte Tag field to the Ethernet frame (EtherType 0x8100). The Tag field has three components in addition to the EtherType:

- **Priority (3 bits)**—The Priority field is used by 802.1p to implement Layer 2 quality of service (QoS).

- **Canonical Format Identifier (CFI) (1 bit)**—The CFI bit is used for compatibility purposes between Ethernet and Token Ring.

- **VLAN ID (VID) (12 bits)**—The VID field is used to distinguish between VLANs on the link.

FCS is recomputed after the 4-byte tag is inserted. IEEE 802.1Q supports up to 4096 VLANs because of the 12-bit length. The IEEE 802.1Q tag is not inserted on the native VLAN, which is the VLAN that the port was assigned to before becoming a trunk port. Figure 4-6 illustrates the IEEE 802.1Q tag format.

Figure 4-6 *IEEE 802.1Q Tag Format*

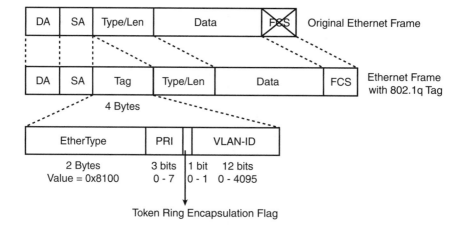

If the adjoining trunk port's native VLAN is different from the local port on the switch, a native mismatch VLAN error occurs. A mismatched native VLAN scenario will bridge VLAN STP information, which translates to having one single STP rather than STP for each VLAN defined. Example 4-1 shows an asterisk on the remote switch's port 1/1, which has a different native VLAN.

Example 4-1 *Detecting a Native VLAN Mismatch*

```
%CDP-4-NVLANMISMATCH:Native vlan mismatch detected on port 1/2
Switch1 (enable) show cdp neighbor
* - indicates vlan mismatch.
# - indicates duplex mismatch.
Port    Device-ID                          Port-ID                   Platform
------- ---------------------------------- ------------------------- -----------
 1/2    Switch#2                           1/1*                      WS-C6506
```

Configuration Best Practices

Trunking has five modes in which it can operate:

- On
- Off
- Desirable
- Auto
- Nonegotiate

In nonegotiate mode, the switch will form a trunk, but will not send DTP frames. The other end switch has to be in On or Nonegotiate mode for nonegotiate to work. Typically, this type of setup is used for connecting a third-party switch that does not support DTP. Table 4-2 provides the details on the various trunking modes.

Table 4-2 *Summary of Five Trunking Modes*

Mode	Description
On	Forces the port to become a trunk port and persuades the neighboring port to become a trunk port. The port becomes a trunk port even if the neighboring port does not agree to become a trunk.
Off	Forces the port to become a non-trunk port and persuades the neighboring port to become a non-trunk port. The port becomes a non-trunk port even if the neighboring port does not agree to become a non-trunk port.
Desirable	Causes the port to negotiate actively with the neighboring port to become a trunk link.

continues

Table 4-2 *Summary of Five Trunking Modes (Continued)*

Mode	Description
Auto	Causes the port to become a trunk port if the neighboring port tries to negotiate a trunk link.
Nonegotiate	Forces the port to become a trunk port but prevents it from sending DTP frames to its neighbor.

Cisco recommends Desirable-Desirable mode for all trunk ports.

VLAN Trunking Protocol

In Figure 4-4, two VLANs extend over multiple switches using trunking. Because each switch sharing trunks must support common VLAN information for the trunks to function correctly, Cisco created the VLAN Trunking Protocol (VTP) for creating and managing that VLAN information. It should be noted that any VLAN created on a switch is in an inactive state until VTP is configured.

A collection of switches that are under the same administrative control and will support the same range of configured VLANs are said to be in the same *VTP domain*. A domain name is simply a unique identifier up to 32 characters long used to identify the switches that will share the same VTP information. The domain name is also case sensitive.

VTP packets are sent to destination address 01-00-0C-CC-CC-CC with a SNAP type of 0x2003. Each switch can operate in one of three modes:

- Server (default)
- Client
- Transparent

In server mode, the switch has a list of all the VLANs for that domain. It can add, delete, or rename any VLAN, and the configuration information is stored in nonvolatile random-access memory (NVRAM). In client mode, the switch obtains its information for the VLAN database from a VTP server, and it cannot make any modifications to it. The information learned by the client switch is not stored in NVRAM. If the client switch is rebooted, the switch must dynamically learn all the VLAN information again from a VTP server. In transparent mode, a switch does not participate in VTP; it merely passes the VTP advertisements to other switches. In transparent mode, the switch can be configured to add, delete, and modify, and the information is stored in NVRAM.

Certain requirements must be met before VTP can be used to manage a domain and distribute VLAN information. Each switch must have a configured trunk port, use the same domain name, and be directly connected. As noted earlier, the trunk port is used to send the

VTP information to the adjacent switch. VTP can automatically distribute VLAN information to all other switches in the same domain through a trunk port, or allow manually for each switch to be configured. The dynamic process using server/client mode is administratively palatable because it is easy to implement; a server switch is configured with VLANs, and the rest of the switches in that domain receive that information. On the other hand, server/client mode can pose potential risks on the network, which will be discussed in this section shortly. Transparent mode requires manually configuring each switch.

VTP has four types of messages:

- Summary advertisements (0x01)
- Subset advertisement (0x02)
- Advertisement requests (0x03)
- Join (0x04)

The two types of VTP versions, version 1 and version 2, have some major differences. Version 2 has support for Token Ring. In version 2, switches running in transparent mode forward VTP advertisements they receive regardless of VTP version or domain name; switches configured for VTP version 1 ignore VTP advertisements with a different VTP domain name than the one configured. Cisco switches default to version 1.

Summary Advertisement

A switch configured as a VTP server sends a summary advertisement every 5 minutes to inform other connected switches of the domain name and revision number. The revision number is tied to changes in VLAN information and increments each time a modification is made on the VTP server switch. When a switch receives a revision number, it compares it to its own. If the number is the same or lower, the switch ignores the summary advertisement.

In Example 4-2, the debug output shows that the switch received a summary advertisement that has a lower revision number than the one that is currently on the switch. Therefore, the switch will ignore the VTP message.

Example 4-2 *Debug Output of Summary Advertisement*

```
VTP: domain Cisco, current rev = 6 found for summary pkt
VTP: summary packet rev 2 lower than domain Cisco rev 6
```

If the revision number is higher, it will update the VLAN database with the information received. The VTP revision number is extremely important because a higher value revision number always wins. Imagine a situation where a switch used only for testing is accidentally connected to a production network. If the test switch is configured with the same VTP domain name as the production network and has a higher revision number, all production switches in that domain will synchronize to it. All previously used VLAN information is overwritten in favor of the VLAN database on the test switch. If the test switch has not been configured for the same VLANs as the production environment, switched ports will revert back to being members of VLAN 1, resulting in loss of connectivity. Always check the revision number of a new switch before bringing it on the network regardless if the switch is going to operate in client or server mode. Make sure the revision number is lower than the production server mode switch. An easy way to ensure that a new switch does not affect the operation of the other switches in the VTP domain is to simply change the domain name of the new switch to something bogus and back to the valid domain name. At this point, it is safe to bring the new switch to the production network, because any time a VTP domain name is changed, the revision number is reset. A reboot will also reset the revision number.

Subset Advertisement

Subset advertisement sends the list of VLANs to the client and server switches. This is the actual database that is being pushed to the switches. The subset advertisement gives information about the name of the VLAN, its status, type, and so on. More than one switch can be configured as a VTP server, and VTP servers will negotiate VLAN information until their databases are synchronized using subset advertisement messages. In Example 4-3, the switch receives information about VLANs 12, 30, 34, 100, and notification of a new VLAN, 111. This output can be collected using the **set trace vtp** command on the switch. Only during networking troubleshooting and as a last measure should the **set trace** command be used because the command taxes the resources of the switch.

Example 4-3 *Debug of Subset Advertisement*

```
VTP/Active: Opening vlan_EVENT_ET event - vlan=vlan12 mode=3
VTP/Active: Closing event
VTP/Active: Opening vlan_EVENT_ET event - vlan=vlan30 mode=3
VTP/Active: Closing event
VTP/Active: Opening vlan_EVENT_ET event - vlan=vlan34 mode=3
VTP/Active: Closing event
VTP/Active: Opening vlan_EVENT_ET event - vlan=vlan0100 mode=3
VTP/Active: Closing event
VTP/Active: Opening vlan_EVENT_ET event - vlan=vlan0111 mode=1
vtp_vlan_change_notification: vlan = 111, mode = 1
2003 Sep 04 10:44:16.110 setVtpVlanInformation: vlanNo [111], mode [1], remoteSp
an [0], remote_span [0] primary[0] PType[0], mistp[0]
2003 Sep 04 10:44:16.250
```

Advertisement Request

An advertisement request is sent when a switch has rebooted, the domain name has been changed, or the VTP summary revision number is higher than what is locally on the switch.

As noted in Example 4-4, the switch is requesting VTP database information from its directly connected neighbor.

Example 4-4   *VTP Advertisement Request*

```
VTP: tx vtp request, domain Cisco, start value
```

Join

VTP join messages prevent the upstream switches from pruning a VLAN on a trunk. The "VLAN Pruning" section later in this chapter will expand the role of this message type.

VTP Example 1

Figure 4-7 shows two switches participating in VTP domain. The server switch will propagate its VLAN information to the client switch. Any VLAN changes must occur on Switch1. The client, Switch2, will not lose its VLAN information if its connection is severed to the VTP server. However, VLAN information will be lost if the client switch is rebooted.

Figure 4-7   *VTP Between Two Switches*

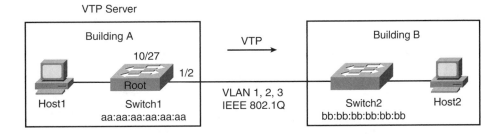

VTP Example 2

Switch1 is a VTP server that is configured with VLANs 2 and 3 (see Example 4-5). Switch2, a new device on the network, is connected on the same VTP domain as Switch1, as shown in Figure 4-7.

Normally, bringing a new switch on the network is a rudimentary process, but in this case, the revision number of Switch2 is higher than Switch1. The higher VTP revision number will cause Switch1 to synchronize to Switch2. Switch1 believes that Switch2 has newer information than it. Using the **set trace** command, the router will generate a log message (see Example 4-6).

Example 4-5 *Output of show vlan Command on Switch1*

```
Switch1 (enable) show vlan
VLAN Name                              Status    IfIndex Mod/Ports, Vlans
---- -------------------------------- --------- ------- -----------------------
1    default                          active    5       1/1
                                                        2/1-2
                                                        6/1-48
                                                        10/7-48
2    vlan2                            active    157      10/1-3
3    Vlan3                            active    173     10/4-6
```

Example 4-6 *Debug of VTP on Switch1 Learning of a Higher Revision Number*

```
VTP: i summary, domain = Cisco, rev = 4, followers = 1
VTP: domain Cisco, current rev = 1 found for summary pkt
VTP: summary packet rev 4 greater than domain Cisco rev 1
```

As a result, Switch1 loses VLANs 2 and 3, and any ports associated with those VLANs default back to VLAN 1. Remember, the highest revision number wins regardless of the mode of the switch. The output from Example 4-7 shows all ports are once again associated with VLAN 1.

Example 4-7 *Output of show vlan Command on Switch1 After Synchronizing with Switch2*

```
Switch1 (enable) show vlan
VLAN Name                              Status    IfIndex Mod/Ports, Vlans
---- -------------------------------- --------- ------- -----------------------
1    default                          active    5       1/1
                                                        2/1-2
                                                        6/1-48
                                                        10/1-48
1002 fddi-default                     active    6
1003 token-ring-default               active    9
1004 fddinet-default                  active    7
1005 trnet-default                    active    8
```

VTP Mode Best Practices

Some environments still deploy VTP server/client mode, while others stick with transparent mode. It is recommended that you configure VTP for transparent mode for a number of reasons, aside from the revision number issue. If an engineer accidentally erases a VLAN, the switch through the VTP mechanism will propagate that information to the rest of the domain. In addition, VTP server/client mode currently only supports VLANs 1-1024. The extended VLAN range, 1024-4096, requires the switch to be configured in transparent mode. The rule of thumb is keep everything simple, because in the long run it can save time and money.

Thus far, the discussion throughout this chapter has been on theory and design considerations. The following section introduces some rudimentary examples on configuring the aforementioned topics. Cisco provides quite a bit of information on its site about how to configure various protocols, features, and so forth. Chapter 5, "Using Catalyst Software," is exclusively dedicated to providing configuration examples that will familiarize the reader on the more common configurations seen in the enterprise network.

Configuring VTP/VLAN/Trunk

Figure 4-8 illustrates multiple switches across the campus network. IEEE 802.1Q is used for trunking method. VLANs 2 and 3 are configured as well. VTP is used to propagate the VLAN information to the rest of the switches.

Figure 4-8   *Configure Switch1 for VTP/VLAN/Trunk*

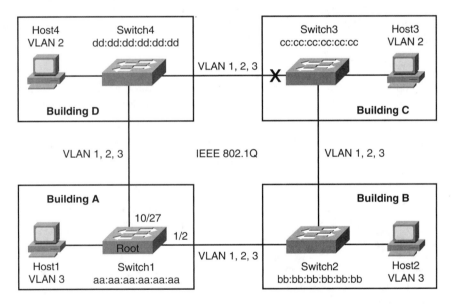

The first thing to do is define the VTP domain, which allows VTP to manage switches that are under its domain. This command is programmed on all four switches:

> **set vtp domain cisco**

VTP domain names and passwords are case sensitive. A VTP domain name is only required for server/client mode. By default, Cisco switches will operate in server mode. For redundancy purposes, the recommendation is to have multiple VTP servers in the switch network. Therefore, only Switch2 and Switch3 will be configured for client mode. Switch1 and

Switch4 will operate in server mode so that they may provide redundancy. Use the following command to change Switch2 and Switch3 to client mode:

set vtp mode client

If a VTP domain name is not configured for server/client mode, or if the switch is not programmed to be in transparent mode, any VLANs created will be in inactive state.

The next step is to create VLANs 2 and 3. The **set vlan** command is used to create VLAN 3 on Switch1:

set vlan 3

Host1 is connected to port 10/3 and is configured to be a member of VLAN 3:

set vlan 3 10/3

By default, all ports are configured with VLAN 1. Hence, any trunks created will have their native VLAN as VLAN 1. Port 1/2 of Switch1 will be used to form a trunk with Switch2 so that Switch1 can pass VTP information to Switch2. The following command will force the native VLAN for trunk 1/2 to be VLAN 2:

set vlan 2 1/2

Typically, it is recommended to assign native VLANs rather than using VLAN 1. The "Understanding VLAN 1" section of this chapter provides greater insight as to why this is necessary.

The port is configured to be an IEEE 802.1Q trunk port with the next command. Dot1q is the equivalent of IEEE 802.1Q on Cisco switches:

set trunk 1/2 dot1q

Recall from earlier discussions of trunking that trunking mode must also be configured. The recommended method is to set trunking mode to desirable:

set trunk 1/2 desirable

Port 1/2 will attempt to actively form a trunk with its directly connected link because it has the desirable parameter configured. Port 10/27 will similarly be configured to form a trunk to Switch4.

VLAN Pruning

One of the major problems with extending Layer 2 architecture is excessive unwanted traffic on the network. A pruning method can be implemented on Cisco switches to prune VLANs from going to switches that do not have any hosts for that VLAN. It is important to note that although pruning can prevent some unnecessary traffic from being circulated across the network, pruning VLANs does not simplify the spanning-tree topologies.

By default, a trunk port allows all VLANs through the trunk as shown in Example 4-8.
Trunk 10/27 goes from Switch1 to Switch4.

Example 4-8 *Output of **show trunk** Command Connected to Switch4*

```
Switch1 (enable) show trunk 10/27
* - indicates vtp domain mismatch
Port       Mode          Encapsulation  Status         Native vlan
--------   -----------   -------------  ------------   -----------
10/27      auto          n-dot1q        trunking       1

Port       Vlans allowed on trunk
--------   --------------------------------------------------------------------
10/27      1-1005,1025-4094

Port       Vlans allowed and active in management domain
--------   --------------------------------------------------------------------
10/27      1-3

Port       Vlans in spanning tree forwarding state and not pruned
--------   --------------------------------------------------------------------
10/27      1-3
```

An example helps clarify this material. Looking back at Figure 4-8, the trunk ports are
permitting all VLAN traffic across the Layer 2 network. Host1 and Host2 are part of VLAN 3.
Host3 and Host4 are in VLAN 2. Any broadcast, multicast, or unicast traffic generated by
Host2 is received by all the switches. There is absolutely no need for Switch3 and Switch4
to receive these packets because these switches do not have any hosts that are part of VLAN 3.
Switch3 and Switch4 will simply drop these packets upon receiving them. Therefore, this
exercise is going to demonstrate how to filter or prune the unnecessary traffic from ever
hitting Switch3 and Switch4.

Pruning VLAN 3 from Switch3 and Switch4 can happen in one of two ways. The first
method discussed is VTP pruning, which is a dynamic process that VTP handles. The
second method involved is manually pruning VLANs. Enterprise customers have used both
methods to prune VLANs. However, manual pruning is preferred because VTP pruning
requires VTP client/server mode operation.

VTP pruning is a global command and affects all the switches in the VTP domain. It only
needs to be configured on one switch. All VLANs by default are prune eligible, which
means that all VLANs can be pruned. To block specific VLANs from the pruning mechanism, use the **clear vtp pruneeligible** command. Example 4-9 demonstrates how to configure Switch1 so that it does not forward VLAN 3 traffic to switches that do not have hosts
that are part of VLAN 3.

Example 4-9 *Enabling VTP Pruning on Switch1*

```
Switch1 (enable) set vtp pruning enable
This command will enable the pruning function in the entire management domain.
All devices in the management domain should be pruning-capable before enabling.
Do you want to continue (y/n) [n]? y
VTP domain Cisco modified
```

After turning pruning on, port 10/27, which is connected to Switch4, now only receives traffic from VLANs 1 and 2 from Switch1 as the output from Example 4-10 shows. Furthermore, because VTP pruning is a global command, Switch1 sends only VLAN 1 and 3 traffic to Switch2.

Example 4-10 *Output of **show trunk** Command to Switch4 After Pruning Is Enabled*

```
Switch1 (enable) show trunk 10/27
* - indicates vtp domain mismatch
Port      Mode        Encapsulation  Status        Native vlan
--------  ----------  -------------  ------------  -----------
10/27     auto        n-dot1q        trunking      1

Port      Vlans allowed on trunk
--------  ------------------------------------------------------------------
10/27     1-1005,1025-4094

Port      Vlans allowed and active in management domain
--------  ------------------------------------------------------------------
10/27     1-3

Port      Vlans in spanning tree forwarding state and not pruned
--------  ------------------------------------------------------------------
10/27     1-2
```

Now, consider a situation where Host4 on Switch4 is now part of VLAN 3. Switch4 will be forced to send VTP Join messages back to Switch1 for VLAN 3. As a result, Switch1 will once again start sending VLAN 3 traffic toward Switch4. VTP pruning is a dynamic process that allows or blocks VLAN traffic from the directly connected switches. VTP statistics can be gathered through the **show vtp statistics** command as shown in Example 4-11. The command shows the number of VTP Join messages transmitted and received. The command can also be used for troubleshooting if any VTP pruning errors occur.

Example 4-11 *Output of **show vtp statistics** Command on Switch2*

```
Switch4 (enable) show vtp statistics VTP pruning statistics:
Trunk    Join Transmitted Join Received Summary advts received from GVRP PDU
                                        non-pruning-capable device  Received
-------- ---------------- ------------- --------------------------- ----------
10/27    777              780           0                           0
!output omitted for brevity
```

The second method of pruning involves manually filtering VLANs from trunks. Manual pruning explicitly requires configuring the switch to filter specific VLANs on a trunk. In Figure 4-8, Switch1 must clear the VLAN 3 off the trunk to prevent VLAN 3 traffic from hitting Switch4. In VTP pruning, trunks dynamically allow and prune VLANs based on VTP Join messages. In the manual process, this is not the case. Typically, manual pruning is configured on trunks that will not have any hosts associated with the filtered VLAN. Pruning also affects spanning-tree topology. Using the **clear trunk** command, manual pruning removes the VLAN from the spanning-tree topology on that switch. Example 4-12 demonstrates removing VLAN 3 from trunk 10/27.

Example 4-12 *Removing VLAN 3 from Trunk 10/27*

```
Switch1 (enable) clear trunk 10/27 3
Removing Vlan(s) 3 from allowed list.
Port 10/27 allowed vlans modified to 1-2,4-1005,1025-4094.
```

The output from Example 4-13 shows the changes after manually pruning VLAN 3. The only active VLANs now on port 10/27 are VLANs 1 and 3.

Example 4-13 *VLAN 3 Is Removed from Trunk 10/27*

```
Switch1 (enable) show trunk 10/27
* - indicates vtp domain mismatch
Port        Mode          Encapsulation  Status        Native vlan
--------    -----------   -------------  ------------  -----------
10/27       desirable     dot1q          trunking      2

Port        Vlans allowed on trunk
--------    ----------------------------------------------------------------
10/27       1-2,4-1005,1025-4094

Port        Vlans allowed and active in management domain
--------    ----------------------------------------------------------------
10/27       1-2

Port        Vlans in spanning tree forwarding state and not pruned
--------    ----------------------------------------------------------------
10/27       1-2
```

Traffic from VLANs 1, 2, and 3 are now going through a single connection, as shown earlier in Figure 4-8. At some point, more bandwidth is needed to help deal with the volume of traffic passing through these switches. Assuming that altering the design of the network is not an option, you can either upgrade to a faster port such as Gigabit or bundle the existing ports into one, thereby, creating a bigger bandwidth connection.

EtherChannel

Companies require greater and cheaper bandwidth to run their networks. Users are becoming more impatient with any sort of latency that occurs in the network. The insatiable appetite of customers for faster networks and higher availability of the networks has made the competition intense between vendors. A few years ago, Cisco came up with a method to not only provide substantially higher bandwidth but with lower cost overhead.

EtherChannel is a technology originally developed by Cisco Systems as a LAN switch-to-switch technique of inverse multiplexing of multiple Fast or Gigabit Ethernet switch ports into one logical channel. Its benefit is that it is effectively cheaper than higher-speed media while using existing switch ports, as shown in Figure 4-9.

Figure 4-9 *4-Port EtherChannel*

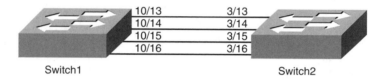

Switch1   Switch2

EtherChannel has developed into a cross-platform method of load balancing between servers, switches, and routers. EtherChannel can bond two, four, or eight ports (Catalyst 6500) to develop one logical connection with redundancy. The three major aspects to EtherChannel are

- Frame distribution
- Management of EtherChannel
- Logical port

EtherChannel does not do frame-by-frame forwarding on a round-robin fashion on each of the links. The load-balancing policy or frame distribution used is contingent upon the switch platform used. For instance, in a Catalyst 5500 switch platform, the load-balancing operation performs an X-OR calculation on the two lowest-order bits of the source and destination MAC address. An X-OR operation between a given pair of addresses will use the same link for all frames. One of the primary benefits of the X-OR operation is to prevent out-of-order frames on the downstream switch. The other advantage is redundancy. If the active channel used by a connection is lost, the existing traffic can traverse over another active link on that EtherChannel. The one disadvantage to X-OR operation is the load on the channels might not be equal because the load-balancing policy is done on a specific header as defined by the platform or user configuration. On a Catalyst 6500 switch, the load-balancing operation can be performed on MAC address, IP address, or IP + TCP/UDP depending on the type of Supervisor/PFC used. Use the **show port capabilities** command to check the module for EtherChannel feature.

The default frame distribution behavior for the Catalyst 6500 is IP. Example 4-14 is based off a Supervisor II/PFC2 card (WS-X6K-SUP2-2GE/WS-F6K-PFC2). This specific Supervisor can support the load-balancing policy up to Layer 4. Some of the older Catalyst 6500 Supervisors do not have this feature available. It is worth noting that most enterprise customers have deployed Catalyst 6500 Supervisor IIs in their networks. Load-balancing policies cannot be configured on Catalyst 5000, and the older Catalyst 4000 Supervisors. The newer Catalyst 4000s with Supervisor II-plus and higher do support load-balancing policies.

Example 4-14 *Output of the* **set port channel** *Command*

```
Switch1 (enable) set port channel all distribution ?
  ip                       Channel distribution ip
  mac                      Channel distribution mac
  session                  Channel distribution session
```

The management of the EtherChannel is done by Port Aggregation Protocol (PAgP). PAgP packets are sent every 30 seconds using multicast group MAC address 01-00-0C-CC-CC-CC with protocol value 0x0104. PAgP checks for configuration consistency and manages link additions and failures between two switches. It ensures that when EtherChannel is created that all ports have the same type of configuration. In EtherChannel, it is mandatory that all ports have the same speed, duplex setting, and VLAN information. Any port modification after the creation of the channel will also change all the other channel ports.

Finally, the last component of EtherChannel is creation of the logical port. The logical port, or Agport, is composed of all the links that make up the EtherChannel. The actual functionality and behavior of the Agport is no different than any other port. For instance, the spanning-tree algorithm treats Agport as a single port.

Example 4-15 shows the recommended steps for configuring EtherChannel on a Catalyst 6500, as shown in Figure 4-9. The ports used by Switch1 for EtherChannel are 10/13-16, and are configured with desirable mode. The desirable mode stipulates that a port actively initiate a channel setup.

Example 4-15 *Output of the* **show port channel group** *Command*

```
Switch1 (enable) show channel group
Admin Group   Ports
-----------   ------------------------------------------------
272           10/1-4
273           10/5-8
274           10/9-12
```

continues

Example 4-15 *Output of the* **show port channel group** *Command (Continued)*

```
275           10/13-16
276           10/17-20
277           10/21-24
278           10/25-28
279           10/29-32
280           10/33-36
281           10/37-40
282           10/41-44
283           10/45-48
```

The Admin Group defines the range of the ports that are going to be used by the EtherChannel. In Example 4-15, the Admin Group is 275, which covers the ports that fall in the range of 13-16. Ports 10/9-12 are configured as a channel using Admin Group 274. If a new Ether-Channel needs to be configured on ports 10/11-14, two separate channels would form because the ports are part of two different Admin Groups. The Admin Group for an Ether-Channel needs to be the same. The Admin Group can be reassigned with the following command in Example 4-16 to allow ports 10/11-14 to be in a single EtherChannel.

Example 4-16 *Output of the* **set port channel** *Command*

```
Switch1 (enable) set port channel 10/10-14 ?
  <admin_group>              Admin group
  mode                       Channel mode
```

Example 4-17 shows how to configure ports 13-16 on module 10 for EtherChannel.

Example 4-17 *Enabling a 4-Port EtherChannel*

```
Switch1 (enable) set port channel 10/13-16 mode desirable
```

The **show port channel** command shown in Example 4-18 shows ports that are configured for channeling. The Admin Group is 275, and the Channel ID for the EtherChannel is 871.

Example 4-18 *Viewing EtherChannel Configuration*

```
Switch1 (enable) show port channel
Port   Status      Channel               Admin Ch
                   Mode                  Group Id
-----  ----------  --------------------  ----- -----
10/13 connected    desirable silent        275   871
10/14 connected    desirable silent        275   871
10/15 connected    desirable silent        275   871
10/16 connected    desirable silent        275   871
-----  ----------  --------------------  ----- -----
```

Example 4-18 *Viewing EtherChannel Configuration (Continued)*

```
Port  Device-ID                             Port-ID                    Platform
----- ------------------------------------- -------------------------- ---------------
10/13 TBA04081025(Switch#2)                 3/13                       WS-C6506
10/14 TBA04081025(Switch#2)                 3/14                       WS-C6506
10/15 TBA04081025(Switch#2)                 3/15                       WS-C6506
10/16 TBA04081025(Switch#2)                 3/16                       WS-C6506
```

Channel ID distinguishes between different EtherChannels on the switch. Silent/Non-Silent modes are involved with unidirectional link failures. It is possible for a fiber connection to remain up even if one of its transceivers has become faulty. Non-Silent mode detects faulty RX/TX transceivers on a fiber port. PAgP will reset the port for 1.6 seconds to force the other side to shut down as well. A unidirectional link can cause black holing of traffic because the return traffic is not received by the RX transceiver. The detection of unidirectional link by a PAgP is about 3.5 * 30 seconds. On the other hand, UniDirectional Link Detection (UDLD) can detect the failure less than 50 seconds versus PAgP. UDLD will be discussed later in Chapter 10, "Implementing and Tuning Spanning Tree." In Silent mode, PAgP does not look for faulty transceivers. The recommendation is to leave Silent/Non-Silent modes at their default values because UDLD better addresses this problem. However, for devices that do not support UDLD, configure Non-Silent mode. Example 4-19 provides useful information about the channel that was created.

Example 4-19 *Output from the* **show port channel information** *Command*

```
Switch1 (enable) show port channel information
Switch Frame Distribution Method: ip both

Port  Status     Channel              Admin Channel Speed Duplex VLAN
                 mode                 group id
----- ---------- -------------------- ----- ------- ----- ------ ----
10/13 connected  desirable silent      275     871 a-100 a-full    1
10/14 connected  desirable silent      275     871 a-100 a-full    1
10/15 connected  desirable silent      275     871 a-100 a-full    1
10/16 connected  desirable silent      275     871 a-100 a-full    1
----- ---------- -------------------- ----- ------- ----- ------ ----


Port  ifIndex Oper-group Neighbor    Oper-Distribution PortSecurity/
                         Oper-group  Method            Dynamic port
----- ------- ---------- ----------  ----------------- -------------
10/13 132             49 65          ip both
10/14 132             49 65          ip both
10/15 132             49 65          ip both
10/16 132             49 65          ip both
----- ------- ---------- ----------  ----------------- -------------
```

The key point here is the load-balancing policy used by the switch. According to Example 4-19, the method used for load balancing is IP. To find out which IP address pairing is using a specific link on the EtherChannel, use the hidden command, as shown in Example 4-20. The **show bundle hash** provides the same information in the newer codes.

Example 4-20 *Output of* **show bundle hash** *Command*

```
Switch1 (enable) show bndlhash 871 10.1.11.3 10.1.34.4
Selected port: 10/14
```

As noted, for source 10.1.11.3 to get to destination 10.1.34.4, it must use the 10/14 link of the EtherChannel.

The **show channel traffic** command shown in Example 4-21 provides utilization information on each of the EtherChannel links.

Example 4-21 *Output of the* **show channel traffic** *Command*

```
Switch1 (enable) show channel traffic
ChanId Port   Rx-Ucst Tx-Ucst Rx-Mcst Tx-Mcst Rx-Bcst Tx-Bcst
------ -----  ------- ------- ------- ------- ------- -------
   869 10/11  26.08%   0.00%  20.10%  51.70%   0.00%  26.13%
   869 10/12  17.39%  40.00%  19.57%  25.69%   0.00%   5.68%
   869 10/13  30.43%  60.00%  40.21%  11.14% 100.00%  64.77%
   869 10/14  26.10%   0.00%  20.12%  11.45%   0.00%   3.40%
```

For troubleshooting purposes, it is important to note if the switch is sending and receiving PAgP packets on the wire as revealed in Example 4-22. This is one of the first commands that needs to be looked at to ensure that adjacent devices configured for EtherChannel support PAgP, and/or the devices are configured correctly.

Example 4-22 *Output of the* **show port channel statistics** *Command*

```
Switch1 (enable) show port channel statistics
Port   Admin   PAgP Pkts    PAgP Pkts PAgP Pkts PAgP Pkts PAgP Pkts PAgP Pkts
       Group   Transmitted  Received  InFlush   RetnFlush OutFlush  InError
-----  -------  -----------  --------- --------- --------- --------- ---------
10/13    275        180         149        0         0         0         0
10/14    275        181         150        0         0         0         0
10/15    275        148         130        0         0         0         0
10/16    275        152         133        0         0         0         0
-----  -------  -----------  --------- --------- --------- --------- ---------
```

Example 4-23 is a hidden command on the Catalyst switch. The **show agport** command provides the assignment of the logical port, 14/39.

Example 4-23 *Output of the* **show agport** *Command*

```
Switch1 (enable) show agport
--- 14/39 ---
old_mem_cnt = 0; path_cost = 8; path_VLAN_cost = 0
trunk_id = 870, time_stamp = 233242506, agifindex = 132
chnl_list = 10/13-16
agport_list = 10/13-16
bndlctrl: prtcnt = 4, num_map = f0, dist_req = 2, dist_port = 0
mod  port bndl_port bndl_sel bndl_sel* act_flag no_bits
10   13   0         c0       c0        2        2
10   14   1         30       30        2        2
10   15   2         0c       0c        2        2
10   16   3         03       03        2        2
0    0    0         00       00        0        0
0    0    0         00       00        0        0
0    0    0         00       00        0        0
0    0    0         00       00        0        0
```

The agport_list parameter shows the active ports on the channel. For instance, if the 10/13 link is lost, the agport_list will take the port out from the list. Notice that in Example 4-24, agport_list does not have port 10/13 as member of the channel.

Example 4-24 *Output of* **show agport** *with Link 10/13 Nonfunctional*

```
Switch1 (enable) show agport
--- 14/39 ---
old_mem_cnt = 0; path_cost = 8; path_VLAN_cost = 0
trunk_id = 870, time_stamp = 233242506, agifindex = 132
chnl_list = 10/13-16
agport_list = 10/14-16
bndlctrl: prtcnt = 4, num_map = f0, dist_req = 2, dist_port = 0
mod  port bndl_port bndl_sel bndl_sel* act_flag no_bits
10   13   0         00       00        0        0
10   14   1         30       30        2        2
10   15   2         8c       8c        2        3
10   16   3         43       43        2        3
0    0    0         00       00        0        0
0    0    0         00       00        0        0
0    0    0         00       00        0        0
0    0    0         00       00        0        0
```

In On mode, the agport_list field is never adjusted because PAgP is disabled. Remember that PAgP is responsible for the addition and deletion of links on the channel.

From spanning tree's perspective, the EtherChannel is seen as a single port, as shown in Example 4-25.

Example 4-25 *Output of the* **show spantree** *Command Using an EtherChannel*

```
Switch1 (enable) show spantree
VLAN 1
Spanning tree mode          PVST+
Spanning tree type          ieee
Spanning tree enabled

Designated Root             00-05-74-18-04-80
Designated Root Priority    4097
Designated Root Cost        0
Designated Root Port        1/0
Root Max Age    20 sec    Hello Time 2  sec    Forward Delay 15 sec

Bridge ID MAC ADDR          00-05-74-18-04-80
Bridge ID Priority            4097  (bridge priority: 4096, sys ID ext: 1)
Bridge Max Age 20 sec    Hello Time 2  sec    Forward Delay 15 sec

Port                     VLAN Port-State    Cost      Prio Portfast Channel_id
------------------------ ---- ------------- --------- ---- -------- ----------
10/13-16                 1    forwarding              8    32 disabled 871
```

The valid EtherChannel configurations are

- Desirable-Desirable
- Desirable-Auto
- On-On
- Off-Off

Cisco recommends Desirable-Desirable mode configuration for EtherChannel. This is beneficial because ports will actively negotiate setting up a channel and will allow the operation of PAgP. It is also recommended to leave Silent/Non-Silent parameters to their default values if UDLD is supported.

Table 4-3 describes the type of channel states that will develop depending on the configuration of the adjacent switches. Spanning tree shuts down (errdisable) channels that are misconfigured, as noted in Table 4-3.

Table 4-3   *Channeling Modes Between Switches*

Switch-A Channel Mode	Switch-B Channel Mode	Channel State
On	On	Channel
On	Off	Not Channel (errdisable)
On	Auto	Not Channel (errdisable)
On	Desirable	Not Channel (errdisable)
Off	On	Not Channel (errdisable)

Table 4-3   *Channeling Modes Between Switches (Continued)*

Switch-A Channel Mode	Switch-B Channel Mode	Channel State
Off	Off	Not Channel
Off	Auto	Not Channel
Off	Desirable	Not Channel
Auto	On	Not Channel (errdisable)
Auto	Off	Not Channel
Auto	Auto	Not Channel
Auto	Desirable	Channel
Desirable	On	Not Channel (errdisable)
Desirable	Off	Not Channel
Desirable	Auto	Channel
Desirable	Desirable	Channel

Understanding VLAN 1

It is important to understand the significance of VLAN 1. By default, all switch ports are part of VLAN 1. VLAN 1 contains control plane traffic and can contain user traffic. It is recommended that user traffic be configured on VLANs other than VLAN 1, primarily to prevent unnecessary user broadcast and multicast traffic from being processed by the Network Management Processor (NMP) of the supervisor. Although VLAN 1 user traffic can be pruned from a trunk, it is not the case with control plane traffic. In fact, in older Cisco Catalyst Software versions (5.4 or earlier), VLAN 1 could not be removed at all from a trunk. Control plane traffic such as VTP, CDP, and PAgP protocols are tagged with VLAN 1 information and are forwarded on a trunk regardless if the trunk has pruned VLAN 1.

Management VLAN, discussed in the next section, is used to monitor and manage the switches on the network. This section also introduces best practices involving management VLAN.

Management VLAN

The internal switch interface, sc0, is used for management of the switch. Management VLAN is used for purposes such as telnet, SNMP, and syslog. By default, VLAN 1 is the management VLAN. Ensure that there are no redundant links for the management VLAN. This practice eliminates the need to rely on the spanning-tree algorithm. This prevents the management VLAN from having any potential issues with spanning-tree loops. If the Layer 2 configuration does not provide an option to eliminate redundancy for the management

VLAN, separate physical connections supporting only the management VLAN should be considered. Ensure that the management VLAN does not have any user traffic on it by only allowing switch management interfaces to be members of that VLAN.

Management VLAN Best Practices

With the introduction of Cisco's powerful switches and VLAN feature, most companies started to deploy a switched network with VLANs extending throughout the LAN campus. Perhaps the strongest driving force to deploying a Layer 2 network was that Layer 3 devices could not keep up with Layer 2 switching engines. The phrase "the network is as fast as its slowest link" comes to mind. These days Layer 3 engines are no longer bottlenecks and can keep pace with Layer 2 engines. For example, the Catalyst 6500 is not the only Layer 3/Layer 2 switching device, but it has the most features and highest switching performance on the market today.

Perhaps the biggest issue with extending VLANs across multiple switches is spanning-tree loops. Spanning Tree Protocol (STP) is a loop-avoidance protocol designed to provide redundancy in a switch fabric network. Host3 will take the path via Switch2 to send traffic to the rest of the hosts on that segment that is not on Switch3 (see Figure 4-8). This works relatively well. If a failure occurs between Switch2 and Switch3, STP can bring up the redundant link, and traffic will be forwarded again after spanning tree converges.

Consider a situation where an STP loop occurs because of a bad transceiver that maintains a link but passes traffic unidirectional, or a hardware failure that results in missed STP BPDUs. This loop will degrade the performance on the switch network, users will have intermittent connectivity, and eventually, the network will be saturated. In a spanning-tree loop, an engineer at times has to console into the device because of slow telnet sessions because of excessive traffic on the network. Any time a VLAN is extended to various switches with redundant links, the network is vulnerable to such an event.

The other chronic issue with Layer 2 design is broadcast, multicast, and unicast flooding. A broadcast message is sent to MAC address FF-FF-FF-FF-FF-FF, which is received by all hosts on the VLAN. When Host1 sends an Address Resolution Protocol (ARP) for Host2, all other devices will also receive the broadcast message. In a huge network, with a great number of users and multiple switches involved, broadcast traffic can unnecessarily eat up bandwidth. Each device will look at the packet at Layer 3 to see if the packet belongs to it; if not, the packet is thrown away. The process of looking at the packet at Layer 3 requires CPU cycles, and as result, devices are functioning sub-optimally. Typically, ARP does not really cause that much trouble, but if in-house applications exist that communicate via broadcast, the application can adversely affect the network for the aforementioned reasons. If a broadcast storm occurs, it can and will bring the segment down completely. The real solution is to keep the segment small regardless whether the discussion is based on physical or logical segment. The rule of thumb is that the broadcast traffic should not be greater than 20 percent of the total traffic on the VLAN or segment.

To prevent excessive broadcasts on a segment, especially in a broadcast storm situation, Cisco switches have a mechanism to control the upper limits of broadcast traffic on a port. Cisco switches monitor the level of broadcast activity in 1-second intervals. They do this by looking at the individual/group destination address in the Ethernet frame. This value is compared with a predefined threshold set by the user. If the sample rate per second exceeds the threshold, the suppression mechanism is enabled, which filters broadcast packets on that port for a specified period of time. By default, broadcast suppression is disabled on Catalyst switches. In this example, the threshold is set to 50%, and anything higher will be dropped.

Broadcast suppression can easily be configured on the switch. According to the following command, any broadcast traffic that exceeds 50% on port 10/1 will be dropped:

set port broadcast 10/1 50%

The actual threshold value is contingent up the engineer's knowledge of the traffic on that segment. This feature does not allow broadcast storms to consume all available bandwidth and melt the network down.

Pruning can also be configured on the switches to reduce the diameter of the broadcast domain. Options are available to control the broadcast domain; these would require time and strategic planning to make Layer 2 somewhat resilient to a broadcast storm.

Some engineers believe that VLANs should never leave the box. In other words, keep Layer 2 small, which can help address issues with VTP client/server mode, and more importantly, spanning tree. The practice also means that trunking is not necessary. Essentially, the engineers want to push for a Layer 3 model. A Layer 3 design has many positive and negative attributes, but it does have one big advantage: Layer 3 does a better job of controlling the spread of the outage in the network.

Avoid extending VLANs, if at all possible. If this is not possible, keep the diameter of the Layer 2 switches small. Spanning tree recommends no more than seven switches between hosts. Avoid VTP client/server mode, and if pruning is required, use manual pruning.

Private VLANs

Common VLAN implementation allows for any-to-any communication. Each host on the VLAN can communicate with any other host on that segment. Preventing communication between hosts on the same VLAN requires moving the users off the VLAN to their own separate VLANs. In the past, VLANs generally had a homogenous pool of users. The users in the VLAN had some type of commonality that allowed them to share the same resources and have the same access on the network. As a result, there was no need to filter traffic between users on the same segment. For instance, vendors or contractors who needed onsite access to the customer network were typically segregated in their own VLAN. Scalability was not an issue because the number of these groups was small and manageable (see Figure 4-10).

Figure 4-10 *Contractors on a Separate VLAN*

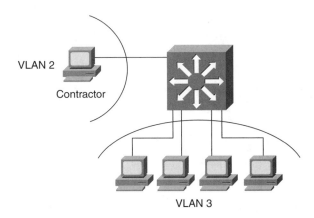

However, the numbers of these third-party groups have dramatically grown and are ubiquitous throughout the customer network, specifically government contractors. To isolate them in their own VLANs would require many IP addresses and VLANs. Figure 4-10 illustrates contractors in VLAN 2. VLAN 3 consists of company workers. Isolating contractors in their own VLANs is not practical and also would require some effort to maintain these VLANs. Private VLANs can help mitigate some of these issues. Private VLANs have the capability to restrict users on the same segment without the necessity of Layer 3 architecture. This translates to fewer IP address used and fewer new VLANs created on the network.

Figure 4-11 shows the contractors have been moved from VLAN 2 and are now members of VLAN 3.

Figure 4-11 *Contractors on the Same VLAN*

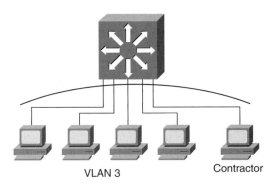

Private VLANs can also help protect hosts from each other on a segment (see Figure 4-12). Recently, corporate networks have been hit with various forms of worms. Typically, a worm infects a machine, and then it tries to form connections with other machines on the network through the infected machine. In a private VLAN environment, the infected machine has restrictions on it as to what ports it can communicate with. As a result, not all ports on that VLAN will be affected by this worm originated by the infected machine. Restrictions on a port might not give you all the protection in the world; however, as mentioned, restrictions can provide some benefits that cannot be overlooked.

Figure 4-12 *Contractor Host Prevented from Communicating to Other Members on the Same VLAN*

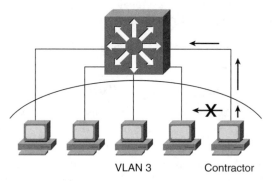

VLAN 3   Contractor

A private VLAN is an extension of the common VLAN to help restrict traffic from users on the same VLAN. It accomplishes this by assigning port designations, which include the following:

- Promiscuous
- Isolated
- Community
- Two-way community

All ports on the VLAN are assigned as part of the primary VLAN. Each port is also defined by a secondary VLAN.

The promiscuous port can communicate with any other host on the primary VLAN. It is usually the MSFC router port, Catalyst 6500 running Catalyst OS. The isolated port communicates only with the promiscuous port and no other host on the segment. It cannot communicate with other isolated ports. There can only be one isolated secondary VLAN in the primary VLAN. Community ports can communicate with the promiscuous port and other ports that are members of the community VLAN. Two different communities cannot communicate with each other.

Flows coming from the isolated or community ports are tagged internally on the switch with a secondary VLAN identifier. The identifier is used to forward the packet to the appropriate destination ports. For insolated ports, it is always going to be the promiscuous port, which internally tags all traffic destined to designated ports with primary VLAN information. If a Layer 2 access list is applied (VLAN Access List-[VACL]), the access list will only affect traffic coming from the secondary VLAN (isolated or community port) to the promiscuous port. The Layer 2 access list does not affect traffic going to the secondary VLAN because the promiscuous port will tag all traffic internally with a primary VLAN identifier. In other words, the promiscuous port cannot apply access lists going to a specific secondary VLAN. In a two-way community configuration, the router will remember the secondary VLAN information. As a result, it will be able to apply Layer 2 access list outbound to the secondary VLAN group.

Some caveats to private VLAN implementation include the following:

- VTP must be configured in transparent mode.

- Private VLANs can use VLANs 2-1000 and 1025-4096.

- Both primary and secondary VLANs can traverse a trunk, and will participate in spanning tree. Any modifications to the primary VLAN spanning tree will affect the secondary VLAN spanning-tree algorithm.

- Private VLANs cannot be configured on trunk, dynamic VLAN, or channel ports. By default, the configuration will automatically disable trunking on the port.

- BPDU guard gets enabled. The BPDU guard protects against a portfast enabled port sending BPDU messages.

- Internet Group Management Protocol (IGMP) snooping is not supported on the private VLANs.

The primary VLAN is 3 with two secondary VLANs, 13 and 15. These secondary VLANs have been associated with a primary VLAN with specific ports defined in Example 4-26. Then the primary and its secondary VLANs have been mapped to the promiscuous port, 15/1.

Example 4-26 *Configuring Private VLANs*

```
Switch1 (enable) set vlan 3 pvlan-type primary
Switch1 (enable) set vlan 13 pvlan-type isolated
Switch1 (enable) set vlan 15 pvlan-type twoway-community
Switch1 (enable) set pvlan 3 13 10/1
Vlan 13 configuration successful
Ports 10/1-12 trunk mode set to off.
Successfully set the following ports to Private Vlan 3,13:
10/1

Switch1 (enable) set pvlan 3 15 10/2-3
Vlan 15 configuration successful
```

Example 4-26 *Configuring Private VLANs (Continued)*

```
Ports 10/1-12 trunk mode set to off.
Ports 10/1-12 trunk mode set to off.
Successfully set the following ports to Private Vlan 3,15:
10/2-3
Switch1 (enable) show pvlan
Primary Secondary Secondary-Type    Ports
------- --------- ---------------- -----------
3       13        isolated          10/1
3       15        twoway-community 10/2-3

Switch1 (enable) set pvlan mapping 3 13 15/1
Successfully set mapping between 3 and 13 on 15/1
Switch1 (enable) set pvlan mapping 3 15 15/1
Successfully set mapping between 3 and 15 on 15/1
Switch1 (enable) show pvlan mapping
Port Primary Secondary
---- ------- ---------
15/1 3       13,15
```

Referring to Figure 4-12, the contractor now cannot communicate with Hosts1, 2, and 3. The other hosts can communicate with each other, but not with the contractor. All hosts including the contractor can communicate with the promiscuous port. Any broadcast or unicast floods generated by any of these hosts including contractor will be contained in their secondary VLAN environment. If contractor sends a broadcast message, the other hosts will not receive the broadcast message.

Private VLANs are relatively new in the enterprise network. Private VLAN offers many features, and it will become popular in the near future, especially in parts of the network where devices need to be protected from other users and possible network attacks.

Summary

This chapter focused on VLAN fundamentals including the roles of VLANs, trunking, and VTP. The two most popular trunking implementations are ISL and IEEE 802.1Q. The preferred trunking configuration is Desirable-Desirable with IEEE 802.1Q implementation. VTP transparent mode is preferred over client/server mode because it is less likely to cause unexpected problems on the network. The discussion moved forward to address the significance behind pruning, Etherchannel, and VLAN 1. Management VLAN needs to have its own separate VLAN with non-redundant links as discussed. The chapter concluded with a discussion of private VLANs and their increased role in today's networks.

This chapter covers the following topics:

- Hybrid versus native
- Downloading Catalyst software
- New software packaging

CHAPTER 5

Using Catalyst Software

As much as Project Synergy represents the origins of the Catalyst 5000 platform, the Cisco acquisition of Crescendo Communications on September 21, 1993, represents the origins of software for the Catalyst platforms. The Crescendo interface came to Cisco as part of the acquisition, and has come to be known today as the Catalyst Operating System (Catalyst OS). Catalyst OS supports only Layer 2 functions and relies on traditional Cisco IOS software for Layer 3 support. As a result, the term *hybrid* describes a Catalyst switch using both Catalyst OS for Layer 2 switching and traditional Cisco IOS for Layer 3 routing.

Hybrid Versus Native

Anyone who configured a Catalyst switch during the last 10 years encountered the Catalyst OS interface and its series of **set**, **clear**, and **show** commands. Switches running Catalyst OS must rely upon a separate version of Cisco IOS to support any Layer 3 or router functions if a Router Switch Module (RSM) or Multilayer Switch Feature Card (MSFC) is installed. Therefore, the term *hybrid* became popular to describe a Catalyst switch running both Catalyst OS for Layer 2 functions, and Cisco IOS for Layer 3 functions. Although Catalyst switches account for more than 50% of the Cisco total sales volume each year, Cisco is known best as a company that makes high-speed routers. As a result, the look and feel of the traditional Cisco IOS interface became available for switches as an alternative to the hybrid look and feel. This alternative is dubbed *native* to indicate the look and feel of the original Cisco IOS applied to a switching platform. The next section of this chapter provides an overview of the look and feel of a Catalyst 6500 series switch running hybrid software, followed by a an overview of the look and feel of a Catalyst 6500 running native software.

The Look and Feel of Hybrid Software

As previously mentioned, the Catalyst OS relies primarily on a series of **set**, **clear**, and **show** commands for configuration. Chapter 6, "Understanding Multilayer Switching," and Chapter 8, "Understanding Quality of Service on Catalyst 6500," include detailed examples of configurations using the Catalyst OS. Only basic configurations sufficient to illustrate the general look and feel of each operating system are provided in this chapter. After a console connection is created into a switch running the Catalyst OS, issuing the **help** or **?** command displays the available commands in user mode. Example 5-1 shows the top level of help available in user mode by issuing the **?** command. Any of the commands displayed in Example 5-1 can be followed by a **?** parameter to obtain detailed help on that command.

Example 5-1 *Help in User Mode in Catalyst OS*

```
Console> ?
  cd                          Set default flash device
  dir                         Show list of files on flash device
  enable                      Enable privileged mode
  help                        Show this help screen
  history                     Show contents of history substitution buffer
  l2trace                     Layer2 trace between hosts
  ping                        Send echo packets to hosts
  pwd                         Show default flash device
  quit                        Exit from the Admin session
  session                     Tunnel to ATM or Router module
  set                         Set commands, use 'set help' for more info
  show                        Show commands, use 'show help' for more info
  traceroute                  Trace the route to a host
  verify                      Verify checksum of file on flash device
  wait                        Wait for x seconds
  whichboot                   Which file booted
```

For example, a **session ?** command can be issued to obtain detailed help on the session command.

The help output in Example 5-1 indicates the show command is available from user mode, so the first thing to do is determine what type of switch is being used and which versions of software are running. This is accomplished with the **show version** command (see Example 5-2).

Example 5-2 *Output of* **show version** *Command*

```
Console> show version
WARNING: This product contains cryptographic features and is subject to United
States and local country laws governing import, export, transfer and use.
Delivery of Cisco cryptographic products does not imply third-party authority
to import, export, distribute or use encryption. Importers, exporters,
distributors and users are responsible for compliance with U.S. and local
country laws. By using this product you agree to comply with applicable
laws and regulations. If you are unable to comply with U.S. and local laws,
return this product immediately.

WS-C6513 Software, Version NmpSW: 8.1(3)
Copyright (c) 1995-2003 by Cisco Systems
```

Example 5-2   *Output of* **show version** *Command (Continued)*

```
NMP S/W compiled on Oct 10 2003, 13:09:37

System Bootstrap Version: 7.7(1)
System Boot Image File is 'bootflash:cat6000-sup720k9.8-1-3.bin'
System Configuration register is 0x10f

Hardware Version: 1.0  Model: WS-C6513  Serial #: TSC073602JS

PS1  Module: WS-CAC-2500W    Serial #: ART0725E0RV

Mod Port Model                Serial #    Versions
--- ---- -------------------- ----------- -------------------------------------
1    16  WS-X6516A-GBIC       SAL0734K96L Hw : 1.0
                                          Fw : 7.2(1)
                                          Sw : 8.1(3)
7    2   WS-SUP720-BASE       SAD0734007W Hw : 2.3
                                          Fw : 7.7(1)
                                          Fw1: 8.1(3)
                                          Sw : 8.1(3)
                                          Sw1: 8.1(3)
15   1   WS-SUP720            SAD073305H8 Hw : 1.5
                                          Fw : 12.2(17a)SX1
                                          Sw : 12.2(17a)SX1


       DRAM                    FLASH                   NVRAM
Module Total   Used    Free    Total   Used    Free    Total Used  Free
------ ------- ------- ------- ------- ------- ------- ----- ----- -----
7      524288K 360393K 163895K 65536K  14706K  50830K 2048K 249K  1799K

Uptime is 0 day, 0 hour, 6 minutes
```

The **show version** output in Example 5-2 indicates the platform is a Catalyst 6513 with a
Supervisor 720, running Catalyst OS version 8.1(3). The **show version** indicates there is
a module 15, running IOS version 12.2(17a)SX1. Because this chassis only supports 13
physical modules, module 15 is a logical number representing the MSFC3 daughterboard
on the Supervisor 720. If a second Supervisor 720 were installed, a module 16 would also
be listed. This configuration represents a hybrid implementation using both Catalyst OS
and IOS. The output of the **show version** command in Example 5-2 indicates there is an
MSFC version 3 in module 15 on the switch. Modules 15 and 16 on the Catalyst 6500 series
are "virtual" and are reserved for the MSFC. Module 15 is used by the MSFC integrated
into the first Supervisor, while module 16 is used by the MSFC integrated into a second
Supervisor, if installed.

With Catalyst OS, Ethernet connections are called *ports* and are Layer 2-only connections.
A list of available ports can be obtained using the **show port** command. The **show port**
command has a number of optional parameters, including the capability to specify an entire
module or a specific port on a module. (See Example 5-3.)

Example 5-3   *Output of* **show port 1/1** *Command*

```
Console> show port 1/1
* = Configured MAC Address

Port  Name                 Status    Vlan      Duplex Speed Type
----- -------------------- --------- --------- ------ ----- ------------
 1/1                       disable   1            full  1000 No Connector


Port  Security Violation Shutdown-Time Age-Time Max-Addr Trap     IfIndex
----- -------- --------- ------------- -------- -------- -------- -------
 1/1  disabled shutdown              0        0        1 disabled      12

Port  Num-Addr Secure-Src-Addr   Age-Left Last-Src-Addr    Shutdown/Time-Left
----- -------- ----------------- -------- ---------------- ------------------
 1/1         0         -              -        -              -      -        -

Port  Flooding on Address Limit
----- ------------------------
 1/1             Enabled

Port     Broadcast-Limit Multicast Unicast Total-Drop            Action
-------- --------------- --------- ------- -------------------- -----------
 1/1           -             -        -                         0 drop-packets

Port  Send FlowControl  Receive FlowControl   RxPause    TxPause
      admin     oper    admin     oper
----- -------- -------- --------- --------- ----------- ----------
 1/1  desired  off      off       off         0           0

Port  Status     Channel              Admin Ch
                 Mode                 Group Id
----- ---------- -------------------- ----- -----
 1/1  disable    auto silent             3     0

Port  Status     ErrDisable Reason    Port ErrDisableTimeout Action on Timeout
----  ---------- -------------------- ---------------------- -----------------
 1/1  disable                       - Enable                 No Change

Port  Align-Err  FCS-Err    Xmit-Err   Rcv-Err    UnderSize
----- ---------- ---------- ---------- ---------- ---------
 1/1          0          0          0          0         0

Port  Single-Col Multi-Coll Late-Coll  Excess-Col Carri-Sen Runs    Giants
----- ---------- ---------- ---------- ---------- --------- --------- ---------
 1/1          0          0          0          0        0         0         0

Port  Last-Time-Cleared
----- -------------------------
 1/1  Sun Oct 30 2003, 22:33:34

Idle Detection
----------------
```

Because all ports in Catalyst OS are Layer 2 only, an Internet Protocol (IP) address cannot be assigned directly to this port, and no IP or other Layer 3 protocol information is displayed in the **show port 1/1** output.

The Catalyst OS relies on **set** and **clear** commands to change parameters. In contrast, the Cisco IOS relies on only the command word to enable a command, and the **no** parameter to disable the command. Just like with Cisco IOS, Catalyst OS requires the user be in enable mode to make any changes to the switch configuration. By default, no console or enable password are set. The user enters enable mode by issuing the **enable** command at the console prompt, and pressing enable because no password has yet been established (see Example 5-4).

Example 5-4 *Entering Enable Mode*

```
Console> enable

Enter password:
Console> (enable)
```

Because a blank enable password is not a best practice, a **set enablepass** command is issued, allowing the password to be changed (see Example 5-5). This is in contrast to the **enable password** or **enable secret** commands that would be issued in Cisco IOS.

Example 5-5 *Setting the Enable Password*

```
Console> (enable) set enablepass
Enter old password:
Enter new password:
Retype new password:
Password changed.
Console> (enable)
```

After the password is changed, a console password can be established by issuing the **set password** command (see Example 5-6). Cisco IOS, on the other hand, uses the **line con 0** command to access the console configuration, and a simple **password** command to change the password.

Example 5-6 *Setting the Console Password*

```
Console> (enable) set password
Enter old password:
Enter new password:
Retype new password:
Password changed.
Console> (enable)
```

The **set system name** command updates the system with a new device name (see Example 5-7).

Example 5-7 *Setting the System Name*

```
Console> (enable) set system name SW1
System name set.
SW1> (enable)
```

Unlike Cisco IOS, Catalyst OS supports a command called **show system,** which provides general system information ranging from the specified location of the device, to the status of the power supplies (see Example 5-8).

Example 5-8 *Output of* **show system** *Command*

```
SW1> (enable) show system
PS1-Status PS2-Status
---------- ----------
ok         none

Fan-Status Temp-Alarm Sys-Status Uptime d,h:m:s Logout
---------- ---------- ---------- -------------- ---------
ok         off        ok         0,02:21:41     20 min

PS1-Type                PS2-Type
-------------------- --------------------
WS-CAC-2500W            none

Modem   Baud  Backplane-Traffic Peak Peak-Time
------- ----- ----------------- ---- ------------------------
disable 9600  0%                  0% Sun Nov 30 2003, 22:33:50

PS1 Capacity: 2331.00 Watts (55.50 Amps @42V)

System Name             System Location         System Contact          CC
-------------------- -------------------- ------------------------ ---
SW1                     Cisco Lab               David Barnes

Fab Chan Speed Input Output
-------- ----- ----- ------
      0    8G    0%     0%
      1   n/a    0%     0%
      2   n/a    0%     0%
      3   n/a    0%     0%
      4   20G    0%     0%
      5   n/a    0%     0%
      6   n/a    0%     0%
      7   n/a    0%     0%
      8   n/a    0%     0%
      9   n/a    0%     0%
     10   n/a    0%     0%
```

Example 5-8 *Output of* **show system** *Command (Continued)*

```
        11   n/a    0%     0%
        12   n/a    0%     0%
        13   n/a    0%     0%
        14   n/a    0%     0%
        15   n/a    0%     0%
        16   n/a    0%     0%
        17   n/a    0%     0%

Core Dump               Core File
----------------------  ----------------------
disabled                disk0:crashinfo

System Logging  Host            File                                  Interval
--------------  --------------  ------------------------------------  --------
Disabled        -               tftp:sysinfo                          1440
Index           System Command
------          ------------------------------------------------------------

Syslog Dump             Syslog File
----------------------  ----------------------
disabled                disk0:sysloginfo
SW1> (enable)
```

Example 5-8 indicates the switch resides in the Cisco Lab, a single 2500 watt power supply is installed, and the 16-port Gigabit Ethernet card installed in slot 1 has only a single 8-Gbps connection into the Switch Fabric. To obtain similar information from Cisco IOS, a combination of **show environment** and **show controller** commands would be required.

Another difference between Catalyst OS and IOS command-line interfaces is in the way the configuration of a device is displayed. Anyone familiar with Cisco IOS has used the **show running-config** command to display the running configuration of a router. Routers utilize both a saved configuration and a running configuration. Changes made to a router's configuration are not committed to memory until a copy or write memory command is issued. Catalyst OS uses the **show config** command to display the configuration of a switch, and no concept of a saved configuration and a separate running configuration exists. Any changes entered at the command line in Catalyst OS are automatically saved. With the introduction of Catalyst OS version 6.3(1) and later, a **show running-config** command was introduced. Example 5-9 shows the optional parameters for the **show running-config** command in Catalyst OS.

Example 5-9 **show running-config** *Options for Catalyst OS*

```
SW1 (enable) show running-config ?
  all                      Show default and non-default runtime config
  qos                      Show QoS configuration
  system                   Show system configuration
  <mod>                    Module number
```

In contrast to Cisco IOS, the **show running-config** command in Catalyst OS only displays commands that have changed from their default values. The addition of the **all** optional parameter displays all configuration commands including the defaults.

The output from the **show tech-support** command is typically the first thing requested by the Cisco Technical Assistance Center when beginning troubleshooting. The **show tech-support** command, long available in Cisco IOS, was finally introduced in Catalyst OS 5.3(1). For versions prior to Catalyst OS 5.3(1), a combination of various **show** commands is required to gather the same information. Example 5-10 shows the optional parameters for the **show tech-support** command in Catalyst OS.

Example 5-10   **show tech-support** *Options for Catalyst OS*

```
SW1 (enable) show tech-support ?
  config                  Show Tech-Support information using config option
  memory                  Show Tech-Support information using memory option
  mistp-instance          Show MISTP information for Tech-support
  mst                     Show MST information for Tech-support
  module                  Show module information for Tech-Support
  port                    Show port information for Tech-Support
  vlan                    Show vlan information for Tech-Support
```

When setting up a Catalyst switch in hybrid mode, Layer 3 functionality is provided by a Router Switch Module (RSM), Router Switch Feature Card (RSFC), or some version of Multilayer Switch Feature Card (MSFC). These Layer 3 devices cannot be configured from the Catalyst OS command line. Configuration of these modules requires accessing the device directly by using the session command.

Connecting to the command-line interface of the MSFC3 is as simple as issuing a **session** command from the Catalyst OS command line, as shown in Example 5-11.

Example 5-11   *Connecting to the MSFC*

```
SW1> (enable) session 15
Trying Router-15...
Connected to Router-15.
Escape character is '^]'.

SW1-MSFC3>
```

After a session is established to the MSFC3 on SW1, standard IOS commands can be issued to configure the router. Issuing an **exit** command returns the device back to the Catalyst OS command-line interface.

In hybrid mode, the individual Ethernet ports configurable from the Catalyst OS cannot be viewed or modified by the MSFC. Layer 3 routing is accomplished by creating VLAN interfaces on the MSFC that correspond to the VLANs created in the Catalyst OS. In Example 5-12, all the ports on module 1 are set to VLAN 10 using the **set vlan** command.

Example 5-12 *Configuring Port VLAN Membership on Module 1*

```
SW1> (enable) set vlan 10 1/1-1/16
VLAN  Mod/Ports
----  ----------------------
10    1/1-16
```

At this point, all ports on module 1 are members of VLAN 10, but no Layer 3 routing functionality is set up on the MSFC. After accessing the MSFC by again issuing the **session 15** command, a Layer 3 VLAN interface can be configured using the **interface VLAN 10** command. To issue the **interface** command, the user must first be in enable and config terminal modes. Example 5-13 shows VLAN 10 being configured on the MSFC3 in SW1.

Example 5-13 *Configuring VLAN 10 on the MSFC3*

```
SW1-MSFC3>enable
Password:
SW1-MSFC3#config t
Enter configuration commands, one per line.  End with CNTL/Z.
SW1-MSFC3(config)#interface vlan10
SW1-MSFC3(config-if)#end
SW1-MSFC3#
```

After the VLAN 10 interface is configured, it can be viewed by issuing a **show interface** command, as in Example 5-14.

Example 5-14 *Output of **show interface** on VLAN 10*

```
SW1-MSFC3#show interface vlan10
Vlan10 is administratively down, line protocol is down
  Hardware is Cat6k RP Virtual Ethernet, address is 000d.662c.64fc (bia 000d.662
c.64fc)
  MTU 1500 bytes, BW 1000000 Kbit, DLY 10 usec,
     reliability 255/255, txload 1/255, rxload 1/255
  Encapsulation ARPA, loopback not set
  ARP type: ARPA, ARP Timeout 04:00:00
  Last input never, output never, output hang never
  Last clearing of "show interface" counters never
  Input queue: 0/75/0/0 (size/max/drops/flushes); Total output drops: 0
  Queueing strategy: fifo
  Output queue: 0/40 (size/max)
  5 minute input rate 0 bits/sec, 0 packets/sec
  5 minute output rate 0 bits/sec, 0 packets/sec
     0 packets input, 0 bytes, 0 no buffer
     Received 0 broadcasts, 0 runts, 0 giants, 0 throttles
     0 input errors, 0 CRC, 0 frame, 0 overrun, 0 ignored
     0 packets output, 0 bytes, 0 underruns
     0 output errors, 1 interface resets
     0 output buffer failures, 0 output buffers swapped out
```

By default, the interface is administratively down and no Layer 3 address is assigned. In Example 5-15, an IP address is assigned and the interface is enabled.

Example 5-15 *Assigning an IP Address to VLAN 10*

```
SW1-MSFC3#config terminal
Enter configuration commands, one per line.  End with CNTL/Z.
SW1-MSFC3(config)#interface vlan10
SW1-MSFC3(config-if)#ip address 10.10.10.1 255.255.255.0
SW1-MSFC3(config-if)#no shut
```

After the IP address is configured and the interface is enabled, the switch will recognize that ports 1/1 through 1/16 are assigned to VLAN 10 via the Catalyst OS interface and VLAN 10 will come up. (See Example 5-16.)

Example 5-16 **show interface** *Output for VLAN 10*

```
SW1-MSFC3#show interface vlan10
Vlan10 is up, line protocol is up
  Hardware is Cat6k RP Virtual Ethernet, address is 000d.662c.64fc (bia 000d.662
c.64fc)
  Internet address is 10.10.10.1/24
  MTU 1500 bytes, BW 1000000 Kbit, DLY 10 usec,
     reliability 255/255, txload 1/255, rxload 1/255
  Encapsulation ARPA, loopback not set
  ARP type: ARPA, ARP Timeout 04:00:00
  Last input never, output never, output hang never
  Last clearing of "show interface" counters never
  Input queue: 0/75/0/0 (size/max/drops/flushes); Total output drops: 0
  Queueing strategy: fifo
  Output queue: 0/40 (size/max)
  5 minute input rate 0 bits/sec, 0 packets/sec
  5 minute output rate 0 bits/sec, 0 packets/sec
     0 packets input, 0 bytes, 0 no buffer
     Received 0 broadcasts, 0 runts, 0 giants, 0 throttles
     0 input errors, 0 CRC, 0 frame, 0 overrun, 0 ignored
     0 packets output, 0 bytes, 0 underruns
     0 output errors, 2 interface resets
     0 output buffer failures, 0 output buffers swapped out
```

At this point, the VLAN 10 interface is processing traffic for any device connected to a port assigned to VLAN 10. Catalyst switches in a hybrid setup require at least one Layer 2 port to be assigned to the same VLAN as the Layer 3 VLAN interface before it can be enabled.

The Look and Feel of Native

With the introduction of Cisco IOS 12.0(7)XE, the familiar command-line interface look and feel from the Cisco popular line of routers became available for the Catalyst 6500 platform. As previously mentioned, this IOS for switches is commonly referred to as native IOS. One of the most noticeable differences in the look and feel between Catalyst OS and native IOS running on a switch is the way connections are treated. With Catalyst OS, Ethernet connections are called *ports*, and with native IOS, those same connections are called *interfaces*. Example 5-3, earlier in the chapter, displayed the output of a **show port** command for port 1/1. Example 5-17 shows the output from the **show interface** command for the same Gigabit Ethernet connection running native IOS 12.1(13)E9.

Example 5-17   **show interface gigabitethernet 1/1** *Command Output*

```
SW1#show interface gigabitethernet 1/1
GigabitEthernet1/1 is administratively down, line protocol is down (disabled)
  Hardware is C6k 1000Mb 802.3, address is 0001.c9db.8814 (bia 0001.c9db.8814)
  MTU 1500 bytes, BW 1000000 Kbit, DLY 10 usec,
     reliability 255/255, txload 1/255, rxload 1/255
  Encapsulation ARPA, loopback not set
  Full-duplex mode, link type is autonegotiation, media type is SX
  output flow-control is unsupported, input flow-control is unsupported, 1000Mb/s
  Clock mode is auto
  input flow-control is off, output flow-control is off
  ARP type: ARPA, ARP Timeout 04:00:00
  Last input never, output never, output hang never
  Last clearing of "show interface" counters never
  Input queue: 0/2000/0/0 (size/max/drops/flushes); Total output drops: 0
  Queueing strategy: fifo
  Output queue :0/40 (size/max)
  5 minute input rate 0 bits/sec, 0 packets/sec
  5 minute output rate 0 bits/sec, 0 packets/sec
     0 packets input, 0 bytes, 0 no buffer
     Received 0 broadcasts, 0 runts, 0 giants, 0 throttles
     0 input errors, 0 CRC, 0 frame, 0 overrun, 0 ignored
     0 input packets with dribble condition detected
     0 packets output, 0 bytes, 0 underruns
     0 output errors, 0 collisions, 1 interface resets
     0 babbles, 0 late collision, 0 deferred
     0 lost carrier, 0 no carrier
     0 output buffer failures, 0 output buffers swapped out
```

Most of the information displayed using both the **show port** command in the Catalyst OS and **show interface** in native IOS is the same, with only a few exceptions; the primary difference is in the formatting of the output.

Unlike the hybrid configuration, only a single interface exists for configuring connections, and each Ethernet connection can be configured as a switched port (Layer 2) or a routed interface (Layer 3). By default, each connection defaults to being a Layer 3 routed interface and is shut down. Configuring the interface for Layer 3 routing is as simple as assigning an IP address and enabling the interface. (See Example 5-18.)

Example 5-18 *Configuring IP on a Gigabit Interface*

```
SW1#config terminal
Enter configuration commands, one per line.  End with CNTL/Z.
SW1(config)#interface gigabitethernet 1/1
SW1(config-if)#ip address 10.10.10.1 255.255.255.0
SW1(config-if)#no shutdown
SW1(config-if)#end
SW1#
```

Now that the interface is configured with an IP address, a quick check of the interface can be accomplished with the **show interface gigabitethernet 1/1** command, as demonstrated in Example 5-19.

Example 5-19 *Output of* **show interface gigabitethernet 1/1** *Command*

```
SW1#show interface gigabitethernet 1/1
GigabitEthernet1/1 is up, line protocol is up
  Hardware is C6k 1000Mb 802.3, address is 000b.fc38.540a (bia 000b.fc38.540a)
  Internet address is 10.10.10.1/24
  MTU 1500 bytes, BW 1000000 Kbit, DLY 10 usec,
     reliability 255/255, txload 1/255, rxload 1/255
  Encapsulation ARPA, loopback not set
  Keepalive not set
  Full-duplex mode, link type is autonegotiation, media type is SX
  output flow-control is unsupported, input flow-control is unsupported, 1000Mb/s
  Clock mode is auto
  input flow-control is off, output flow-control is off
  ARP type: ARPA, ARP Timeout 04:00:00
  Last input never, output 00:02:14, output hang never
  Last clearing of "show interface" counters never
  Input queue: 0/75/0/0 (size/max/drops/flushes); Total output drops: 0
  Queueing strategy: fifo
  Output queue :0/40 (size/max)
  5 minute input rate 0 bits/sec, 0 packets/sec
  5 minute output rate 0 bits/sec, 0 packets/sec
  L2 Switched: ucast: 3 pkt, 1230 bytes - mcast: 0 pkt, 0 bytes
  L3 in Switched: ucast: 0 pkt, 0 bytes - mcast: 0 pkt, 0 bytes mcast
  L3 out Switched: ucast: 0 pkt, 0 bytes
     0 packets input, 0 bytes, 0 no buffer
     Received 0 broadcasts, 0 runts, 0 giants, 0 throttles
     0 input errors, 0 CRC, 0 frame, 0 overrun, 0 ignored
     0 input packets with dribble condition detected
     0 packets output, 0 bytes, 0 underruns
     0 output errors, 0 collisions, 4 interface resets
     0 babbles, 0 late collision, 0 deferred
     0 lost carrier, 0 no carrier
     0 output buffer failures, 0 output buffers swapped out
```

Example 5-20 shows the configuration of GigabitEthernet interface 1/1.

Example 5-20 *GigabitEthernet 1/1 Running Configuration*

```
SW1#show run interface gigabitethernet 1/1
Building configuration...

Current configuration : 87 bytes
!
interface GigabitEthernet1/1
 ip address 10.10.10.1 255.255.255.0
end
```

The same Gigabit Ethernet interface can be configured as a switched port with a few simple configuration commands. First, a VLAN is created to contain the switch port. In Example 5-21, as in the Catalyst OS configuration, VLAN 10 is used.

Example 5-21 *Creating VLAN 10 in Native Mode*

```
SW1#config terminal
Enter configuration commands, one per line.  End with CNTL/Z.
SW1(config)#vlan 10
SW1(config-vlan)#end
SW1#
```

Issuing a **switchport** command puts the interface into a Layer 2-only mode. This command must be issued before any additional switchport commands can be issued. The **switchport mode access** command configures the port as an access port and prevents the port from becoming a trunk. The **switchport access** command allows the assignment of a VLAN. In this case, VLAN 10 is assigned to GigabitEthernet 1/1. (See Example 5-22.) Issuing a **no switchport** command on the interface removes all Layer 2 configuration and returns the interface to a Layer 3 configuration.

Example 5-22 *Configuring a Layer 2 Switch Port*

```
SW1#configure terminal
Enter configuration commands, one per line.  End with CNTL/Z.
SW1(config)#interface gigabitethernet 1/1
SW1(config-if)#switchport
SW1(Config-if)#switchport mode access
SW1(config-if)#switchport access vlan 10
SW1(Config-if)#no shutdown
SW1(config-if)#end
SW1#
```

When using native to configure multiple connections as switch ports, Layer 3 routing of those switch ports is accomplished using VLAN interfaces in the same way as with hybrid.

A comparison between the look and feel of hybrid and native is illustrated by contrasting the configuration of VLAN Trunking Protocol (VTP) in both environments in Table 5-1.

Table 5-1 *Configuring VTP in Hybrid Versus Native*

Catalyst OS	Cisco IOS Software
SW1# **set vtp domain Cisco**	SW1#**configure terminal**
SW1#**set vtp mode server**	SW1(config)#**vtp mode server**
SW1#**set vlan 10 name Lab**	SW1(config)#**vtp domain Cisco**
SW1#**set vlan 10 1/1 – 16**	SW1(config)#**vlan 10**
	SW1(config-vlan)#**name Lab**
	SW1(config)#**interface range fastethernet 1/1 – 16**
	SW1(config-if-range)#**switchport**
	SW1(config-if-range)#**switchport mode access**
	SW1(config-if-range)#**switchport access vlan 10**

Table 5-2 shows a list of commonly used commands and their syntax in both Catalyst OS and Cisco IOS for Catalyst switches.

Table 5-2 *Catalyst OS and Cisco IOS Command Comparison*

Catalyst OS	Cisco IOS Software
reset system	**reload**
session	**remote-login**
set system name	**hostname**
set test diaglevel	**diagnostic level**
set boot config-register	**config-register**
set boot system flash	**boot system flash**
set module power down/up	**power enable module**
set port disable	**shutdown** (interface mode)
set port duplex	**duplex**
**set port flowcontrol send [desired	off |on]**	**flowcontrol send [desired	off	on]**
**set port flowcontrol receive [desired	off |on]**	**flowcontrol receive [desired	off	on]**
set port negotiation *<mod/port>* **enable/disable**	**speed nonegotiate**
set port speed	**speed**
set cam	**mac-address-table**
set port jumbo	**mtu 9216**

Table 5-2   *Catalyst OS and Cisco IOS Command Comparison (Continued)*

Catalyst OS	Cisco IOS Software
set port channel	**channel-group** *<group>* **mode** (interface mode)
set trunk (default mode is auto)	**switchport mode trunk** (VLAN database command)
set udld	**udld**
set vlan *<vlan id>* **port**	**switchport** **switchport mode access** **switchport access vlan <>**
set vtp	**vtp**
set spantree backbonefast	**spanning-tree backbonefast**
set spantree enable/disable	**spanning-tree vlan**
set spantree portfast	**spanning-tree portfast**
set qos enable	**mls qos**
set port dot1qtunnel	**switchport mode dot1qtunnel**
show cam dynamic	**show mac-address-table dynamic**
show channel info or **show port channel**	**show etherchannel summary**
show mac	**show interface counters**
show port *<slot/port>*	**show interface** *<type slot/port>*
show mls cef	**show mls cef**
show port	**show interface status**
show port capabilities	**show interface capabilities**
show span	**show monitor**
show spantree	**show spanning-tree**
show qos	**show mls qos**
show trace	**show debugging**
show trunk or **show port trunk**	**show interfaces trunk**
show udld	**show udld**
show vlan	**show vlan**
show vtp domain	**show vtp status**
clear cam	**clear mac-address-table**

Choosing Between Hybrid and Native

A very common question posed to Cisco is "Should I run in a hybrid or native configuration?" The answer is, "it depends." Although there is no wrong answer, the choice should be influenced by a number of considerations. Are personnel responsible for configuring and maintaining the switch more familiar with one interface or another? If personnel are already familiar with configuring Cisco routers, but not switches using Catalyst OS, native might be a better choice. As of the writing of this text, some differences in feature support exist between hybrid and native, with more software features typically available in hybrid. On the other hand, some of the newest Cisco modules for platforms such as the Catalyst 6500 and some of the newest Cisco switches such as the 4500 series run only on native.

The Cisco official position on hybrid versus native is that eventually feature parity will exist between both types of software, and that even switches without Layer 3 routing capabilities, such as a Catalyst 6500 without an MSFC, will be able to run native. Although native appears to be becoming more popular because of the capability to have one look and feel of interface to learn and support, Cisco is committed to developing and supporting Catalyst OS for many, many years to come. As a result, many companies have both hybrid and native switches in their networks, and a choice between the types of software comes down to current hardware and/or feature support. As of this writing Table 5-3 compares the feature support between Catalyst OS and native IOS on the Cisco flagship switching platform, the Catalyst 6500.

Table 5-3 *Software Feature Comparison*

Software Feature	Catalyst OS	Cisco IOS
VLAN ranges: up to 4096 VLAN SVIs (Layer 3 VLAN interfaces)	x	x
Inter-VLAN routing	x	x
4096 Layer 2 VLANs	x	x
Private VLANs	x	x
Dynamic VLANs	x	
Trunking: IEEE 802.1q, ISL	x	x
DTP, VTP	x	x
VTPv3	x	
IEEE 802.1q tunneling	x	x
Layer 2 Protocol tunneling	x	x
Spanning Tree: PortFast, UplinkFast, BackboneFast, BPDU Guard, PRRST+, PVRST	x	x
IEEE 802.1s and 802.1w	x	x

Table 5-3   *Software Feature Comparison (Continued)*

Software Feature	Catalyst OS	Cisco IOS
Jumbo frames	x	x
EtherChannel, Port Aggregation Protocol (PAgP)	x	x
EtherChannel, IEEE 802.3ad (LACP)	x	x
Local and Remote Span (RSPAN)	x	x
Multicast Services: PIM, IGMP snooping, RGMP	x	x
QoS Marking, Policing, Scheduling	x	x
QoS ACLs	x	x
Routing ACLs	x	x
VLAN ACLs	x	x
Cisco IOS Server Load Balancing		x
Broadcast suppression	x	x
Protocol filtering, Cisco IOS support on Supervisor Engine 1A systems only	x	x
Port security	x	x
IEEE 802.1X	x	x
Time Domain Reflectometer (TDR)	x	x
AutoQoS	x	
ARP Inspection	x	
Network-Based Application Recognition (NBAR)	x	x
User-Based Rate Limiting		x
Cisco Discovery Protocol	x	x
NetFlow Data Export (NDE)	x	x
Unidirectional Link Detection (UDLD)	x	x
Voice VLAN ID (VVID) and inline power for Cisco IP Phones	x	x
Supervisor redundancy and failover	x	x
Stateful Supervisor Switchover	x	
Multiprotocol Label Switching (MPLS), EoMPLS, MPLS VPN		x
Distributed Cisco Express Forwarding (dCEF)		x

Refer to Cisco.com for a current list of hardware and feature support in Catalyst OS and Cisco IOS for Catalyst switches.

Downloading Catalyst Software

Cisco Catalyst operating systems are available via the Cisco Software Center at http://www.cisco.com/public/sw-center/. Users should read the documentation and release notes for each software version before downloading and installing on any Catalyst switch. The Cisco documentation lists minimum and recommended software versions for each Catalyst platform, modules, and linecards. Although Catalyst OS does not offer different levels of software images based on feature requirements, Cisco IOS for switches does offer various feature sets depending on the platform. Cisco offers differentiated features sets so that customers may choose and pay for a combination of features they require. For example, a customer requiring only IP routing may not choose the more expensive Enterprise feature set.

CAUTION	It is extremely important to read the software release notes before attempting an upgrade of Catalyst software of any kind. The software release notes provide information on minimum boot ROM versions, minimum DRAM requirements, and minimum software versions to support specific hardware.

This section illustrates some of the steps required to locate and download Cisco software for the Catalyst 6000/6500, 4500, and 3750 series switches.

Software for Catalyst 6000/6500

After a decision has been made to run either hybrid or native, the software can be downloaded from the Cisco Software Center. Figure 5-1 is a snapshot of what users see when selecting Catalyst 6000 from the LAN Switching menu in the Cisco Software Center.

As seen in Figure 5-1, users are faced with a number of choices when downloading Catalyst 6000/6500 software. Users are often confused about which link to choose based on their need to download Catalyst OS, IOS for the MSFC running in hybrid, or IOS for the Supervisor running in native mode.

Figure 5-2 indicates that selecting Download Supervisor & Related Interface Cards Software in the section Download Catalyst 6000 Series Software Images provides users with access to Catalyst OS software images to be used standalone on Layer 2-only Catalyst 6000/6500 switches, or in hybrid mode with separate IOS images on MSFCs.

Each Catalyst OS image filename for Catalyst 6000/6500 Supervisors begins with cat6000-sup. For example, the filename cat6000-sup6-4-6.bin represents the Catalyst OS software version 6.4(6).

Figure 5-1   *Catalyst 6000 Software Center*

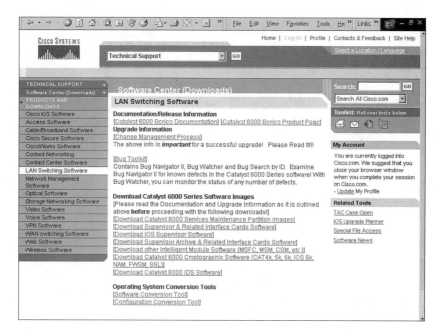

Figure 5-2   *Link to Catalyst OS Software*

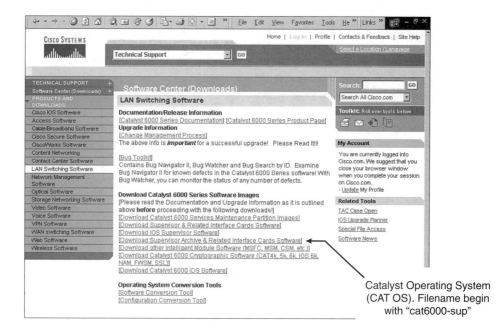

Catalyst Operating System
(CAT OS). Filename begin
with "cat6000-sup"

Figure 5-3 indicates that selecting Download IOS Supervisor Software provides uses with access to native IOS software images for the Catalyst 6000/6500 Supervisors.

Each native IOS image filename for the Catalyst 6000/6500 begins with c6sup. For example, the filename c6sup22-jsv-mz.121-13.E9 represents native IOS for the Catalyst version 12.1(13)E9.

Figure 5-4 indicates that selecting Download other Intelligent Module Software (MSFC, MSM, CSM, and so on) provides user access to IOS software images for the MSFCs. These software images when paired with Catalyst OS images on the Supervisor create a hybrid configuration.

Each IOS image filename for the MSFC begins with c6msfc. For example, the filename c6msfc2-jsv-mz.121-13.E11 is IOS for the MSFC2 version 12.1(13)E11.

Figure 5-3   *Link to Native Software*

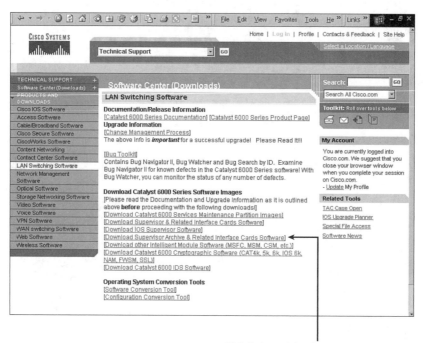

IOS Software for Supervisors (Native).
Filenames begin with "c6sup"

Figure 5-4 *Link to MSFC Software*

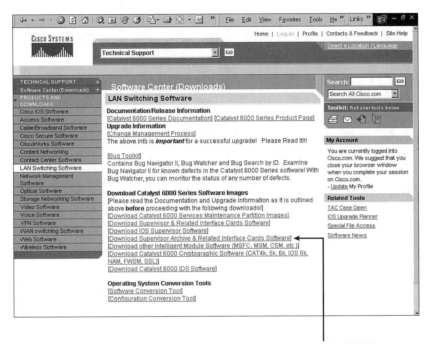

IOS Software for MSFCs
(Hybrid). Filenames begin with "c6msfc"

The following excerpt from the Catalyst documentation on Cisco.com describes the naming conventions used by Catalyst OS and Cisco IOS images:

- Catalyst OS on the Supervisor and Cisco IOS on the MSFC (hybrid):
  - Catalyst OS image naming conventions for Supervisor Engines I, II, and Supervisor Engine 720 and Cisco IOS image naming conventions for the MSFC1, MSFC2, and MSFC3 are described later in this chapter.
  - Catalyst OS naming conventions for the Supervisor Engine I, IA, II, and 720
  - cat6000-sup: Supervisor 1 and 1A
  - cat6000-sup2: Supervisor II
  - cat6000-sup720: Supervisor 720
  - Cisco IOS naming conventions for the MSFC1, 2, and 3

- — c6msfc : MSFC1
- — c6msfc2: MSFC2
- — c6msfc3: MSFC3
- — c6msfc-boot: MSFC1 boot image
- — c6msfc2-boot: MSFC2 boot image
- Examples of Catalyst OS images for the Supervisor and Cisco IOS images for the MSFC:
  - — cat6000-supk8.8-1-1.bin is the Catalyst 6500/6000 Supervisor I and IA Catalyst OS image, version 8.1(1)
  - — cat6000-sup720k8.8-1-1.bin is the Catalyst 6500/6000 Supervisor 720 Catalyst OS image, version 8.1(1)
  - — c6msfc-boot-mz.121-19.E is the Catalyst 6500/6000 MSFC 1 Cisco IOS Boot image, version 12.1(19)E
  - — c6msfc-ds-mz.121-19.E is the Catalyst 6500/6000 MSFC 1 Cisco IOS image, version 12.1(19)E
  - — c6msfc2-jsv-mz.121-19.E is the Catalyst 6500/6000 MSFC 2 Cisco IOS image, version 12.1(19)E
  - — c6msfc3-jsv-mz.122-14.SX2 is the Catalyst 6500 MSFC 3 Cisco IOS image, version 12.2(14)SX2
- Cisco IOS (native) images:
  - — Cisco IOS (native) image naming conventions for the Supervisor Engines I, IA, II, and Supervisor Engine 720 are described later in this chapter.
  - — Cisco IOS (native) naming conventions for the Supervisor IA and II
- The c6supxy indicates the Supervisor/MSFC combination upon which it will run, where x is the Supervisor version and y is the MSFC version:
  - — c6sup—original name for native IOS image, runs on the Supervisor I, MSFC1.
  - — c6sup11—Supervisor I, MSFC1
  - — c6sup12—Supervisor I, MSFC2
  - — c6sup22—Supervisor II, MSFC2
- Examples of Cisco IOS (native) images for the Supervisor I and II:
  - — c6sup-is-mz.120-7.XE1 is the Catalyst 6500/6000 Cisco IOS image (with Supervisor I/MSFC1), version 12.0(7)XE1
  - — c6sup11-dsv-mz.121-19.E1 is the Catalyst 6500/6000 Cisco IOS image (with Supervisor I/MSFC1), version 12.1(19)E1

- — c6sup12-js-mz.121-13.E9 is the Catalyst 6500/6000 Cisco IOS image (with Supervisor I/MSFC2), version 12.1(13)E9

- — c6sup22-psv-mz.121-11b.EX1 is the Catalyst 6500 Cisco IOS image (with Supervisor II/MSFC2), version 12.1(11b)EX1

- Cisco IOS (native) naming conventions for the Supervisor 720:

  The s720xy indicates the MSFC/Policy Feature Card (PFC) combination on the Supervisor Engine 720, where x is the MSFC version and y is the PFC version.

  s72033—MSFC3, PFC3

  Example of Cisco IOS (native) naming convention for the Supervisor 720:

  - — s72033-jk9s-mz.122-14.SX is the Catalyst 6500 Supervisor 720 Cisco IOS image (with Supervisor 720/MSFC 3/PFC 3a), version 12.2(14)SX

Software for Catalyst 4500

The Supervisors for the Catalyst 4500 run native IOS images, which come in a choice of two feature sets, Basic or Enhanced. The Basic image supports only RIP version 1 and 2, along with Static Routes, AppleTalk, and IPX. The Enhanced feature set includes more robust dynamic routing capabilities such as OSPF, EIGRP, and IS-IS. While Enhanced feature sets are available for the Supervisor III and IV on the Catalyst 4500, only the Basic feature set is available for the Supervisor II+. Figure 5-5 shows the links to software for the Supervisor II+, III, IV, and V on the Catalyst 4500 on Cisco.com.

Catalyst 4500 software uses the following naming convention:

- Basic: cat4000-**i9**s-mz

- Enhanced: cat4000-**i5**s-mz

For example, the latest Enhanced image for the Supervisor IV at time of publication is 12.1(20)EW1, which has a filename of cat4000-i5s-mz.121-20.EW1.bin. Upgrading from a basic image to the Enhanced image on the Supervisor III or IV is as simple as purchasing the Enhanced image and loading it onto the Supervisor.

Software for Catalyst 3750

Like the Catalyst 4500, the Catalyst 3750 platform offers two levels of software images, both utilizing a native IOS interface. Catalyst 3750 series switches support running either a Standard Multilayer Image (SMI) or an Enhanced Multilayer Image (EMI). SMI supports only static routing and RIP version 1 and 2; EMI supports OSPF and EIGRP.

Figure 5-5   *Catalyst 4500 Software*

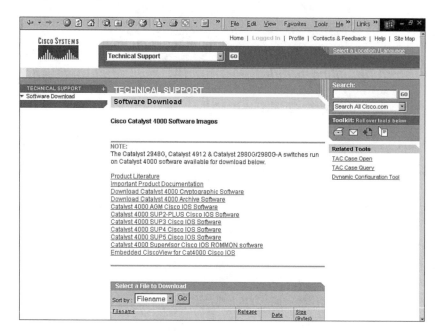

Catalyst 3750 software uses the following naming convention:

- Basic: c3750-**i9**-mz

- Enhanced: c3750-**i5**-mz

For example, the latest Enhanced image for the Catalyst 3750 series at the time of publication is 12.1(19)EA1a, which has a filename of c3750-**i5**-mz.121-19.EA1a.bin. Upgrading from a standard image to the Enhanced image on the 3750 is as simple as purchasing the Enhanced image and loading it onto the switch.

One important difference between the Catalyst 3750 series and other Catalyst switching platforms, such as the 4500 and 6000/6500 is the Cluster Management Software (CMS) included with each Catalyst 3750 series switch. CMS is free with each 3750 series switch and provides a Graphical User Interface (GUI) for configuration of either an individual switch or a stack of 3750 series switches. Accessing CMS is as simple as pointing a browser to the IP address of the management interface on a 3750 switch. CMS requires a java plug-in to be installed before it can be used. Users may download the CMS plug-in from the software download center on Cisco.com. Figure 5-6 shows the links to Catalyst 3750 software and the CMS plug-in on Cisco.com. Figure 5-7 is a snapshot of the front panel configuration mode in CMS. The user has selected multiple interface in the switch cluster to be configured with the same parameters.

Figure 5-6   *Catalyst 3750 Software*

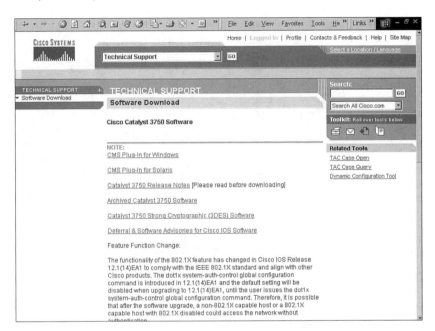

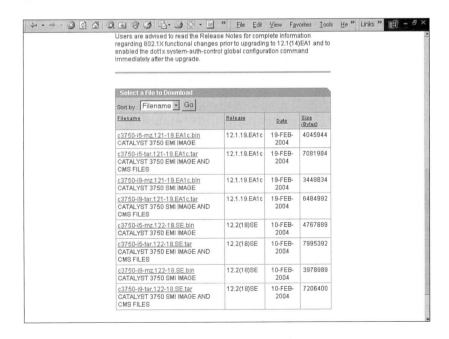

Figure 5-7 *CMS Front Panel View*

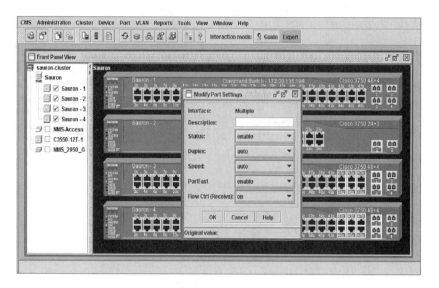

New Software Packaging

In April of 2003, Cisco announced new simplified packaging of Cisco IOS beginning with release 12.3 on the 1700, 2600, and 3700 series router platforms. Goals of the simplification effort are to reduce the number of available packages from 44 to 8, while providing consistent image names across the various platforms Cisco offers. Beginning with 12.2S and 12.3T, simplified packaging is available for all platforms running Cisco IOS. This new packaging extends to Catalyst switches running IOS, while a similar simplification effort will extend to Catalyst OS.

Packaging for Routers

Figure 5-8 represents the eight new packages for Cisco IOS devices.

As mentioned earlier, consistent imaging naming is one of the benefits of the new packaging structure. Table 5-4 is an example of the eight packages available on the 2600 series router. The same abbreviation is used across all platforms.

As of this writing, none of the Catalyst switching platforms run Cisco IOS either native or hybrid in release trains that support the new packaging (12.2S, 12.3, or 12.3T), but they eventually will follow a similar packaging system.

Figure 5-8   *Software Packaging for Routers*

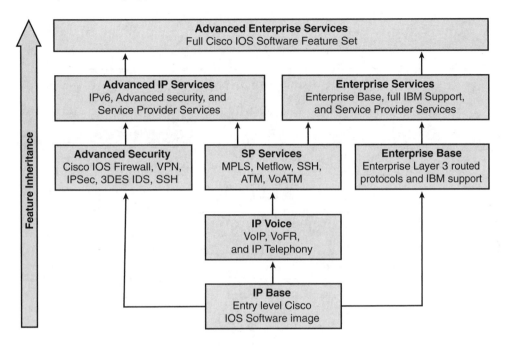

Table 5-4   *Feature Sets for the 2600 Series Routers*

Feature Set	Image Name
IP Base	C2600-ipbase-mz
IP Voice	C2600-ipvoice-mz
Enterprise Base	C2600-entbase-mz
Advanced Security	C2600-advsecurityk9-mz
SP Services	C2600-spservicesk9-mz
Advanced IP Services	C2600-advipservicesk9-mz
Enterprise Services	C2600-entservicesk9-mz
Advanced Enterprise Services	C2600-adventerprisek9-mz

Packaging for Switches

Figure 5-9 represents proposed packaging for Catalyst switches running native IOS.

Figure 5-9 *Native IOS Packaging for Catalyst Switches*

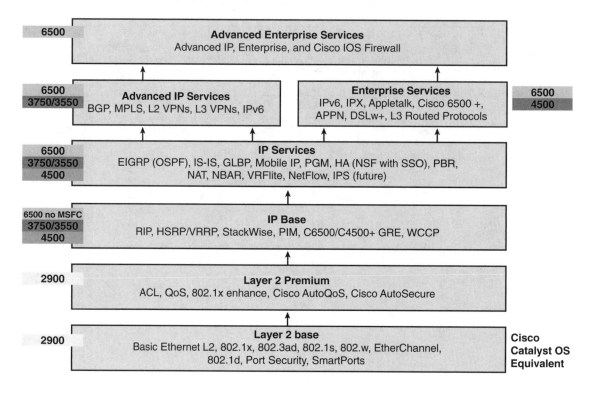

The packaging outlined in Figure 5-9 closely resembles the new software packaging for traditional Cisco routers. Again, this software packaging does not affect devices running Catalyst OS. There are no plans currently to change the way Catalyst OS is offered.

Summary

This chapter provided an overview of hybrid and native software for the Catalyst switching platforms, along with look and feel differences between Catalyst OS and Cisco IOS for switches. In addition, procedures for converting a Catalyst 6000/6500 from hybrid to native and back to hybrid were provided, along with an overview of the software available for the Catalyst 3750, 4500, and 6000/6500 series switching platforms.

This chapter covers the following topics:

- Why MLS
- Introducing MLS
- Understanding the MLS packet flow
- Configuring MLS
- Router access lists
- MLS on Catalyst 6500
- Understanding the need for Cisco Express Forwarding

CHAPTER 6

Understanding Multilayer Switching

Multilayer switching (MLS) is a cache-based forwarding model. After the initial packet is handled by the router, all subsequent packets are forwarded by the hardware switching engine. The phrase "route once, switch many" comes to mind. Traditionally, the router has two primary tasks:

- It must participate with other routers to learn and populate routes in the routing table.
- It must software switch packets between its interfaces.

The chapter focuses on the switching component of the router and the role of a switch in taking over most of this responsibility. Newer hardware gear, such as Catalyst 6500 with Supervisor II and Supervisor 720, allows for all packets to bypass the router and directly switch in hardware.

Why MLS?

The first Cisco switches did not have any Layer 3 routing capability. They merely switched frames at Layer 2 between hosts on the same VLAN. All inter-VLAN switching was forwarded to the router. The switch was many times faster in switching packets than the router. A router had greater latency when it had to forward packets at Layer 3. To get around this problem, as mentioned in earlier chapters, VLANs were extended throughout the LAN campus, minimizing the role of routers in the LAN network.

The actual connection between the switch and the router came in two forms. The first was one physical link per VLAN that was configured on the switch. The second method involved one physical cable between the switch and router with trunking enabled. The former was widely deployed because most LAN designs did not require trunking between a router and switch. After the packet arrived on a router's interface, the router did the Media Access Control (MAC) rewrite and software switched the packet out of one of its other interfaces. A popular router at that time, 4000 router, could only fast switch packets at a rate of 14,000 packets per second (pps). The enterprise router, 7500 family with an RSP2 card, could only do 150,000 pps. A Catalyst 5000 switch can switch packets at millions of pps (Mpps).

The multilayer switching mechanism enabled the use of Catalyst 5000 hardware to switch packets between different subnets in hardware, which translated into higher performance of packet handling on the network.

Newer hardware for Catalyst 6500 with Cisco Express Forwarding (CEF) implementation can switch packets at very high rates. For example, Supervisor II with a Switch Fabric Module (SFM) card can switch packets at rates as high as 210 Mpps. The Supervisor 720 can go as high as 400 Mpps. The discussion at the moment is with MLS and its role in Cisco switches.

Introducing MLS

MLS was first introduced for the Catalyst 5000 in version 4.1(1) of the switch operating system, and a NetFlow Feature Card (NFFC) was also required. The MLS-enabled switch keeps track of the initial packet destined to the router, and any subsequent packets from the same flow destined to the router are intercepted by the switch. The switch now does the forwarding for the router. The process greatly increases the number of packets switched between VLANs.

MLS offers low latency at Layer 3. It uses the existing network infrastructure in place, assuming the Catalyst 5000 product line. Aside from a daughter card and software upgrade, MLS does not have any other major requirements. MLS handles packet switching and rewrite function at the ASIC level, whereas the router does this at the software level. A Catalyst 6500 switch automatically is configured for MLS, and its architecture is vastly different from the Catalyst 5000 product line.

The following are the requirements for enabling MLS on the Catalyst 5000 product line:

- Switching Engines (MLS-SE)
  - Cat5k—Supervisor Engine SW 4.1(1) or later
  - Supervisor IIG, or IIIG
  - Supervisor III w/NFFC I or II
  - CAt6k—Supervisor Engine SW 5.3(1)CSX or later
  - Supervisor IA w/MSFC and PFC
- Routing Processors (MLS-RP)
  - RSM, Cisco 7500, 7200, 4700, 4500 series routers
  - SW 11.3(2)WA4(4)
  - SW 11.3(8)WA4(11) or later (ATM Media)
  - RSFC—SW 12.0(3c)W5(8a) or later
  - 3600—12.0(2) or later
  - MSFC—12.0(3)XE or later

Example 6-1 shows the output from a Catalyst 5500 device. As the output shows, the supervisor is a Supervisor III, WS-X5530, running 4.5(5) Catalyst Operation System (Catalyst OS) software, which means it can support MLS. Furthermore, it has an NFFC II, WS-F5531A, card installed.

Example 6-1 *Supervisor Information*

```
Switch3> (enable) show module 1
Mod Module-Name       Ports Module-Type           Model     Serial-Num Status
--- ----------------- ----- --------------------- --------- ---------- -------
1                     0     Supervisor III        WS-X5530  030061500 faulty
Mod MAC-Address(es)                         Hw     Fw         Sw
--- --------------------------------------- ------ ---------- -----------------
1   00-90-86-66-50-00 to 00-90-86-66-53-ff 3.5    5.1(2)     4.5(5)
Mod Sub-Type Sub-Model Sub-Serial Sub-Hw
--- -------- --------- ---------- ------
1   NFFC II  WS-F5531A 0030060943 2.2
```

There are three components to MLS:

- **Multilayer Switching Route Processor (MLS-RP)**—The router component responsible for the initial packet forwarding. It informs the Multilayer Switching Engine (MLS-SE) of what MAC address it used for rewrite, and any changes to the interface, such as routing, access list, and so on.

- **Multilayer Switching Engine (MLS-SE)**—Understands Layer 3 flow, rewrites MAC, and switches packets.

- **Multilayer Switching Protocol (MLSP)**—MLSP is the means by which MLS-RP and MLS-SE communicate. MLSP uses Cisco Group Management Protocol (CGMP) multicast MAC address 01-00-0c-dd-dd-dd. The MLSP packet contains VLAN Trunking Protocol (VTP) domain name, version number, router ID, and sequence number. It also sends information regarding access list and routing table changes/ updates. The switch adds a 1-byte XTAG for the purpose of identifying all MAC addresses associated with a single router. Hellos are sent every 15 seconds, with dead timer set at 45 seconds.

MLS can be programmed on an internal or external router. Cisco introduced various routing capable modules for the Catalyst 5000 product line. These modules supported almost all features and functions of a typical router. These modules include Route Switch Module (RSM) and Route Switch Feature Card (RSFC), with RSM being the most popular. RSM could software switch packets at 114,000 pps. It is basically an RSP2 card in the Catalyst 5000/5500 chassis. The combination of fast internal router and the switching engine allowed for robust forwarding of packets with low latency. MLS can also be programmed on an external router such as 75xx, 72xx, and so on that is connected to a Catalyst switch. Many Catalyst 5500 MLS implementations used an RSM.

Understanding the MLS Packet Flow

It is critical for the MLS-enabled switch to see the full initial packet flow. In other words, the switch must see the initial packet destined to the inbound router interface, and then, it must also see the packet on the outbound interface of the router. If the switch does not know the outbound interface for the flow of the traffic, it will not have the information to rewrite the MAC at the ASIC level.

As the packet enters the port destined to another VLAN, the switch will forward the packet to the RSM (see Figure 6-1). This is known as the Candidate packet. Assuming the switch sees the outbound interface, the packet now becomes an Enable packet. The RSM will do a MAC rewrite and forwards the packet out its other interface. The RSM uses fast switching, which is on by default depending on the router code used, to forward the packet. During this process, the switch, MLS-SE, keeps track of this flow. Any other subsequent packets destined to Host2 will be MLS switched by the MLS-SE. At this point, the router will not do any further switching from Host1 to Host2. The router does not even know that the switch is forwarding the packet on its behalf. As a result, debugging or IP accounting commands on the router will not provide any useful information, because the packet is not traversing through the router. The MLS feature not only helps reduce latency in the network, but it also allows for the RSM to do more important functions such as ensuring that it has proper routes and neighbor relationships with its routing peers.

Figure 6-1 *Initial Flow Between Two Hosts on Different VLANs*

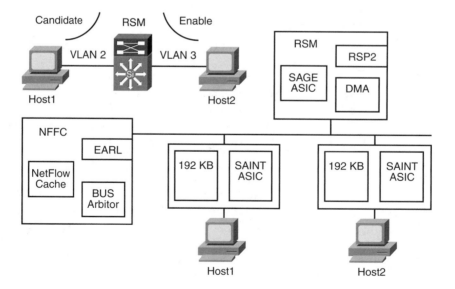

The actual flow of the packet follows. This process is based on a Catalyst 5500 platform. Although the actual implementation might vary slightly depending on the hardware used, the idea is the same:

1   Host1 sends traffic to Host2 that resides on a separate VLAN. The router's MAC address is used at the frame level.

2   The packet arrives at the ingress port. The switch stores the packet in the SAINT ASIC and does a FCS check on the packet. If the FCS check is bad, it will drop the packet. Assuming the packet is good, the SAINT will forward the packet to all other ports.

3   The EARL2, which is on the NFFC card, looks at the 6-byte destination MAC address and informs all other ports via the INDEX bus to keep or flush the packet.

4   At this point, the EARL2 sees the router interface as the destination MAC address because it periodically receives MLSP hellos from the router.

5   The EARL2 checks to see if there is an MLS flow for this traffic. If not, it will forward the packet to the router. The packet becomes a Candidate packet now. A partial MLS entry is created.

6   The SAGE ASIC (higher DMA in place of interface for Ethernet port, but otherwise similar in function to SAINT ASIC) on the RSM is instructed by the EARL2 to accept the packet.

7   The RSM looks at the packet at Layer 3. It checks its routing table to forward the packet out of the correct interface. In Figure 6-1, it is VLAN 3.

8   RSM does a MAC rewrite.

9   RSM forwards the packet out of the VLAN 3 interface.

10   The switch sees the router MAC address again as the source for the partial flow that was created.

11   Having seen the router's MAC address for the flow, the switch will complete the MLS entry. The packet is now an Enable packet.

12   The switch sends Layer 3 flow cache to the rewrite engine. The rewrite engine will be responsible for the header rewrite: Source/Destination MAC, TTL, and CRC.

13   When the packet for this flow arrives at the SAINT, the EARL2 searches the NetFlow cache, and will forward the packet to a Layer 3 logic that is embedded in the EARL2 ASIC. It instructs all other ports including the RSM to flush the packet from their SAINT and SAGE ports, respectively. Some line cards have one rewrite engine per switching bus on the EARL2, while other line cards have the rewrite engine on the card itself.

Figure 6-2 uses an external router trunked to the switch with MLS enabled. This example allows for the Layer 3 shortcut to take place because the switch sees the full flow of the traffic.

Figure 6-2   *MLS on an External Router*

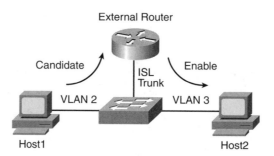

In Figure 6-3, Host2 is two hops away from Host1. The initial packet from Host1 is sent to R1. The XTAG will be that of R1's. The R1 sends the flow back down the ISL trunk to the switch. This causes the first shortcut to be created. The next partial flow is from R1 to R2, where the switch creates an XTAG for R2. When the traffic from R2 is sent back to the switch to Host2, the second full flow is completed. In this setup, the EARL2 will do a look up at the NetFlow cache twice.

Figure 6-3   *Two Layer 3 Shortcuts Created*

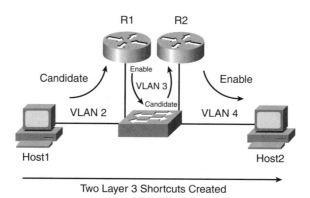

The partial flow is created as the packet from Host1 goes to R1 (see Figure 6-4). Because the switch does not see the packet back from the router, an MLS entry is not created.

Figure 6-4   *Shortcut Is Not Created*

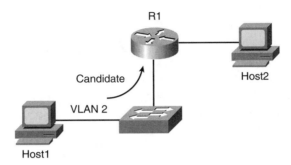

Both switches will create the Layer 3 shortcut in Figure 6-5. The only caveat here is
Switch2's Layer 3 shortcut will time out because all subsequent traffic is handled by
Switch1.

Figure 6-5   *Multiple Switches Involved*

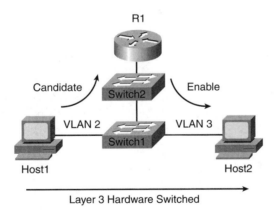

Configuring MLS

This section provides a sample MLS configuration. To check if MLS is enabled, type the
show mls command on the switch, as shown in Example 6-2.

Example 6-2 *MLS Output from the Switch*

```
Switch3 (enable) show mls
Multilayer switching enabled
Multilayer switching aging time = 256 seconds
Multilayer switching fast aging time = 0 seconds, packet threshold = 0
Current flow mask is Destination flow
Configured flow mask is Destination flow
Total packets switched = 0
Active shortcuts = 0
Netflow Data Export disabled
Netflow Data Export port/host is not configured.
Total packets exported = 0
MLS-RP IP        MLS-RP ID      XTAG MLS-RP MAC-Vlans
---------------  -----------    ---- --------------------------------
10.1.2.10        0010f6b34800    2 00-10-f6-b3-48-00  2-3
```

Example 6-2 provides a wealth of information, such as the status of MLS, MLS aging timer, the type of flow configured, and so on. The NetFlow Data Export section of the output is optional. This feature is important for billing purposes. For instance, a department is charged by the volume of the traffic generated on the network. Another important field is the MLS-RP IP section. This IP address belongs to the router, which also has an XTAG value associated with it. This router is responsible for traffic created on VLAN 2 and VLAN 3. For each of these VLANs, the MLS-enabled switch will create a shortcut. Any other VLANs that are not configured for MLS will be fast switched by the router itself.

The commands in Example 6-3 enable MLS on the internal router (refer to Figure 6-1). As noted, MLS-RP IP must be globally turned on. The **mls-rp management** command needs to be enabled on one interface only. All interfaces must have **mls rp ip** and **mls rp vtp-domain** commands configured. The switch component should already have MLS enabled. If not, **set mls enable** will do the trick.

Example 6-3 *Configuring MLS on the RSM*

```
RSM(config)#mls rp ip
RSM(config)#int vlan2
RSM(config-if)#mls rp vtp-domain Cisco
RSM(config-if)#mls rp ip
RSM(config-if)#mls rp management-interface
RSM(config-if)#int vlan 3
RSM(config-if)#mls rp vtp-domain Cisco
RSM(config-if)#mls rp ip
MLS-5-ROUTERADD:Route Processor 10.1.2.10 a Dded
```

The syslog message in Example 6-3 is generated when the switch finds the Route Processor (RP) through MLSP.

In Example 6-4, the MLS entry has been defined per destination, which is the default for the Catalyst switch. As noted in the output, the destination IP addresses are given with their associated VLAN and port numbers.

Example 6-4 *MLS Entry on the Switch*

```
Switch3 (enable) show mls entry
                  Last Used         Last    Used
Destination IP  Source IP         Prot DstPrt SrcPrt Destination Mac    Vlan Port
--------------- ----------------  ---- ------ ------ ----------------- ---- -----
MLS-RP 10.1.2.10:
10.1.2.1        0.0.0.0            0     -      -     00-04-c0-d0-a8-54 2    7/3
10.1.3.5        0.0.0.0            0     -      -     00-02-fc-76-c4-38 3    7/2
```

The MLS entries were created because of Host1-generated pings toward Host2. Keep in mind the MLS is one direction only. When traffic returns, the switch must also create a shortcut for the return traffic. Again, the flow defined in Example 6-4 is based on destination only. If more granular MLS entries are required, full flow can be configured. Quite a bit more information is now available regarding the flow. There is a memory cost associated with enabling MLS full flow. Most networks leave the per-destination flow on.

Example 6-5 illustrates how to enable MLS full flow and then examine the MLS table. Configuring MLS full flow is more resource intensive because more information is gathered about the traffic flow, such as source IP address and port type.

Example 6-5 *Configuring the Switch to Full Flow*

```
Switch3 (enable) set mls flow full
Switch3 (enable) show mls entry
Destination IP  Source IP         Prot DstPrt SrcPrt Destination Mac    Vlan Port
--------------- ----------------  ---- ------ ------ ----------------- ---- -----
MLS-RP 10.1.2.10:
10.1.3.5        10.1.2.1          ICMP -      -     00-02-fc-76-c4-38 3    7/2
10.1.2.1        10.1.3.5          ICMP -      -     00-04-c0-d0-a8-54 2    7/3
```

The default timer for the MLS entry is 256 seconds. This can be changed by manipulating the aging timer. The aging timer is a multiple of 8. In Example 6-6, the aging time was set at 100, which is not a multiple of 8. The switch changed the 100 to 104 to make it a multiple of 8.

Example 6-6 *Configuring Aging Time*

```
Switch3 (enable) set mls agingtime 100
Switch3 (enable) show mls
Multilayer switching enabled
Multilayer switching aging time = 104 seconds
```

MLS also provides some statistics that can be useful when troubleshooting networks. For instance, the statistics parameters provide information on how much a protocol is generating traffic (see Example 6-7).

Example 6-7 *Statistics for Protocols*

```
Switch3 (enable) show mls statistics protocol
Protocol     TotalFlows  TotalPackets  TotalBytes
----------   ----------  ------------  --------------
Telnet       0                      0             0
FTP          0                      0             0
WWW          0                      0             0
SMTP         0                      0             0
X            0                      0             0
DNS          0                      0             0
Others       3                      9          1022
Total        3                      9          1022
```

Some of this data can also be extrapolated from the router using **show mls rp**.

Router Access Lists

The router access list does not affect the MLS flow. After the packets hit the access list, any subsequent packets will be MLS switched. The role of the access list is in the initial flow. If the router access list denies the traffic from Host1 to Host2, the MLS entry will never be created.

If the log parameter is enabled in the access list, all traffic will be process switched. The log parameter can be CPU intensive and dramatically affect the performance of the router. The access list 1 is created to log all IP traffic that traverses through the router. This is only for testing purposes and should not be enabled in the production network. If the log parameter will be used, ensure that it is very specific and granular (see Example 6-8). The matching number of the access list shows the number of packets that has hit this access list. Also note that there is no entry in the MLS table under the **show mls entry** in Example 6-8.

Example 6-8 *Creating the Access List*

```
RSM(config)# access-list 1 permit any log
RSM#show access-lists 1
Standard IP access list 1
    permit any log (2443 matches)
Switch3 (enable) show mls entry
Destination IP  Source IP        Prot DstPrt SrcPrt Destination Mac    Vlan Port
--------------- ---------------- ---- ------ ------ ----------------- ---- -----
MLS-RP 10.1.2.10:
 No entries
```

MLS on Catalyst 6500

Supervisor 1 with MSFC1/2 with PFC 1 can do MLS internally. MLS on the Catalyst 6500 is enabled by default. No configuration changes are necessary on MSFC or the Catalyst switch. The communication between MSFC and PFC is done via Serial Communication Protocol (SCP). PFC handles all the shortcuts created. It can store up to 128 K entries, but typically, the range is in the 30–40 K entries. If many entries are in the MLS table, the timers can be tuned to flush some of the older entries from the table. Naturally, this puts more stress on the switch because it has to repopulate the table periodically. Using the Fast Aging Timer feature, **set mls agingtime fast**, allows for a more manageable MLS table. To disable MLS for a VLAN, use the **no mls ip** on the desired interface. This is generally done for debugging purposes.

The rewrite function is the same as a Catalyst 5000 switch. The PFC changes the MAC destination address to point toward Host2 rather than the MSFC (see Figure 6-6). It also changes the source MAC address from Host1 to the MSFC MAC address. The PFC decrements the TTL and does a Layer 3 checksum on the packet. Layer 3 information remains the same. The result is the packet is now Layer 3 switched by the PFC.

Figure 6-6   *Catalyst 6500 with MSFC*

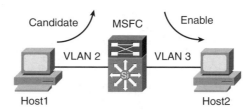

In this environment, the MSFC is performing the MLS-RP for the Catalyst 5500 that is connected to the Catalyst 6500 switch. The Catalyst 5500 will be able to create the Layer 3 shortcut between Host1 and Host2 (see Figure 6-7).

Figure 6-7   *Catalyst 6500 with MSFC as the RP for Catalyst 5500*

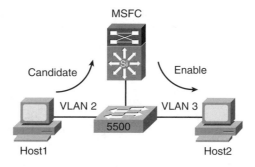

The PFC off the Catalyst 6500 will not perform MLS-SE in a Catalyst 5500, as shown in Figure 6-8. The Layer 3 shortcut does not occur in the Catalyst 6500. It does, however, occur on the Catalyst 5500 that houses the RSM.

Figure 6-8   *PFC Does Not Act as MLS-SE for Catalyst 5500 Switches*

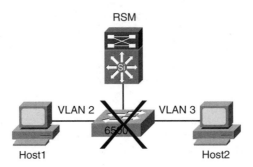

The following process is illustrated using a Supervisor 1A with PFC1 as the packet enters a Catalyst 6500 ingress port, shown in Figure 6-9:

1   Host1 sends traffic to Host2 that resides on a separate VLAN.

2   The packet arrives at the ingress port. The switch stores the packet in the Pinnacle ASIC and does a FCS check on the packet. If the FCS check is bad, it will drop the packet. Assuming the packet is good, the Pinnacle requests access to the data bus (dBUS) from the Local Arbitrator. The port adds 256-bit dBus header. The header contains sequence number, source port, index, VLAN, and so on.

3   The Central Arbitrator provides Local Arbitrator on the module access to the dBus in a round-robin fashion.

4   The packet is forwarded to all other ports. PFC1 has four main engines:

— Layer 2 Forwarding engine

— Layer 3 Forwarding engine

— Access List engine

— Multicast Replication engine

These engines also have an interface to the dBus and will receive the traffic that was generated by the ingress port. The packet lookups by these engines happen simultaneously.

5   The Layer 2 engine does a lookup in the Layer 2 forwarding table for the 6-byte destination MAC address. If the destination is the router MAC, the Layer 2 engine will signal the Layer 3 engine to take over. This is the first Layer 2 lookup. The Layer 2 engine may require a second lookup depending on what happens on the other engines.

6 While Layer 2 is examining the packet, Layer 3 also does a lookup on the packet to see if it has a NetFlow table for the destination.

7 The ACL engine checks to see if there is an inbound/outbound access list defined for the port. It will forward this information to the Layer 3 engine.

8 The Layer 3 engine with its interaction with the Layer 2 engine will have the rewrite information for the flow. If there is no entry in the NetFlow table, the Layer 2 engine will create a Candidate entry and send the traffic toward the MSFC.

9 The rewrite information will be sent via the results bus (rBus) to the destination port for rewrite by the router.

10 The Layer 3 engine forwards Layer 3 rewrite information along with the ACL information to the Layer 2 engine for future use.

11 Layer 2 does a second lookup for the final destination, Host2. The Layer 2 engine must know the MAC address of Host2, or otherwise, the Enable entry will not take place.

12 Any subsequent packets will be hardware switched.

Again, no configuration changes are needed to enable MLS on a Catalyst 6500 switch with Supervisor 1A. To check the status of MLS on the MSFC, use the **show mls status** command. The **show mls rp** command is only relevant to MSFC acting as an RP for an external Catalyst 5000 family.

Example 6-9 shows an MLS table for the Catalyst 6500 switch.

Example 6-9 *MLS Table*

```
Switch2 (enable) show mls entry
Destination-IP  Source-IP       Prot  DstPrt SrcPrt Destination-Mac    Vlan EDst
ESrc DPort      SPort      Stat-Pkts  Stat-Bytes Uptime   Age
--------------- --------------- ----- ------ ------ ----------------- ---- ----
---- --------- --------- ---------- ----------- -------- --------
MSFC 10.1.30.20 (Module 15):
10.1.3.3        10.1.34.4       ICMP  0      0      00-05-74-18-04-bc 30   ARPA
ARPA 1/1        3/2       4          400        00:00:35 00:00:35
10.1.34.4       10.1.3.3        ICMP  0      0      00-04-c1-5f-78-81 34   ARPA
ARPA 3/2        1/1       4          400        00:00:35 00:00:35
```

In Example 6-10, the **rlog** command provides information about whether the PFC is getting traffic from MSFC or not. This can be useful in troubleshooting MLS issues. The output in Example 6-10 shows the MSFC and PFC are communicating because the router port is added to the MLS table with its associated XTAG value.

Figure 6-9 *Catalyst 6500 with MSFC*

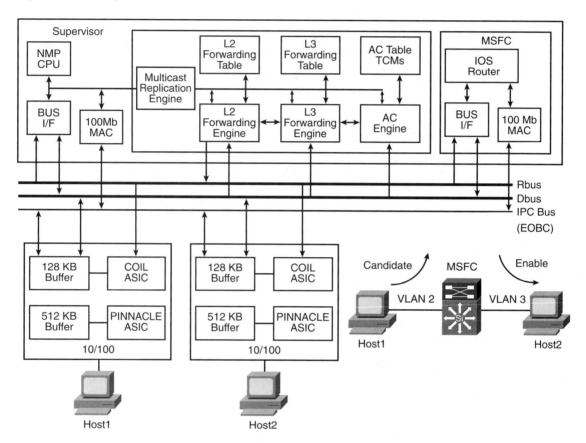

Example 6-10 rlog *Output*

```
Switch2 (enable) show mls rlog l2
SWLOG at 81f53810: magic 1008, size 51200, cur 81f55c14, end 81f60020
Current time is: 09/23/03,16:21:42
538 09/22/03,17:51:16:(RouterConfig)Router_Cfg(2793): ClearL3Entries xtag 1, vla
n 25
537 09/22/03,17:51:16:(RouterConfig)Router_cfg: router_add_mac_to_earl 00-30-b6-
3e-53-c4  added for mod 15/1 Vlan 25 Earl AL =0
536 09/22/03,17:51:16:(RouterConfig)Router_Cfg: Process add mls entry for mod 15
/1 vlan 25 i/f 1, proto 0, LC 0
535 09/22/03,17:51:16:(RouterConfig)Router_Cfg(2793): ClearL3Entries xtag 1, vla
n 25
```

Understanding the Need for Cisco Express Forwarding

To appreciate the advantages offered by Cisco Express Forwarding (CEF), it is important to understand some of the shortfalls of flow-based switching mechanisms, such as MLS, described in the previous sections. MLS works well for the most part. After the first packet, all other packets are hardware switched. The switching of the packet at hardware provides higher performance many times over than software-based switching done by a router. The problem with MLS implementation is that the first packet always hits the router. Any network changes caused by neighbor resets, route flaps, and aging timers can cause the MLS table for those specific entries to get flushed. This puts unnecessary burden on the router to perform the initial packet switching again. If the numbers of these network changes are high enough in a short period of time, there would be a massive performance hit on the network. The router will be churning to repopulate the MLS table. The aging timers can also affect the performance of MLS. If there are too many flows to different destinations, many MLS entries are created. A problem occurs when these flows are short lived, therefore causing some flows to be in the MLS table for a longer period than they need to. At the same time, new flows are constantly being created, causing a bigger MLS table.

Another issue with MLS-based switching is limited storage space. Depending on what type of flow mask is used, the MLS entries might get filled up. A ceiling issue exists with enabling MLS. Also, the algorithms used for lookups are not as efficient, which is why CEF was introduced.

CEF-based switching does not rely on the router to handle the first packet. In the Catalyst 6500 with a Supervisor II/MSFC2, for the most part, the MSFC2 (router component) does not software switch any data packets (with the exception of subnet broadcasts, NAT'd packets, unsupported route-map statements, and a few other cases). All data packets are handled by the PFC2 hardware. The only packets that hit the MSFC are those that are destined to the router, such as routing updates, SNMP queries, and any other control traffic.

The two major components of CEF are Forwarding Information Base (FIB) and the adjacency table. These two tables make CEF scalable and robust. The FIB table is an exact replica of the routing table. Any additions or deletions in the routing table are also changed on the FIB table. The FIB table consists of four levels of hierarchy to correspond with the 4 bytes of an IPv4 address. CEF searches for the longest match in the hierarchical structure to switch the packet. The Catalyst 6500 with Supervisor II can store up to 256 K FIB entries, plus 16 K multicast entries. The adjacency table maps Layer 2 MAC addresses to the associated Layer 3 IP addresses. The combination of the two allows for packets to be switched at a high rate.

The MSFC2 in Supervisor II obtains routing information from its routing protocol peers, and it creates the appropriate adjacencies for the corresponding IP address. After having built these two tables, it pushes them down to the PFC2 card. The PFC2 card now handles all data switching for the MSFC2. The MSFC2 job at this point is minimal. It primarily handles control traffic that is essential for network connectivity. The Supervisor II/PFC2/ MSFC2 only operates in CEF mode.

The following process outlines a packet as it traverses a Supervisor II using CEF (see Figure 6-10):

1 Host1 sends traffic to Host2 that resides on a separate VLAN.

2 The Layer 2 and Layer 3 forwarding engines receive packet header from the dBus.

3 The Layer 2 engine does a lookup for the 6-byte destination MAC address, checks for input quality of service (QoS)/ACL/Security ACL. The Layer 3 engine simultaneously does a FIB and NetFlow table lookup. Some of the tasks are undone simultaneously by the engines to reduce packet latency on the switch.

4 The results from QoS/ACL/Security ACL are forwarded to Layer 3 by the Layer 2 engine. In parallel, the Layer 3 engine sends to Layer 2 the destination VLAN for the packet.

5 Layer 3 performs adjacency lookup. Layer 2 does any outbound QoS/ACL/Security ACL.

6 Layer 2 QoS/ACL/Security ACL information is sent to the Layer 3 engine. The Layer 3 engine will implement specific policy such as filter, QoS, and so on for the packet.

7 Layer 3 computes the rewrite result and forwards to Layer 2. Layer 3 updates adjacency and NetFlow table statistics. These steps occur in parallel.

8 The Layer 2 engine does a lookup on the destination MAC address that it receives from Layer 3. Layer 2 chooses between its result and the one it received from Layer 3 and forwards on the rBUS.

There are a handful of commands available both on the MSFC2 and Supervisor II to view CEF-related information. For example, the adjacency command provides information about the IP address and the corresponding MAC address. Most of the output in Example 6-11 is obvious with the exception of adjacency type.

Example 6-11 *CEF Adjacency*

```
Switch1 (enable) show mls enable cef adjacency
Mod:              16
Destination-IP:   10.1.3.40          Destination-Mask:  255.255.255.255
FIB-Type:         resolved
AdjType  NextHop-IP      NextHop-Mac      Vlan Encp Tx-Packets   Tx-Octets
-------  --------------- ---------------- ---- ---- ------------ ------------
connect  10.1.3.40       00-10-f6-b3-48-00  3 ARPA           5          500
```

Figure 6-10 *Catalyst 6500 with Supervisor II*

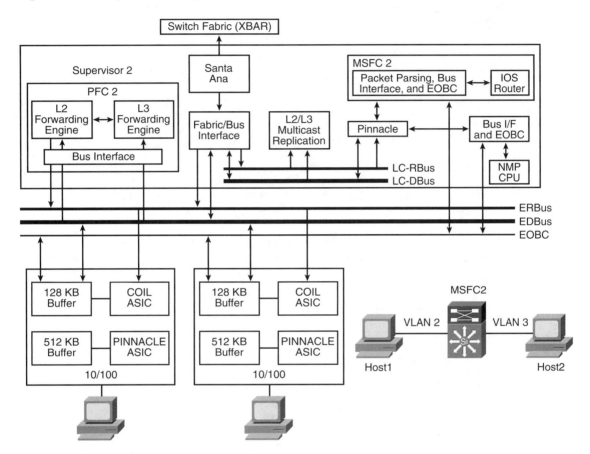

There are five different types of adjacency states, as shown in Table 6-1.

Table 6-1   *Five Types of Adjacency States*

Adjacency Type	Description
Connect	Complete rewrite information. Most entries will be connected.
Punt	Traffic is software switched by the MSFC2.
No R/W	Rewrite information is incomplete and must be handled by MSFC2.
FRC DRP	Entry used to drop packets because of ARP throttling.
Drop, Null, Loopbk	Entries used to drop packets.

NOTE	Do not get confused with the word MLS on the Catalyst 6500 with Supervisor II/MSFC2. The switching is CEF not MLS.

The FIB table is listed in Example 6-12 with relevant next hops.

Example 6-12 *MLS Table*

```
Switch1 (enable) show mls entry
Mod FIB-Type  Destination-IP  Destination-Mask  NextHop-IP        Weight
--- --------  --------------  ----------------  --------------    ------
16 resolved  10.1.3.40        255.255.255.255   10.1.3.40            1
16 resolved  10.1.3.2         255.255.255.255   10.1.3.2             1
 16 resolved  10.1.3.3          255.255.255.255   10.1.3.3            1
```

The volume of traffic through the switch can be ascertained through the **show mls cef** command. As noted in Example 6-13, IPX and IP multicast are also hardware switched.

Example 6-13 *MLS Statistics*

```
Switch1 (enable) show mls cef
Total L3 packets switched:              123504682
Total L3 octets switched:             183111880220
Total route entries:                        38
IP route entries:                       37
IPX route entries:                       1
IPM route entries:                       0
IP load sharing entries:                     0
IPX load sharing entries:                    0
Forwarding entries:                         11
Bridge entries:                             24
Drop entries:                                3
```

The output in Example 6-14 was gathered from the MSFC2. The MAC address, 0004C0D0AC38, is the actual Layer 2 address of the host machine. The router MAC address along with 0800 makes the number 0005741804BC0800 as listed in the output. All this information is needed for the rewrite information. The Cisco IOS CEF commands have information on CEF summary information, next hop addresses, and so on.

Example 6-14 *Adjacency Information Off the Router*

```
msfc_15#show adjacency detail
Protocol Interface              Address
IP       Vlan3                  10.1.3.2(7)
0 packets, 0 bytes
0004C0D0AC38
0005741804BC0800
                                ARP        02:57:46
```

CEF addresses numerous issues that MLS could not. First and foremost, it is more scalable than MLS. Enterprise networks have grown in size and the types of services it has made available to its users in the past three years. The creation and deletion of a high number of flows affected the performance of the switch, and subsequently created greater latency on the network. Therefore, CEF had to address scalability issues. The second major problem was the flow-based switching algorithm's inefficient cache table lookup. CEF, as mentioned earlier, offers a better mechanism to do lookups and allows for latency to be low. The obvious advantage was that most traffic never hit the router; the packets were hardware switched. CEF, as a result, addressed issues with scalability, latency, and overall robustness.

Summary

MLS has proven to be very useful over the years. It minimized the latency problem that was associated with the router by essentially taking over the switching function from the router. MLS was ideal in the enterprise network, where traffic is deterministic and less volatility is involved as compared to the Internet arena. Despite CEF taking over the reigns, MLS continues to play an important role. This chapter attempted to address the details of MLS on issues regarding designs, and the life of a packet as it traversed through various Catalyst platforms.

CEF switching is becoming more popular for both router as well as switching platforms. It has been widely deployed in the enterprise environment the past few years. The newer Cisco Catalyst 6500 switches only do CEF switching. Details on CEF components and implementation were cited in this chapter. CEF provides greater stability and scalability than MLS.

This chapter covers the following topics:

- An ounce of planning
- Configuration overview
- Initial configuration
- Connecting the switches
- Configuring the access layer
- Configuring SNMP

CHAPTER 7

Configuring Switches

Now that you have learned about the concepts behind Layer 2 and Layer 3 switching in some detail, you will focus on a start-to-finish configuration of a relatively simple campus switching design in this chapter.

An Ounce of Planning

Everyone has probably heard the old joke "ready, fire, aim." Unfortunately, this phrase can sometimes describe the implementation of some networks given what appears to be a lack of basic planning prior to configuration. The daily operation of a switched environment can be greatly simplified and future problems avoided by applying a few best practices and a little bit of planning. This begins with planning the method for remotely accessing the switch, followed by basic configuration of the switch, and then configuring connections between switches.

Management Interfaces

Believe it or not, one of the first things to think about when configuring a new network is management, primarily because network management typically is the last thing to be thought of when the network is implemented, and seemingly one of the most tedious things to change or improve after the network is operational. One item to consider is how to handle remote access to the switch. Catalyst switches support both in-band and out-of-band management. In-band management interfaces are connected to the switching fabric and participate in all the functions of a switchport including spanning tree, Cisco Discovery Protocol (CDP), and VLAN assignment. Out-of-band management interfaces are not connected to the switching fabric and do not participate in any of these functions.

Out-of-band management is achieved initially through the serial console port on the Supervisor module. Each Catalyst switch ships with the appropriate console cable and connectors to connect to a host such as a Windows workstation or terminal server. Consult the Catalyst documentation at Cisco.com to determine the kind of connectors and cables appropriate for each platform. After a physical connection is made between the console port on a Catalyst switch and a serial port on a workstation or terminal server, the administrator has full access to the switch for configuration. At this point, the administrator can assign an IP address to either an out-of-band management (sl0) interface via the Serial Line Internet Protocol (SLIP), a predecessor to the Point-to-Point Protocol (PPP), or assign an IP address to an in-band management interface (sc0 or sc1). Supervisors for the Catalyst 4500 series switches offer an additional out-of-band management interface via a 10 Mbps or 10/100 Mbps Ethernet interface (me1) depending on the Supervisor model.

The choice between out-of-band and in-band management is often not an easy one because each has its pros and cons. An in-band management connection is the easiest to configure and the most cost effective because management traffic rides the same infrastructure as user data. Downsides to in-band management include a potential for switches to be isolated and unmanageable if connectivity to the site or individual device is lost, for example in a spanning-tree loop or if fiber connections are cut accidentally. In addition, if the management interface is assigned to a VLAN that has other ports as members, any broadcast or multicast traffic on that VLAN is seen by the management interface and must be processed by the supervisor.

As the speed of processors has improved with newer supervisors, the risk of overwhelming a supervisor with broadcast/multicast traffic has declined somewhat, but has not been eliminated completely. With these drawbacks to in-band management, why doesn't everyone just use out-of band management? The answer is simple: time and money. Out-of-band management requires a secondary infrastructure to be built out around the devices such as terminal servers, switches, and modems. The benefit of an out-of-band management solution is that it offers a completely separate method of connecting to the devices for management that does not rely upon a properly functioning data infrastructure to work.

Many administrators find themselves implementing both in-band and out-of-band management solutions depending on the reliability of the data infrastructure between the networks that contain the management stations and the devices being managed. For example, Catalyst switches in a typical headquarters location are likely to be on reliable power grids, potentially with backup power, and have redundant connections between devices. A Catalyst switch in a remote office connected to headquarters via a router and a single nonredundant Frame Relay connection might justify out-of-band management. The remote router and switch could be connected to a terminal server and an analog dial-up connection for configuration and remote management. In an ideal world, networking devices would all be accessible via an out-of-band connection, if possible. Sometimes it takes only a wake-up call at 3:00 a.m. or an unplanned road trip to a remote location to compel an organization to install an out-of-band management solution.

sc0 and VLAN 1

All switchports must be members of a VLAN, and, by default, it is VLAN 1. Because VLAN 1 was selected as the default VLAN for all switchports, it was also chosen to handle special traffic such as VLAN Trunking Protocol (VTP) advertisements, CDP, Port Aggregation Protocol (PAgP), or Link Aggregation Control Protocol messages (LACP). By default, in-band management interfaces such as sc0 are members of VLAN 1.

Over the years, a common scenario involving VLAN 1 and the management interface developed. In this scenario, administrators assigned an IP address to sc0, left it in VLAN 1, and created other VLANs for all user traffic. All ports not changed or enabled remain in VLAN 1. Trunked ports between switches are created to connect VLANs, and, by default, all VLANs (1-1005 or 1-4096 depending on trunk type and switch software version) are allowed across a trunk. Because each switch will have a management interface, likely sc0, this can result in VLAN 1 spanning the entire switched network. Remember that IEEE spanning tree only allows seven switch hops between end stations, and many times large networks that allow all VLANs to be trunked can approach or exceed the limit, especially for VLAN 1. When a spanning tree exceeds seven switch hops, the spanning-tree topology can become unpredictable during a topology change and reconvergence can be slow if the spanning tree reconverges at all. A few different options should be considered to alleviate this problem. The first option is to use a different VLAN other than VLAN 1 for the management interfaces in the network. As of Catalyst OS version 5.4(1) and later, VLAN 1 can be cleared from both Inter-Switch Link (ISL) Protocol and 802.1q trunks, thus removing VLAN 1 from the spanning-tree topology on those trunks. Simply substituting a different VLAN number does not alleviate the problem of new VLAN spanning the switched network and potentially exceeding the allowed number of hops. To avoid the problem, either multiple VLANs must be dedicated to network management or the management interfaces must be placed in multiple VLANs along with user traffic. Either way, the management interfaces must be reachable by the network management stations. In the configuration examples later in this chapter, the sc0 interface is placed in a user VLAN along with other ports.

Figure 7-1 shows a simple network diagram of a small remote office with multiple switches. In this figure, VLAN 501 is used as the management VLAN at the remote office.

In a configuration like this, the VLAN numbers in the remote office are only locally significant. This is true because a Layer 3 routed connection separates the remote office from the headquarters location, and VLAN 501 is not carried across the WAN. As a result, the remote office could use any VLAN number for management including VLAN 1.

The example could get trickier if the routers and WAN connections are replaced by switches and a high-speed Gigabit connection between buildings in a campus environment. In this situation, as long as the links between buildings can still be Layer 3 connections and VLAN 501 is cleared from the trunks, it can yield the same result, as in Figure 7-1. Unfortunately, many times with existing implementations, because of legacy Layer 2-only implementations or application design considerations, the links between locations are Layer 2 trunks carrying all VLANs. As a result, VLAN 501 gets carried to the home office switches, and potential spanning-tree problems can result.

Figure 7-1 *Remote Office Using VLAN 501 for Management*

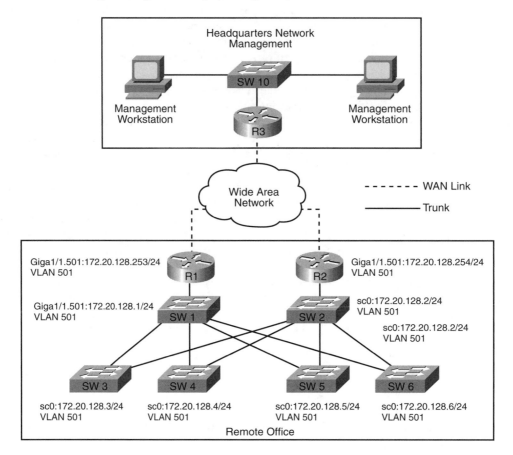

It is important to remember that even when VLAN 1 is cleared from a trunk, the previously mentioned special traffic, such as CDP, PAgP, and VTP, is still forwarded across the trunk with a VLAN 1 tag, but no user data is sent using VLAN 1. All trunks default to a native VLAN of 1 unless changed. In the case of an 802.1q trunk, where the native VLAN is untagged, 802.1q IEEE Bridge Protocol Data Units (BPDUs) are forwarded untagged on the common spanning-tree VLAN 1 for interoperability with other vendors, unless VLAN 1 has been cleared from the trunk. Cisco Per-VLAN Spanning Tree (PVST+) BPDUs are sent and tagged for all other VLANs. Refer to the sections on ISL and 802.1q trunking in Chapter 4, "Layer 2 Fundamentals," of this book for more information on trunking and native VLAN operation.

It is a good idea, if possible, to adopt some standards for VLAN numbering. Using consistent VLAN numbers for similar functions at multiple locations can many times help in the operation and troubleshooting of the networks later on. For example, many companies reserve certain VLAN ranges for specific functions. Table 7-1 is a sample of what a company might start with when implementing VLANs on existing and new networks.

Table 7-1   *Sample Plan for VLAN Numbering*

VLAN Numbers	Function
1	Not in use; clear from all trunks
2–99	Management VLANs (sc0)
100–399	Access layer devices
400–599	Data center devices
600–699	Internet and partner connections
700–899	Reserved for future use
900–999	Point-to-point links between switches (Layer 3)

Although this sample uses VLAN numbers in the 1–1005 range, newer versions of Cisco Catalyst OS and IOS support 4096 VLANs using 802.1q trunks. Again, because VLAN numbers are only locally significant when they are carried on trunks between switches, the sample numbering scheme provides great flexibility, and some companies may adopt a much more granular VLAN numbering system. For example, they may dictate that VLAN 50 be used as the management VLAN on all switches at all locations instead of allowing any VLAN in the range from 2–99 to be used. No hard and fast rules exist for VLAN numbering plans, and Table 7-1 represents one approach.

Configuration Overview

Figure 7-2 shows a diagram of four switches that are yet to have any connections configured. These four switches comprise the primary components of the network that will be configured and added onto throughout the remainder of this chapter.

Figure 7-2   *Four Primary Switches*

A mix of platforms, software levels, and interfaces was chosen to provide a variety of configuration examples. Table 7-2 lists the switches in use.

Table 7-2 *Switch Information*

Switch Name	Platform	Software Type	Software Version(s)
SW1	6513	Native	12.1(8b)E16
SW2	6506	Native	12.1(8b)E16
SW3	5500	Hybrid	4.5(5) Catalyst OS
			12.2(10a) IOS
SW4	4506	Native	12.1(19)E

The software versions installed on these switches are not recommendations for these platforms, only versions that support the modules and features required for these exercises. Administrators should utilize the tools on the Cisco Software Center at Cisco.com, such as the IOS Upgrade Planner, Software Advisor, and Cisco Bug Navigator, to help select a satisfactory software level. After a software level has been selected, administrators should reference the release notes for a list of Open and Resolved Caveats in that version.

Initial Configuration

Configuration begins with naming each switch and assigning an IP address to a management interface on each switch shown in Figure 7-2. Refer to Chapter 5, "Using Catalyst Software," for examples of setting system and host names, along with setting an enable password. Private IP addresses described in Request for Comments (RFC) 1918 will be used in all the examples in this chapter.

NOTE RFC 1918 along with others can be viewed online at http://www.ietf.org/rfc. RFC 1918 defines private address ranges as

- 10.0.0.0–10.255.255.255 (10/8 prefix)

- 172.16.0.0–172.31.255.255 (172.16/12 prefix)

- 192.168.0.0–192.168.255.255 (192.168/16 prefix)

In this chapter, addresses from the 172.16.0.0–172.31.255.255 range are used.

Before implementing any IP equipment, take the time to develop an IP addressing standard. Going back and readdressing devices in production can be quite time consuming. Although development of an IP addressing standard is beyond the scope of this book, a few important items should be considered when developing a standard, including

- Planning the IP address space so it can be summarized, resulting in as few routes as possible being required to reach any network.

- Determining whether private, public, or a mix of private and public addressing will be used and how.

- Planning the IP address space to scale to the necessary number of devices. For example, assigning a network of 172.16.200.0/24 to a user VLAN on a switch provides 254 host addresses for user devices, but if 300 devices need to be supported, you must decide either to assign a second class C or /24 VLAN for the additional 46 devices or assign a larger network of 172.16.200/22.

In preparation for the configuration examples throughout the rest of this chapter, Table 7-3 provides a simple IP addressing scheme.

Table 7-3   *IP Address Ranges*

Function	IP Address Range
User VLANs	172.16.192–223.0 255.255.255.0
Loopback interfaces	172.16.224–239.0 255.255.255.255
Point-to-point links	172.16.240.4–252 255.255.255.252

Using the preceding ranges, IP addresses are plentiful because private addressing space is being used, but it is always a good practice to conserve addressing space whenever possible. The address ranges in Table 7-3 can all be summarized into a single 172.16.192.0/18 route advertisement.

Configuring VTP

Chapter 4 discussed the various modes and capabilities of VTP in detail. In this chapter, VTP transparent mode is used on all the example switches. A VTP domain name of Cisco is used. A VTP password is unnecessary in transparent mode but should be carefully chosen in client/server mode. Prior to Cisco IOS version 12.1(11b)E, VTP and VLANs could only be configured in VLAN database mode on IOS devices. In IOS version 12.1(11b)E and later, VTP and VLANs can be configured either in database mode or in global configuration mode. In either case, the VTP and VLAN configuration information is stored in a vlan.dat file and is not part of the running configuration. To properly back up a native IOS configuration, both the running-configuration and the vlan.dat file must be saved. CiscoWorks Resource Manager Essentials, starting with version 3.5, automatically saves the vlan.dat file. Using Examples 7-1 through 7-4, VTP is configured on each switch along with a VLAN that will be used for user devices later in the chapter.

Example 7-1 *Configuring VTP Using VLAN Database Mode on SW1*

```
SW1#vlan database
SW1(vlan)#vtp transparent
Setting device to VTP TRANSPARENT mode.
SW1(vlan)#vtp domain Cisco
Changing VTP domain name from NULL to Cisco
SW1(vlan)#vlan 110
VLAN 110 added:
    Name: VLAN0110
SW1(vlan)#exit
APPLY completed.
Exiting....
SW1#
```

Example 7-2 *Configuring VTP Using VLAN Database Mode on SW2*

```
SW2#vlan database
SW2(vlan)#vtp transparent
Setting device to VTP TRANSPARENT mode.
SW2(vlan)#vtp domain Cisco
Changing VTP domain name from NULL to Cisco
SW2(vlan)#vlan 120
VLAN 120 added:
    Name: VLAN0120
SW2(vlan)#exit
APPLY completed.
Exiting....
```

Example 7-3 *Configuring VTP on SW3 in Catalyst OS*

```
SW3 (enable) set vtp mode transparent
VTP domain  modified
SW3 (enable) set vtp domain Cisco
VTP domain Cisco modified
SW3 (enable) set vlan 130
Vlan 130 configuration successful
SW3 (enable)
```

Example 7-4 *Configuring VTP on SW4 in Global Configuration Mode*

```
SW4#config t
Enter configuration commands, one per line.  End with CNTL/Z.
SW4(config)#vtp mode transparent
Setting device to VTP TRANSPARENT mode.
SW4(config)#vtp domain Cisco
```

Example 7-4 *Configuring VTP on SW4 in Global Configuration Mode (Continued)*

```
Changing VTP domain name from NULL to Cisco
SW4(config)#vlan 140
SW4(config-vlan)#end
SW4#
```

When created, you can delete VLANs one at a time using either a **clear** command in
Catalyst OS or the **no** form of the VLAN command in IOS. To delete all VTP and VLAN
information in Catalyst OS, you can use the **clear config all** command. Although there is
no vlan.dat file in Catalyst OS, the vlan.dat file is stored in NVRAM on Catalyst 6000/
6500s in const_nvram: and 4000/4500s running native in cat4000_flash:. To delete all VTP
and VLAN information in native IOS on the Catalyst 6000/6500, use the **erase const_
nvram:** command. On the Catalyst 4000/4500 running native IOS, use the **erase cat4000_
flash:**. As shown in Example 7-5, vlan.dat files can be copied to flash or to a TFTP server
using the copy command.

Example 7-5 *Copying vlan.dat to Flash in Slot0:*

```
SW1#copy const_nvram:
SW1#copy const_nvram:vlan.dat slot0:
Destination filename [vlan.dat]?
660 bytes copied in 0.328 secs
```

Configuring sc0 and LO0

Because SW3 is running hybrid, it will be configured with both a sc0 management interface
in Catalyst OS and a Loopback 0 (LO0) interface in IOS on the Route Switch Module
(RSM). Figure 7-3 shows the management interfaces assigned to each of the four switches.

Figure 7-3 *IP Addresses Assigned to Management Interfaces*

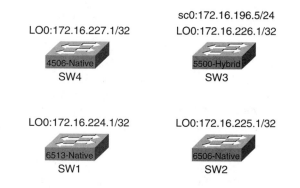

To prevent the use of a separate VLAN for switch management, the choice is made to place the sc0 interface in the user VLAN 130. Switches 1, 2, and 4 running native IOS are configured with only a Loopback interface (LO0), just like any other Cisco router. The primary benefit of a loopback interface is that it never goes down unless manually shut down. Example 7-6 shows the configuration of LO0 on SW1.

Example 7-6   *Configuring LO0 on SW1 (Native)*

```
SW1#config t
1w5d: %SYS-5-CONFIG_I: Configured from console by console
Enter configuration commands, one per line.  End with CNTL/Z.
SW1(config)#interface loopback0
SW1(config-if)#ip address 172.16.224.1 255.255.255.255
SW1(config-if)#end
1w5d: %SYS-5-CONFIG_I: Configured from console by console
SW1#show interface loopback0
Loopback0 is up, line protocol is up
  Hardware is Loopback
  Internet address is 172.16.224.1/32
  MTU 1514 bytes, BW 8000000 Kbit, DLY 5000 usec,
     reliability 255/255, txload 1/255, rxload 1/255
  Encapsulation LOOPBACK, loopback not set
  Last input never, output never, output hang never
  Last clearing of "show interface" counters never
  Input queue: 0/75/0/0 (size/max/drops/flushes); Total output drops: 0
  Queueing strategy: fifo
  Output queue :0/0 (size/max)
  5 minute input rate 0 bits/sec, 0 packets/sec
  5 minute output rate 0 bits/sec, 0 packets/sec
  L2 Switched: ucast: 0 pkt, 0 bytes - mcast: 0 pkt, 0 bytes
  L3 in Switched: ucast: 0 pkt, 0 bytes - mcast: 0 pkt, 0 bytes mcast
  L3 out Switched: ucast: 0 pkt, 0 bytes
     0 packets input, 0 bytes, 0 no buffer
     Received 0 broadcasts, 0 runts, 0 giants, 0 throttles
     0 input errors, 0 CRC, 0 frame, 0 overrun, 0 ignored, 0 abort
     0 packets output, 0 bytes, 0 underruns
     0 output errors, 0 collisions, 0 interface resets
     0 output buffer failures, 0 output buffers swapped out
SW1#
```

In Example 7-6, an IP address of 172.16.224.1 is assigned using a 32-bit subnet mask. The output of the **show interface loopback0** command shows the interface in the UP/UP state. Because this is a loopback, the interface will show up even though no connectivity to the switch exists, and the loopback interface is, at the moment, unreachable. Example 7-7 shows the configuration of LO0 on SW2.

In Example 7-8, sc0 is assigned an IP address of 172.16.196.5/24 in VLAN 130. The default route added for sc0 will eventually point to the IP address of the VLAN 130 interface on the RSM.

Example 7-7 *Configuring LO0 on SW2 (Native)*

```
SW2#config t
Enter configuration commands, one per line.  End with CNTL/Z.
SW2(config)#interface loopback0
SW2(config-if)#ip address 172.16.225.1 255.255.255.255
SW2(config-if)#end
```

Example 7-8 *Configuring sc0 on SW3 (Hybrid-Catalyst OS)*

```
SW3> (enable) set int sc0 130 172.16.196.5 255.255.255.0
Interface sc0 vlan set, IP address and netmask set.
SW3> (enable) set ip route default 172.16.196.1
Route added.
```

Example 7-9 shows the configuration of LO0 on SW3.

Example 7-9 *Configuring LO0 on SW3 (Hybrid-IOS)*

```
SW3 (enable) show module
Mod Module-Name      Ports Module-Type          Model      Serial-Num Status
--- ----------------- ----- -------------------- ---------- ---------- -------
1                     0     Supervisor III       WS-X5530   030061500  faulty
3                     1     Route Switch         WS-X5304   006578507  ok
4                     24    10/100BaseTX Ethernet WS-X5224  009607843  ok
6                     12    100BaseTX Ethernet   WS-X5113   002503515  ok
7                     24    10/100BaseTX Ethernet WS-X5234  019554483  ok
8                     24    10/100BaseTX Ethernet WS-X5225R 013458239  ok
13                          ASP/SRP

Mod MAC-Address(es)                            Hw     Fw         Sw
--- ------------------------------------------ ------ ---------- -----------------
1   00-90-86-66-50-00 to 00-90-86-66-53-ff 3.5   5.1(2)     4.5(5)
3   00-e0-1e-91-b9-7c to 00-e0-1e-91-b9-7d 7.7   20.22      12.2(10a)
4   00-10-7b-78-57-00 to 00-10-7b-78-57-17 1.4   3.1(1)     4.5(5)
6   00-40-0b-b0-95-40 to 00-40-0b-b0-95-4b 1.2   1.2        4.5(5)
7   00-30-7b-b7-77-00 to 00-30-7b-b7-77-17 1.0   4.5(2)     4.5(5)
8   00-d0-06-9b-83-10 to 00-d0-06-9b-83-27 3.3   4.3(1)     4.5(5)

Mod Sub-Type Sub-Model Sub-Serial Sub-Hw
--- -------- --------- ---------- ------
1   NFFC II  WS-F5531A 0030060943 2.2
SW3 (enable) session 3
Trying Router-3...
Connected to Router-3.
Escape character is '^]'.

RSM1>en
RSM1#config t
```

continues

Example 7-9 *Configuring LO0 on SW3 (Hybrid-IOS) (Continued)*

```
Enter configuration commands, one per line.  End with CNTL/Z.
RSM1(config)#int loopback0
RSM1(config-if)#ip address 172.16.226.1 255.255.255.255
RSM1(config-if)#end
RSM1#sh interface loopback0
Loopback0 is up, line protocol is up
  Hardware is Loopback
  Internet address is 172.16.226.1/32
  MTU 1514 bytes, BW 8000000 Kbit, DLY 5000 usec,
     reliability 255/255, txload 1/255, rxload 1/255
  Encapsulation LOOPBACK, loopback not set
  Last input never, output never, output hang never
  Last clearing of "show interface" counters never
  Input queue: 0/75/0/0 (size/max/drops/flushes); Total output drops: 0
  Queueing strategy: fifo
  Output queue :0/0 (size/max)
  5 minute input rate 0 bits/sec, 0 packets/sec
  5 minute output rate 0 bits/sec, 0 packets/sec
     0 packets input, 0 bytes, 0 no buffer
     Received 0 broadcasts, 0 runts, 0 giants, 0 throttles
     0 input errors, 0 CRC, 0 frame, 0 overrun, 0 ignored, 0 abort
     0 packets output, 0 bytes, 0 underruns
     0 output errors, 0 collisions, 0 interface resets
     0 output buffer failures, 0 output buffers swapped out
RSM1#
```

In Examples 7-8 and 7-9, the switch is running hybrid Catalyst OS/IOS and the connection is to the console port on the supervisor. The first step is to determine in which slot the RSM is installed, and then session to the RSM. In this case, the RSM is installed in slot 3. After a session to the module in slot 3 is established, the loopback interface is configured the same way as in native. (See Example 7-10.)

Example 7-10 *Configuring LO0 on SW4 (Native)*

```
SW4(config)#interface loopback0
SW4(config-if)#ip address 172.16.227.1 255.255.255.255
SW4(config-if)#end
SW4#
```

In each of the loopback configuration examples, the loopback interface is administratively up and the line protocol is up even though no active ports are configured on the switch. This again is because loopback interfaces are special and cannot go down unless administratively shut down. This is not true for VLAN interfaces because of a feature called autostate. It is important to understand how autostate operates, as you learn in the next section.

Autostate

Hybrid and native switches have a feature called *autostate*. The feature is enabled by default and can only be disabled in hybrid. In hybrid, logical VLAN interfaces configured on the RSM/RSFC, MSFC, or Layer 3 module on the Catalyst 4000 rely on ports in Catalyst OS to be active in the same VLANs before communication is possible. For example, it is possible to configure a VLAN interface on an MSFC for VLAN 100 without any switchports in Catalyst OS belonging to VLAN 100, or VLAN 100 even being defined in Catalyst OS for that matter. Because this is possible, the Cisco IOS portion of the hybrid configuration attempts to prevent a routing "black hole" by placing the VLAN interface in a down/down state. After one or more active ports or a trunk is configured in the same VLAN as the interface in Cisco IOS, the VLAN interface changes to an up/up state. This checking mechanism is the result of the autostate feature. One exception to this feature is for the VLAN assigned to the management interface (sc0) on the switch. The sc0 interface can be shut down administratively.

To further prevent black holes, the autostate feature on the Catalyst 6000/6500 waits for the valid Layer 2 port(s) to transition into a forwarding state before allowing the Layer 3 VLAN interface to transition to an UP/UP state. The autostate on the Catalyst 6000/6500 feature began synchronizing with spanning tree in this way starting in 5.5(10) and 6.1(1) Catalyst OS software.

The commands in Example 7-11 disable autostate depending on the platform.

Example 7-11   *Disabling Autostate on Catalyst 6000/6500 Hybrid*

```
Switch (enable) set msfcautostate disable
Switch (enable) show msfcautostate
MSFC Auto port state: disabled
Switch (enable)
```

A Catalyst 6000/6500 with dual MSFCs would require autostate to be disabled to allow traffic to flow between the MSFCs on that VLAN if no active ports existed. In most situations, this is not necessary, and autostate should be enabled unless a specific need exists to disable it. Example 7-12 shows autostate being disabled on a Catalyst 5500 with an RSM.

Example 7-12 *Disabling Autostate on Catalyst 5000/5500 with RSM*

```
Switch (enable) set rsmautostate disable
RSM port auto state disabled.
Switch (enable) show rsmautostate
RSM Auto port state: disabled
Multi-RSM Option: enabled
Switch (enable)
```

If autostate is enabled and no active ports exist on a specific VLAN in the switch, the interface on the RSM remains up if there is more than one RSM. Essentially, the RSMs see each other's interfaces as valid. This allows traffic to flow between the two RSMs on that VLAN without disabling the autostate feature. The autostate feature is enhanced for multi-RSM configurations starting in 6.1(2) Catalyst OS software. Multi-RSM allows the interfaces on two RSMs to go down when the last active port on that VLAN in the switch goes down. Example 7-13 shows autostate being disabled on a Catalyst 4000 using hybrid software.

Example 7-13 *Disabling Autostate on Catalyst 4000 Hybrid with a Layer 3 Module*

```
Router#autostate disable
Disabling Autostate
Router#show autostate entries
Autostate Feature is currently disabled on the system.
```

System Logging

Cisco devices including Catalyst switches generate a variety of system messages for events such as changes in interface status, environmental conditions, parity memory errors, and security alerts. These messages are displayed on the system console by default. Console logging is a high-priority task in Cisco IOS, and, in some cases, enough console messages can effectively hang the router or switch and render the console unusable. Cisco recommends disabling console and monitor logging and configuring the switch or router to send console messages to an internal buffer that is adjustable in size. Disabling monitor logging prevents system messages from being displayed on terminal lines. Table 7-4 lists the levels of syslog messages supported on a Cisco device.

Table 7-4 *Syslog Severity Levels, Types, and Descriptions*

Severity Level	Severity Type	Description
0	Emergencies	System unusable
1	Alerts	Immediate action is required
2	Critical	Critical condition
3	Errors	Error conditions
4	Warnings	Warning conditions
5	Notifications	Normal, but significant condition
6	Informational	Informational messages
7	Debug	Debugging messages

Examples 7-14 and 7-15 show console logging being disabled and logging to a buffer being enabled on both native and hybrid software.

Example 7-14 *Disabling Console and Monitor Logging and Enabling Logging Buffered (Native)*

```
SW1(config)#no logging console
SW1(config)#no logging monitor
SW1(config)#logging buffered 16384
SW1(config)#end
SW1#
```

Example 7-15 *Disabling Console and Monitor Logging and Enabling Logging Buffered (Hybrid-Catalyst OS)*

```
SW3> (enable) set logging console disable
System logging messages will not be sent to the console.
SW3> (enable) set logging buffer 500
System logging buffer size set to <500>
SW3> (enable)
```

The logging buffers in Examples 7-14 and 7-15 are specified in bytes and are circular, meaning the oldest log messages will be overwritten by the newest messages after the buffer is full. The maximum logging buffer size in Catalyst OS is 500 bytes. To view the contents of the logging buffer, use the **show log** command. One problem with relying only on the logging buffer is that it is wiped clean during a reload. A more effective solution for logging system messages is the addition of a syslog server. A *syslog server* is simply a machine running a syslog daemon conforming to the Berkley Standard Distribution (BSD) standard. A syslog server stores the messages in the order received for later viewing. Many network management tools such as CiscoWorks and HP Openview can operate as a syslog server. In larger environments, it is generally recommended to set up a dedicated syslog server because of the number of messages that can be generated each day by dozens or hundreds of Cisco devices. Example 7-16 shows the configuration of logging to a syslog server using native software.

Example 7-16 *Completing the Logging Configuration (Native)*

```
SW1#config t
Enter configuration commands, one per line.  End with CNTL/Z.
SW1(config)#logging 10.10.10.1
SW1(config)#logging facility local7
SW1(config)#logging trap notifications
SW1(config)#logging source-interface lo0
SW1(config)#
```

In Example 7-16, the switch is pointed to a syslog server at IP address 10.10.10.1 and sets the default logging facility for logging. The syslog server specified should also be set for the same facility/level. The switch is configured to send notification level (5) messages and above to the syslog server and not send informational and debug level (6 and 7, respectively) messages because of the sheer number of level 6 and 7 messages generated during operation. Finally, the switch is configured to send log messages with a source address of loopback0. Example 7-17 shows the configuration of logging to a syslog server using hybrid software.

Example 7-17 *Completing the Logging Configuration (Hybrid-Catalyst OS)*

```
SW3> (enable) set logging server 10.10.10.1
10.10.10.1 added to System logging server table.
```

In Example 7-17, the switch is pointed to the same syslog server at 10.10.10.1. Catalyst OS does not support a loopback interface and log messages are sent with a source address of sc0.

By default, syslog messages are not time stamped. This can cause major issues when attempting to troubleshoot the switch because not knowing when the message occurred can sometimes render the messages almost useless. In Example 7-18, a switch running native software is configured for time stamping of syslog messages and system debug messages.

Example 7-18 *Configuring Debug and Log Message Time Stamps (Native)*

```
SW1#config t
Enter configuration commands, one per line.  End with CNTL/Z.
SW1(config)#service timestamps debug datetime localtime show-timezone msec
SW1(config)#service timestamps log datetime localtime show-timezone msec
SW1(config)#end
SW1#
```

In Example 7-19, a switch running hybrid software is configured for time stamping of syslog messages and system debug messages.

Example 7-19 *Configuring Log Message Time Stamps (Hybrid-Catalyst OS)*

```
SW3> (enable) set logging timestamp enable
System logging messages timestamp will be enabled.
```

NOTE   A discussion of external time sources is beyond the scope of this book. You should reference documentation on the Network Time Protocol (NTP) on Cisco.com, along with publicly available information on the types of time sources that can be purchased for or accessed in networking environments.

Logging levels can be adjusted in both Catalyst OS and Cisco IOS for a wide variety of facilities or features. For example, spanning tree in Catalyst OS defaults to generating log messages for level 2 and higher, but is many times adjusted to level 6 so that more information is recorded during spanning-tree changes. Consult the Cisco web page at Cisco.com for a complete listing of facilities and their default levels for each platform and operating system.

Connecting the Switches

Now that a good portion of the "housekeeping" configuration items are complete, connections between the four switches in Figure 7-4 can be configured. All the physical connections between the switches are already in place.

Figure 7-4   *Physical Links Between Switches*

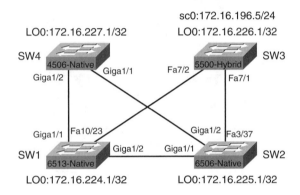

IOS Port/Interface Types

Because a combination of platforms is being used in the examples throughout this chapter, it is important to understand the different types of port/interface types that can be configured on a switch running IOS. Table 7-5 outlines the types of port/interfaces and their uses.

Configuring the Connections

The first connection to bring up is the Gigabit connection between SW1 and SW2. This connection is a single Gigabit link and will not be configured as a trunk, but as a routed physical interface. All interfaces on Catalyst 6000/6500s running native IOS default to routed physical interfaces.

Table 7-5   *Port/Interface Types in IOS*

Port/Interface Type	Function	Sample Configuration
Routed Physical Interface	Traditional Cisco IOS routed interface. Each interface represents a unique Layer 3 network.	**interface gigabitethernet 1/1** **no switchport** **ip address 172.16.100.1 255.255.255.0**
Routed Switch Virtual Interface (SVI)	Single routed interface for all the switchports assigned to a VLAN.	**interface vlan 901** **ip address 172.16.200.1 255.255.255.0**
Access Switch-Port Interface	To group a range of Layer 2 ports into a single VLAN.	**interface range fastethernet 2/1-48** **switchport mode access** **switchport access vlan 130**

In Example 7-20, the current configuration of the GigabitEthernet1/2 interface shows the interface is shut down and no IP address is assigned. In Example 7-20, a /30 IP address is assigned from the range for point-to-point links defined in Table 7-3, earlier in this chapter.

Example 7-20   *Configuring the GigabitEthernet Link on SW1*

```
SW1#show run interface gigabitethernet 1/2
Building configuration...

Current configuration : 61 bytes
!
interface GigabitEthernet1/2
 no ip address
 shutdown
end

SW1#config t
Enter configuration commands, one per line.  End with CNTL/Z.
SW1(config)#interface gigabitethernet 1/2
SW1(config-if)#ip address 172.16.240.5 255.255.255.252
SW1(config-if)#no shutdown
SW1(config-if)#end
SW1#
```

In Example 7-21, the GigabitEthernet interface on SW2 is configured.

Example 7-21   *Configuring the GigabitEthernet Link on SW2*

```
SW2#show run interface gig
SW2#show run interface gigabitethernet 1/1
Building configuration...

Current configuration : 61 bytes
```

Example 7-21 *Configuring the GigabitEthernet Link on SW2 (Continued)*

```
!
interface GigabitEthernet1/1
 no ip address
 shutdown
end

SW2#config t
Enter configuration commands, one per line.  End with CNTL/Z.
SW2(config)#interface GigabitEthernet1/1
SW2(config-if)#ip address 172.16.240.6 255.255.255.252
SW2(config-if)#no shut
SW2(config-if)#end
SW2#
1w6d: %SYS-5-CONFIG_I: Configured from console by console
```

In Example 7-22, a **show interface gigabitethernet1/1** command is issued to determine if the interface is now UP/UP, and a **ping** command is issued to the IP address of the GigabitEthernet1/2 interface on SW1 to determine success.

Example 7-22 *Testing the Connection Between SW1 and SW2*

```
SW2#show interface gigabitethernet 1/1
GigabitEthernet1/1 is up, line protocol is up
  Hardware is C6k 1000Mb 802.3, address is 0001.6471.d968 (bia 0001.6471.d968)
  Internet address is 172.16.240.6/30
!output truncated

SW2#ping 172.16.240.5

Type escape sequence to abort.
Sending 5, 100-byte ICMP Echos to 172.16.240.5, timeout is 2 seconds:
!!!!!
Success rate is 100 percent (5/5), round-trip min/avg/max = 1/1/1 ms
SW2#
```

Figure 7-5 shows the network as it is configured at this stage, and the IP addressing information assigned thus far.

Figure 7-5 *Link Operational Between SW1 and SW2*

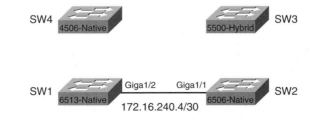

Next, the connection between SW2 and SW3 is configured, as shown in Example 7-23.

Example 7-23 *Configuring the Connection on SW2 to SW3*

```
SW2#config t
Enter configuration commands, one per line.  End with CNTL/Z.
SW2(config)#interface fastEthernet 3/37
SW2(config-if)#ip address 172.16.240.9 255.255.255.252
SW2(config-if)#no shutdown
SW2(config-if)#end
SW2#
```

Because SW3 is running hybrid software, the Layer 2 connection in Catalyst OS is configured first, and then the switched virtual interface (SVI) on the RSM is configured. VLAN 901 is selected from the range of VLANs allocated to point-to-point Layer 2 links. Example 7-24 shows VLAN 901 being created and port 7/1 assigned to VLAN 901. The next step is to configure the RSM with a VLAN 901 interface.

Example 7-24 *Configuring the Connection on SW3 to SW2 (Catalyst OS)*

```
SW3> (enable) set vlan 901
Vlan 901 configuration successful
SW3> (enable) set vlan 901 7/1
VLAN 901 modified.
VLAN 1 modified.
VLAN  Mod/Ports
----  ----------------------
901   7/1

SW3> (enable)
SW3> (enable) show port 7/1
Port  Name              Status     Vlan       Level  Duplex Speed Type
----- ----------------- ---------- ---------- ------ ------ ----- -----------
 7/1                    connected  901               normal a-full a-100 10/100BaseTX
!Output truncated
SW3> (enable)
```

Example 7-25 shows VLAN 901 being configured on the RSM of SW3.

Example 7-25 *Configuring VLAN 901 on the RSM on SW3*

```
RSM1>en
RSM1#config t
Enter configuration commands, one per line.  End with CNTL/Z.
RSM1(config)#interface vlan901
RSM1(config-if)#ip address 172.16.240.10 255.255.255.252
RSM1(config-if)#no shut
RSM1(config-if)#end
RSM1#
```

In Example 7-26, the **show interface vlan901** command is issued to determine if the interface is now UP/UP, and a **ping** is issued to the IP address of the FastEthernet3/37 interface on SW2 to determine success.

Example 7-26 *Testing the Connection Between SW3 and SW2*

```
RSM1#show interface vlan901
Vlan901 is up, line protocol is up
  Hardware is Cat5k Virtual Ethernet, address is 0010.f6b3.4800 (bia 0010.f6
800)
  Internet address is 172.16.240.10/30
!output truncated

RSM1#ping 172.16.240.9

Type escape sequence to abort.
Sending 5, 100-byte ICMP Echos to 172.16.240.9, timeout is 2 seconds:
!!!!!
Success rate is 100 percent (5/5), round-trip min/avg/max = 1/9/40 ms
RSM1#
```

Figure 7-6 shows the network as it looks at this stage, and the IP addressing information assigned thus far.

Figure 7-6 *Link Operational Between SW3 and SW2*

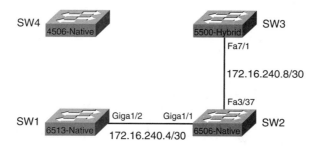

Next, the connection between SW3 and SW1 is configured (see Example 7-27). Again, the Layer 2 connection in Catalyst OS is configured first, followed by the SVI on the RSM. VLAN 902 is used for this link.

Example 7-27 *Configuring the Connection on SW3 to SW1 (Catalyst OS)*

```
SW3> (enable) set vlan 902
Vlan 902 configuration successful
SW3> (enable) set vlan 902 7/2
VLAN 902 modified.
```

continues

Example 7-27 *Configuring the Connection on SW3 to SW1 (Catalyst OS) (Continued)*

```
VLAN 1 modified.
VLAN  Mod/Ports
----  ----------------------
902   7/2

SW3> (enable) show port 7/2
Port  Name              Status     Vlan       Level  Duplex Speed Type
----- ----------------- ---------- ---------- ------ ------ ----- ------------
 7/2                    connected  902        normal a-full a-100 10/100BaseTX
!output truncated
```

The next step is to configure the RSM with a VLAN902 interface, as shown in Example 7-28.

Example 7-28 *Configuring VLAN902 on the RSM on SW3*

```
RSM1#config t
Enter configuration commands, one per line.  End with CNTL/Z.
RSM1(config)#interface VLAN902
RSM1(config-if)#ip address 172.16.240.13 255.255.255.252
RSM1(config-if)#no shutdown
RSM1(config-if)#end
```

Now that the SW3 side of the connection is configured, the other side is configured on SW1 (see Example 7-29).

Example 7-29 *Configuring the Connection Between SW1 and SW3*

```
SW1#show run interface FastEthernet10/23
Building configuration...

Current configuration : 60 bytes
!
interface FastEthernet10/23
 no ip address
 shutdown
end

SW1#config t
Enter configuration commands, one per line.  End with CNTL/Z.
SW1(config)#interface FastEthernet10/23
SW1(config-if)#ip address 172.16.240.14 255.255.255.252
SW1(config-if)#no shutdown
SW1(config-if)#end
SW1#
```

In Example 7-30, a **show interface FastEthernet10/23** command is issued to determine if the interface is now UP/UP, and a **ping** is issued to the IP address of the VLAN902 interface on SW3 to determine success.

Example 7-30   *Testing the Connection Between SW1 and SW3*

```
SW1#show interface FastEthernet10/23
FastEthernet10/23 is up, line protocol is up
  Hardware is C6k 100Mb 802.3, address is 0005.7418.048a (bia 0005.7418.048a)
  Internet address is 172.16.240.14/30
!output truncated

SW1#ping 172.16.240.13

Type escape sequence to abort.
Sending 5, 100-byte ICMP Echos to 172.16.240.13, timeout is 2 seconds:
!!!!!
Success rate is 100 percent (5/5), round-trip min/avg/max = 1/1/4 ms
SW1#
```

Figure 7-7 shows the network as it looks at this stage, and the IP addressing information assigned thus far.

Figure 7-7   *Link Operational Between SW3 and SW1*

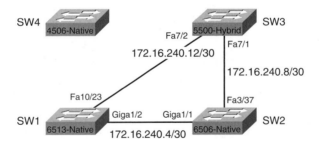

Next, the connection between SW1 and SW4 is configured, as shown in Example 7-31.

Example 7-31   *Configuring the Connection on SW1 to SW4*

```
SW1#show run interface gigabitethernet 1/1
Building configuration...

Current configuration : 61 bytes
```

continues

Example 7-31   *Configuring the Connection on SW1 to SW4 (Continued)*

```
!
interface GigabitEthernet1/1
 no ip address
 shutdown
end

SW1#config t
Enter configuration commands, one per line.  End with CNTL/Z.
SW1(config)#interface gigabitethernet 1/1
SW1(config-if)#ip address 172.16.240.17 255.255.255.252
SW1(config-if)#no shutdown
SW1(config-if)#end
SW1#
```

Next, the connection between SW1 and SW4 is configured, as shown in Example 7-32.

Example 7-32   *Configuring the Connection on SW4 to SW1*

```
SW4#show run interface gigabitethernet 1/2
Building configuration...

Current configuration : 36 bytes
!
interface GigabitEthernet1/2
end

SW4#config t
Enter configuration commands, one per line.  End with CNTL/Z.
SW4(config)#interface gigabitethernet 1/2
SW4(config-if)#no switchport
SW4(config-if)#ip address 172.16.240.18 255.255.255.252
SW4(config-if)#end
SW4#
```

It is important to understand that the Catalyst 4500 series switch defaults to all interfaces being configured as Access Port Switch Interfaces. To convert the gigabitethernet1/2 interface from a Layer 2 switchport to a Layer 3 routed physical interface, the **no switchport** command must be used prior to assigning the IP address in Example 7-32.

In Example 7-33, the **show interface gigabitethernet1/2** command is issued to determine if the interface is now up/up and a **ping** is issued to the IP address of the GigabitEthernet 1/1 interface on SW1 to determine success.

Figure 7-8 shows the network as it looks at this stage, and the IP addressing information assigned thus far.

Example 7-33 *Testing the Connection Between SW4 and SW1*

```
SW4#show interface gigabitethernet 1/2
GigabitEthernet1/2 is up, line protocol is up (connected)
  Hardware is Gigabit Ethernet Port, address is 000b.fdd5.62bf (bia 000b.fdd5
bf)
  Internet address is 172.16.240.18/30
!output truncated

SW4#ping 172.16.240.17

Type escape sequence to abort.
Sending 5, 100-byte ICMP Echos to 172.16.240.17, timeout is 2 seconds:
!!!!!
Success rate is 100 percent (5/5), round-trip min/avg/max = 4/4/4 ms
SW4#
```

Figure 7-8 *Link Operational Between SW1 and SW4*

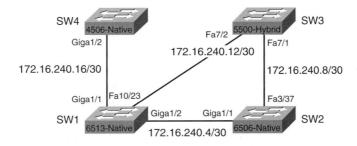

Finally, the connection between SW4 and SW2 is configured, starting with SW4. (See Example 7-34.)

Example 7-34 *Configuring the Connection from SW4 to SW2*

```
SW4#show run interface GigabitEthernet1/1
Building configuration...

Current configuration : 36 bytes
!
interface GigabitEthernet1/1
end

SW4#config t
Enter configuration commands, one per line.  End with CNTL/Z.
```

continues

Example 7-34 *Configuring the Connection from SW4 to SW2 (Continued)*

```
SW4(config)#interface GigabitEthernet1/1
SW4(config-if)#no switchport
SW4(config-if)#ip address 172.16.240.21 255.255.255.252
SW4(config-if)#end
SW4#
```

The connection is completed by configuring the GigabitEthernet1/2 interface on SW2, as shown in Example 7-35.

Example 7-35 *Configuring the Connection from SW2 to SW4*

```
SW2#show run interface GigabitEthernet1/2
Building configuration...

Current configuration : 61 bytes
!
interface GigabitEthernet1/2
 no ip address
 shutdown
end

SW2#config t
Enter configuration commands, one per line.  End with CNTL/Z.
SW2(config)#interface GigabitEthernet1/2
SW2(config-if)#ip address 172.16.240.22 255.255.255.252
SW2(config-if)#no shutdown
SW2(config-if)#end
SW2#
```

In Example 7-36, the **show interface gigabitethernet 1/2** command is issued to determine if the interface is now UP/UP, and a **ping** is issued to the IP address of the GigabitEthernet 1/1 interface on SW4 to determine success.

Example 7-36 *Testing the Connection Between SW2 and SW4*

```
SW2#show interface gigabitethernet 1/2
GigabitEthernet1/2 is up, line protocol is up
  Hardware is C6k 1000Mb 802.3, address is 0001.6471.d969 (bia 0001.6471.d969)
  Internet address is 172.16.240.22/30
!output truncated

SW2#ping 172.16.240.21

Type escape sequence to abort.
Sending 5, 100-byte ICMP Echos to 172.16.240.25, timeout is 2 seconds:
!!!!!
Success rate is 100 percent (5/5), round-trip min/avg/max = 4/4/4 ms
SW2#
```

Figure 7-9 shows the completed switch connections, and all the network addresses assigned.

Figure 7-9   *Completed Connections Between All Four Switches*

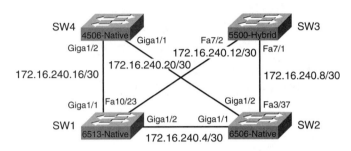

Now that the basic connections between switches have been established, ports to be used for access layer devices, such as workstations and servers, will be configured.

Configuring the Access Layer

Switchports on the Catalyst 5500 SW3 and interfaces on the Catalyst 4506 SW4 will be configured in VLANs to support access layer devices. Figure 7-10 shows the IP network numbers assigned to these VLANs.

Figure 7-10   *Addition of Access Layer VLANs*

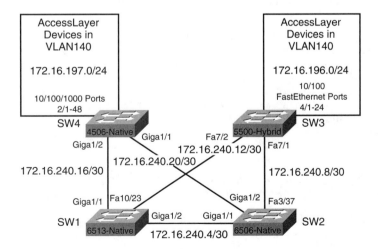

Configuring the access layer begins with configuring ports on SW3 to be in VLAN 130. VLAN 130 is one of the access layer VLANs in the VLAN addressing scheme outlined in Table 7-1 earlier in this chapter. Remember VLAN 130 was created on SW3 earlier in VTP configuration (refer to Example 7-3). In Example 7-37, module 4 on SW3 is a 24-port 10/100 Mb FastEthernet module, and will have all ports assigned to VLAN 130.

Example 7-37 *Configuring Ports on SW3 as Members of VLAN 130*

```
SW3> (enable) show mod 4
Mod Module-Name         Ports Module-Type           Model     Serial-Num Status
--- ------------------- ----- --------------------- --------- --------- -------
4                       24    10/100BaseTX Ethernet WS-X5224  009607843 ok

Mod MAC-Address(es)                          Hw     Fw         Sw
--- --------------------------------------- ------ ---------- -----------------
4   00-10-7b-78-57-00 to 00-10-7b-78-57-17 1.4    3.1(1)     4.5(5)
SW3> (enable)

SW3> (enable) set vlan 130 4/1-24
VLAN 130 modified.
VLAN 1 modified.
VLAN  Mod/Ports
----- ---------------------
130   4/1-24

SW3> (enable)
```

For these ports to be reachable from other networks, an SVI must be configured on the RSM for VLAN 130. The SVI for VLAN 130 is configured in Example 7-38. Remember sc0 on the switch is already assigned to VLAN 130 with an IP address of 172.16.196.5/24 in Example 7-8, earlier in the chapter.

Example 7-38 *Configuring a SVI for VLAN 130 on the RSM of SW3*

```
RSM1#config t
Enter configuration commands, one per line.  End with CNTL/Z.
RSM1(config)#int vlan130
RSM1(config-if)#ip address 172.16.196.1 255.255.255.0
RSM1(config-if)#end
RSM1#
```

In Example 7-39, the **show interface vlan130** command is issued to confirm the SVI is UP/UP, and a **ping** from the SVI to the sc0 interface on the supervisor is issued.

In Example 7-40, the interfaces on module 2 of SW4 are configured for VLAN 140. Module 4 on the SW4 is a 48-port 10/100/1000BASE-TX module.

Example 7-39   *Verifying the Status of the VLAN130 Interface and sc0*

```
RSM1#show interface vlan130
Vlan130 is up, line protocol is up
  Hardware is Cat5k Virtual Ethernet, address is 0010.f6b3.4800 (bia 0010.f6b3.4
800)
  Internet address is 172.16.196.1/24
(output truncated)

RSM1#ping 172.16.196.5

Type escape sequence to abort.
Sending 5, 100-byte ICMP Echos to 172.16.196.5, timeout is 2 seconds:
!!!!!
Success rate is 100 percent (5/5), round-trip min/avg/max = 1/23/112 ms
```

Example 7-40   *Configuring Ports 2/1-48 on SW4 for VLAN 140*

```
SW4#config t
Enter configuration commands, one per line.  End with CNTL/Z.
SW4(config)#interface range gigabitethernet 2/1 - 48
SW4(config-if-range)#switchport mode access
SW4(config-if-range)#switchport access vlan 140
SW4(config-if-range)#end
SW4#

SW4#show vlan

VLAN Name                             Status    Ports
---- -------------------------------- --------- -------------------------------
1    default                          active
140  VLAN0140                         active    Gi2/1, Gi2/2, Gi2/3, Gi2/4
                                                Gi2/5, Gi2/6, Gi2/7, Gi2/8
                                                Gi2/9, Gi2/10, Gi2/11, Gi2/12
                                                Gi2/13, Gi2/14, Gi2/15, Gi2/16
                                                Gi2/17, Gi2/18, Gi2/19, Gi2/20
                                                Gi2/21, Gi2/22, Gi2/23, Gi2/24
                                                Gi2/25, Gi2/26, Gi2/27, Gi2/28
                                                Gi2/29, Gi2/30, Gi2/31, Gi2/32
                                                Gi2/33, Gi2/34, Gi2/35, Gi2/36
                                                Gi2/37, Gi2/38, Gi2/39, Gi2/40
                                                Gi2/41, Gi2/42, Gi2/43, Gi2/44
                                                Gi2/45, Gi2/46, Gi2/47, Gi2/48
!output truncated
```

The **interface range** command must be entered exactly as shown in Example 7-40 with
spaces to be accepted. The output of the **show vlan** command shows ports 2/1–48 assigned
successfully to VLAN 140.

Now that these ports have been assigned, an SVI must be created on SW4 so that VLAN 140 can be reached from other networks. The SVI for VLAN 140 on SW4 is created in Example 7-41.

Example 7-41 *Configuration of a SVI on SW4 for VLAN 140*

```
SW4#config t
Enter configuration commands, one per line.  End with CNTL/Z.
SW4(config)#interface VLAN140
SW4(config-if)#ip address 172.16.197.1 255.255.255.0
SW4(config-if)#no shutdown
SW4(config-if)#end
SW4#
```

In Example 7-42, the **show interface vlan140** command is issued to confirm the SVI is UP/UP.

Example 7-42 *Verifying the Status of the VLAN140 Interface*

```
SW4#show interface vlan140
Vlan140 is up, line protocol is up
  Hardware is Ethernet SVI, address is 000b.fdd5.62bf (bia 000b.fdd5.62bf)
    Internet address is 172.16.197.1/24
```

Dynamic Routing

Now that the Layer 3 connections between the four switches are configured, the access layer VLANs created, and access ports assigned, a dynamic routing protocol is configured to allow connectivity between VLANs. In these examples, EIGRP is used as the dynamic routing protocol. EIGRP will be enabled on all four switches using Autonomous System (AS) 100, starting with SW1. Refer to the documentation on Cisco.com for more information about EIGRP and other dynamic routing protocols. Example 7-43 shows EIGRP being configured on SW1.

Example 7-43 *EIGRP Configured on SW1*

```
SW1(config)#router eigrp 100
SW1(config-router)#network 172.16.192.0 0.0.63.255
SW1(config-router)#end
SW1#show ip eigrp interfaces
IP-EIGRP interfaces for process 100

                    Xmit Queue   Mean   Pacing Time   Multicast    Pending
Interface   Peers   Un/Reliable  SRTT   Un/Reliable   Flow Timer   Routes
Gi1/1         0        0/0         0        0/10          0           0
Gi1/2         0        0/0         0        0/10          0           0
Fa10/23       0        0/0         0        0/10          0           0
Lo0           0        0/0         0        0/10          0           0
SW1#
```

The output of the **show ip eigrp interfaces** command in Example 7-43 indicates the four interfaces that have been configured on SW1 with IP addresses in the previous exercises now part of EIGRP AS 100. The same commands are repeated on SW2 in Example 7-44, on SW3 in Example 7-45, and on SW4 in Example 7-46.

Example 7-44 *EIGRP Configured on SW2*

```
SW2#config t
Enter configuration commands, one per line.  End with CNTL/Z.
SW2(config)#router eigrp 100
SW2(config-router)#network 172.16.192.0 0.0.63.255
SW2(config-router)#end
SW2#show ip eigrp interfaces
IP-EIGRP interfaces for process 100

                     Xmit Queue   Mean   Pacing Time   Multicast    Pending
Interface    Peers   Un/Reliable  SRTT   Un/Reliable   Flow Timer   Routes
Gi1/1          1        0/0        1044      0/10         5216          0
Gi1/2          0        0/0          0       0/10            0          0
Fa3/37         0        0/0          0       0/10            0          0
Lo0            0        0/0          0       0/10            0          0
SW2#
```

Example 7-45 *EIGRP Configured on the RSM of SW3*

```
RSM1(config)#router eigrp 100
RSM1(config-router)#network 172.16.192.0 0.0.63.255
RSM1(config-router)#end
RSM1#show ip eigrp interfaces
IP-EIGRP interfaces for process 100

                     Xmit Queue   Mean   Pacing Time   Multicast    Pending
Interface    Peers   Un/Reliable  SRTT   Un/Reliable   Flow Timer   Routes
Vl130          0        0/0          0       0/10            0          0
Vl901          1        0/0        726       0/10         3632          0
Vl902          1        0/0        752       0/10         3760          0
Lo0            0        0/0          0       0/10            0          0
RSM1#
```

Example 7-46 *EIGRP Configured on SW4*

```
SW4#config t
Enter configuration commands, one per line.  End with CNTL/Z.
SW4(config)#router eigrp 100
SW4(config-router)#network 172.16.192.0 0.0.63.255
SW4(config-router)#end
SW4#show ip eigrp interfaces
IP-EIGRP interfaces for process 100
```

continues

Example 7-46 *EIGRP Configured on SW4 (Continued)*

```
                      Xmit Queue   Mean   Pacing Time   Multicast    Pending
Interface     Peers  Un/Reliable  SRTT   Un/Reliable   Flow Timer   Routes
Vl140         0      0/0          0      0/10          0            0
Gi1/1         1      0/0          0      0/10          0            0
Gi1/2         1      0/0          0      0/10          0            0
Lo0           0      0/0          0      0/10          0            0
SW4#
```

Now that dynamic routing for network 172.16.192.0 and its subnets has been configured
on all four switches, a look at the routing table of SW1 in Example 7-47 shows that the
networks for the access layer VLANs (172.16.196.0 and 172.16.197.0) are now reachable
via the uplinks to those switches.

Example 7-47 *Output of* **show ip route** *on SW1*

```
SW1#show ip route
Codes: C - connected, S - static, I - IGRP, R - RIP, M - mobile, B - BGP
       D - EIGRP, EX - EIGRP external, O - OSPF, IA - OSPF inter area
       N1 - OSPF NSSA external type 1, N2 - OSPF NSSA external type 2
       E1 - OSPF external type 1, E2 - OSPF external type 2, E - EGP
       i - IS-IS, L1 - IS-IS level-1, L2 - IS-IS level-2, ia - IS-IS inter area
       * - candidate default, U - per-user static route, o - ODR
       P - periodic downloaded static route

Gateway of last resort is not set

     172.16.0.0/16 is variably subnetted, 11 subnets, 3 masks
C       172.16.240.12/30 is directly connected, FastEthernet10/23
D       172.16.240.8/30
           [90/28416] via 172.16.240.6, 00:03:08, GigabitEthernet1/2
C       172.16.240.4/30 is directly connected, GigabitEthernet1/2
D       172.16.240.20/30
           [90/3072] via 172.16.240.6, 00:03:11, GigabitEthernet1/2
           [90/3072] via 172.16.240.18, 00:03:11, GigabitEthernet1/1
D       172.16.225.1/32
           [90/130816] via 172.16.240.6, 00:03:08, GigabitEthernet1/2
C       172.16.240.16/30 is directly connected, GigabitEthernet1/1
C       172.16.224.1/32 is directly connected, Loopback0
D       172.16.227.1/32
           [90/130816] via 172.16.240.18, 00:03:11, GigabitEthernet1/1
D       172.16.226.1/32
           [90/156160] via 172.16.240.13, 00:06:00, FastEthernet10/23
D       172.16.196.0/24
           [90/30720] via 172.16.240.13, 00:06:00, FastEthernet10/23
D       172.16.197.0/24
           [90/3072] via 172.16.240.18, 00:03:12, GigabitEthernet1/1
C    127.0.0.0/8 is directly connected, EOBC0/0
SW1#
```

Channeling and Trunking

All the configuration examples thus far have assumed it is possible to restrict a VLAN to a single switch. Although this is the cleanest and simplest configuration, it is not always possible. Many times, connections between access layer and distribution layer switches are Layer 2, and VLANs must span many switches because of application or administrative requirements. Chapter 11, "Design and Implementation Best Practices," discusses additional design options and considerations.

In Figure 7-11, a requirement for two additional VLANs with ports on both SW1 and SW2 is introduced. VLANs 401 and 402 are used for the exercises. VLANs 401 and 402 have been created on SW1 and SW2 using the same procedures as in Examples 7-1 through 7-4. While the Gigabit connection between SW1 and SW2 could be converted to a trunk to carry these additional VLANs, some unused FastEthernet ports will be configured in a channel to carry only these new VLANs and VLAN 1.

Figure 7-11 *Addition of VLANs 401 and 402*

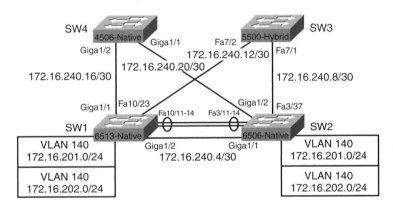

Configuration begins with creating the channel group on SW1, as shown in Example 7-48.

Example 7-48 *Creating the Channel Group on SW1*

```
SW1#config t
Enter configuration commands, one per line.  End with CNTL/Z.
SW1(config)#interface range fastEthernet 10/11 - 14
SW1(config-if-range)#no ip address
SW1(config-if-range)#switchport
SW1(config-if-range)#switchport trunk encapsulation dot1q
SW1(config-if-range)#switchport mode trunk
SW1(config-if-range)#switchport mode dynamic desirable
SW1(config-if-range)#switchport trunk allowed vlan remove 2-400,403-1005
```

continues

Example 7-48   *Creating the Channel Group on SW1 (Continued)*

```
SW1(config-if-range)#channel-group 1 mode desirable
SW1(config-if-range)#no shutdown
SW1(config-if-range)#end
SW1#
```

The channel is completed by configuring the other side on SW2, as shown in Example 7-49.

Example 7-49   *Creating the Channel Group on SW2*

```
SW2(config)#interface range fastEthernet 3/11 - 14
SW2(config-if-range)#no ip address
SW2(config-if-range)#switchport

SW2(config-if-range)#switchport trunk encapsulation dot1q
SW2(config-if-range)#switchport mode trunk
SW2(config-if-range)#switchport mode dynamic desirable
SW2(config-if-range)#switchport trunk allowed vlan remove 2-400,403-1005
SW2(config-if-range)#channel-group 1 mode desirable
Creating a port-channel interface Port-channel1
SW2(config-if-range)#no shutdown
SW2(config-if-range)#end
SW2#
```

Issuing a **show run interface fastEthernet 3/11** command displays the configuration of one of the ports in the channel (see Example 7-50).

Example 7-50   *Verifying the Configuration on SW2*

```
SW2#show run interface fastEthernet 3/11
Building configuration...

Current configuration : 182 bytes
!
interface FastEthernet3/11
 no ip address
switchport
 switchport trunk encapsulation dot1q
 switchport trunk allowed vlan 1,401,402
 channel-group 1 mode desirable
end
```

The operation of the new channel group can be verified by issuing a **show interfaces port-channel 1** command. The operation of the trunk can be verified by issuing the **show interfaces trunk** command, as shown in Example 7-51.

Example 7-51 *Output of the* **show interfaces port-channel** *and* **show interfaces trunk** *Commands on SW1*

```
SW1#show interfaces port-channel 1
Port-channel1 is up, line protocol is up
  Hardware is EtherChannel, address is 0009.1267.9ffa (bia 0009.1267.9ffa)
  MTU 1500 bytes, BW 400000 Kbit, DLY 100 usec,
     reliability 255/255, txload 1/255, rxload 1/255
  Encapsulation ARPA, loopback not set
  Full-duplex, 100Mb/s
  Members in this channel: Fa10/11 Fa10/12 Fa10/13 Fa10/14
!output truncated

SW1#show interfaces trunk

Port        Mode            Encapsulation  Status          Native vlan
Po1         desirable       802.1q         trunking        1

Port        Vlans allowed on trunk
Po1         1,401-402

Port        Vlans allowed and active in management domain
Po1         1,401-402

Port        Vlans in spanning tree forwarding state and not pruned
Po1         1,401-402
SW1#
```

The bandwidth reported on the channel is 400000 Kbit, and the members of the channel are listed in the output.

Configuring UniDirectional Link Detection

One best practice to follow when configuring a network like the one used in this chapter is the configuration of UniDirectional Link Detection (UDLD) in Aggressive mode. UDLD is designed to mitigate certain fault conditions on fiber and copper Ethernet interfaces. UDLD is designed to shutdown any miswired ports or unidirectional links by putting the port in an errDisabled state. UDLD is a Layer 2 protocol and, when run in combination with autonegotiation Layer 1 mechanisms, UDLD can validate the physical (Layer 1) and logical (Layer 2) integrity of a link. UDLD accomplishes this task by learning about neighbors and keeping neighbor status in a cache. Neighbors are learned by the sending of UDLD echo or hello messages.

The UDLD Aggressive feature provides additional protection against unidirectional link conditions in certain situations, and attempts to re-establish a connection with the neighbor when a failure is detected. UDLD Aggressive works by detecting when one side of a link remains up while the other side of the link has gone down, and after eight failed retries, transitions the port to an errDisabled state and generates a syslog message.

Cisco recommends configuring UDLD in Aggressive mode on point-to-point FastEthernet/
GigabitEthernet links between Cisco switches, and setting the message interval to 15 seconds.
UDLD is globally disabled by default and can be enabled globally or on a port–by-port
basis. In the examples in this section, UDLD Aggressive should be configured on all the
links between switches. An example of this configuration on a per-port basis is shown in
Example 7-52 using SW1 and SW2.

Example 7-52 *Enabling Aggressive UDLD on SW1 and SW2*

```
SW1#config t
Enter configuration commands, one per line.  End with CNTL/Z.
SW1(config)#interface range gigabitethernet 1/1 - 2
SW1(config-if-range)#udld enable
SW1(config-if-range)#udld aggressive
SW1(config-if-range)#end

SW2#config t
Enter configuration commands, one per line.  End with CNTL/Z.
SW2(config)#interface range gigabitethernet 1/1 - 2
SW2(config-if-range)#udld enable
SW2(config-if-range)#udld aggressive
SW2(config-if-range)#end
SW2#
```

The output of the **show udld** command on SW1 shows the status of the UDLD configuration. In the output in Example 7-53, SW1 detects SW2 as a UDLD neighbor, because both
SW1 and SW2 have been configured, but does not detect SW4 on GigabitEthernet1/1
because it has yet to be configured.

Example 7-53 *Output of* **show udld** *Command on SW1*

```
SW1#show udld

Interface Gi1/1
- - -
Port enable administrative configuration setting: Enabled / in aggressive mode
Port enable operational state: Enabled / in aggressive mode
Current bidirectional state: Unknown
Current operational state: Advertisement
Message interval: 7
Time out interval: 5
No neighbor cache information stored

Interface Gi1/2
- - -
Port enable administrative configuration setting: Enabled / in aggressive mode
Port enable operational state: Enabled / in aggressive mode
Current bidirectional state: Bidirectional
Current operational state: Advertisement - Single neighbor detected
Message interval: 60
```

Example 7-53 *Output of* **show udld** *Command on SW1 (Continued)*

```
Time out interval: 5

    Entry 1
    - - -
    Expiration time: 168
    Device ID: 1
    Current neighbor state: Bidirectional
    Device name: SAD04281ARM
    Port ID: Gi1/1
    Neighbor echo 1 device: SAD050814BH
    Neighbor echo 1 port: Gi1/2

    Message interval: 5
    CDP Device name: SW2
```

Portfast and BPDU Guard

You can find a detailed discussion of portfast and BPDU Guard in Chapter 10, "Implementing and Tuning Spanning Tree," but the configuration of the access layer ports in this chapter's examples would not be complete without enabling portfast and BPDU Guard.

Portfast is a feature that bypasses the normal spanning-tree operation of listening and learning and places a port immediately into forwarding when a port is connected. Portfast should only be used on ports connecting to end-station devices such as workstations and servers. Portfast is disabled by default and is enabled on a port-by-port basis.

The addition of BPDU Guard as an additional protection allows the switch to place any port configured with portfast into an errDisabled state if a BPDU is received on that port. Because ports 2/1 through 2/48 on SW4 were configured for access layer devices in VLAN 140 in Example 7-40 earlier in the chapter, those ports will have portfast and BPDU Guard enabled as follows in Example 7-54.

Example 7-54 *Enabling Portfast and BPDU Guard on SW4*

```
SW4#config t
Enter configuration commands, one per line.  End with CNTL/Z.
SW4(config)#interface range gigabitethernet 2/1 - 48
SW4(config-if-range)#spanning-tree portfast
%Warning: portfast should only be enabled on ports connected to a single
  host. Connecting hubs, concentrators, switches, bridges, etc... to this
  interface  when portfast is enabled, can cause temporary bridging loops.
  Use with CAUTION
%Portfast will be configured in 48 interfaces due to the range command
  but will only have effect when the interfaces are in a non-trunking mode.

SW4(config-if-range)#spanning-tree bpduguard enable
SW4(config-if-range)#end
```

Configuring SNMP

Now that the sample network in this chapter has been configured and is operational, the switches should be configured so that management stations can gather information via the Simple Network Management Protocol (SNMP). SNMP is used to gather statistics, counters, and tables in the Management Information Base (MIB) of a device.

The SNMP framework consists of three parts:

- SNMP manager
- SNMP agent
- MIB

The SNMP manager is a host that monitors the activities of network devices using SNMP. The SNMP manager is typically referred to as the Network Management Station (NMS). The SNMP agent is software running on the device being monitored by the SNMP manager. A MIB is a virtual storage area for network management information consisting of collections of managed objects. MIBs are written in the SNMP MIB module language as defined in RFCs 2578, 2579, and 2580. SNMP agents can be configured to allow read-only or read-write access to the device. Management stations like CiscoWorks use the read-only functions of the agent to monitor the device, and can use the read-write functions of the agent to make changes to the device configuration. SNMP uses passwords called *community strings* to grant access to the SNMP agent. Access to the agents can be further limited via SNMP access lists.

A detailed discussion of SNMP and network management is beyond the scope of this book. SNMP MIB information for each Cisco device can be found on Cisco.com.

You should configure SNMP on each Cisco device to be monitored by NMS. A sample SNMP configuration is shown on SW1 in Example 7-55.

Example 7-55 *Sample SNMP Configuration on SW1*

```
SW1#config t
Enter configuration commands, one per line.  End with CNTL/Z.

SW1(config)#access-list 10 permit 10.10.10.2
SW1(config)#snmp enable
SW1(config)#snmp-server community alpha ro 10
SW1(config)#snmp-server community beta rw 10
SW1(config)#snmp-server contact John Smith (555)789-2653
SW1(config)#snmp-server location Denver Data Center
SW1(config)#snmp enable traps
SW1(config)#snmp trap-source lo0
```

After SNMP is configured on SW1, the statistics can be viewed using the **show snmp** command, as shown in Example 7-56.

Example 7-56 *Output of* **show snmp** *Command on SW1*

```
SW1#show snmp
Chassis: SAD050814BH
Contact: John Smith (555)789-2653
Location: Denver Data Center
0 SNMP packets input
    0 Bad SNMP version errors
    0 Unknown community name
    0 Illegal operation for community name supplied
    0 Encoding errors
    0 Number of requested variables
    0 Number of altered variables
    0 Get-request PDUs
    0 Get-next PDUs
    0 Set-request PDUs
0 SNMP packets output
    0 Too big errors (Maximum packet size 1500)
    0 No such name errors
    0 Bad values errors
    0 General errors
    0 Response PDUs
    0 Trap PDUs

SNMP logging: disabled
```

Summary

This chapter provided configuration examples for connecting switches running both native and hybrid software configurations, and offers examples of both Layer 3 and Layer 2 connectivity between switches. The material in this chapter can serve as a reference for initial configuration of either hybrid or native switches, and illustrates some options and best practices when configuring access layer ports, trunks, channels, and point-to-point Layer 3 links. In each of the examples, no logical Layer 2 loops were created, so spanning-tree issues are avoided. Avoiding spanning tree is not always possible, so you should reference Chapter 10 of this book when attempting to optimize and troubleshoot a network with logical loops.

A detailed look at other design options and implementation best practices can be found in Chapter 11.

This chapter covers the following topics:

- QoS services
- Class of service
- Type of service
- QoS operational model
- QoS caveats

CHAPTER 8

Understanding Quality of Service on Catalyst 6500

Quality of service (QoS), at a rudimentary level, is defined as providing preferential treatment for priority traffic. It does this on the expense of low-priority traffic. The motivation behind QoS is to allow network- and user-critical data to have consistent and reliable access to the network. QoS deployment is central to converged networks where IP telephony has merged with traditional data network. QoS helps with management of latency and bandwidth on the network. Some general terms will be outlined, but the bulk of this chapter will be dedicated to the life of a QoS packet through a Catalyst 6500 switch.

QoS objectives are to provide reliable and available resources for applications and services on the network. In addition, QoS should offer some predictability of traffic flow seen on the network. Most networks today are implementing QoS for these very same reasons. Customers are looking for cheaper alternate means than simply increasing bandwidth on the network to support the various services they are supporting. However, bandwidth scarcity is not the only reason for QoS. Some applications are delay sensitive and require special handling on the network device itself.

QoS helps mitigate the following issues seen on the network:

- End-to-end delay
  - Fixed delay
  - Variable delay (also known as jitter)
- Bandwidth capacity issues
- Packet loss

QoS Services

Two types of QoS architectures are currently available: Integrated Services (IntServ) and Differentiated Services (DiffServ). IntServ is designed to provide guaranteed resources on the network for applications. For example, a network application via Resource Reservation Protocol (RSVP), a signaling protocol, requests specific bandwidth from the network for a given flow. RSVP visiting each network hop toward the IP destination address will attempt to allocate network bandwidth resources. If the results are positive, the application can send its traffic on the network. RSVP in addition to bandwidth allotment can also help allocate resources for delay-sensitive applications as well as provide the traditional best-effort service. The idea behind IntServ is that if specific application traffic flow requirements are met, the likelihood of network affecting the performance of the application is minimized. IntServ requires all devices along the path of the traffic flow to support RSVP. Most networks today cannot meet this requirement.

The second type of QoS architecture is DiffServ. Essentially, some user-defined traffic will have a higher priority than other traffic on the network. For example, the network engineer might provide more network resources for voice traffic over data traffic, and so on. Unlike IntServ, DiffServ is not an all-or-none mechanism. No admission controls mechanism exists in DiffServ as in IntServ. Each network device along the traffic flow will appropriately handle the traffic based on that particular device configuration. Most networks today operate using the DiffServ model because it is more scalable and flexible than IntServ. The discussion of this chapter will be based on DiffServ model.

Class of Service

QoS implementation can occur at both Layer 2 and Layer 3, and also work in conjunction to provide end-to-end QoS for services on the network. QoS implementation at Layer 2 is known as class of service (CoS). A Layer 2 device, such as a Catalyst switch, will provide preferential treatment for traffic that has higher Layer 2 CoS settings.

Packets are given priority based on their CoS value. The CoS values range from 0 to 7, with 7 as the highest priority level. The CoS resides inside the IEEE 802.1Q and Inter-Switch Link (ISL) headers. The three most significant bits in the 4-byte Tag field in IEEE 802.1Q are used for CoS. In the ISL header, the three least significant bits in the 1-byte User field carry the CoS value. Chapter 4, "Layer 2 Fundamentals," can be referenced for detailed discussion on the format of IEEE 802.1Q and Cisco ISL frames.

A network administrator can set, for example, voice traffic with a higher CoS value as the voice traffic passes through the switch. If this configuration is not made, the voice traffic on the switch will not be given preferential treatment by the switch and, as a result, will have to compete for bandwidth and incur latency similar to other nonpriority traffic. In other words, for QoS implementation to be effective, QoS requires both Layer 2 and Layer 3 device configuration.

Type of Service

To give priority for traffic at Layer 3, type of service (ToS), or now known as the DS byte, needs to be manipulated. The ToS field is composed of 1 byte in the IP packet. IP precedence is the three most significant bits. As a result, a total of 8 different types of priorities are found in IP precedence. Types 6 and 7 are used by control traffic.

The Differentiated Services Code Point (DSCP) uses the first 6 bits of ToS byte rather than the original 3 as mentioned, which can provide up to 64 different types of priorities. DSCP is backward compatible to IP precedence as the mapping shows in Example 8-1.

Example 8-1   *ToS to DSCP Map*

```
IP Precedence 0 =0 DSCP
IP Precedence 1 =8 DSCP
IP Precedence 2 =16 DSCP
IP Precedence 3 =24 DSCP
IP Precedence 4 =32 DSCP
IP Precedence 5 =40 DSCP
IP Precedence 6 =48 DSCP
IP Precedence 7 =56 DSCP
```

QoS Operational Model

Thus far, the discussion has laid out the fundamentals of QoS and the types of roles it can play, and has defined some general terms such as CoS, ToS, and DCSP. This section will explore the various steps necessary for a QoS packet to traverse from a Catalyst 6500 switch's ingress to egress port.

Catalyst QoS operational model consists of five steps:

1 Classification

2 Input scheduling

3 Marking and policing

4 Marking

5 Output scheduling

Classification

Classification is the initial step that needs to be discussed. The Catalyst switch needs to distinguish one incoming frame from another so that it can appropriately forward the packet through the switch.

Figure 8-1 depicts the path the frame takes before going to the switching engine (PFC/PFC2) for further instructions. By default, Catalyst 6500 switch's port is programmed to be untrusted, which means that any frame received on the port will have its CoS value reset to 0. The default CoS value of 0 can be changed, and any incoming frames on that untrusted port will inherit the new configured CoS setting. Now, that having been said, the port can be configured to be trusted, in which case the incoming frame's CoS value will be maintained. An ingress port can be configured with the following options:

- **Untrusted**—Incoming frame will lose its CoS value, and inherit default or configured value on the ingress port.
- **Trust-cos**—Incoming frame will maintains its CoS value.
- **Trust-dscp**—Incoming packet will maintain its DSCP value.
- **Trust-ipprec**—Incoming packet will maintain its IP precedence value.

Figure 8-1 *Classification of Incoming Frame*

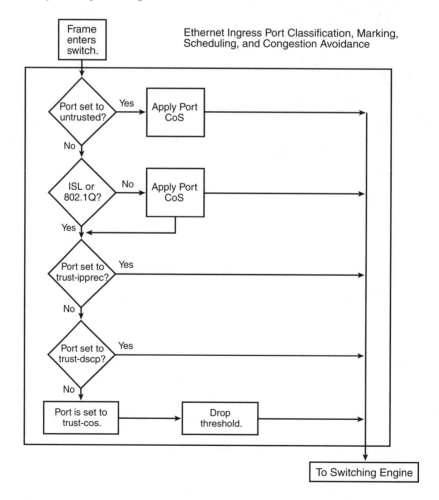

A Layer 3 switching engine is required to configure trust-dscp and trust-ipprec options. Configuring a port's trust status can be done with the **set port qos** command:

```
Switch1 (enable) set port qos 1/2 trust trust-cos
```

The configuration has been modified to allow for port 1/2 to be trusted. The command was performed on a gigabit port. Now, any incoming packet with CoS value set will be forwarded on without change. It is worth noting an importing caveat regarding 10/100 cards (for example, the WS-X6248-xx or WS-X6348-xx) and classification. The 10/100 cards do not support any trust-type configuration. So, for instance in Example 8-2, port 10/3 is configured as a CoS trust port. However, the switch generates a syslog message that trust-cos feature is not supported and that Receive thresholds are enabled. It is also worth noting that even though the trust-type is not supported on a 10/100 card, the command still needs to be performed to enable Receive thresholds. The "Input Scheduling" section of this chapter will discuss Receive thresholds.

Example 8-2   *Configuring a 10/100 Port as a CoS Trusted Port*

```
Switch1 (enable) set port qos 10/3 trust trust-cos
Trust type trust-cos not supported on this port.
Receive thresholds are enabled on port 10/3.
Port 10/3 qos set to untrusted.
```

The repercussion of a 10/100 card not supporting trust-type is that incoming frames with CoS values set will be reset to 0. A workaround can be implemented using an access list as outlined in the following steps for incoming frames to retain their CoS values:

Step 1   Enable the 10/100 card for **trust-cos**, as follows:

```
Switch1 (enable) set port qos 10/3 trust trust-cos
Trust type trust-cos not supported on this port.
Receive thresholds are enabled on port 10/3.
Port 10/3 qos set to untrusted.
```

Step 2   Create an access list:

```
Switch1 (enable) set qos acl ip list1 trust-cos any
```

Step 3   Commit the changes to nonvolatile random-access memory (NVRAM):

```
Switch1 (enable) commit qos acl list1
```

Step 4   Map the access list to the port:

```
Switch1 (enable) set qos acl map list1 10/3
ACL list1 is successfully mapped to port 10/3.
The old ACL mapping is replaced by the new one.
```

Example 8-3 shows an excerpt from the **show port qos** command. A point of interest in the output is that access list, list1, is applied to port 10/3 and for IP traffic only.

Example 8-3 *QoS Parameters for a Single Port*

```
Switch1 (enable) show port qos 10/3
Config:
Port  ACL name                           Type
----- -------------------------------    ----
10/3  list1                              IP
```

QoS access list can either be implemented for a specific port, **port-based**, or to the entire VLAN, **vlan-based**. Access list, list1, was created for port-based only, which means the access list will not affect other hosts on the same VLAN. By default, Cisco switches are configured for port-based. However, if needed, the **set port qos** command can be used to change the QoS access list configuration to vlan-based.

```
Switch1 (enable) set port qos 10/3 vlan-based
```

Input Scheduling

Input scheduling is the next step involved in handling the frame after the frame has arrived at the ingress port, assuming the port has been configured for trust-cos (refer to Figure 8-1). Input scheduling basically assigns incoming frames to queues. If trust-cos is not configured, the incoming frames will bypass the Receive threshold (also known as the drop threshold) queue and are forwarded directly to the switching engine. Each queue has its own drop threshold level, which means that frames are dropped after the threshold value is exceeded.

The number of queues and their associated drop threshold values are dependent on the hardware used. Example 8-4 shows features available for port 10/3 off the WS-X6248-xx module. Note the QoS scheduling field shaded in the example. There are two defined queues: rx-(1q4t),tx-(2q2t). Input scheduling deals with rx-(1q4t). The tx-(2q2t) will be discussed later in the chapter. The 1q4t is defined as 1 queue with 4 drop thresholds. Newer line cards have 1p1q4t, translating to 1 priority queue, 1 normal queue, with 4 drop threshold queues. Each of these thresholds is set to drop incoming packets. The packets are dropped based on their CoS setting and the amount of buffer used.

Example 8-4 *Type of QoS Scheduling*

```
Switch1 (enable) show port capabilities 10/3
Model              WS-X6248-RJ-45
Port               3/1
Type               10/100BaseTX
Speed              auto,10,100
Duplex             half,full
Trunk encap type   802.1Q,ISL
```

Example 8-4 *Type of QoS Scheduling (Continued)*

```
Trunk mode             on,off,desirable,auto,nonegotiate
Channel                yes
Broadcast suppression  percentage(0-100)
Flow control           receive-(off,on),send-(off)
Security               yes
Dot1x                  yes
Membership             static,dynamic
Fast start             yes
QOS scheduling         rx-(1q4t),tx-(2q2t)
CoS rewrite            yes
ToS rewrite            DSCP
UDLD                   yes
Inline power           no
AuxiliaryVlan          1..1000,1025..4094,untagged,dot1p,none
SPAN                   source,destination
COPS port group        3/1-48
Link debounce timer    yes
Dot1q-all-tagged       yes
```

Since 1q4t has only 1 queue, all incoming frames will be placed in this single queue. However, if the queue starts to become congested, frames will be dropped based on their CoS values. The following lists the defaults for each CoS value:

- CoS 0 and 1 are mapped to threshold 1 (set at 50 percent)
- CoS 2 and 3 are mapped to threshold 2 (set at 60 percent)
- CoS 4 and 5 are mapped to threshold 3 (set at 80 percent)
- CoS 6 and 7 are mapped to threshold 4 (set at 100 percent)

Any incoming packet with CoS setting of 0 or 1 that is mapped to threshold 1 will be dropped if the port buffer is at 50 percent or higher. The **show qos info** command in Example 8-5 shows the default mapping for CoS and its associated drop threshold level on a Catalyst switch.

Example 8-5 *Default Parameters for 1q4t rx*

```
Switch1 (enable) show qos info config 1q4t rx
QoS setting in NVRAM for 1q4t receive:
QoS is enabled
Queue and Threshold Mapping for 1q4t (rx):
Queue Threshold CoS
----- --------- ---------------
1     1         0 1
1     2         2 3
1     3         4 5
1     4         6 7
```

continues

Example 8-5 *Default Parameters for **1q4t rx** (Continued)*

```
Rx drop thresholds:
Queue #  Thresholds - percentage
-------  ------------------------------------
50% 60% 80% 100%
Rx WRED thresholds:
WRED feature is not supported for this port type.
Rx queue size ratio:
Rx queue size-ratio feature is not supported for this port type.
```

The 1p1q4t has an extra queue called the strict priority queue, which is associated with CoS value of 5. The strict priority queue, queue 2, takes precedence over the standard queue, queue 1. Traffic in the strict priority queue is always serviced first. Typically critical user traffic is marked with CoS 5 at Layer 2 and the equivalent of DSCP value of 40 at Layer 3. The reason user traffic is not marked with higher CoS values such as CoS 6 or 7 is that these values are generally associated with control traffic. The bulletins outline the two queues and their associated drop threshold levels:

- CoS 0 and 1 are mapped to threshold 1/standard queue (set at 50 percent)
- CoS 2 and 3 are mapped to threshold 2/standard queue (set at 60 percent)
- CoS 4 is mapped to threshold 3/standard queue (set at 80 percent)
- CoS 5 is mapped to priority queue (set at 100 percent)
- CoS 6 and 7 are mapped to threshold 4/standard queue (set at 100 percent)

Both the queue and threshold settings can be changed, if necessary. For example, using the **set qos map** command, the CoS 4 has now been mapped to drop threshold level 2:

```
Switch1 (enable) set qos map 1p1q4t rx 1 2 cos 4
QoS rx priority queue and threshold mapped to cos successfully.
```

The switch, however, will not allow for the priority queue to be associated with any threshold other than its own threshold. The following configuration attempted to link threshold 4 with CoS value of 6 with priority 2 queue. This example would have worked if the threshold had been set at 1:

```
Switch1 (enable) set qos map 1p1q4t rx 2 4 cos 6
Incompatible queue/threshold number with port-type specified.
```

The following changes the drop threshold for threshold 1 from 50 percent to 60 percent:

```
Switch1 (enable) set qos drop-threshold 1q4t rx queue 1 60 60 80 100
Receive drop thresholds for queue 1 set at 60% 60% 80% 100%
```

Marking and Policing

The next step after input scheduling is for the frame to be forwarded to the switching engine (PFC/PFC2). The switching engine will mark every frame with an internal DSCP value.

This marking will help the switching engine to appropriately service the frame. The internal DSCP value is not arbitrary. It is derived from the following sources: DSCP or IP precedence value of the packet at Layer 3, CoS value of frame at Layer 2, or from a user-defined access list.

Example 8-6 shows the mapping between CoS and DSCP values. This mapping that occurs is strictly based on the architectural design of the Catalyst 6500 switch.

Example 8-6 *CoS to DSCP Map*

```
Switch1 (enable) show qos map runtime cos-dscp-map
CoS - DSCP map:
CoS   DSCP
---   ----
  0   0
  1   8
  2   16
  3   24
  4   32
  5   40
  6   48
  7   56
```

Figure 8-2 shows the flow of the traffic through the switching engine. It might be bit a confusing to have classification on the switching engine along with marking and policing, but classification has to be done on the switching engine at times (for example, the list1 access list given earlier in the chapter to help assist the port to distinguish incoming traffic).

After the traffic has been marked, the switching engine checks to see if policing is configured for the traffic and if the traffic is within the bandwidth guidelines. The motivation behind policing is to curb bandwidth use. The policing mechanism places a ceiling on the amount of bandwidth utilized. Traffic is either dropped or its priority marked down if the bandwidth policy is exceeded.

A token bucket conceptual model is used to demonstrate the policing behavior (see Figure 8-3). The objective is to ensure the bucket does not overflow. There are three elements of interest:

- **Incoming rate**—Incoming packet rate is what the user is currently sending.
- **Bucket size**—The bucket size equates to the burst allowed.
- **Output rate**—Output rate is the allowed bandwidth given to the user. The rate interval is set at 0.25 milliseconds for a Catalyst 6500 switch.

Figure 8-2 *Traffic Flow Through the Switching Engine*

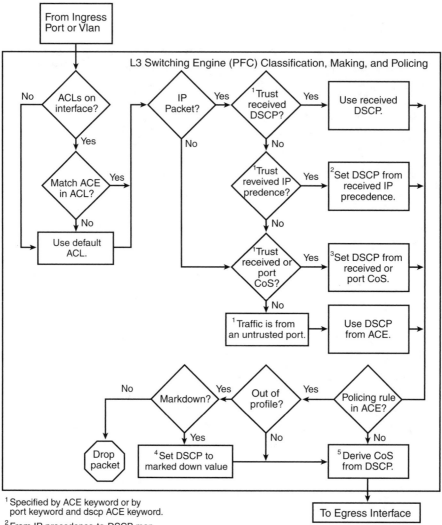

[1] Specified by ACE keyword or by
port keyword and dscp ACE keyword.

[2] From IP precedence-to-DSCP map.

[3] From CoS-to-DSCP map.

[4] From DSCP markdown map.

[5] From DSCP-to-CoS map.

Figure 8-3   *Token Bucket Model*

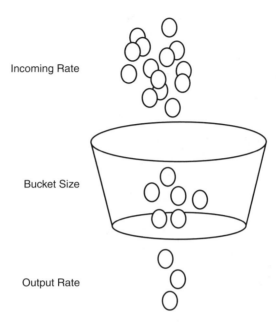

Incoming Rate

Bucket Size

Output Rate

Initially, the bucket will be empty because there is no traffic flow. If the incoming rate is below the rate limiting parameter configured, the leak rate is able to keep up with incoming rate of packets. As a result, the bucket is not filled. If the rate coming in is higher than the allowed leak rate, an overflow will occur. At this point, policing kicks in.

There are two types of policing defined in Catalyst switches: microflow and aggregate. A microflow policing mechanism looks at each individual flow. These individual flows are defined by their Layer 3 and Layer 4 properties. A Catalyst switch can support up to 63 microflows on Catalyst 6500. Aggregate policing, on the other hand, looks at many individuals flows at a time. Aggregate policing supports up to 1023 policing configurations.

The following steps detail, in brief, how to configure and apply a microflow policer for traffic that has a DSCP value of 40:

Step 1   Define the policing parameters:

```
Switch1 (enable) set qos policer microflow police1 rate 64 burst 128
    drop
QoS policer for microflow police1 created successfully.
```

Step 2 Assign an access list with its associated policing parameter:

```
Switch1 (enable) set qos acl ip list1 dscp 40 microflow police1 ip any
    10.1.1.1
```

Step 3 Apply the access list to the NVRAM:

```
Switch1 (enable) commit qos acl list1
```

Step 4 Map the access list to the specific port:

```
Switch1 (enable) set qos acl map list1 10/3
```

All IP traffic from port 10/3 to 10.1.1.1 will be policed at 64 kbps with a burst up to 128 kbps. On the other hand, the following aggregate configuration applies policing to all IP traffic:

Step 1 Define an aggregate policy. The rate has been configured to be 2000, but because rate and burst are increments of 32, the switch sets the rate to 1984, which is the closest increment of 32 to the 2000 user-defined rate value:

```
Switch1 (enable) set qos policer aggregate police2 rate 2000 burst 4000
    drop
QoS policer for aggregate police2 created successfully.
```

Step 2 Link the aggregate policy to an access list:

```
Switch1 (enable) set qos acl ip list1 dscp 40 aggregate police2 ip any
    any
```

Step 3 Apply the access list to the NVRAM:

```
Switch1 (enable) commit qos acl list1
```

Step 4 Map the access list to the specific port:

```
Switch1 (enable) set qos acl map list1 10/3
```

The aggregate policy has been defined that allows for all IP traffic from port 10/3 to not exceed 2 Mbps throughput with 4 Mbps burst.

Marking

The switching engine forwards the traffic to the egress port. The internal DSCP values assigned to the traffic at the switching engine are marked back to their respected CoS or DSCP/IP precedence values at the egress port. For example, the incoming frames at the ingress port had a value of CoS 5, the switching engine assigned an internal DSCP value of 40 for these frames as the switching engine switched these frames. At the egress port, the DSCP value of 40 was marked back to the original value of CoS 5. Same principle applies for incoming packets that have IP precedence or DSCP values set. Figure 8-4 shows the flow of the traffic coming from the switching engine, PFC, or MSFC.

Figure 8-4   *Traffic Forwarded to Egress Port*

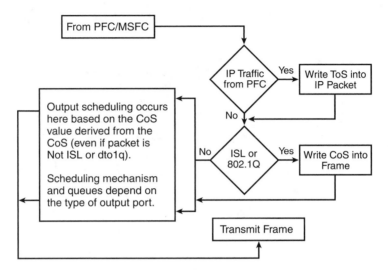

Output Scheduling

After marking, the traffic is forwarded to the appropriate transmit queue on the egress port (see Figure 8-5). Depending on the hardware module used, the number of queues and drop thresholds varies. The reason behind the queues on the egress port is to service higher priority traffic first. It is equally important that during congestion, certain steps should be taken to minimize dropping of critical traffic. This is done via congestion avoidance implemented on Cisco switches.

Figure 8-5   *Traffic Handling on the Egress Port*

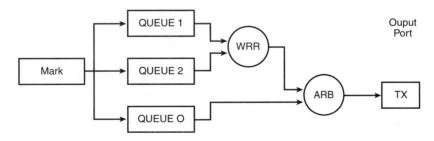

The older line cards such as WS-X6348-xx have two queues with two drop thresholds, 2q2t. In 2q2t, the size of queue 1, which corresponds to low-priority traffic, is 80 percent of total transmit queue size. Queue 2 is allocated the remaining 20 percent for high-priority traffic.

As noted in the output (see Example 8-7), CoS values 4-7 are sent to queue 2. The drop threshold is set at 80 percent for CoS 0 and 1 on queue 1, and CoS 4 and 5 on queue 2. The drop threshold is at 100 percent for CoS values 2 and 3 on queue 1 and 6 and 7 on queue 2.

Example 8-7   *QoS Information for 2q2t tx*

```
Switch1 (enable) show qos  information config 2q2t tx
QoS setting in NVRAM for 2q2t transmit:
QoS is enabled
Queue and Threshold Mapping for 2q2t (tx):
Queue Threshold CoS
----- --------- ---------------
1    1          0 1
1    2          2 3
2    1          4 5
2    2          6 7
Tx drop thresholds:
Queue #  Thresholds - percentage
-------  ------------------------------------
1         80% 100%
2         80% 100%
Tx WRED thresholds:
WRED feature is not supported for this port type.
Tx queue size ratio:
Queue #  Sizes - percentage
-------  ------------------------------------
1         80%
2         20%
WRR Configuration of ports with 2q2t:
Queue #  Ratios
-------  ------------------------------------
1         5
2         255
```

Example 8-7 shows default values for 2q2t; these values can be changed, if necessary, using the **set qos map** command. For example, frames with CoS 2 value are now associated with drop threshold 1 rather than its default of 2:

```
set qos map 2q2t tx 1 1 cos 2
```

Congestion avoidance helps the two queues in Example 8-7 from filling up. Typically, if congestion avoidance mechanism is not used, when the two queues are filled up, any incoming traffic to the queues is dropped. This is known as a tail drop. Congestion avoidance mechanisms such as Random Early Detection (RED) and Weighted Random Early Detection (WRED) help with minimizing the risk of queues being filled up.

Example 8-7 shows that WRED feature is not supported on this port, which means it can only do tail drop. Random RED and WRED accomplish two things:

- Proactive queue management

- Queue size control (minimizing queuing delays)

RED simply drops packets randomly regardless of the traffic priority. However, with WRED, high-priority packets are preferred over low-priority packets, and the dropping of the packets is done at random. This randomness prevents global synchronization, which prevents TCP conversations throttling back at the same time. It is a big plus to have hardware that supports WRED.

The newer cards have 1 priority queue, 2 standard queues, and 2 thresholds, 1p2q2t. For 1p2q2t, the standard/low priority queue size is 70 percent of total transmit queue size. The standard/high priority queue and strict priority queue each have 15 percent of the total transmit queue size. Also, note (see Example 8-8) that queue 3 is associated with strict priority queue. The strict priority queue is defined for the CoS 5 traffic.

Example 8-8   *QoS Information for 1p2q2t tx*

```
Switch1 (enable) show qos information config 1p2q2t tx
QoS setting in NVRAM for 1p2q2t transmit:
QoS is enabled
Queue and Threshold Mapping for 1p2q2t (tx):
Queue Threshold CoS
----- --------- ---------------
1     1         0 1
1     2         2 3
2     1         4 6
2     2         7
3     -         5
Tx drop thresholds:
Tx drop-thresholds feature is not supported for this port type.
Tx WRED thresholds:
Queue #  Thresholds - percentage
-------  ---------------------------------------------
1        40%:70% 70%:100%
2        40%:70% 70%:100%
Tx queue size ratio:
Queue #  Sizes - percentage
-------  ---------------------------------------------
1        70%
2        15%
3        15%
WRR Configuration of ports with 1p2q2t:
Queue #  Ratios
-------  ---------------------------------------------
1        5
2        255
```

After the traffic is in the appropriate queues, the Weighted Round Robin (WRR) is used to service each of the queues. WRR is used for standard/high and standard/low queues. The strict priority is always serviced first before the other two queues. The default behavior is to service standard/high queue 70 percent of time, and standard/low the remaining 30 percent.

QoS Caveats

Caveats regarding QoS and the Catalyst 6500 switch include the following:

- **Etherchannel**—Etherchannel ports require identical QoS configurations on the individual ports.
- **IGMP snooping**—QoS does not support IGMP traffic, if IGMP snooping is enabled on the switch.
- **MSFC**—Any traffic sourced from MSFC to the egress port has a CoS value of 0.
- **Flexwan**—Traffic incoming from a Flexwan module has its CoS value always set to 0.

Summary

This chapter explains some of the basics involved with enabling QoS on a Catalyst switch. QoS does not create additional bandwidth. Prioritization of certain applications and protocols are becoming essential in today's network. Converged networks that include voice, video, and legacy mainframe traffic have specific delay and bandwidth requirements. Hence, the need for QoS is critical.

This chapter primarily focused on QoS implementation on the Catalyst 6500 switch. In a nutshell, incoming traffic with QoS label at Layer 2 or at Layer 3 is received on the ingress port. The ingress port either allows for the incoming traffic to retain its label or assigns one to the traffic. If trust-cos is enabled on the port, the traffic is forwarded to input scheduling. The next step in the process is to forward the traffic to the switching engine (PFC/PFC2). The PFC/PFC2 marks each frame or packet with an internal DSCP value. If PFC is configured for policing, it will ensure the traffic is within the policy guidelines. The traffic is finally forwarded to the egress port, where the internal DSCP value is marked back to the original label on the traffic. The traffic is put in the egress queue for output scheduling, and subsequently is serviced by WRR.

This chapter covers the following topics:

- Understanding IGMPv1 and IGMPv2
- Multicast flooding
- IGMP snooping
- CGMP
- IGMP snooping versus CGMP

CHAPTER 9

Implementing Multicast on Catalyst Switches

Multicast deployments have increased exponentially over the past 4 years. A single host sources traffic to a multicast group, which has multiple members associated with the group. Instead of forwarding unicast traffic to each host on the network, multicast allows the source to send the traffic once, and any host that joins that specific multicast group can receive the stream. As a result, multicast is a one-to-many model that helps reduce network traffic. This chapter will cover Internet Group Management Protocol (IGMP) snooping and Cisco Group Management Protocol (CGMP) in detail.

Understanding IGMPv1 and IGMPv2

Communication between the router and the host is done via the IGMP, which has two versions. In IGMPv1, two IGMP packets are defined. The first packet is a membership query sent by the query router every 1 minute on the segment to find out what multicast groups are still in use. The second packet is a membership report. The hosts use a membership report to inform the query router of their interest for a specific multicast traffic. No leave process exists in IGMPv1. If the query router does not receive a membership report within 3 minutes, the router will prune the interface. A pruned interface stops receiving the multicast feed for that group. The **show mroute** command displays which interface has been pruned for a specific multicast stream. In IGMPv1, no selection process exists for the query router. The designated router (DR) is responsible for forwarding multicast traffic and also performs the query router function.

Example 9-1 shows the packet format for IGMPv1. As noted in Example 9-1, Protocol number 2 in IP protocol is defined for IGMP. The source address is 10.1.3.5 and the multicast group is 239.1.1.1. Any host interested in receiving the multicast stream from 10.1.3.5 will join the 239.1.1.1 group.

Example 9-1 *IGMP Sniffer Trace*

```
IP: Protocol       = 2 (IGMP)
IP: Header checksum = 8455 (correct)
IP: Source address  = [10.1.3.5]
IP: Destination address = [239.1.1.1]
IP: No options
IP:
```

continues

Example 9-1 *IGMP Sniffer Trace (Continued)*

```
        IGMP: ----- IGMP header -----
            IGMP:
            IGMP: Version       = 1
          IGMP: Type        = 2 (Ver1 Membership Report)        IGMP: Unused
  = 0x00
            IGMP: Checksum      = AC99 (correct)
            IGMP: Group Address = [239.1.1.1]
            IGMP:
            IP: Protocol       = 2 (IGMP)
!Protocol is IGMP
            IP: Header checksum = 8455 (correct)
```

IGMPv2 has additional functionality defined by the following IGMP packet types and is currently deployed in today's networks:

- **Query election process**—All routers on the segment send query messages to all hosts, 224.0.0.1. The router with the lowest IP address wins and becomes the query router. Re-election process starts after 250 seconds if the query router is not heard from.

- **Maximum Response Time field**—This field tweaks the report suppression mechanism (default is 10 seconds). The purpose of this field is to reduce burstiness, especially on segments with a lot of multicast receivers. In large segments, it is desirable to tune this value higher to prevent multiple hosts sending membership reports.

- **Group-specific query message**—After the query router has received a leave group message, the router sends a group-specific query message to ensure no other hosts require the multicast flow. The maximum response time field for a group-specific query message is 1 second to keep the latency short. The other query message is a general membership query message also found in IGMPv1.

- **Leave group messages**—The host sends a leave group message to all routers 224.0.0.2 that it is leaving a specific multicast group. The query router sends back a group-specific query message to ensure no other hosts are part of the multicast group. It does this twice for a total of 2 seconds and then it stops sending that specific multicast flow down to the segment.

Multicast Flooding

Because no specific host is associated with the multicast MAC address in the content-addressable memory (CAM) table, multicast traffic is flooded throughout the VLAN. (See Figure 9-1.) This type of setup creates unnecessary traffic on the VLAN and wastes precious network resources. Each host machine has to process the packet as it arrives on the interface card, thus, wasting CPU cycles. If the volume of the multicast stream is high enough, it could potentially cause other relevant and control traffic to be dropped. This problem worsens if the VLAN is extended to various other campus switches.

Figure 9-1   *Each Host Receives the Multicast Stream*

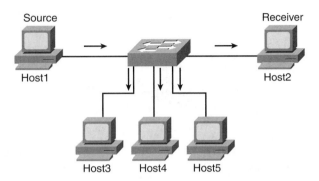

One easy method to address this problem is to manually map the ports that require the multicast traffic to the multicast MAC address. For example, Host2 on port 10/1 is interested in receiving the multicast stream 239.1.1.1 as shown in Figure 9-2.

Figure 9-2   *Multicast Traffic Is Sent Only to Host2*

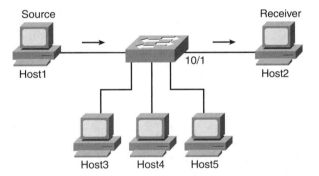

To manually configure ports to receive the multicast stream, it is important to know how to derive the Layer 2 MAC address for the multicast group 239.1.1.1. The first 4 bits of the 32-bit address are defined as a Class D address (1110); now, only 28 bits of meaningful address space remain. A Layer 2 MAC address has 48 bits. The first 25 bits are static (01005e), leaving only 23 bits for the IP address to be placed. Because there are 28 bits of meaningful IP addresses, 5 bits must be thrown away to allow the remaining 23 bits to fit. As a result of the 5 bits thrown away, 32 multicast IP addresses (2^5) are mapped to a single Layer 2 MAC address.

The calculation in Figure 9-3 shows how to derive the Layer 2 MAC address for multicast group 239.1.1.1.

Figure 9-3 *Calculating MAC Address for Multicast Group*

25 Bits (Static = 01005e) + Last 23 Bits from IP Address

IP Address 239.1.1.1

11101111.00000001.00000001.00000001 ← First 9 bits are thrown away.
0000001.00000001.00000001 ← Convert to hex.
01-00-5e-01-01-01 ← Finally, the MAC address.

Port 10/1 is configured to accept the 239.1.1.1 stream on VLAN 3. (See Example 9-2.) All other ports should not receive this traffic anymore because the CAM table has only one port associated with the multicast traffic. After the configuration change, the **show mac** command shows port 10/1 as the recipient for the multicast traffic.

Example 9-2 *Creating a Static CAM Entry*

```
Switch1 (enable) set cam static 01-00-5e-01-01-01 10/1 3
Static multicast entry added to CAM table.
Switch1 (enable) show mac 10/1
Port     Rcv-Unicast           Rcv-Multicast         Rcv-Broadcast
-------- --------------------- --------------------- ---------------------
10/1                        2                     5                       0
Port     Xmit-Unicast          Xmit-Multicast        Xmit-Broadcast
-------- --------------------- --------------------- ---------------------
10/1                        1                 13766                       0
Port     Rcv-Octet             Xmit-Octet
-------- --------------------- ---------------------
10/1                      504              20684066
```

Realistically, manually associating ports with specific multicast streams is not a viable option. Each time a new multicast stream is generated, manual intervention is required to configure specific ports to receive the traffic. In a different situation, if Host3 now wants to receive 239.1.1.1 traffic or Host2 no longer wants the traffic, this, too, must be manually configured. Multicast support on a switch needs to be efficient, dynamic, and relatively easy to implement.

IGMP Snooping

IGMP snooping prevents multicast flows from flooding to all ports on a VLAN by monitoring the Layer 3 IGMP packets. Multicast streams are sent to ports that explicitly request the flow. The switch via the IGMP snooping mechanism listens to the conversation between the router and the host machine. The switch learns at Layer 3 which port is signaling for or leaving a multicast group. The switching engine forwards this message to the Network Management Processor (NMP), where the port is added to or removed from the Layer 2 multicast forwarding group based on the IGMP message type.

The first step that is required for IGMP snooping is that the switch needs to learn the router port. Typically, a Protocol Independent Multicast (PIM) hello message signals the switch where the router port is located. The following messages are used for locating the router port:

- IGMP Group Membership Queries (01-00-5e-00-00-01 or 224.0.0.1)
- PIM v1 Queries (01-00-5e-00-00-02 or 224.0.0.2)
- PIM v2 Queries (01-00-5e-00-00-0d or 224.0.0.13)
- DVMRP messages (01-00-5e-00-00-04 or 224.0.0.4)
- MOSPF messages (01-00-5e-00-00-05 or 224.0.0.5 and 01-00-5e-00-00-06 or 224.0.0.6)

Figure 9-4 shows that the source and receivers are directly connected to the same switch. The switch has a multilayer switch feature card (MSFC), which will handle inter-VLAN communication. Therefore, the MSFC, port 15/1, will be the router port.

Figure 9-4   *IGMP Snooping*

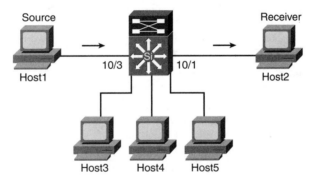

Membership Report

This section reviews various IGMP snooping scenarios.

Scenario 1: IGMP Snooping Process Between Source and Receiver on the Same VLAN

This scenario will go step by step through the IGMP snooping process (refer to Figure 9-4). The first objective is to know what the configuration looks like on the router, as shown in Example 9-3. The router is configured with PIMv2 and the PIM query interval is set at 30 seconds. The DR is the local router, MSFC, 10.1.3.10. At this point, only VLAN 3 is configured for multicast.

Example 9-3 *IGMP Configuration on the Router and Switch*

```
msfc_15#show ip pim interface vlan3
Address            Interface                Version/Mode    Nbr   Query    DR
                                                            Count Intvl
10.1.3.10          Vlan3                    v2/Sparse-Dense 1     30       10.1.3.10
```

In Catalyst 6500 switches, IGMP snooping is enabled by default. (See Example 9-4.) Note that RGMP and GMRP are beyond the scope of this book and will not be discussed.

Example 9-4 *Supervisor Multicast Information*

```
Switch1 (enable) show multicast protocols status
IGMP enabled
IGMP fastleave disabled
RGMP disabled
GMRP disabled
```

Example 9-5 shows the IGMP max query response set at 10 seconds. A router must receive a membership report within the max query response time interval, or else it will prune the interface. The Last member query response interval allows for the router to check once more before pruning the interface. The Multicast groups joined shows the multicast groups that the router knows on VLAN 3.

Example 9-5 *IGMP Interface Information*

```
msfc_15#show ip igmp interface vlan 3
Vlan3 is up, line protocol is up
  Internet address is 10.1.3.10/24
  IGMP is enabled on interface
  Current IGMP host version is 2
  Current IGMP router version is 2
  IGMP query interval is 60 seconds
  IGMP querier timeout is 120 seconds
  IGMP max query response time is 10 seconds
  Last member query response interval is 1000 ms
  Inbound IGMP access group is not set
  IGMP activity: 2 joins, 0 leaves
  Multicast routing is enabled on interface
  Multicast TTL threshold is 0
  Multicast designated router (DR) is 10.1.3.10 (this system)
  IGMP querying router is 10.1.3.10
  Multicast groups joined (number of users):
      239.1.1.1(1) 224.0.1.40(1)
```

The **show igmp groupinfo**, a hidden command, will show whether or not the multicast traffic from the source has any receivers. In Example 9-6, the multicast source only field is set at false, which means that receivers exist for the 239.1.1.1 traffic. If the value was set at true, the source is sending traffic but no receivers exist to get the multicast stream. The **show IGMP groupinfo** command can be useful when troubleshooting multicast-related issues.

Example 9-6   *Multicast Source Only*

```
Switch1 (enable) show igmp groupinfo 3 01-00-5e-01-01-01
MAC Address:                01-00-5e-01-01-01
Multicast Flag:             TRUE
confMask:                   [0-4-0-0]
ltl_index:                  0x500
mcast_info->protocol_type 2 = PROTO_TYPE_IGMP
mcast_info->protocol_type->info::
tx_v1_report:               FALSE
tx_v2_report:               TRUE
wait_count:                 0
mcast_source_only:          FALSE
IP Address:                 239.1.1.1
Host List::                 15/1
Router Port  List::         10/1,15/1
User Conf Port List::       <null>
V1 Host List::
report_rx_portlist::        15/1
```

The following steps outline the IGMP snooping process for the first host on VLAN 3 that sends a membership report for group 239.1.1.1:

Step 1   Host2 sends an unsolicited IGMP membership report to 239.1.1.1. The MSFC, port 15/1, is the router port for this traffic:

```
Switch1 (enable) show multicast router
Port        Vlan
---------- ----------------
15/1         3
Total Number of Entries = 3
'*' - Configured
'+' - RGMP-capable
```

Step 2   The switch that intercepted the IGMP message creates an EARL entry for Host2:

```
MCAST-IGMPQ:recvd an IGMP V2 Report on the port 10/1 vlanNo 3 GDA
   239.1.1.1
     In ModifyMulticastEarlEntry
     Creating new entry because it's the first Node
     Creating initial node in ModifyMulticast
     Updating portlist for initial hostlist add
```

The entry now is in the multicast forwarding table for the Group Destination Address (GDA), 239.1.1.1 (01-00-5e-01-01-01):

```
Switch1 (enable) show multicast group 01-00-5e-01-01-01
VLAN  Dest MAC/Route Des   [CoS]  Destination Ports or VCs/[Protocol Type]
----  -----------------    -----  ----------------------------------------
3     01-00-5e-01-01-01            10/1,15/1
```

Multicast MAC addresses that appear in the forwarding table are stored as static entries in the CAM table. From the switch perspective, 239.1.1.1 is now associated with ports 10/1 and 15/1 on VLAN 3:

```
Switch1 (enable) show cam static 3
* = Static Entry. + = Permanent Entry. # = System Entry. R = Router Entry.
X = Port Security Entry $ = Dot1x Security Entry
VLAN  Dest MAC/Route Des   [CoS]  Destination Ports or VCs/[Protocol Type]
----  -----------------    -----  ----------------------------------------
3     01-00-5e-00-01-28            10/1,15/1
3     01-00-5e-01-01-01            10/1,15/1
```

Step 3 The switch then sends the IGMP packet to the MSFC on port 15/1:

```
        MCAST-RELAY:Relaying packet on port 15/1 vlanNo 3
        MCAST-SEND: Inband Transmit Succeeded for IGMP RELAY msg on port
    15/1 vlanNo 3
```

Step 4 The router receives the unsolicited IGMP Join from the receiver, Host2 with an IP address of 10.1.3.2:

```
    *Sep 30 05:58:47.830: IGMP: Received v2 Report on Vlan3 from 10.1.3.2
      for 239.1.
    1.1
```

Step 5 The MSFC updates its IGMP membership table. The IGMP group membership provides information on the last host that requested the multicast traffic for that subnet:

```
    msfc_15#show ip igmp group
    IGMP Connected Group Membership
    Group Address    Interface         Uptime    Expires   Last Reporter
    239.1.1.1        Vlan3             00:21:54  00:02:39  10.1.3.2
```

Step 6 Next, the MSFC populates the mroute table, which is the equivalent of the IP route table for multicast. It will create the (*, g) and (S, G) entries for 239.1.1.1 and forward the traffic out on VLAN 3:

```
    msfc_15#show ip mroute 239.1.1.1
    IP Multicast Routing Table
    Flags: D - Dense, S - Sparse, s - SSM Group, C - Connected, L - Local,
           P - Pruned, R - RP-bit set, F - Register flag, T - SPT-bit set,
           J - Join SPT, M - MSDP created entry, X - Proxy Join Timer Running
```

```
                    A - Advertised via MSDP, U - URD, I - Received Source Specific Host
                       Report
             Outgoing interface flags: H - Hardware switched
             Timers: Uptime/Expires
             Interface state: Interface, Next-Hop or VCD, State/Mode
             (*, 239.1.1.1), 00:06:25/00:02:59, RP 0.0.0.0, flags: DJC
               Incoming interface: Null, RPF nbr 0.0.0.0
               Outgoing interface list:
                 Vlan3, Forward/Sparse-Dense, 00:06:25/00:00:00
             (10.1.3.5, 239.1.1.1), 00:00:18/00:02:41, flags: PCT
               Incoming interface: Vlan3, RPF nbr 0.0.0.0
               Outgoing interface list: Null
```

Step 7 Multicast multilayer switching (MMLS) is enabled by default on
Catalyst 6500 switches. In this case, because both source and destination
are on the same VLAN, no hardware shortcut is created on the MSFC.
This flow is already being handled by hardware switching. As a result,
there will be no multicast MLS entry:

```
msfc_15#show mls ip multicast group 239.1.1.1
Multicast hardware switched flows:
Total hardware switched flows : 0
Switch1 (enable) show mls multicast entry
Router-IP       Dest-IP         Source-IP        Pkts            Bytes
         InVlan Type OutVlans
-------------- --------------- --------------- ------------------- -
--------- ------ ---- ---------------------------------------------
Total Entries Displayed: 0 (0 complete flow (C) and 0 partial flow (P))
```

Scenario 2: IGMP Snooping Process Between the Source and a Second Receiver on the Same VLAN

Figure 9-5 illustrates what happens when a second host from the same VLAN sends a
membership report to the router.

Figure 9-5 *Host3 Sends a Membership Report*

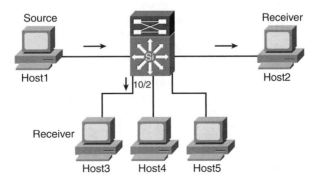

The following explains the process:

Step 1 Host3, on port 10/2, sends an unsolicited IGMP membership report to 239.1.1.1.

Step 2 The switch intercepts the IGMP message:

```
MCAST-IGMPQ:recvd an IGMP V2 Report on the port 10/2 vlanNo 3 GDA
    239.1.1.1
        In ModifyMulticastEarlEntry
```

The multicast forwarding table is updated with port 10/2:

```
Switch1 (enable) show multicast group 01-00-5e-01-01-01
VLAN  Dest MAC/Route Des    [CoS]  Destination Ports or VCs/[Protocol Type]
----  ------------------    -----  ---------------------------------------
3     01-00-5e-01-01-01            10/1-2,15/1
```

Step 3 The switch then sends the IGMP packet to the MSFC on port 15/1:

```
    MCAST-RELAY:Relaying packet on port 15/1 vlanNo 3
    MCAST-SEND: Inband Transmit Succeeded for IGMP RELAY msg on port
15/1 vlanNo 3
```

Step 4 The router receives the unsolicited IGMP Join from the receiver:

```
*Sep 30 06:07:41.434: IGMP: Received v2 Report on Vlan3 from 10.1.3.3
    for 239.1.
1.1
```

Step 5 MSFC updates its IGMP membership table:

```
msfc_15#show ip igmp group
IGMP Connected Group Membership
Group Address    Interface         Uptime    Expires   Last Reporter
239.1.1.1        Vlan3                       00:31:16  00:02:11  10.1.3.3
```

Step 6 Because the MSFC already has an outgoing interface (OIF) for VLAN 3, it will not do anything on the mroute table.

Step 7 No changes are made to the MMLS table. The MSFC does not send any shortcut information to the MMLS-Switching Engine (MMLS-SE) because Host3 is also part of VLAN 3:

```
msfc_15#show mls ip multicast group 239.1.1.1
Multicast hardware switched flows:
Total hardware switched flows : 0
Switch#1 (enable) show mls multicast entry
Router-IP      Dest-IP        Source-IP      Pkts                Bytes
         InVlan Type OutVlans
--------------- -------------- -------------- -------------------- -----------
---------- ------- ---- ---------------------------------------------
Total Entries Displayed: 0 (0 complete flow (C) and 0 partial flow (P))
```

Scenario 3: IGMP Snooping Process Between Source and Receiver on Different VLANs

Host4 from a different VLAN has requested the multicast stream 239.1.1.1. (See Figure 9-6.)

Figure 9-6   *Host4 Sends a Membership Report*

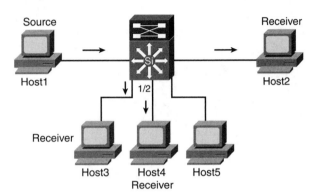

A hardware shortcut is created by the MSFC in this scenario because traffic is between different VLANs:

Step 1   Host4, on port 1/2, sends an unsolicited IGMP membership report to 239.1.1.1.

Step 2   The switch intercepts the IGMP message:

```
MCAST-IGMPQ:recvd an IGMP V2 Report on the port 1/2 vlanNo 30 GDA
    239.1.1.1
        In ModifyMulticastEarlEntry
        Creating new entry because it's the first Node
        Creating initial node in ModifyMulticast
        Updating portlist for initial hostlist add
```

The multicast forwarding table adds an additional line for VLAN 30 and its associate port of 1/2 for Host4:

```
Switch1 (enable) show multicast group
VLAN  Dest MAC/Route Des   [CoS] Destination Ports or VCs/[Protocol Type]
----  -----------------    -----  ----------------------------------------
3     01-00-5e-01-01-01           10/1-2,15/1
30    01-00-5e-01-01-01           1/2,15/1
```

Step 3 The switch then sends the IGMP packet to the MSFC on port 15/1:

```
MCAST-RELAY:Relaying packet on port 15/1 vlanNo 30
MCAST-SEND: Inband Transmit Succeeded for IGMP RELAY msg on port
15/1 vlanNo 30
```

Step 4 The router receives the unsolicited IGMP Join from the receiver:

```
*Sep 30 09:06:58.881: IGMP: Received v2 Report on Vlan30 from 10.1.4.1
for 239.1.1.15. The MSFC updates its IGMP membership table.
```

Step 5 The router updates its IGMP membership table:

```
msfc_15#show ip igmp groups
IGMP Connected Group Membership
Group Address    Interface         Uptime    Expires   Last Reporter
239.1.1.1        Vlan30            00:00:46  00:02:55  10.1.4.1
```

Step 6 Interface VLAN 30 is added to the OIF list. The letter H denotes
hardware switched:

```
msfc_15#show ip mroute 239.1.1.1
IP Multicast Routing Table
Flags: D - Dense, S - Sparse, s - SSM Group, C - Connected, L - Local,
       P - Pruned, R - RP-bit set, F - Register flag, T - SPT-bit set,
       J - Join SPT, M - MSDP created entry, X - Proxy Join Timer Running
       A - Advertised via MSDP, U - URD, I - Received Source Specific Host
           Report
Outgoing interface flags: H - Hardware switched
Timers: Uptime/Expires
Interface state: Interface, Next-Hop or VCD, State/Mode
(*, 239.1.1.1), 00:05:45/00:02:59, RP 0.0.0.0, flags: DJC
  Incoming interface: Null, RPF nbr 0.0.0.0
  Outgoing interface list:
    Vlan3, Forward/Sparse-Dense, 00:01:44/00:00:00
    Vlan30, Forward/Sparse-Dense, 00:05:45/00:00:00
(10.1.3.5, 239.1.1.1), 00:00:21/00:02:59, flags: CT
  Incoming interface: Vlan3, RPF nbr 0.0.0.0, RPF-MFD
  Outgoing interface list:
    Vlan30, Forward/Sparse-Dense, 00:00:21/00:00:00, H
```

Step 7 The packets are now hardware switched between VLAN 3, the multicast
source, and VLAN 30, Host4, for 239.1.1.1 traffic:

```
msfc_15#show mls ip multicast group 239.1.1.1
Multicast hardware switched flows:
(10.1.3.5, 239.1.1.1) Incoming interface: Vlan3, Packets switched:
  508380
Hardware switched outgoing interfaces: Vlan30
RPF-MFD installed
Total hardware switched flows : 1
```

An MMLS entry is created because the multicast packets are hardware switched:

```
Switch1 (enable) show mls multicast entry
Router-IP      Dest-IP         Source-IP       Pkts                Bytes
         InVlan Type OutVlans
--------------- --------------- --------------- -------------------- -----------
--------- ------ ---- ----------------------------------------------
10.1.3.10      239.1.1.1       10.1.3.5        534751              794639986
         3       C    30
Total Entries Displayed: 1 (1 complete flow (C) and 0 partial flow (P))
```

For the MMLS entry to be created and updated, the MMLS-route processor (MMLS-RP), MSFC, and the MMLS-SE, the supervisor, must communicate with each other to ensure consistent data on both devices. The **show multicast statistics** command displays communication information between the MMLS-RP and MMLS-SE. (See Example 9-7.)

Example 9-7 *Multicast Statistics on the Switch*

```
Switch1 (enable) show mls multicast statistics
Router IP        Router Name         Router MAC
---------------  ------------------  -----------------
10.1.3.10        ?                   00-05-5e-96-76-c0
Transmit:
                   Feature Notifications: 0
           Feature Notification Responses: 2
          Shortcut Notification Responses: 3
!Switch's response back to the MSFC regarding the shortcut messages

                     Delete Notifications: 0
                          Flow Statistics: 47
                  Total Transmit Failures: 0
Receive:
                    Feature Notifications: 2
                        Shortcut Messages: 3

! Switch received 3 shortcut messages from the MSFC

              Duplicate Shortcut Messages: 0
                    Shortcut Install TLV: 1
!One hardware shortcut created

                    Selective Delete TLV: 0
                        Group Delete TLV: 0
                              Update TLV: 0
                   Input VLAN Delete TLV: 0
                  Output VLAN Delete TLV: 0
                       Global Delete TLV: 0
                         MFD Install TLV: 1
                          MFD Delete TLV: 0
                   Global MFD Delete TLV: 0
                             Invalid TLV: 0
```

The next section discusses what happens when a receiver leaves a multicast group, and how IGMP snooping handles such an event.

IGMP Leave Process

This section explores two types of leave process. The first leave process involves a single host leaving a multicast session while other hosts from the same VLAN are still receiving the multicast traffic. In the second example, the host is the last member to leave a multicast session.

The IGMP query router, MSFC, will send queries every 60 seconds to both VLAN 3 and VLAN 30 to check for members for the multicast group 239.1.1.1 (refer to Figure 9-6). As these queries are sent by the router to the switch, the switch forwards the queries to ports that are participating in the multicast session. Upon receiving the query message, the hosts will send back an IGMP membership report. The switch again intercepts these IGMP messages from the hosts and only forwards one membership report to the MSFC. A router does not need to receive membership reports from more than one host from a single VLAN for a multicast traffic. So long as there is one host, the multicast stream still needs to be forwarded to that interface. For this reason, the switch drops the other IGMP membership reports.

Scenario 1: IGMP Snooping Leave Process Between the Source and Multiple Receivers on the Same VLAN

Figure 9-7 and the subsequent steps outlined address the issue of a receiver leaving a multicast group while another receiver on the same VLAN is still interested in the traffic.

Figure 9-7 *Host2 Sends an IGMP Leave*

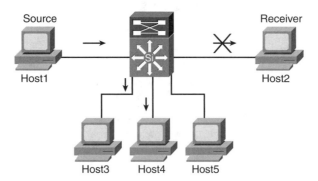

Step 1   Host2 sends a leave group message to all routers, 224.0.0.2, for multicast traffic 239.1.1.1.

Step 2   The Catalyst switch intercepts the IGMP leave message:

```
MCAST-IGMPQ:recvd an IGMP Leave on the port 10/1 vlanNo 3 GDA 239.1.1.1
```

Step 3   The switch sends a MAC-based general query to port 10/1. A random deletion timer value (1 to 3 seconds) will be set. If the host is communicating via IGMPv1, the random deletion timer is set at 10 seconds:

```
MCAST-DEL-TIMER: Deletion Timer Value set to Random Value 3
```

Step 4   If the switch does not hear a membership report during the random deletion timer, it will drop the port from its multicast forwarding table:

```
MCAST-TIMER:IGMPLeaveTimer expired on port 10/1 vlanNo 3 GDA 01-00-5e-
    01-01-01
Delete UpdatePortOnMulticast
```

Step 5   The switch does not send the IGMP leave message to the MSFC because the switch knows that Host3, which is on the same VLAN as Host2, is still accepting the 239.1.1.1 traffic. The MSFC does not even know that Host2 has left the multicast group. Also, no changes have been made to the MMLS table because Host3 on the VLAN 3 is still accepting the traffic.

Scenario 2: IGMP Snooping Leave Process Between the Source and Last Receivers

Figure 9-8 illustrates the last receiver, Host4, on VLAN 30 leaving the multicast group 239.1.1.1. When Host4 leaves the multicast group, both switch and MSFC will have to update their appropriate tables.

Figure 9-8   *Host4 Sends IGMP Leave*

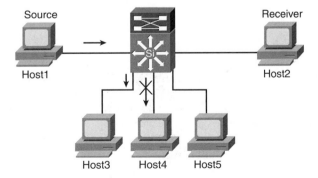

The following steps outline the IGMP snooping process when Host4 leaves the multicast group.

Step 1 Host4 sends a leave group message to all routers, 224.0.0.2, for multicast traffic 239.1.1.1.

Step 2 The Catalyst switch intercepts the IGMP leave message:

```
MCAST-IGMPQ:recvd an IGMP Leave on the port 1/2 vlanNo 30 GDA 239.1.1.1
```

Step 3 The switch sends a MAC-based general query to port 1/2:

```
MCAST-DEL-TIMER: Deletion Timer Value set to Random Value 3
```

Step 4 The switch updates its multicast forwarding table:

```
In ModifyMulticastEarlEntry
      Delete UpdatePortOnMulticast
      Delete UpdatePortOnMulticast - Last Port
```

Step 5 Because Host4 is the last member for the multicast group, the switch forwards an IGMP leave message to the MSFC:

```
MCAST-SEND:Transmitting IGMP Leave msg on port 15/1 vlanNo 30
```

Step 6 Upon receiving the IGMP leave message, the MSFC sends two group-specific queries to check for any members for VLAN 30:

```
IGMP: Received Leave from 10.1.4.1 (Vlan30) for 239.1.1.1
IGMP: Send v2 Query on Vlan4 to 239.1.1.1
IGMP: Send v2 Query on Vlan4 to 239.1.1.1
```

Step 7 Not hearing any response, MSFC deletes multicast traffic 239.1.1.1 to VLAN 30:

```
IGMP: Deleting 239.1.1.1 on Vlan30
```

Step 8 The MSFC updates the MMLS-SE engine to clear the shortcut between VLAN 3 and VLAN 30 for the multicast 239.1.1.1 traffic.

IGMP Fastleave

With IGMP fastleave enabled, the switch removes the port from the multicast forwarding table without sending a MAC-based query to the port. The purpose behind fastleave is to quickly transition the port or VLAN off the multicast stream. Most customers have not deployed fastleave today. Fastleave should not be enabled on ports that have hubs connected to them. For example, two hosts are off the same hub, which is connected to a port on a Catalyst switch with IGMP fastleave enabled. If one host leaves, the switch immediately takes the port off the multicast forwarding table. As a result, the second host on the hub will lose its multicast traffic. IGMP fastleave is disabled on trunk ports.

Address Aliasing

Address aliasing is defined as mapping 32 multicast IP addresses to a single Layer 2 MAC address. A multicast Layer 3 address could map to a system MAC address that is used by the switch, which is a potential risk. Any packets destined to the system CAM entries are directly sent to the NMP because it is assumed that the packets are part of the control traffic rather than user traffic. As a result, network outages can occur if multicast user traffic is mapped to a system CAM entry.

Look at an example to solidify the problem with address aliasing. Both Host1 and Host2 are in VLAN 3 as shown in Figure 9-9. Two types of supervisors are used in this design. Their handling of address aliasing will become apparent shortly.

Figure 9-9   *Address Aliasing*

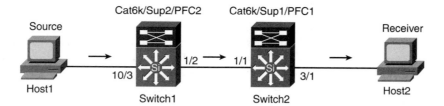

Example 9-8 shows two outputs from Switch1 and Switch2, respectively.

Example 9-8   *System CAM Entries for VLAN 3*

```
Switch1 (enable) show cam system 3
* = Static Entry. + = Permanent Entry. # = System Entry. R = Router Entry.
X = Port Security Entry $ = Dot1x Security Entry
VLAN  Dest MAC/Route Des    [CoS]  Destination Ports or VCs / [Protocol Type]
----  ----------------      -----  -------------------------------------------
3     00-00-0c-07-ac-03 R#         15/1
3     00-05-74-18-04-bc R#         15/1
3     01-00-0c-cc-cc-cc  #         1/3
3     01-00-0c-cc-cc-cd  #         1/3
3     01-00-0c-dd-dd-dd  #         1/3
3     01-80-c2-00-00-00  #         1/3
3     01-80-c2-00-00-01  #         1/3
Total Matching CAM Entries Displayed  =7

Switch2 (enable) show cam system 3
* = Static Entry. + = Permanent Entry. # = System Entry. R = Router Entry.
X = Port Security Entry $ = Dot1x Security Entry
```

continues

Example 9-8 *System CAM Entries for VLAN 3 (Continued)*

```
VLAN  Dest MAC/Route Des     [CoS]  Destination Ports or VCs / [Protocol Type]
----  -----------------      -----  ------------------------------------------
3     01-00-0c-cc-cc-cc   #         1/3
3     01-00-0c-cc-cc-cd   #         1/3
3     01-00-0c-dd-dd-dd   #         1/3
3     01-00-5e-00-00-01   #         1/3
3     01-00-5e-00-00-04   #         1/3
3     01-00-5e-00-00-05   #         1/3
3     01-00-5e-00-00-06   #         1/3
3     01-00-5e-00-00-0d   #         1/3
3     01-00-5e-00-00-16   #         1/3
3     01-80-c2-00-00-00   #         1/3
3     01-80-c2-00-00-01   #         1/3
Total Matching CAM Entries Displayed  =11
```

Unlike Switch1, which has a PFC2 card, Switch2 with its PFC1 card has various multicast MAC addresses in its system table that start with prefix 01005e. Host1 will source 239.0.0.4 multicast traffic that maps to the system CAM entry, 01-00-5e-00-00-04. This MAC entry is also used by DVMRP routers. By sourcing an address that maps to a system CAM entry, the multicast packets will hit the NMP, which will be forced to look at these packets. As a result, the NMP is saturated, causing important control traffic to get dropped. Example 9-9 shows the output generated by Switch2.

Example 9-9 *IGMP Address Aliasing*

```
Total Matching CAM Entries Displayed  =11
Switch2 (enable) 2003 Oct 01 16:15:02 %MCAST-2-IGMP_ADDRAL:IGMP: Address
  Aliasing for 01-00-5e-00-00-04
2003 Oct 01 16:15:02 %MCAST-2-IGMP_FALLBACK:IGMP: Running in FALL BACK mode
2003 Oct 01 16:15:02 %MCAST-2-IGMP_ADDRALDETAILS:IGMP: Multicast address
  aliasing: From 00-05-74-18-04-bc (10.1.3.5) on 1/1 to 01-00-5e-00-00-04
  (239.0.0.4)
```

IGMP Fallback

When the switch receives too much traffic because of address aliasing, it will flush the multicast MAC addresses from the system CAM table. This process is known as *IGMP fallback*.

Compare the **show cam system 3** entries for Switch2 as shown in Example 9-8 and Example 9-10. IGMP fallback has cleared the multicast CAM entries from the system CAM table to protect the switch from pegging at 100 percent.

Example 9-10 *CAM Entries Do Not Have Multicast MAC Addresses*

```
Switch2 (enable) show cam system 3
* = Static Entry. + = Permanent Entry. # = System Entry. R = Router Entry.
X = Port Security Entry $ = Dot1x Security Entry
VLAN  Dest MAC/Route Des    [CoS]  Destination Ports or VCs / [Protocol Type]
----  -----------------     -----  ------------------------------------------
3     01-00-0c-cc-cc-cc  #         1/3
3     01-00-0c-cc-cc-cd  #         1/3
3     01-80-c2-00-00-00  #         1/3
3     01-80-c2-00-00-01  #         1/3
Total Matching CAM Entries Displayed  =4
```

At this point, only IGMP packets are allowed to hit the NMP. IGMP fallback is set for 5 minutes. (See Example 9-11.) If no excessive address aliasing occurs, the switch will reinstall the system MAC addresses in the system CAM table. If address aliasing is still occurring, the switch will cause fallback to occur again. If a third fallback occurs, the switch will stay in fallback mode until IGMP snooping is manually disabled and enabled. A switch reload also removes IGMP fallback state.

Example 9-11 *IGMP Snooping Is Currently in Fallback Mode*

```
Switch2 (enable) show igmp mode
IGMP Mode:                auto
IGMP Operational Mode:    igmp-only
IGMP Address Aliasing Mode: fallback
```

An interesting point worth noting is that Switch1 was not affected by address aliasing. PFC2 cards identify multicast router control traffic based on the destination IP address rather than the Layer 2 MAC address used in PFC and earlier EARLs. Hence, the 32 IP addresses to a single MAC address is not an issue for the PFC2 card.

Cisco Group Management Protocol

Cisco Group Management Protocol (CGMP) is another widely used protocol to forward multicast traffic to appropriate ports. CGMP is a Cisco proprietary protocol. The router communicates IGMP information with the switch via the CGMP protocol at Layer 2. Unlike IGMP snooping, CGMP-enabled switches do not have any insight into the Layer 3 IGMP packet types. All IGMP information is forwarded to the router, which in turn sends a Layer 2 message informing the switch regarding client participation for multicast traffic. The router translates the IGMP report into a CGMP message and forwards it to the switch. Based on what is contained in the CGMP packet, the switch will either add or delete port(s) for the multicast stream. Some of the switches that support CGMP are the 3500XL, 2924XL, and Catalyst 5500 without a NetFlow Feature Card (NFFC) card. The packet type of CGMP is defined as follows:

Version (4 bits): 1 and 2
Type (4 bits):   0= Join
                      1= Leave
Reserved (2 bytes): Not used and is set to 0
Count (1 byte): GDA/USA pairs in the CGMP packet
GDA (6 byte): The translated multicast IP group address
USA (6 bytes): MAC address of the client that initiated the IGMP report

Table 9-1 lists the possible CGMP messages. Entry 3 is used by the router to inform the switch of its location. Hence, when a multicast flow gets created, the router port automatically is associated with the multicast stream. Entry 4 is used by the router to leave a multicast stream. Entries 5 and 6 are used to clear multicast CAM entries.

Table 9-1 *Different Types of GDA*

Entry	GDA	USA	Join/Leave	Meaning
1	Multicast MAC	Client MAC	Join	Add port to group
2	Multicast MAC	Client MAC	Leave	Delete port from group
3	00-00-00-00-00-00	Router MAC	Join	Assign router port
4	00-00-00-00-00-00	Router MAC	Leave	Remove router port
5	Multicast MAC	00-00-00-00-00-00	Leave	Delete group
6	00-00-00-00-00-00	00-00-00-00-00-00	Leave	Delete all group

When CGMP is enabled for a VLAN, the switch will automatically associate the CGMP MAC address 01-00-0c-dd-dd-dd with the system CAM entry for that VLAN. (See Example 9-12.)

Example 9-12 *System CAM Table for VLAN 2*

```
Switch3 (enable) show cam system 2
* = Static Entry. + = Permanent Entry. # = System Entry. R = Router Entry. X = Port
Security Entry
VLAN  Dest MAC/Route Des  Destination Ports or VCs / [Protocol Type]
----  ------------------  -------------------------------------------------
2     00-10-f6-b3-48-00R  3/1
2     01-00-0c-cc-cc-cc#  1/9
2     01-00-0c-cc-cc-cd#  1/9
2     01-00-0c-dd-dd-dd#  1/9
2     01-80-c2-00-00-00#  1/9
2     01-80-c2-00-00-01#  1/9
```

Use the **show cam static** command to view the Layer 2 forwarding table for the multicast traffic on the Catalyst 5000 switches. In Example 9-13, the output from the switch illustrates that Host3 and route switch module (RSM) ports are the only ports accepting the multicast traffic destined to 239.1.1.1 on VLAN 2.

Example 9-13 *239.1.1.1 Is Accepted by Ports 3/1 and 7/3*

```
Switch3 (enable) show cam static 2
* = Static Entry. + = Permanent Entry. # = System Entry. R = Router Entry. X = P
ort Security Entry
VLAN  Dest MAC/Route Des  Destination Ports or VCs / [Protocol Type]
----  -----------------   --------------------------------------------------
2     01-00-5e-01-01-01*  3/1,7/3
```

Figure 9-10 shows Host2 connected to Switch3, a Catalyst 5509 device, which also has an RSM blade. Switch3 is configured for CGMP.

Figure 9-10 *CGMP Communication*

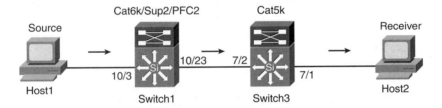

The following steps outline the CGMP process as Host2 sends a membership report for group 239.1.1.1:

Step 1 Host3 sends a IGMP membership report for 239.1.1.1.

Step 2 The switch forwards a message to the RSM.

Step 3 The RSM receives the unsolicited IGMP membership report. It updates its IGMP group table.

Step 4 RSM then updates the mroute table by creating (*, G) and (S, G) for 239.1.1.1. It also puts VLAN 2 in forwarding state to receive 239.1.1.1 traffic.

Step 5 The router translates the IGMP membership report to a Layer 2 CGMP message and forwards it to the switch using CGMP well-known multicast MAC address, 0100.0CDD.DDDD with SNAP value of 0x2001:

— The GDA field will have the translated MAC address of 239.1.1.1= 0010.5e01.0101.

— The User Source Address (USA) will be the MAC address of the client (Host3) that sent the IGMP membership report.

Step 6 The switch examines the CGMP packet. If it does not have a CAM entry for the multicast MAC address, it will create a CAM entry for GDA and associate the router port to it. The switch looks at the USA field and again examines the CAM table. The switch will have a CAM entry for the USA field because Host2 initiated the request for the multicast stream. As a result, the switch also adds the Host2 port to the GDA entry.

Step 7 Any subsequent multicast traffic destined to 239.1.1.1 will be forwarded to the RSM and the host port. In this example, the host port is 7/3.

IGMP Leave Process

The leave process works the same. The router receives the IGMP leave message from the host and translates the information to CGMP and forwards it to the switch. The switch then removes the client port from the CAM entry for that GDA.

Local Leave Process

With more recent implementations, the Catalyst 4000 and 5000 family can actually handle the IGMP leave process locally rather than forwarding it to the router. To enable this feature, use the following command:

```
Switch3 (enable) set cgmp leave <enable | disable>
```

This command will create two multicast MAC entries in the systems CAM table: 01-00-5e-00-00-01 and 01-00-5e-00-00-02. Now, when a host sends an IGMP leave message, the switch intercepts the packet, similar in process to IGMP snooping.

The local leave process is as follows:

Step 1 Host3 sends a leave group message to all routers, 224.0.0.2, for multicast traffic 239.1.1.1.

Step 2 The switch intercepts the IGMP packet. It sends an IGMP general query out the port 7/3.

Step 3   Because port 7/3 is the last host for the multicast traffic, the switch sources an IGMP leave message to the router.

Step 4   Upon receiving the IGMP leave message, the RSM sends two group specific queries to check for any members for VLAN 2:

```
IGMP: Received Leave from 10.1.2.1 (Vlan2) for 239.1.1.1
IGMP: Send v2 Query on Vlan2 to 239.1.1.1
IGMP: Send v2 Query on Vlan2 to 239.1.1.1
```

Step 5   The RSM sends a CGMP message to the switch to delete the GDA from the CAM.

IGMP Snooping Versus CGMP

When comparing IGMP and CGMP, IGMP snooping is a far superior method of handling multicast traffic on a switch. Implementing IGMP snooping over CGMP has various advantages. IGMP is based on a standard whereas CGMP is Cisco proprietary. IGMP can handle IGMP leave message both from GDA and all-routers address. CGMP only understands all-routers address. IGMP is able to handle address aliasing more effectively. CGMP is forwarded to other switches at Layer 2, causing unnecessary traffic on the network. Host leaves are handled sequentially in CGMP because of report suppression. This is not the case with IGMP.

Summary

This chapter illustrated the intricacies involved with IGMP snooping and CGMP. IGMP snooping is enabled by default on Catalyst 6000 switches. CGMP is the default for the Catalyst 5000 family. Unlike IGMP snooping, CGMP requires configuration changes on the router. Via the IGMP snooping feature, the switch is able to listen to the conversation between the router and the host machine. Hence, rather than flooding the VLAN with multicast traffic, the switch forwards the traffic to hosts that explicitly requested the stream. CGMP forwards the IGMP messages to the router, which converts the IGMP packet into a CGMP packet and forwards it back to the switch. Despite CGMP local leave implementation, where the CGMP-enabled switch can intercept the IGMP leave packet and locally query the host, CGMP is slowly becoming obsolete, because all current model Catalyst switches support Layer 3 capabilities.

This chapter covers the following topics:

- Preventing loops with spanning tree
- Spanning-tree convergence
- Introducing Rapid Spanning Tree Protocol
- Understanding Multiple Spanning Tree
- UniDirectional Link Detection

CHAPTER 10

Implementing and Tuning Spanning Tree

Chapter 1, "LAN Switching Foundation Technologies," discussed the fundamentals behind the spanning-tree algorithm. This chapter will explore the intricacies of spanning tree along with Cisco's numerous proprietary features that help with preventing Layer 2 loops on the network. Today's networks require rapid convergence because of the sensitive nature of applications and other network protocols. It becomes imperative for the Spanning Tree Protocol (STP) to handle convergence issues quickly and more effectively. The introductions of Rapid Spanning Tree Protocol (RSTP) and Multiple Spanning Tree (MST) have addressed faster convergence and scalability issues at Layer 2.

Preventing Loops with Spanning Tree

STP (IEEE 802.1D) has two immediate drawbacks. The first issue is with convergence. It just takes too long for Layer 2 networks to converge. Depending on the type of failure, it could take anywhere from 30 to 50 seconds to converge the network. The other issue with STP is potential loops. Loops can be catastrophic, as discussed on numerous occasions throughout this book. Cisco introduced features such as portfast, Root Guard, and Loop Guard to help mitigate loop problems, as discussed in the next sections.

Portfast

The portfast feature skips through various stages of spanning-tree states, and it immediately brings a port from blocking to forwarding state. There are two reasons behind portfast. First, the delay incurred through normal spanning-tree states could cause startup problems. For example, a host machine's user login screen times out because the port is still transitioning through its spanning-tree states. It takes 30 seconds for a port to transition to forwarding state. While the port is transitioning, the Windows software is attempting to log on to the server and subsequently will fail because the host machine does not have full network connectivity. This problem was ubiquitous with users that had Novell Clients.

The second reason behind portfast is that Topology Change Notifications (TCNs) are not generated when a host machine joins or leaves a port. This reason is significant. If portfast is disabled on a host port, anytime a user does a restart or a shutdown on his machine, a TCN is generated by the switch and forwarded on the bridge Root Port. (See Figure 10-1.)

The upstream designated switch sends back a Topology Change Acknowledgment (TCA) to the switch. The process continues until the Root receives the TCN. The Root resets the content-addressable memory (CAM) entries from 5 minutes to 15 seconds (Forward delay), and the duration of the new CAM aging entry will last for 35 seconds (20 Max age + 15 Forward delay) before reverting to the 5-minute timer. The Root sends configuration bridge protocol data units (BPDUs) informing all the switches of topology and timer changes. This process is unnecessary for ports that are not participating in spanning tree. No spanning-tree change occurs when a user machine joins or leaves a bridge. As a result, portfast configuration is preferred on host ports.

Figure 10-1 *TCN Updates*

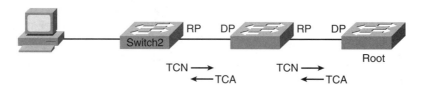

RP = Root Port
DP = Designated Port

Switch-to-switch links should not have portfast enabled because the switches are participating in spanning-tree topology. One small caveat exists for portfast. If the switch receives a configuration BPDU on a portfast-enabled port, it will recycle the port through the normal spanning-tree states. This protects the network from possible loops.

Example 10-1 shows how to configure portfast on host port, 3/1. A warning message is generated when portfast is enabled. The warning message reminds the engineer on what devices portfast should not be enabled.

Example 10-1 *Enabling Portfast*

```
Switch2 (enable) set spantree portfast 3/1 enable
Warning: Spantree port fast start should only be enabled on ports connected
to a single host.  Connecting hubs, concentrators, switches, bridges, etc. to
a fast start port can cause temporary spanning tree loops.  Use with caution.
Spantree port  3/1 fast start enabled.
```

The **spantree** command provides a global view of ports that have been enabled for portfast. (See Example 10-2.)

Example 10-2 *Spanning Tree Information for VLAN 3*

```
Switch2 (enable) show spantree 3
VLAN 3
Spanning tree mode        PVST+
Spanning tree type        ieee
Spanning tree enabled
Designated Root           00-05-74-18-04-80
Designated Root Priority  4099
Designated Root Cost      4
Designated Root Port      1/1
Root Max Age   20 sec   Hello Time 2  sec   Forward Delay 15 sec
Bridge ID MAC ADDR        00-01-63-29-bc-02
Bridge ID Priority        32768
Bridge Max Age 20 sec   Hello Time 2  sec   Forward Delay 15 sec
Port                    Vlan Port-State    Cost      Prio Portfast Channel_id
----------------------- ---- ------------- --------- ---- -------- ----------
3/1                      3    forwarding      100   32 enabled  0
```

Portfast BPDU Guard

BPDU Guard goes one step further in protecting the network from possible loops. Ports enabled with portfast should not receive any BPDUs because these ports are not participating in spanning tree. Hence, any BPDUs received on these ports are invalid. Someone may have mistakenly or intentionally put a new switch on the portfast port or looped the portfast port to another switch. Portfast, by default, brings the port to blocking mode if it receives BPDU messages. It then brings the port up through the normal spanning-tree process, essentially turning off the portfast feature. The BPDU Guard feature error disables the port completely when a BPDU is heard on a portfast port. Manual intervention is required to bring the port out of error disabled (errDisabled) state. BPDU Guard is a global command that affects all the enabled portfast ports, as shown in Example 10-3.

Example 10-3 *Enabling BPDU Guard*

```
Switch2 (enable) set spantree portfast bpdu-guard enable
Spantree portfast bpdu-guard enabled on this switch
```

Example 10-4 illustrates a portfast BPDU Guard–enabled port receiving a BPDU message.

Example 10-4 *BPDU Traffic Seen on Portfast BPDU Guard Port*

```
Switch2 (enable) 2003 Oct 07 15:30:32 %SPANTREE-2-RX_PORTFAST: Received BPDU on
 PortFast enable port. Disabling 3/1
Switch2 (enable) show port 3/1

Port  Name                 Status      Vlan       Duplex Speed Type
----- -------------------- ----------- ---------- ------ ----- -----------
 3/1                       errdisable 3           a-half a-10 10/100BaseTX
```

Portfast BPDU Filter

BPDU Filter is a global command that prevents a switch from transmitting BPDU messages on a portfast-enabled port. (See Example 10-5.) Earlier in the chapter, you learned that BPDUs received on a portfast-enabled port cause the port to cycle back through its normal spanning-tree states; however, with BPDU Filter, the downstream portfast port should never see a BPDU message. BPDU is yet another safety net to prevent potential loops on a network.

Example 10-5 *Enabling BPDU Filter*

```
Switch2 (enable) set spantree portfast bpdu-filter enable
```

In Figure 10-2, Switch2 will not send BPDUs out its portfast port that is connected to Switch3. It will, however, continue to receive BPDU messages from Switch3. To prevent spanning-tree issues, Switch3 will also have to be enabled with BPDU filtering.

Figure 10-2 *BPDU Filtering*

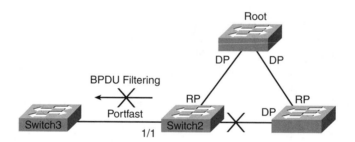

NOTE Note that Figure 10-2 reflects a bad design. This figure is used to illustrate BPDU filtering currently available on Cisco switches.

Root Guard

Root Guard allows a device that is connected to a portfast-enabled port to participate in spanning tree, but will not be allowed to become the root. Example 10-6 outlines Root Guard configuration.

NOTE   Root Guard is not compatible with Loop Guard, which you learn about in the next section.

Example 10-6 *Enabling Root Guard*

```
Switch2 (enable) set spantree guard root 1/1
Enable rootguard will disable loopguard if it's currently enabled on the
  port(s).
Do you want to continue (y/n) [n]? y
Switch2 (enable) 2003 Oct 07 17:40:55 %SPANTREE-5-ROOTCHANGE:Root changed for
  Vlan 2: New root port 0/0. New Root mac address is 00-01-63-29-bc-01.
2003 Oct 07 17:40:55 %SPANTREE-2-ROOTGUARDBLOCK: Port 1/1 tried to become non-
  designated in VLAN 2. Moved to root-inconsistent state
2003 Oct 07 17:40:56 %SPANTREE-6-PORTBLK: Port 1/1 state in VLAN 2 changed to
  blocking
```

If superior BPDUs are heard from a portfast-enabled port, the port state is changed to root inconsistent state. In Example 10-7, Switch2 heard superior BPDUs for VLAN 2 on port 1/1. Root Guard is enabled per port and affects all VLANs that traverse that port.

Example 10-7 *Spanning Tree for VLAN 2*

```
Switch2 (enable) show spantree 2
VLAN 2
Spanning tree mode          PVST+
Spanning tree type          ieee
Spanning tree enabled
Designated Root             00-01-63-29-bc-01
Designated Root Priority    30000
Designated Root Cost        0
Designated Root Port        1/0
Root Max Age    20 sec   Hello Time 2  sec   Forward Delay 15 sec
Bridge ID MAC ADDR          00-01-63-29-bc-01
Bridge ID Priority          30000
Bridge Max Age 20 sec    Hello Time 2  sec   Forward Delay 15 sec
Port                     Vlan Port-State    Cost      Prio Portfast Channel_id
------------------------ ---- ------------- --------- ---- -------- ----------
  1/1                      2   root-inconsis       4   32 enabled  0
```

If Switch2 stops receiving superior BPDUs on port 1/1, it will transition the port back to forwarding. (See Example 10-8.) This is a dynamic process.

Example 10-8 *Port Transitioning Due to New Root*

```
Switch2 (enable) 2003 Oct 07 17:51:07 %SPANTREE-5-MSGAGEEXPIRY: Msg Age timer
  expired on port 1/1 in vlan 2
2003 Oct 07 17:51:07 %SPANTREE-2-ROOTGUARDUNBLOCK: Port 1/1 restored in VLAN 2
2003 Oct 07 17:51:07 %SPANTREE-5-ROOTCHANGE:Root changed for Vlan 2: New root
  port 0/0. New Root mac address is 00-01-63-29-bc-01.
2003 Oct 07 17:51:07 %SPANTREE-6-PORTLISTEN: Port 1/1 state in VLAN 2 changed to
  listening
```

Loop Guard

The Loop Guard feature protects against possible spanning-tree loops by detecting a unidirectional link. With a unidirectional link, a port on one of the link partners is operationally in the up state and transmitting, but is not receiving traffic. At the same time, the other link partner is operating correctly. Loop Guard is enabled on ports that are participating in spanning tree and are redundant at Layer 2. When the switch stops receiving BPDUs on its root or blocking port, it will transition the port to loop inconsistent state, which does not pass traffic.

Loop Guard is configured per port on codes earlier than Catalyst OS 7.1(1). Loop Guard does not work with Root Guard (see Example 10-9), and Loop Guard should not be enabled on portfast ports. One other caveat involving Loop Guard is channeling. The first operational port is used for BPDUs; if the link has a unidirectional failure, Loop Guard will transition all the links off the channel to loop inconsistent state. This is not a desirable effect because the inherent redundancy gained through channeling is lost.

Example 10-9 *Loop Guard Enabled*

```
Switch2> (enable) set spantree guard loop 3/5
Enable loopguard will disable rootguard if it's currently enabled on the port(s).
Do you want to continue (y/n) [n]? y
Switch2> (enable) show spantree guard 3/5
Port                      VLAN Port-State    Guard Type
-------------------- ----- ------------- ----------
3/5                         2    forwarding    loop
```

In Figure 10-3, Switch2 stops receiving BPDUs from Switch3. With Loop Guard enabled, Switch2 transitions the blocking port to loop inconsistent state. The unidirectional link could have resulted from a faulty transmit transceiver on Switch3 or a bad receive transceiver on Switch2. Regardless, Loop Guard changes the port's state to protect the network. If Loop Guard was not enabled, Switch2 would have moved the blocking port to forwarding. As result of this state change, a one-way loop would have occurred going counterclockwise. Loop Guard does not require manual intervention. If Switch2 starts hearing BPDUs again on port 3/5, it will transition the port back to blocking state.

Figure 10-3 *Loop Guard*

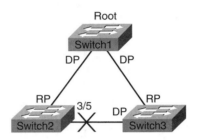

Spanning-Tree Convergence

Spanning-tree convergence issues have been a challenge for network administrators to address. Depending on the size of the Layer 2 network, it can get very complicated. In fact, one of the big selling points of RSTP is its superior convergence capability over the legacy STP. Cisco switches provide numerous commands that can be used to tweak specific spanning-tree timers as introduced in Chapter 1, and discussed in more depth in this section. Cisco has also made available features such as BackboneFast and UplinkFast to help converge the Layer 2 network faster.

Spanning-Tree Timers

Spanning-tree convergence issues can be tricky. It is recommended that you keep things as simple as possible at Layer 2. Keeping timers at default values is recommended because of the large majority of testing, network design certifications, and number of installations using default timers.

Spanning tree has various timers, including the following:

- **Hello**—Root sends configuration BPDUs every 2 seconds.

  set spantree hello interval [vlan]

- **Forward Delay**—The time interval for listening and learning states. It is not, however, the sum of listening and learning state. The default for Forward Delay is set at 15 seconds.

  set spantree fwddelay delay [vlan]

- **Maxage**—The amount of time a switch saves configuration BPDUs. Maxage plays an important role during indirect failures. The default value for Maxage is 20 seconds.

  set spantree maxage agingtime [vlan]

The diameter of the spanning network dictates how flexible the configuration of these parameters are. Typically, Hello and Forward Delay timers are not adjusted. There is some room, however, to adjust the Maxage timer.

Figure 10-4 shows the amount of time it takes for an indirect link failure to occur before a blocking port transitions to forwarding.

Figure 10-4 *Maxage Timer*

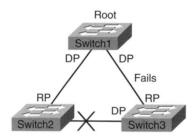

The following steps outline how the Maxage timer works:

Step 1   The connection between Switch1 and Switch3 fails.

Step 2   Switch3 will start generating inferior configuration BPDUs toward Switch2.

Step 3   Switch2 will ignore these BPDUs from Switch3 for 20 seconds, the Maxage timer.

Step 4   After this timer expires, Switch2 will transition the blocking port to forwarding. This will take an additional 30 seconds.

Step 5   Switch2 will forward configuration BPDUs from the Root (Switch1) to Switch2.

Step 6   Switch2 will cease sending inferior BPDUs. The network has now converged.

From the spanning-tree perspective, the network would look like Figure 10-5 after convergence. It took 50 seconds (20 seconds for Maxage + 30 seconds for listening/learning) for the network to converge. This type of outage is referred to as an *indirect failure*. If Switch2 lost its Root Port (RP), the convergence would have been 30 seconds. The blocking port would immediately go to listening state. This is known as a *direct failure*.

Figure 10-5 *Spanning-Tree Convergence*

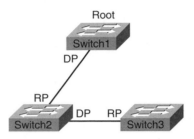

The Maxage timer is composed of two elements. The first component is the diameter of the switches involved between the two hosts. It is generally accepted that there should be no more than seven switches between any two hosts. It is also acceptable that no more than three configuration BPDUs can potentially be lost:

Diameter=((lost BPDU + 1) * Hello Interval) + (Delay * (diameter - 1))
((3 + 1) * 2) + (1 * (7 - 1)) = 14 seconds

The second element involved in Maxage calculation is Message Age Overestimate. Each switch increments the Message Age field by 1 second as the configuration BPDU traverses through the switch. This 1-second value is overstated by the switch. Realistically, the switch can forward the BPDU much quicker than 1 second:

Message Age Overestimate=(diameter - 1) * delay
(7 - 1) * 1 = 6 seconds

Finally, the two values are taken together to come up with the 20-second Maxage default timer:

Maxage= Diameter + Message Age Overestimate
14 + 6 = 20 seconds

For example, if the diameter between two host machines is 3 bridges or switches, the Maxage could be set to 12 (10 + 2):

Diameter: ((3 + 1) * 2) + (1 * (3 - 1)) = 10 seconds
Message Age Overestimate: (3 - 1) * 1 = 2 seconds

BackboneFast

BackboneFast is a Maxage optimizer. (See Figure 10-6.) In other words, BackboneFast helps get rid of the 20 seconds that are associated with Maxage timer, which is used for indirect failures as mentioned in the previous section. BackboneFast does this by first detecting the indirect failure. The trigger for the indirect failure is when the switch receives inferior BPDUs on its blocking port. The second component to BackboneFast is verifying the failure. It does this through Root Link Query (RLQ) protocol. The switch sends RLQ requests to the upstream switch to find the location of the Root. Upon finding the location of the Root, the switch expires the Maxage timer and transitions the blocking port to listening state.

Figure 10-6 *BackboneFast*

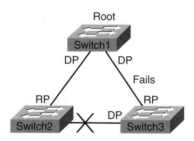

BackboneFast process is outlined in the following steps:

Step 1   The connection between Switch1 and Switch3 fails.

Step 2   Switch3 will start generating inferior configuration BPDUs toward Switch2.

Step 3   Upon receiving the inferior BPDUs, Switch2 sends a RLQ toward the upstream switch.

Step 4   Switch1 sends back a RLQ response that it is the Root.

Step 5   Switch2 now knows that it still has a path to the Root. It can now safely transition the blocked port.

Step 6   Switch2 transitions the blocking port into listening state. It forwards configuration BPDUs to Switch3.

Step 7   After 30 seconds, Switch3 has converged. This is the same amount of time for direct failure convergence.

BackboneFast is a global command, and it should be enabled on all switches, as shown in Example 10-10. BackboneFast does not affect direct failure convergence times.

Example 10-10 *Enable BackboneFast*

```
Switch2 (enable) set spantree backbonefast enable
Backbonefast enabled for all VLANs.
```

UplinkFast

UplinkFast is another feature that helps with the convergence issue. There must be redundant physical links on the access switch to the upstream switches to enable the UplinkFast feature. (See Figure 10-7.) One of the links is used for forwarding and the other link is used for backup. When the forwarding link fails, the backup link comes up and starts forwarding traffic. The convergence time is reduced to 2 to 3 seconds through this process. To help build the CAM table based on the new link, the switch sources all relevant MAC addresses that were associated with the link that failed and advertises them at a rate of 15 packets per 100 ms with a dummy multicast address, 01-00-0C-CD-CD-CD.

Figure 10-7 *UplinkFast*

If the UplinkFast feature is going to be used, it should only be configured on access switches. It is critical that UplinkFast not be enabled on core switches, because it could potentially cause some severe instability issues. In fact, when UplinkFast is enabled, by default, the switch sets the bridge priority to 49152 from its 32768. This is done to ensure that the access switch is not used as Root. Also, the cost on the switch ports is increased by 3000; so the switch is not used as transit by other switches.

In Figure 10-7, Switch2 is defined as the access switch. As noted in the **spantree** information (see Example 10-11), the switch has redundant links for VLAN 4 because one of its ports is in blocking mode. UplinkFast is a global command. The root priority and port cost are automatically adjusted when UplinkFast is enabled.

Example 10-11 *Spanning Tree for VLAN 4*

```
Switch2 (enable) show spantree 4
VLAN 4
Spanning tree mode          PVST+
Spanning tree type          ieee
Spanning tree enabled
Designated Root             00-05-74-18-04-80
Designated Root Priority    24580
Designated Root Cost        19
Designated Root Port        3/11
Root Max Age   20 sec   Hello Time 2  sec   Forward Delay 15 sec
Bridge ID MAC ADDR          00-01-63-29-bc-03
Bridge ID Priority          32768
Bridge Max Age 20 sec   Hello Time 2  sec   Forward Delay 15 sec
```

continues

Example 10-11 *Spanning Tree for VLAN 4 (Continued)*

```
Port                          Vlan Port-State    Cost      Prio Portfast Channel_id
----------------------------  ---- ------------  --------- ---- -------- ----------
3/11                          4    forwarding          19  32   enabled  0
3/12                          4    blocking            19  32   enabled  0
```

Example 10-12 shows the configuration involved in turning UplinkFast on a switch. The defaults for the bridge and ports have been adjusted accordingly.

Example 10-12 *Uplinkfast Enabled*

```
Switch2 (enable) set spantree uplinkfast enable
VLANs 1-4094 bridge priority set to 49152.
The port cost and portvlancost of all ports set to above 3000.
Station update rate set to 15 packets/100ms.
```

As noted, port 3/11 is forwarding while 3/12 is in backup state as shown in Example 10-13.

Example 10-13 *Uplinkfast Currently Active on Port 3/11*

```
Example 10-13
Switch2 (enable) show spantree uplinkfast
Station update rate set to 15 packets/100ms.
uplinkfast all-protocols field set to off.
VLAN           port list
----------------------------------------------
4              3/11(fwd),3/12
```

Introducing Rapid Spanning Tree Protocol

The primary focus thus far has been on legacy STP as defined by IEEE 802.1D. As you have learned in the previous sections, the immediate hindrance of STP is convergence. It takes anywhere from 30 to 50 seconds depending on the type of failure to converge the network. RSTP helps with convergence issues that plague legacy STP. RSTP has additional features similar to UplinkFast and BackboneFast that offer better recovery at Layer 2 than STP.

RSTP is based on IEEE 802.1w standard. Numerous glaring differences exist between RSTP and STP. For starters, RSTP requires full-duplex point-to-point connection between adjacent switches. Half duplex, generally speaking, denotes a shared medium whereby multiple hosts share the same wire; a point-to-point connection cannot reside in this environment. As a result, RSTP cannot work in a half-duplex mode. STP and RSTP also have port designation differences. RSTP has Alternate and Backup port designation, which are absent from the STP environment. Ports not participating in spanning tree are known as *edge ports*. Edge ports should be configured using the **set spantree portfast** command. The edge port becomes a non-edge port immediately if a BPDU is heard on the port. Non-edge ports participate in the spanning-tree algorithm; hence, only non-edge ports generate Topology Changes (TCs) on the network when transitioning to forwarding state only. TCs are not generated for any other RSTP states. In legacy STP, TCNs were generated for any active port that was not configured for portfast.

RSTP port designations include the following:

- **Root Port (RP)**—Defined as port closest metrically to the Root. This designation is also seen in legacy STP.

- **Alternate Port**—Alternate path to get to the Root. Alternate ports do not forward traffic. An alternate port is equivalent to a backup of the RP.

- **Designated Port (DP)**—Port used to forward the best BPDU on each segment.

- **Backup Port**—This port is a backup to the DP on the segment. It does not forward traffic.

These port designations are illustrated in Figure 10-8.

Figure 10-8 *RSTP Port Designations*

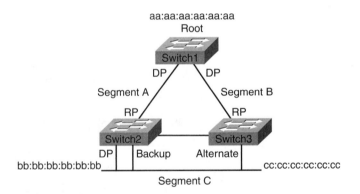

All ports on the Root that are participating in spanning tree will be forwarding on each of the segments. Hence, Root will forward its BPDUs to both Switch2 and Switch3. Switch2 and Switch3 RPs are directly connected to the Root. The RPs will be receiving configuration BPDUs from the Root and will be in forwarding state. Switch2 and Switch3 will be competing as to which switch will forward BPDUs on Segment C. The decision process is the same for both RSTP and STP. As noted in Chapter 1, the decision process involves the following:

- Lowest path cost to the Root
- Lowest Sender Bridge ID (BID)
- Lowest Port ID

In Figure 10-8, the lowest BID will determine which switch will be the DP for Segment C because the cost to the Root is the same for both Switch2 and Switch3. The BID is composed of bridge priority and MAC address. The default priority value is the same for both Switch2 and Switch3; therefore, the decision is going to be based on the lowest MAC address. Switch2 has a lower MAC address than Switch3, and, as a result, will be forwarding on Segment C. As noted in Figure 10-8, the DP is associated with Switch2. The Backup Port on Switch2 will be discarding. It will be backing up DP should it go down. The Alternate Port is in discarding state and will be backing up the RP on Switch3. The only forwarding port on Segment C will be the DP on Switch2.

RSTP States

Table 10-1 shows the different port states between RSTP and legacy STP. The three port states in RSTP are the following:

- Discarding
- Learning
- Forwarding

In Cisco implementation, discarding is replaced with blocking.

Table 10-1 *Port States*

Operational Port State	STP Port State	RSTP Port State
Enabled	Blocking	Discarding
Enabled	Listening	Discarding
Enabled	Learning	Learning
Enabled	Forwarding	Forwarding
Disabled	Discarding	Discarding

RSTP BPDU

The BPDU packet has also changed with RSTP. (See Figure 10-9.) The version field in legacy STP was set at 1, but in RSTP, the version is set at 2. The motivation here is for RSTP to be able to communicate with legacy STP. The Flag field in the STP BPDU packet contained TCN and TCA. In RSTP, the Flag field, 1 byte long, has been modified to accommodate port designations and proposal/agreement between adjacent switches. BPDUs are sent every 2 seconds. Unlike in legacy STP, in RSTP, each switch generates its own BPDUs regardless if it hears BPDUs from the Root. In legacy STP, BPDUs were only generated by the Root and propagated throughout the spanning-tree domain. As a result, when a switch did not receive a configuration BPDU, it did not know where the failure occurred. In RSTP mode, the switch needs only to worry about its immediate neighbors. Hence, BPDUs also serve as keepalive mechanisms between adjacent switches. If the switch does not hear three consecutive BPDUs from its downstream neighbor, it will transition appropriate ports to converge the network.

Figure 10-9 *RSTP BPDU Flag Field*

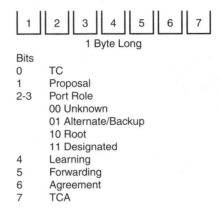

Bits
0   TC
1   Proposal
2-3   Port Role
        00 Unknown
        01 Alternate/Backup
        10 Root
        11 Designated
4   Learning
5   Forwarding
6   Agreement
7   TCA

RSTP Proposal/Agreement

Figure 10-10 depicts adjacent switches participating in RSTP implementation. RSTP switches require BPDUs from their connected neighbors to keep the link up. This mechanism is outlined in the RSTP proposal/agreement process.

Figure 10-10 *RSTP Proposal/Agreement*

The mechanism involved in proposal/agreement between adjacent switches is very fast. It takes less than few seconds to transition a port to the appropriate state, whereas in STP, it took a minimum of 30 seconds. In Figure 10-10, BPDU exchange between Switch1 and Switch2 has not yet taken place. Only in discarding and learning states will proposal BPDUs be sent. Assume that the ports connecting the two switches are in learning state: Switch1, with lower BID, sends a proposal BPDU to Switch2. Switch2 having received the proposal sees that Switch1 has better BPDU; it will accept Switch1 as the Root for the

VLAN. Switch2 will send an agreement BPDU back to Switch1. In a situation where Switch1 does not receive an agreement BPDU, it will fall back to legacy STP mode.

A new connection has been set up between Switch1 and Switch3. (See Figure 10-11.) When this connection comes up, Switch3 will receive a better BPDU from Switch1. It must, therefore, transition its current RP and designate a new RP.

Figure 10-11 *A New Connection Between Switches*

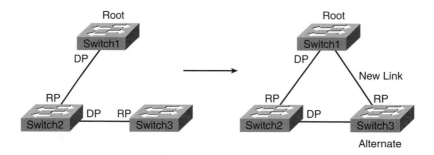

The following steps outline how Switch3 chooses a new RP:

Step 1 A new connection between Switch1 and Switch3 has been set up.

Step 2 Switch3 receives a better BPDU from Switch1. It keeps the new port in blocking state.

Step 3 Switch3 transitions the current RP to Alternate port (discarding state).

Step 4 Switch3 sends an agreement BPDU to Switch1.

Step 5 Switch3 transitions the new RP to forwarding state.

Step 6 Switch1 receives the agreement BPDU and transitions its port to forwarding state as well.

RSTP Legacy Support

RSTP is backward compatible with legacy STP. Typically, RSTP generates BPDUs every 2 seconds on the wire informing the segment of which bridge is the Root. Based on this information, the downstream bridges will appropriately designate their spanning-tree ports. The problem is that legacy STP devices do not understand these BPDU messages that they are receiving from RSTP-enabled devices. As a result, legacy STP devices will continue to generate their own BPDUs and ignore the RSTP BPDUs. Legacy STP BPDUs may have wrong information as to which bridge is the Root in the network. It becomes crucial for RSTP implementation to be backward compatible to prevent such a scenario.

The RSTP device is engineered so that it can deal with legacy STP devices on the same Layer 2 network. RSTP handles the legacy STP device problem through a timer. The RSTP device will wait 4 seconds (2 * hello interval) to see if legacy STP BPDUs will cease. If they do not, RSTP will fall back to legacy STP mode. Now, all the bridges will communicate via legacy STP specifications. Hence, the fast convergence and relative stability gained through RSTP is lost. Manual intervention is required to revert back to RSTP mode. Unfortunately, no mechanism is in place today to allow an RSTP device to revert back to RSTP mode if the legacy STP device disappears.

RSTP Direct Failure

RSTP has natively implemented the same type of mechanisms involved in UplinkFast and BackboneFast. In Figure 10-12, when Switch3 loses its RP, it immediately transitions the Alternate port into forwarding mode. In legacy STP mode, a direct failure of this type would have taken 30 seconds. Unlike the UplinkFast mechanism, the RSTP mechanism does not use dummy multicast generation to flush the CAM entries. TCs generated by RSTP to the upstream switch clear the appropriate CAM entries associated with the broken link.

Figure 10-12 *RSTP Convergence Due to Link Failure*

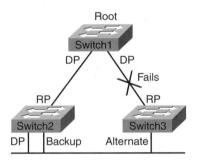

When a TC bit is set, the switch starts a TC While timer equal to 4 seconds (2 * hello interval) for all its non-edge ports. It flushes the MAC addresses that were associated with that port. The upstream switch that received the TC BPDU will flush its MAC addresses from all ports except the port that received the BPDU. This process streamlines the convergence process. In legacy STP, the TCNs first needed to be propagated to the Root, which afterward generated configuration BPDUs that were propagated back to the spanning-tree domain. The amount of time it took to converge the network was contingent upon how big the spanning-tree domain was. In RSTP, the TCs are flooded quickly to non-edge ports and RPs, and the upstream switches flush their CAM entries, resulting in faster convergence time. The downside to this process is some flooding does take place in the network.

RSTP Indirect Failure

Referencing back, Figure 10-6 shows an indirect type of failure that would take 50 seconds for spanning tree to converge. Using BackboneFast, the convergence time is reduced to 30 seconds. Maxage timer does not exist in RSTP. RSTP takes an active role in bringing the network into convergence rather than passively waiting for timers to expire before transitioning a non-edge port.

The following steps outline how RSTP handles indirect link failures:

Step 1　Switch3 loses its RP connection to the Root. As a result, Switch3 starts to generate BPDUs, informing other switches that it is the Root.

Step 2　Switch2 receives the inferior BPDUs from Switch3. Switch2 knows through periodic BPDUs that it still has a connection to the Root.

Step 3　Switch2 sends BPDUs informing Switch3 that Switch1 is still the Root.

Step 4　Upon receiving the superior BPDUs, Switch3 stops sending BPDUs. It transitions its DP to RP.

Configuring RSTP

RSTP is also known as Per VLAN Rapid Spanning Tree Plus (PVRST+). It requires, at minimum, Catalyst OS Release 7.5(1). RSTP simply requires one command to be enabled. The **spantree mode** command globally enables RSTP for the switch. (See Example 10-14.) The command needs to be performed on all switches in the Layer 2 network; otherwise, some switches will be in legacy STP mode.

Example 10-14 *Configuring RSTP on Switches 1, 2, and 3*

```
Switch1 (enable) set spantree mode rapid-pvst+
Switch2 (enable) set spantree mode rapid-pvst+
Switch3 (enable) set spantree mode rapid-pvst+
```

Example 10-15 shows the Root bridge for VLAN 3.

Example 10-15 *Spanning-Tree Information for VLAN 3*

```
Switch2 (enable) show spantree 3
VLAN 3
Spanning tree mode          RAPID-PVST+
!RSTP is enabled
Spanning tree type          ieee
Spanning tree enabled
Designated Root             00-01-63-29-bc-02
!Root bridge is local
Designated Root Priority    32768
Designated Root Cost        0
```

Example 10-15 *Spanning-Tree Information for VLAN 3 (Continued)*

```
Designated Root Port       1/0
Root Max Age   20 sec   Hello Time 2  sec   Forward Delay 15 sec
Bridge ID MAC ADDR         00-01-63-29-bc-02
Bridge ID Priority         32768
Bridge Max Age 20 sec   Hello Time 2  sec   Forward Delay 15 sec
Port                    State         Role Cost     Prio Type
------------------------ ------------ ---- -------- ---- --------------------
3/24                     forwarding    DESG      19   32 P2P
3/47                     forwarding    DESG      19   32 P2P
15/1                      forwarding   DESG       4   32 P2P, Edge
```

Understanding Multiple Spanning Tree

Multiple Spanning Tree (MST) implementation is defined by IEEE 802.1s. MST convergence is fast because it rides on top of RSTP. MST provides load-balancing capability without the scalability issues that are attached with legacy STP. MST allows for very large Layer 2 networks. It can accomplish this through various regions or domains that house specific Layer 2 devices. In the "Introducing Rapid Spanning Tree Protocol" section, the primary focus was on 802.1w. Here, the discussion is on the integration of 802.1s and 802.1w using Cisco switches.

Comparing MST to PVST+/CST

In PVST+, a single spanning-tree topology is built for each VLAN. Each VLAN will have its own legacy STP network. Consider the design shown in Figure 10-13. If there were 50 VLANs running among these three switches, there would have been 50 instances of spanning tree to maintain. PVST+ offers good load-balancing capability because of the granularity offered through 50 instances of spanning tree. For instance, Switch1 could be configured to be the Root for the even VLANs, while Switch2 would be the Root for the odd VLANs. At the same time, the two Root switches can be configured to be the secondary Root for each other's VLANs.

Figure 10-13 *Switches in Triangle Design*

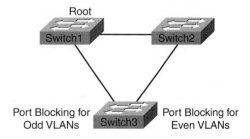

In Common Spanning Tree (CST) implementation, there would be one instance of spanning tree for all the VLANs. In Figure 10-13, Switch1 will be the Root for all the VLANs. As a result, there would be one instance of spanning tree. The negative side to CST is that the load-balancing capability is lost. Now, all user traffic is passed through Switch1. This is inefficient due to waste of critical bandwidth.

MST is a compromise between PVST+ and CST and offers numerous other advantages. Rather than creating 1 or 50 instances of spanning tree as defined by CST and PVST+, respectively, MST only creates two instances of spanning tree for the design shown in Figure 10-13. VLANs can be assigned arbitrarily to any instance. In this example, Switch1 handles even VLANs and Switch2 handles odd VLANs. MST provides load-balancing capability for groups of VLANs rather than each VLAN. It also uses the strength of CST by grouping VLANs to reduce the number of instances of VLANs in the network.

MST Regions

The mechanics involved on how MST manages to create only two instances of spanning tree in Figure 10-13 has to do with regions. A *region*, similar to an administration domain, is a collection of VLANs that have the same configuration and are managed under the same MST umbrella. In the example given, one region has two instances of spanning tree. Each region must have the same configuration for these three elements:

- Region Name (32 bytes)
- Revision Number (16 bits)
- Associating VLANs with spanning-tree instances

Internal Spanning Tree

There must at least be two instances for MST, meaning at least two spanning-tree topologies. The first instance, Internal Spanning Tree (IST), is set at 0. The second instance is user defined. The IST instance extends the CST inside the MST region. The Layer 2 network essentially has two tiers: one CST and multiple MSTIs (MST instances). A total of 15 MSTIs plus 1 IST under one region can be configured.

Figure 10-14 illustrates the importance of IST. This figure shows two regions. Two switches are within Region 10. Switch2, which is part of Region 20, has a higher BID value than the other two switches. Hence, its superior BPDUs are accepted by Switch1 and Switch3 for IST instance. From Switch1 and Switch3's perspective, Switch2 is the Root for all the VLANs for MST 0 instance. Switch1 has an additional role to play. One of its ports is a *boundary port*, meaning that it is connected to a different region. When it receives the BPDU from Switch2, it first modifies the BPDU before forwarding it on to Switch3. It adds an IST Master ID and IST Master Path Cost to the BPDU. By default, the IST Master ID is the bridge ID and the Master Path Cost is 0.

Figure 10-14 *CST Cloud*

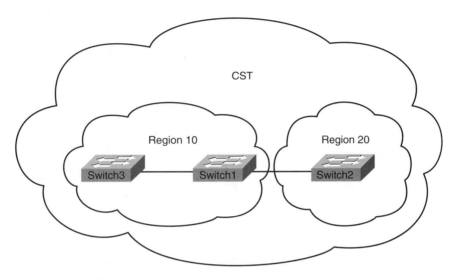

Two distinct methods exist for selecting an IST Master:

- The Root for the CST that is inside the region will also be selected as IST Master. For example, Switch2 will also be the IST Master for Region 20.

- The boundary bridge is defined as the smallest path cost to the CST Root. In Figure 10-14, that would be Switch1, because it has a direct connection to Switch2.

Figure 10-15 shows Switch1 adding the IST Master Path Cost, as depicted by the shaded boxes.

Figure 10-15 *BPDU Entering MST Region*

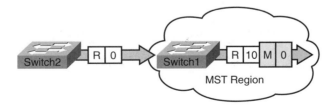

The objective of having an IST is to make the MST region appear as a single bridge. This is an important distinction because it allows for MST to have large Layer 2 networks. For instance, Region 10 is seen by other regions as one bridge with one port participating in spanning tree. The IST master bridge is used as transit by the local bridges within the region.

It is important to understand that one CST is available for the entire Layer 2 network. The CST topology is built based on IST. Also, remember that within the region, another spanning tree is locally significant to the region, as discussed in the next section.

Spanning Tree Inside the Region

In Figure 10-14, Region 10 and Region 20 have their own spanning-tree topology that is different from the CST spanning-tree topology. The locally significant spanning-tree topology is known as MSTI. There could be one instance or multiple instances depending on the design requirements. A region can have up to 15 MSTIs. Keep these three points in mind with respect to MSTI implementation:

- MSTIs exist inside the region.

- MSTIs have no direct interaction with outside the region.

- MST sends 1 BPDU for all the instances in that region. Within the BPDU, an MSTP Record (M-record) is maintained for each of the instances. M-record contains spanning-tree information for an MSTI.

MST Example—All Switches in the Same Region

Take a look at an example to solidify some of these concepts. Remember, MST requires a minimum of 7.1(1) Catalyst OS code. Switch1 will be the Root for even VLANs, and Switch2 will be the Root for odd VLANs. All these switches (see Figure 10-16) will be located in the same MST region. Follow the configuration guidelines in Example 10-16.

Figure 10-16 *Switches in the Same Region*

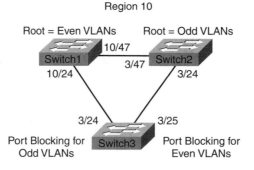

Example 10-16 *MST Configuration*

```
Switch1 (enable) set spantree mst config name grp1
!Defining the name for the MST
Switch1 (enable) set spantree mst config revision 10
!Revision number is set to 10
Switch1 (enable) set spantree mst config commit
!Any changes to name and revision number requires a commit afterwards or else the
changes will not take effect
Switch1 (enable) set spantree mode mst
!Turning MST on. This command disables PVST+
Switch2 (enable) set spantree mst config name grp1
Switch2 (enable) set spantree mst config revision 10
Switch2 (enable) set spantree mst config commit
Switch2 (enable) set spantree mode mst
Switch3 (enable) set spantree mst config name grp1
Switch3 (enable) set spantree mst config revision 10
Switch3 (enable) set spantree mst config commit
Switch3 (enable) set spantree mode mst
```

As mentioned in the "MST Regions" section, the configuration name, revision number, and VLAN mapping need to be the same for all the switches within the same region. The revision number is arbitrary and user defined. Ensure that ports connecting the switches are set to full duplex and are configured with IEEE 802.1Q trunking before commencing with MST configuration.

As noted on Switch1, the MST configuration name is grp1 with revision 10. Example 10-17 shows the only instance of IST that covers VLANS 1-4096. You need to now create two more instances for even and odd VLANs. Also, note in Example 10-17 that you can configure 15 additional MSTIs.

Example 10-17 *MST Region Configuration*

```
Switch1 (enable) show spantree mst config
Current (NVRAM) MST Region Configuration:
Configuration Name: grp1                         Revision: 10
Instance VLANs
-------- ----------------------------------------------------------------
IST      1-4094
  1       -
  2       -
  3       -
  4       -
  5       -
  6       -
  7       -
  8       -
  9       -
 10       -
```

continues

Example 10-17 *MST Region Configuration (Continued)*

```
   11      -
   12      -
   13      -
   14      -
   15      -
   ========================================================================
```

After creating the odd and even VLANs, as outlined in Example 10-18, commit them to the MST group.

Example 10-18 *MST Load-Balancing Configuration*

```
Switch1 (enable)set spantree mst 2 vlan
2,4,6,8,10,12,14,16,18,20,22,24,26,28,30,32,34,36,38,40,42,44,46,48,50
Switch1 (enable)set spantree mst 3 vlan
1,3,5,7,9,11,13,15,17,19,21,23,25,27,29,31,33,35,37,39,41,43,45,47,49
Switch1 (enable)set spantree mst config commit
Switch2 (enable)set spantree mst 2 vlan
2,4,6,8,10,12,14,16,18,20,22,24,26,28,30,32,34,36,38,40,42,44,46,48,50
Switch2 (enable)set spantree mst 3 vlan
1,3,5,7,9,11,13,15,17,19,21,23,25,27,29,31,33,35,37,39,41,43,45,47,49
Switch2 (enable)set spantree mst config commit
Switch3 (enable)set spantree mst 2 vlan
2,4,6,8,10,12,14,16,18,20,22,24,26,28,30,32,34,36,38,40,42,44,46,48,50
Switch3 (enable)set spantree mst 3 vlan
1,3,5,7,9,11,13,15,17,19,21,23,25,27,29,31,33,35,37,39,41,43,45,47,49
Switch3 (enable)set spantree mst config commit
```

Once again, looking at the MSTI table, you can see that instances 2 and 3 are now defined. (See Example 10-19.)

Example 10-19 *Update to MST Region Configuration*

```
Switch1 (enable) show spantree mst config
Current (NVRAM) MST Region Configuration:
Configuration Name: grp1                              Revision: 10
Instance VLANs
-------- ------------------------------------------------------------------
IST      51-4094
   1      -
   2      2,4,6,8,10,12,14,16,18,20,22,24,26,28,30,32,34,36,38,40,42,44
          46,48,50
   3      1,3,5,7,9,11,13,15,17,19,21,23,25,27,29,31,33,35,37,39,41,43
          45,47,49
   4      -
   5      -
   6      -
   7      -
   8      -
```

Example 10-19 *Update to MST Region Configuration (Continued)*

```
 9       -
10       -
11       -
12       -
13       -
14       -
15       -
===========================================================================
```

The last step required is to ensure that the appropriate switches are the Root for the VLANs. Switch1 and Switch2 have been configured to be Roots for even and odd VLANs in Example 10-20, respectively. The priority field has been reduced from 32771 to 24576 for both switches.

Example 10-20 *MST Root for VLAN 2*

```
Switch1 (enable) set spantree root mst 2
Instance 2 bridge priority set to 24576.
Instance 2 bridge max aging time set to 20.
Instance 2 bridge hello time set to 2.
Instance 2 bridge forward delay set to 15.
Switch2 (enable) set spantree root mst 3
Instance 3 bridge priority set to 24576.
Instance 3 bridge max aging time set to 20.
Instance 3 bridge hello time set to 2.
Instance 3 bridge forward delay set to 15.
```

Switch3 correctly recognizes Switch1 and Switch2 for their respective VLANs. The VLANs mapped information shows that Switch1 is the Root for all even VLANs (see Example 10-21), while Switch2 is the Root for all odd VLANs (see Example 10-22). The Role column shows the designation of the port with respect to the spanning-tree topology. Remember that the port role was defined by RSTP. The type field shows that all these ports are point to point, which means they are set at full duplex.

Example 10-21 *MST Information for VLAN 2*

```
Switch3 (enable) show spantree mst 2
Spanning tree mode          MST
Instance                    2
VLANs Mapped:               2,4,6,8,10,12,14,16,18,20,22,24,26,28,30,32,34,36
                            38,40,42,44,46,48,50
Designated Root             00-05-74-18-04-80
Designated Root Priority    24578   (root priority: 24576, sys ID ext: 2)
Designated Root Cost        200000     Remaining Hops 19
Designated Root Port        3/24
Bridge ID MAC ADDR          00-0b-fc-d4-23-80
```

continues

Example 10-21 *MST Information for VLAN 2 (Continued)*

```
Bridge ID Priority      32770  (bridge priority: 32768, sys ID ext: 2)
Port                 State         Role Cost      Prio Type
-------------------- ------------- ---- -------- ---- -------------------
3/24                 forwarding    ROOT  200000   32 P2P
3/25                 blocking      ALTR  200000   32 P2P
15/1                 forwarding    DESG   20000   32 P2P, Edge
```

Example 10-22 *MST Information for VLAN 3*

```
Switch3 (enable) show spantree mst 3
Spanning tree mode        MST
Instance                  3
VLANs Mapped:             1,3,5,7,9,11,13,15,17,19,21,23,25,27,29,31,33,35,37
                          39,41,43,45,47,49
Designated Root           00-01-63-29-bc-00
Designated Root Priority  24579  (root priority: 24576, sys ID ext: 3)
Designated Root Cost      200000     Remaining Hops 19
Designated Root Port      3/25
Bridge ID MAC ADDR        00-0b-fc-d4-23-80
Bridge ID Priority        32771  (bridge priority: 32768, sys ID ext: 3)
Port                 State         Role Cost      Prio Type
-------------------- ------------- ---- -------- ---- -------------------
3/24                 blocking      ALTR  200000   32 P2P
3/25                 forwarding    ROOT  200000   32 P2P
15/1                 forwarding    DESG   20000   32 P2P, Edge
```

You might have noticed the high costs associated with each port, as shown in Examples 10-21 and 10-22. These high values for ports are due to 802.1t implementation, which is mandatory with MST; 802.1t sets a 32-bit cost on port bandwidth. For instance, in legacy STP, the port cost for 10BASE-T port was at 100; now it is at 2,000,000. Table 10-2 shows the new values for each port based on its speed.

Table 10-2 *New Values for Ports*

Bandwidth (Mbps)	New Value (802.1t)	Original Value
10	2,000,000	100
100	200,000	19
1,000	20,000	4
10,000,000	2	

In legacy STP, the BID field was composed of 2-byte priority plus 6-byte MAC address. Because 802.1t steals 12 bits from the priority field to compose the VLAN number, the priority field can now only take 16 values by increments of 4096. The new BID is as follows:

BID = Priority (4 bits) + VLAN number (12 bits) + MAC (6 bytes)

MST Example—Multiple Regions

This section illustrates the significance of IST and multiple MSTIs by describing a simple example where two different regions are implemented. In Figure 10-17, Switch1 and Switch3 are in Region 10. Switch2 is in Region 20. The default IST is the only other instance.

Figure 10-17 *Multiple Regions*

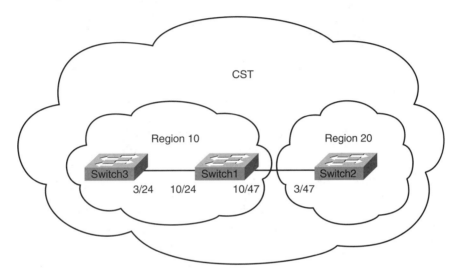

The first task is to define the two regions. Both Switch1 and Switch3 will have the same configuration. (See Example 10-23.)

Example 10-23 *MST Configuration for Two Regions*

```
Switch1 (enable) set spantree mst config name grp1
Switch1 (enable) set spantree mst config revision 10
Switch1 (enable) set spantree mst config commit
Switch1 (enable) set spantree mode mst
Switch3 (enable) set spantree mst config name grp1
Switch3 (enable) set spantree mst config revision 10
Switch3 (enable) set spantree mst config commit
Switch3 (enable) set spantree mode mst
Switch2 (enable) set spantree mst config name grp2
Switch2 (enable) set spantree mst config revision 20
Switch2 (enable) set spantree mst config commit
Switch2 (enable) set spantree mode mst
```

Switch1 and Switch2 in Example 10-24 are configured for grp1 and grp2, respectively.

Example 10-24 *MST Region Configuration for Regions 10 and 20*

```
Switch1 (enable) show spantree mst config
Current (NVRAM) MST Region Configuration:
Configuration Name: grp1                         Revision: 10
Instance VLANs
-------- --------------------------------------------------------------
IST       1-4094
Switch2 (enable) show spantree mst config
Current (NVRAM) MST Region Configuration:
Configuration Name: grp2                         Revision: 20
Instance VLANs
-------- --------------------------------------------------------------
IST       1-4094
```

IST instance makes a region appear as one bridge to the rest of the network. The MST 0 instance is the IST instance. From the output shown in Example 10-25, the bridge for the CST is Switch2, 00-01-63-29-bc-00. The designated RP to Switch2 correctly shows 10/47, which is directly connected to Switch2. Also, notice Master ID MAC address and IST Master Path Cost are different for the two regions. All other internal switches within the region will use the master bridge as a transit to other regions. The boundary key in the type field shows that ports 3/47 and 10/47 are connected to a different region.

Example 10-25 *IST Spanning Tree Information for Switch1 and Switch2*

```
Switch1 (enable) show spantree mst 0
Spanning tree mode         MST
Instance                   0
VLANs Mapped:              1-4094
Designated Root            00-01-63-29-bc-00
!Correctly sees Switch2 as the root for CST
Designated Root Priority   24576   (root priority: 24576, sys ID ext: 0)
Designated Root Cost       200000
Designated Root Port       10/47
Root Max Age   20 sec   Hello Time 2  sec   Forward Delay 15 sec
IST Master ID MAC ADDR        00-05-74-18-04-80
!the local bridge is the master bridge
IST Master ID Priority     32768
IST Master Path Cost       0            Remaining Hops 20
Bridge ID MAC ADDR         00-05-74-18-04-80
Bridge ID Priority         32768   (bridge priority: 32768, sys ID ext: 0)
Bridge Max Age 20 sec   Hello Time 2  sec   Forward Delay 15 sec   Max Hops 20
Port                    State          Role Cost    Prio Type
--------------------    -------------  ---- -------- ---- --------------------
10/24                   forwarding     DESG  200000   32 P2P
10/47                   forwarding     ROOT  200000   32 P2P, Boundary
15/1                    forwarding     DESG   20000   32 P2P, Edge
```

Example 10-25 *IST Spanning Tree Information for Switch1 and Switch2 (Continued)*

```
Switch2 (enable) show spantree mst 0
Spanning tree mode        MST
Instance                  0
VLANs Mapped:             1-4094
Designated Root           00-01-63-29-bc-00
!Root for the CST
Designated Root Priority  24576  (root priority: 24576, sys ID ext: 0)
Designated Root Cost      0
Designated Root Port      1/0
Root Max Age  20 sec  Hello Time 2  sec   Forward Delay 15 sec
IST Master ID MAC ADDR    00-01-63-29-bc-00
!The local bridge is the master bridge
IST Master ID Priority    24576
IST Master Path Cost      0            Remaining Hops 20
Bridge ID MAC ADDR        00-01-63-29-bc-00
!The local bridge is the root for CST
Bridge ID Priority        24576  (Bridge priority: 24576, sys ID ext: 0)
Bridge Max Age 20 sec  Hello Time 2  sec   Forward Delay 15 sec  Max Hops 20
Port                    State          Role Cost     Prio Type
----------------------- -------------- ---- -------- ---- -------------------
3/47                    forwarding     DESG  200000   32 P2P, Boundary
!Connected to a different region or legacy STP network
15/1                    forwarding     DESG   20000   32 P2P, Edge
```

Switch3 accepts Switch1 as the master bridge, as shown in Example 10-26.

Example 10-26 *IST Spanning Tree Information for Switch3*

```
Switch3 (enable) show spantree mst 0
Spanning tree mode        MST
Instance                  0
VLANs Mapped:             1-4094
Designated Root           00-01-63-29-bc-00
!Switch2 is seen as the Root for CST
Designated Root Priority  24576  (root priority: 24576, sys ID ext: 0)
Designated Root Cost      200000
Designated Root Port      3/24
Root Max Age  20 sec  Hello Time 2  sec   Forward Delay 15 sec
IST Master ID MAC ADDR    00-05-74-18-04-80
!Switch1 is seen as the master bridge for Region 10
IST Master ID Priority    32768
IST Master Path Cost      200000       Remaining Hops 19
Bridge ID MAC ADDR        00-0b-fc-d4-23-80
Bridge ID Priority        32768  (bridge priority: 32768, sys ID ext: 0)
Bridge Max Age 20 sec  Hello Time 2  sec   Forward Delay 15 sec  Max Hops 20
Port                    State          Role Cost     Prio Type
----------------------- -------------- ---- -------- ---- -------------------
3/24                    forwarding     ROOT  200000   32 P2P
15/1                    forwarding     DESG   20000   32 P2P, Edge
```

So far, the discussion has been with the IST spanning tree. Let us create an MSTI within the regions. In Region 10, Switch1 will be the Root for the 50 VLANs. Also make Switch2 the Root for the same VLANs in Region 20. A red flag should rise. How can there be two Roots for the same VLANs? The simple answer is regions. Each region can have its own spanning-tree instances and they do not affect the spanning-tree instances of other regions. Follow the configuration shown in Example 10-27.

Example 10-27 *Configuring Roots for VLANs 1-50*

```
Switch1 (enable) set spantree mst 1 vlan 1-50
Switch1 (enable) set spantree mst config commit
Switch2 (enable) set spantree mst 1 vlan 1-50
Switch2 (enable) set spantree mst config commit
Switch3 (enable) set spantree mst 1 vlan 1-50
Switch3 (enable) set spantree mst config commit

Switch1 (enable) set spantree root mst 1
Instance 1 bridge max aging time set to 20.
Instance 1 bridge hello time set to 2.
Instance 1 bridge forward delay set to 15.

Switch2 (enable) set spantree root mst 1
Instance 1 bridge priority set to 24576.
Instance 1 bridge max aging time set to 20.
Instance 1 bridge hello time set to 2.
Instance 1 bridge forward delay set to 15.
```

Both Switch1 and Switch2 have been configured to be the Roots for VLANs 1-50 in their respective regions. Because these VLANs are only locally significant, no information exists regarding master bridge/path cost. An additional port designation appears under the Role Column. (See Example 10-28.) The BDRY role appears in the MSTI when the port is connected to a different region or legacy STP.

Example 10-28 *Spanning-Tree Information for MST Instance 1*

```
Switch1 (enable) show spantree mst 1
Spanning tree mode        MST
Instance                  1
VLANs Mapped:             1-50
Designated Root           00-05-74-18-04-80
!Notice Switch1 is the root for vlan 1-50
Designated Root Priority  24577  (root priority: 24576, sys ID ext: 1)
Designated Root Cost      0              Remaining Hops 20
Designated Root Port      1/0
Bridge ID MAC ADDR        00-05-74-18-04-80
Bridge ID Priority        24577  (bridge priority: 24576, sys ID ext: 1)
```

Example 10-28 *Spanning-Tree Information for MST Instance 1 (Continued)*

```
Port                       State         Role Cost     Prio Type
------------------------   ------------  ---- --------  ---- --------------------
10/24                      forwarding    DESG 200000    32 P2P
10/47                      forwarding    BDRY 200000    32 P2P, Boundary
15/1                       forwarding    DESG  20000    32 P2P, Edge
Switch2 (enable) show spantree mst 1
Spanning tree mode         MST
Instance                   1
VLANs Mapped:              1-50
Designated Root            00-01-63-29-bc-00
!Switch2 is the root in Region 20 for vlan 1-50
Designated Root Priority   24577  (root priority: 24576, sys ID ext: 1)
Designated Root Cost       0             Remaining Hops 20
Designated Root Port       1/0
Bridge ID MAC ADDR         00-01-63-29-bc-00
Bridge ID Priority         24577  (bridge priority: 24576, sys ID ext: 1)
Port                       State         Role Cost     Prio Type
------------------------   ------------  ---- --------  ---- --------------------
3/47                       forwarding    BDRY 200000    32 P2P, Boundary
15/1                       forwarding    DESG  20000    32 P2P, Edge
```

From Switch3's perspective, it sees only Switch1 as the Root for VLANs 1-50. (See Example 10-29.)

Example 10-29 *Spanning-Tree Information for MST Instance 1*

```
Switch3 (enable) show spantree mst 1
Spanning tree mode         MST
Instance                   1
VLANs Mapped:              1-50
Designated Root            00-05-74-18-04-80
!Switch1 is the Root
Designated Root Priority   24577  (root priority: 24576, sys ID ext: 1)
Designated Root Cost       200000        Remaining Hops 19
Designated Root Port       3/24
Bridge ID MAC ADDR         00-0b-fc-d4-23-80
Bridge ID Priority         32769  (bridge priority: 32768, sys ID ext: 1)
Port                       State         Role Cost     Prio Type
------------------------   ------------  ---- --------  ---- --------------------
3/24                       forwarding    ROOT 200000    32 P2P
15/1                       forwarding    DESG  20000    32 P2P, Edge
```

MST Example—MST Connected to PVST+ Network

MST through IST will also be able to communicate with a non-MST bridge such as PVST+. From PVST+'s perspective, the MST region appears as one bridge. In Figure 10-18, Switch2 will now be PVST+ bridge. Switch1 recognizes its port 10/47 is connected to a non-MST bridge.

Figure 10-18 *MST Connected to PVST+ Switch*

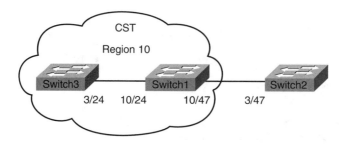

The BPDU it received contains information regarding who the Root is and the path cost to the Root. Switch1 will add the IST Master ID along with Master Path Cost and forwards the new BPDU to Switch3. This setup and behavior are no different if Switch2 was an MST-bridge. The only caveat is that because PVST+ does not understand 802.1w, the ports in the IST instance will lose their RSTP capability. Therefore, it is not recommended to have multiple modes of spanning tree in the network. Example 10-30 shows how to change back Switch2 to PVST+ mode.

Example 10-30 *Changing the Switch to PVST+ Mode*

```
Switch2 (enable) set spantree mode pvst+
Switch1 (enable) show spantree mst 0
Spanning tree mode        MST
Instance                  0
VLANs Mapped:             51-4094
Designated Root           00-01-63-29-bc-00
!The root is Switch2
Designated Root Priority  32768   (root priority: 32768, sys ID ext: 0)
Designated Root Cost      200000
Designated Root Port      10/47
Root Max Age   20 sec  Hello Time 2  sec   Forward Delay 15 sec
IST Master ID MAC ADDR    00-05-74-18-04-80
!Master bridge is local
IST Master ID Priority    32768
IST Master Path Cost      0              Remaining Hops 20
Bridge ID MAC ADDR        00-05-74-18-04-80
Bridge ID Priority        32768  (bridge priority: 32768, sys ID ext: 0)
Bridge Max Age 20 sec  Hello Time 2  sec   Forward Delay 15 sec  Max Hops 20
Port                      State         Role Cost      Prio Type
------------------------- ------------- ---- --------- ---- -------------------
10/24                     forwarding    DESG 200000    32 P2P
10/47                     forwarding    ROOT 200000    32 P2P, Boundary(PVST)
15/1                      forwarding    DESG 20000     32 P2P, Edge
```

UniDirectional Link Detection

Although the UniDirectional Link Detection (UDLD) protocol falls outside of STP, UDLD has numerous benefits that make it essential in a Layer 2 network. UDLD's function is to prevent a one-way communication between adjacent devices. When UDLD detects one-way conversation, it can do one of two things depending on whether UDLD is configured in Normal mode or Aggressive mode. In Normal mode, UDLD simply changes the UDLD-enabled port to undetermined state if it stops receiving UDLD messages from its directly connected neighbor. Aggressive mode was introduced in Catalyst OS 5.4(3); it will make eight attempts to re-establish the UDLD neighbor relation before error disabling the port. Aggressive mode is the preferred method of configuring UDLD. Bottom line, by preventing this one-way communication, UDLD can be very useful in spanning-tree networks.

UDLD was first introduced in Catalyst OS 5.1(1). UDLD is a Layer 2 protocol that is enabled between adjacent switches. It uses MAC 01-00-0c-cc-cc-cc with SNAP HDLC protocol type 0x0111. Example 10-31 illustrates the UDLD packet format.

Example 10-31 *UDLD Packet*

```
Multicast Address:      01-00-0c-cc-cc-cc
LLC:                          0xAAAA03
Org ID:                       0x00000c
HDLC Protocol Type: 0x0111
      TVLs (Type Length and Value):
      0x0001:          Device ID
      0x0002:          Port ID
      0x0003:          Echo LV
      0x0004:          Message Interval TLV
      0x0005:          Timeout Interval TLV
```

For example, in Figure 10-19, the TX transceiver from Switch1 goes faulty and is not sending configuration BPDUs to Switch3. To make matters worse, Switch1 is not detecting the faulty transceiver and, as a result, it will not bring the port down. Because Switch3 is not receiving the BPDUs, it assumes that it has lost its connection to the Root. It will transition its blocking port to forwarding state. It will change its original RP that was directly connected to Switch1 to DP. Switch3 will assign the port that is connected to Switch2 as its RP. The network now is no longer loop free. A potential for a counterclockwise one-way loop exists. If a host from Switch2 sends a broadcast message, both Switch1 and Switch2 will receive the broadcast. Switch3 will forward the broadcast to Switch1, which, in turn, will forward it back to Switch2, and so on. UDLD, in Aggressive mode, helps spanning tree in this type of an event by error disabling the port.

Figure 10-19 *Bad Transceiver*

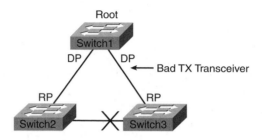

The two adjacent devices send UDLD packets at intervals of 15 seconds. The packets are echoed back by the adjacent switch to its neighbor, informing the upstream switch that it received the UDLD message. In Example 10-32, Switch1 receives a UDLD packet from Switch2's port 1/1. Because it received a UDLD packet, Switch1 will reset its UDLD neighbor cache table. The function of the UDLD neighbor cache table is to ensure that the neighbor is still active. If the cache table times out, UDLD will error disable the port as is in the case of Aggressive mode. Any time a UDLD message is received, the cache table timers are reset.

Example 10-32 *UDLD syslog Message*

```
Switch1 (enable) UDLD(1,2)Rcvd msg #1 from TBA04081025(Switch#2) port 1/1
UDLD(1,2)Found my own ID pair in 2way conn list
UDLD(1,2)Udld packet memory released
UDLD(1,2)[80974]InbandTransmit succeeded
UDLD(1,2)[81343]Received packet, parsing...
UDLD(1,2)New_entry = 835f2e90
UDLD()Entry added: 2 entries cached
```

UDLD needs to be first globally enabled, and then at the port level running Catalyst OS code, as shown in Example 10-33.

Example 10-33 *Enabling the UDLD Feature*

```
Switch1 (enable) set udld enable
UDLD enabled globally
Switch1 (enable) set udld enable 1/2
UDLD enabled on port 1/2.
Warning: UniDirectional Link Detection should be enabled on all
  the ends of the connection in order to work properly.
```

Table 10-3 shows the four different types of port states defined by UDLD. To check a port's link state, use the **show udld port** command, as shown in Example 10-34.

Table 10-3   *UDLD Port States*

Port State	Function
Undetermined	Currently attempting to detect neighbor or neighbor is not configured for UDLD.
Not Applicable	UDLD is disabled on the port.
Shutdown	UDLD is detected and port is shutdown.
Bidirectional	UDLD is working fine. Adjacent devices see each other's UDLD messages.

Example 10-34 *Display UDLD Configuration for Port 1/2*

```
Switch1 (enable) show udld port 1/2
UDLD             : enabled
Message Interval : 15 seconds
Port      Admin Status  Aggressive Mode  Link State
--------  ------------  ---------------  ---------------
 1/2      enabled       disabled         bidirectional
```

Example 10-35 is a hidden command that shows the UDLD state of the neighbor. The output shows the neighbor is in bidirectional state with Switch1.

Example 10-35 *Hidden UDLD Command*

```
Switch1 (enable) show udld neighbor
Port     Device Name                     Device ID     Port-ID OperState
-------- ------------------------------- ------------- ------- -------------
 1/2     TBA04081025(Switch2)            00016329bc00 1/1      bidirectional
```

Finally, Example 10-36 shows how to configure UDLD for Aggressive mode.

Example 10-36 *Enabling UDLD Aggressive Mode*

```
Switch1 (enable) set udld aggressive-mode enable 1/2
Aggressive UDLD enabled on port 1/2.
Warning: Aggressive Mode for UniDirectional Link Detection
should be enabled only on ports not connected to hubs,
media converters or similar devices.
Switch1 (enable) show udld port 1/2
UDLD             : enabled
Message Interval : 15 seconds
Port      Admin Status  Aggressive Mode  Link State
--------  ------------  ---------------  ---------------
 1/2      enabled       enabled          bidirectional
```

Summary

Legacy STP has numerous drawbacks with respect to convergence time and potential loops. Features such as portfast, Root Guard, and UplinkFast help address some the shortcomings of legacy STP. RSTP, 802.1w, has recently become available in 7.5(1) Catalyst OS code. Prior to this code, it was not possible to run RSTP alone. MST, 802.1s, implementation in Cisco devices also requires 802.1w and 802.1t protocols. Essentially, MST runs on top of RSTP. RSTP addresses the issue with convergence time. It natively has features similar to UplinkFast and BackboneFast. Unlike legacy STP, RSTP BPDUs have been modified to include port designation and proposal/agreement mechanism between adjacent bridges. MST helps scale Layer 2 networks while at the same time provides load-balancing capability. MST is a compromise between PVST+ and CST. Finally, this chapter also addressed UDLD protocol and its benefits.

This chapter covers the following topics:

- Layer 3 designs
- Building blocks
- Campus design
- Catalyst Supervisor and switch fabric redundancy

CHAPTER 11

Design and Implementation Best Practices

One goal of every network design is to provide users as much bandwidth as possible, as often as possible. Sounds easy, right? Network administrators often use terms such as highly available, redundant, scalable, and resilient to describe their network designs. To make good on the implied promises of these terms, administrators should adopt certain best practices.

Many long-time Cisco customers respond to the latest switching design best practices by saying "Just a few years ago I was told to switch where possible and route where I must, now I am told to route where possible and switch only where I must. What is the deal?" A best practice is only a best practice until your requirements or a technology change sufficiently to invalidate the best practice in favor of a new one. The term best practice does not indicate that only one way exists to accomplish a task, it only indicates that in the majority of circumstances experience demonstrates a certain solution to be a success. In the case of LAN switching, customers were told for years to implement Layer 2-only solutions to achieve high-speed Ethernet data transfer rates. With almost universal support of Transmission Control Protocol/Internet Protocol (TCP/IP) for applications and much improved hardware capabilities, these same customers are now being advised to implement Layer 3/4 solutions in those same networks.

The best network design is the one that meets the needs of its users. No one "correct" switched design exists, only proven design principles that should be incorporated where possible. Designs can differ based on a number of real-world factors including budgets, available existing hardware, application requirements, and implementation timelines. The key is to understand and weigh the pros and cons of each design principle against the overall goals for the design.

Layer 3 Designs

Designs that incorporate Layer 3/4 aware hardware rather than Layer 2-only aware hardware have many proven benefits including, first and foremost, a reduced reliance on spanning tree for redundancy, followed by more intelligent routing or treatment of traffic. Cisco's current recommendations for switching designs focus on the three-tiered core/distribution/access model, implementing Layer 3 connections between the core and distribution devices, and Layer 2 connections between the distribution and access layers. As

Layer 3 switching capabilities become common even in the least expensive access layer switch platforms, the three-tiered model is likely to adopt a Layer 3 switching approach everywhere, not just in the core and distribution layers. Figure 11-1 illustrates a relatively simple three-layer core, distribution, and access design model.

Figure 11-1 *Three-Layer Design Model*

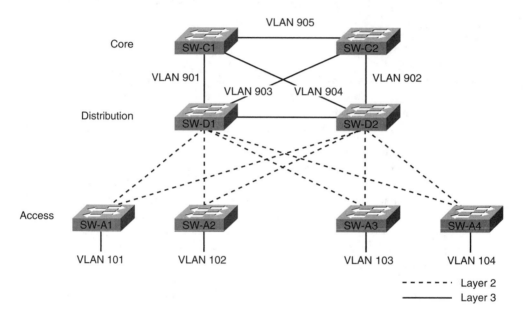

NOTE   The switching examples used in this chapter use a slightly different naming convention than previous chapters, incorporating the layer into the switch name. For example, SW-D2 indicates Switch2 in the distribution layer.

In the first few examples, such as Figure 11-1, each access layer switch is assigned a single VLAN for user data, and that VLAN does not extend beyond that access layer switch. This is similar to the configuration examples in Chapter 7, "Configuring Switches." Although it often makes sense to assign more than one VLAN to an access-layer switch, in an ideal design those VLANs would not be trunked between access-layer switches. Although not trunking, these VLANs might be more difficult to do with switched infrastructures that have evolved over a period of years; new designs should adopt this best practice, and existing designs can be converted incrementally. One of the main benefits of assigning data VLAN on a per-switch basis is an elimination of Layer 2 loops in spanning tree, resulting in a much-simplified troubleshooting process.

In contrast to the configuration examples in Chapter 7, each access layer switch in Figure 11-1 has a Layer 2 connection to both SW-D1 and SW-D2. Like the examples in Chapter 7, the connections between the distribution and core switches are routed Layer 3 connections and use VLAN numbers 901–905 that are not utilized for any access layer devices. No Layer 2 spanning-tree loops exist in the design illustrated in Figure 11-1. Even though no spanning-tree loops exist in this configuration, spanning tree is not disabled. Spanning tree is enabled by default and should remain on even in loop-free topologies as a loop-prevention mechanism.

Before finalizing and implementing any switching design, it is vitally important to understand as much as possible about the anticipated traffic flow. Not understanding the traffic flow might result in high-bandwidth connections being underutilized and lower bandwidth connections being overrun with traffic. Figure 11-1 represents an almost fully meshed design from a core and distribution perspective, with each core and distribution switch connecting to every other with the exception of switches SW-D1 and SW-D2.

Building Blocks

When designing a switched network, following a modular approach is a good practice. These modules can be thought of as the building blocks of an overall network. After the design and configuration of the basic building blocks are well understood inside an organization, additional building blocks can be added as the network grows, without greatly increasing the complexity of troubleshooting and operating the network. Following this approach, Figure 11-2 illustrates a simple building block that could be used to handle switching in a single location. In this figure, each access layer switch services a single floor of users in a facility, with each access switch having dual connections to the distribution switches. In the smallest of networks, this may be the only infrastructure that exists, and in this case, the distribution switches also function as core switches in what is termed a collapsed backbone. In this situation, a trunk carrying the two access layer VLANs connects the core/distribution switches and forms simple loops for VLANs 101 and 102 that spanning tree will block. In this connection, users connected to either switch have connections to both distribution layer switches, and the distribution switches provide Layer 3 routing via switched virtual interfaces (SVIs) for each VLAN. In addition, Hot Standby Router Protocol (HSRP) can be configured so that SW-D1 is the active router for VLAN 101, while SW-D2 is the active router for VLAN 102. Administrators then point workstation default gateways to the appropriate HSRP IP address for their respective VLANs.

Figure 11-2 *Simple Building Block*

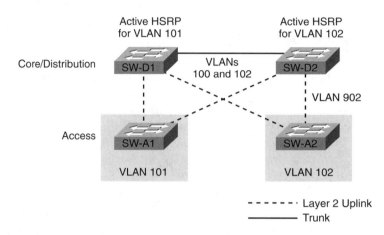

The building block design in Figure 11-2 represents a very simple spanning tree. With this simple design and improvements made using the Rapid Spanning Tree Protocol (RSTP) discussed in Chapter 10, "Implementing and Tuning Spanning Tree," administrators are unlikely to encounter spanning-tree reconvergence problems. In this configuration, HSRP communication occurs directly between the two HSRP peers—SW-D1 and SW-D2—via the trunk between those two switches. As the need to expand the network arises, more building blocks can be added. Figure 11-2 shows VLANs 101 and 102 shaded to indicate that all ports on SW-A1 and SW-A2 will be members of those VLANs. The shading is not a boundary for VLANs 101 and 102. For example, the ports linking SW-A1 and SW-D1 are in VLAN 101, as are the ports linking SW-A1 to SW-D2.

Figure 11-3 illustrates a typical configuration for remote offices where a single router with a T1 or similar speed connection into a Frame Relay network connects to both distribution switches via either 10 Mbps or 10/100 Mbps Ethernet. In this case, the bandwidth bottleneck is not the 10/100 Mbps connection from the distribution switches, but the T1 connection (1.536 Mbps) connection to a home office or other larger location.

As mentioned in the auto-negotiation section in Chapter 1, "LAN Switching Foundation Technologies," connections between switches and external routers should be manually configured for the appropriate speed and duplex, and not allowed to auto-negotiate. In Figure 11-3, two different VLANs not in use elsewhere in the network are used to connect the switches to the routers. IP subnets with a 30-bit subnet mask like the kind used in the examples in Chapter 7 can be used for these connections, assuming the distribution switches have Layer 3 routing capabilities.

Figure 11-3 *Typical Remote Office Design*

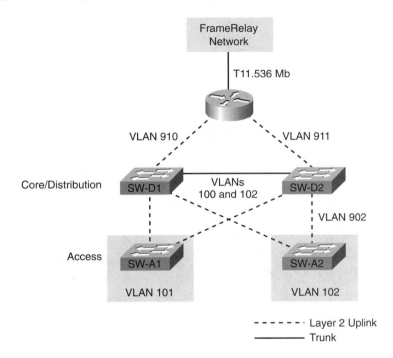

Figure 11-4 shows the converged state of the spanning trees for VLANs 101 and 102 when SW-D1 is the root bridge for VLAN 101 and SW-D2 is the root bridge for VLAN 102. Host 1 is connected to a port on SW-A1 in VLAN 101, and Host 2 is connected to a port on SW-A2 in VLAN 102. Refer to Chapter 10 for a refresher on spanning-tree configuration or on spanning-tree terminology. In Figure 11-4, the port on SW-A1 connecting the switch to SW-D2 is in a blocking state for VLAN 101 because that port is farthest from the root bridge, SW-D1. The same blocking state occurs for VLAN 102 for the port on SW-A2 connecting the switch to SW-D1. When Host 1 on VLAN 101 needs to communicate with Host 2 on VLAN 102, it sends its traffic to its configured default gateway, in this case SW-D1, which is the active HSRP router for VLAN 101. Although SW-D1 has a direct physical connection to VLAN 102 and SW-A2, spanning tree is blocking the connection, and the traffic is forced to take an indirect path through SW-D2 to reach SW-A2 and, ultimately, Host 2.

Figure 11-4 *Converged Spanning Tree*

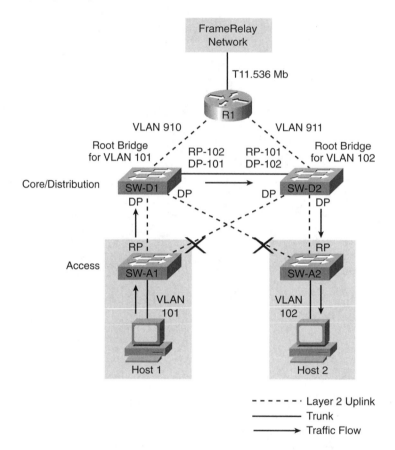

In Figure 11-5, the trunk between SW-D1 and SW-D2 is removed. In this configuration, no loops exist for VLANs 101 and 102, so all ports on SW-D1 and SW-D2 are now forwarding. The arrows indicating traffic flow now show traffic originating on Host 1 being sent directly to SW-A2 by SW-D1, bypassing SW-D2 altogether. This configuration works well when VLANs can be isolated to a single switch, and when connections to the distribution layer are dual-homed. Again, in this scenario, HSRP traffic for switches SW-D1 and SW-D2 flows through the access layer. This type of building block will be used in the "Campus Design" section of this chapter.

Figure 11-5 *Removal of Trunk Between SW-D1 and SW-D2*

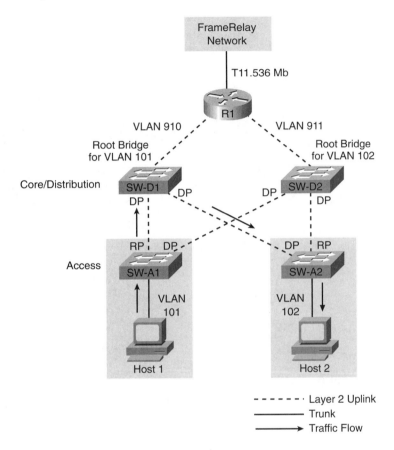

Removing the link between SW-D1 and SW-D2 if other critical devices are single attached to only one of the distribution switches could create potential pitfalls. Figure 11-6 shows the addition of a router R2 with a single attachment to SW-D2, and a server with a single attachment to SW-D2. As long as nothing goes wrong and all the interfaces stay up and running, reaching these new devices from anywhere in the network should not be a problem. Should a connection between an access layer switch and a distribution switch fail, as illustrated in Figure 11-6, communication is disrupted. Single-attached devices also represent a single point of failure in the design should the switch they are attached to fail completely.

Figure 11-6 *Single-Attached Router and Server*

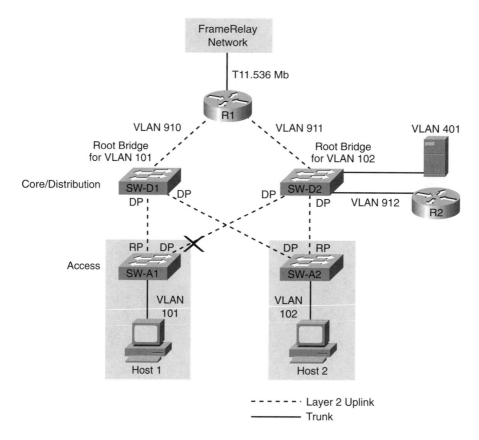

In Figure 11-6, the link between SW-A1 and SW-D2 fails. Because no connection exists between SW-D1 and SW-D2 carrying VLAN 101, and no inter-VLAN routing has been configured, Host 1 cannot communicate with the server in VLAN 401 or R2. It may seem obvious to avoid these kinds of single-attached configurations by dual attaching each router and dual attaching each server, but, often times, the responsibility of overall network administration is segmented into LAN, WAN, and application teams. In some circumstances, servers might get added without the knowledge of the LAN team, and problems do not surface unless a failure of the LAN infrastructure occurs. The next section, "Campus Design," outlines a few options to prevent such problems from occurring.

Campus Design

Although it is difficult to capture a "typical" campus network design in a single illustration, campus networks, in general, experience many common demands including support of large numbers of end users, servers, and the need for WAN connectivity to either the Internet or to other locations. Figure 11-7 illustrates a simple campus network design using the three-tiered core, distribution, access design principle, with the addition of a building block of dual-attached switches to accommodate servers.

Figure 11-7 *Simple Campus Design*

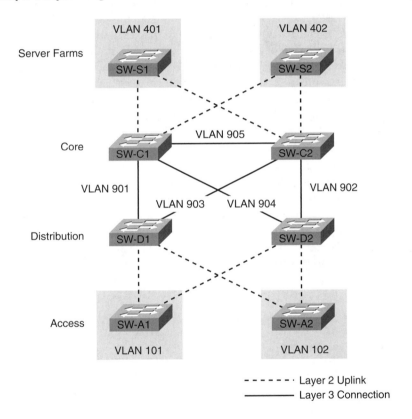

In this design, the building block outlined in the previous section is used at the access and distribution layer without the connection between SW-D1 and SW-D2. This design differs from the previous collapsed backbone design by incorporating a true core layer of switches with fully meshed connections to the distribution layer. Figure 11-7 uses the VLAN numbering scheme outlined in Chapter 7. The switches in the core and distribution layer are all capable of Layer 3 routing and are using networks with 30-bit subnet masks for VLANs 901–905. This creates a routed core infrastructure with only the access layer and server switches utilizing Layer 2 uplinks. Administrators that have experience with Cisco routers might recognize that the links between core switches are providing the functionality that was once provided by high-speed WAN links. In this configuration, the core and distribution switches are configured to run some type of dynamic routing protocol, such as OSPF or EIGRP, to facilitate routing and form neighbor relationships across their direct connections in VLANs 901–905. Refer to Chapter 7 for details on configuring dynamic routing protocols on Catalyst switches. It is assumed that in most designs the core and distribution switches will be higher-end platforms with more switching capacity, and links between core and distribution switches will be high speed. As a result, it is a good practice to avoid allowing the core and distribution switches to route traffic via access layer or server VLANs, such as 101 and 102 or 401 and 402. Routing via the access layer or server block can be disabled in most routing protocols by issuing a **passive-interface** command for each interface connecting to those VLANs. Example 11-1 changes gigabitethernet 1/1 on SW-D1 to passive mode for EIGRP.

TIP   Although the assignment of a VLAN number to Layer 3 interfaces is not necessary on switches using native software or the Cisco IOS interface, it is a best practice to follow a defined IP addressing and VLAN numbering scheme. Administrators may elect to pair VLAN numbers with IP network numbers even though actual configuration of those VLAN numbers on the switch is not necessary. This way, platforms that run hybrid software and require VLANs to be assigned can follow the same IP and VLAN numbering scheme.

Example 11-1 *Passive Interface Command for EIGRP*

```
SW-D1#config terminal
Enter configuration commands, one per line.  End with CNTL/Z.
SW-D1(config)#router eigrp 100
SW-D1(config-router)#passive-interface gigabitethernet 1/1
SW-D1(config-router)#end

SW-D1#show ip protocol
Routing Protocol is "eigrp 100"
  Outgoing update filter list for all interfaces is
  Incoming update filter list for all interfaces is
  Default networks flagged in outgoing updates
```

Example 11-1 *Passive Interface Command for EIGRP (Continued)*

```
Default networks accepted from incoming updates
EIGRP metric weight K1=1, K2=0, K3=1, K4=0, K5=0
EIGRP maximum hopcount 100
EIGRP maximum metric variance 1
Redistributing: eigrp 100
Automatic network summarization is in effect
Routing for Networks:
   172.16.192.0/18
Passive Interface(s):
   GigabitEthernet1/1
Routing Information Sources:
   Gateway         Distance      Last Update
   172.16.240.13        90       00:00:33
   172.16.240.6         90       2w2d
   172.16.240.18        90       1w0d
Distance: internal 90 external 170
```

After the **passive-interface** command is issued successfully, the output from the **show ip protocols** command in Example 11-1 indicates the gigabitethernet 1/1 interface is passive for EIGRP. Refer to the documentation on Cisco.com for more information about disabling routing for protocols, such as OSPF and EIGRP, for specific interfaces.

Often, overlap exists between core, distribution, and access layer positioning when it comes to selecting a switching platform for each layer. As the switching capabilities of each of the Cisco platforms continue to grow, switches once used in a network core are sometimes redeployed in a distribution or even access layer as newer models or capabilities become available. This is no different than a Pentium II fileserver installed in 2000 being reused for a simpler function in 2004 in favor of a Pentium IV system. Cisco positions its higher-end platforms such as the Catalyst 6000/6500 as core and distribution switches, the Catalyst 4500 as a distribution and high-capacity closet switch, and the Catalyst 3750 as an access layer switching solution. Platform positioning is simply a guideline for placement of switches in a network and is not a hard and fast rule. Many networks run exclusively Catalyst 6500s in the core, distribution, and access layer, and others use what is typically considered a distribution switch in the core. The key is to match the switch capabilities with current and future network traffic.

In Figure 11-7, traffic routed between VLANs 101 and 102 is accomplished by the distribution switches SW-D1 and SW-D2, because no Layer 2 loops exist on those VLANs. Figure 11-8 again introduces Host 1 and Host 2 and illustrates the traffic flow between them should a link between the access layer and distribution layer fail.

Figure 11-8 *Access Layer Link Failure*

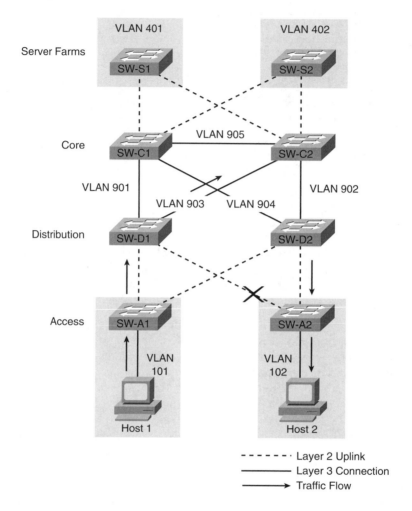

Because traffic from Host 1 is being sent to the active HSRP address on SW-D1 to be routed, when the link between SW-A2 and SW-D1 fails, SW-D1 recognizes a path in its routing table to VLAN 102 via SW-C2. This is due to SW-D2 advertising VLAN 102 via a dynamic routing protocol to each of its neighbors SW-C1 and SW-C2. The path from SW-A1 to VLAN 102 through SW-C2 is the shortest, assuming the bandwidth of each of the links connecting the core and distribution switches is identical, and no customization of routing metrics has been configured. In most networks, link failures between switches are not a frequent occurrence, and temporary routing of using an indirect path through the core is not an issue. If links between the switches in an environment fail often, bigger issues likely exist. One alternative to this design is to add another Layer 3 link between the distribution switches. This option and the resulting traffic flow are illustrated in Figure 11-9.

Figure 11-9 *Addition of a Link Between SW-D1 and SW-D2*

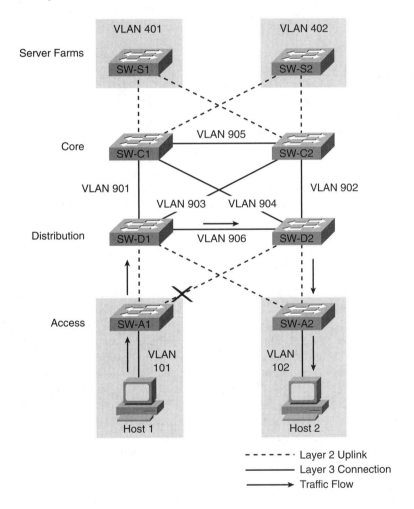

The link between SW-D1 and SW-D2 continues the VLAN numbering convention by using VLAN 906, and a dynamic routing neighbor relationship is formed between SW-D1 and SW-D2 using this link. As a result, when the link between the SW-A2 and SW-D1 is lost, traffic bypasses the core switches and is routed via the distribution layer. Seeing this new traffic flow, administrators may wonder why any design would exclude the link between SW-D1 and SW-D2. Although there is certainly nothing wrong with adding the link, it does add cost to the design because each pair of distribution switches will require an extra connection, and is really only useful in a scenario where an access layer link has failed or when a device is single attached to a distribution layer switch. Access layer failures should be rare, and single-attached devices to the distribution layer should be avoided whenever possible.

Traffic Flows

When designing any network, it is important to understand how the expected traffic from source to destination will be accommodated by the design. Figure 11-10 illustrates the expected traffic flow between Host 1 and Server 1.

Host 1 is configured to use the active HSRP address for VLAN 101 on SW-D1 as its default gateway, and Server 1 is configured to use the active HSRP address for VLAN 401 on SW-C1 as its default gateway. Assuming all the links between the core and distribution switches are of equal speed, SW-D1 will have two paths in its routing table to VLAN 401. Dynamic routing protocols, such as EIGRP, automatically load balance traffic using up to four equal cost paths by default. You can adjust this behavior to use fewer than four paths or up to eight paths using the **maximum-paths** command. (See Example 11-2.) Normally, the default of four maximum paths is sufficient and should not be changed.

The same situation exists on the return path from Server 1 to Host 1 because SW-C1 has equal paths in its routing table to VLAN 101 via SW-D1 and SW-D2. In this situation, traffic returning from Server 1 to Host 1 might take a different path than traffic originating from Host 1 to Server 1. This behavior is described as asymmetrical routing and is typically not an issue for most types of traffic. Because return traffic can take multiple paths, some packets may be received out of order and must rely upon the application to reassemble the packets in the correct order. If a requirement exists to limit the traffic flow to one well-known path unless a link failure occurs, administrators might adjust the parameters of dynamic routing protocols to favor one path over another. In the case of EIGRP, you can adjust the delay parameter so that one route is preferred over another. Delay, and not bandwidth, should be increased on the links that should not be used during normal traffic flow. Once adjusted, if the preferred link fails, the link with the additional delay will be used. Example 11-3 shows the default delay of 10 microseconds on a GigabitEthernet interface and the possible values for delay. Delay is adjusted on an interface-by-interface basis.

Figure 11-10 *Traffic Flow Between Host 1 and Server 1*

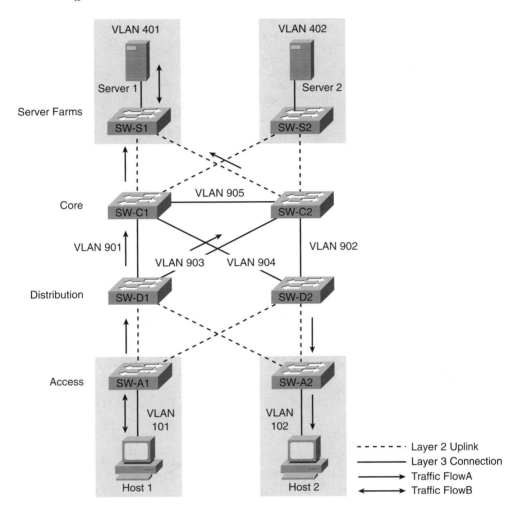

Example 11-2 *Maximum Paths Command for EIGRP*

```
SW-D1#config t
Enter configuration commands, one per line.  End with CNTL/Z.
SW-D1(config)#router eigrp 100
SW-D1(config-router)#maximum-paths ?
  <1-8>  Number of paths
```

Example 11-3 *Increasing EIGRP Delay*

```
SW-D1#show interface gigabitethernet 1/1
GigabitEthernet1/1 is up, line protocol is up
  Hardware is C6k 1000Mb 802.3, address is 0005.7418.048a (bia 0005.7418.048a)
  Internet address is 172.16.240.17/30
  MTU 1500 bytes, BW 1000000 Kbit, DLY 10 usec,
    reliability 255/255, txload 1/255, rxload 1/255
  Encapsulation ARPA, loopback not set
  Keepalive set (10 sec)
  Full-duplex, 1000Mb/s
  ARP type: ARPA, ARP Timeout 04:00:00
  (output truncated)

SW-D1#config t
SW-D1#)config)interface GigabitEthernet1/1
SW-D1(config-if)#delay ?
  <1-16777215>  Throughput delay (tens of microseconds)
```

Single Points of Failure

All networking organizations are forced to make choices about where they allow single points of failure to be designed into their networks. These choices are generally based on the cost to benefit ratio of eliminating each single point of failure. As a result, some single points of failure get eliminated, and some remain and are simply lived with. In Figure 11-11, one single point of failure from the previous figures has been eliminated by installing dual-network interface cards (NICs) into Server 1 and Server 2. Previously, a single cable failure from the server to the switch, a single NIC failure on the server, a single port or module failure on the switch, or an entire switch failure, would render the server unavailable. In Figure 11-11, each server is connected to both SW-S1 and SW-S2 to prevent those single points of failure from occurring.

Although a wide range of NIC redundancy or "teaming" solutions exists from many vendors, virtually all require the two connections to be members of the same VLAN. In Figure 11-11, VLAN 402 is eliminated from the design and VLAN 401 is allowed to span both SW-S1 and SW-S2. This situation is an example of an unavoidable need to span VLANs across switches, and creates a Layer 2 loop in the topology that spanning tree must block. Other applications, such as wireless, currently rely on access points to be installed in the same VLAN for roaming to occur between access points. As a result, VLANs must span switches creating logical loops that must be managed by spanning tree.

With few exceptions, end-user hosts are always single attached to their access switches and are vulnerable to the same single component failures as servers. Because of the costs associated with creating redundant connections for each end user and the capability for most organizations to continue with minimal impact if a single user is down, this single point of failure is almost always not eliminated.

Figure 11-11 *Dual NICs in Servers 1 and 2*

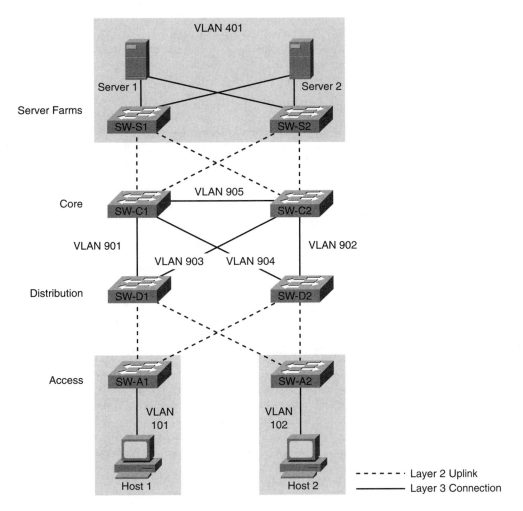

In reality, users don't care that Server 1 or Server 2 is available, they only care that applications running and data stored on Server 1 or Server 2 are available. Other options for eliminating a server single point of failure include content networking devices such as the Cisco CSS 11500 series, the server load-balancing features of Cisco IOS, and content services modules for the Catalyst 6500 series switches. Content networking allows you to load balance applications between multiple physical or "real" servers, while allowing users to point their workstations to one "virtual" server for their needs. Details on load-balancing operation and products can be found on the Cisco Systems website at Cisco.com.

Catalyst Supervisor and Switch Fabric Redundancy

A question often asked of Cisco is "Where should I have Supervisor redundancy, and where should I not?" Although it seems like a relatively simple question, the answer is not always a simple one. Not all switching platforms support Supervisor redundancy. For example, the option to install redundant supervisors on the Catalyst 4000/4500 series did not become available until the introduction of the 4507R, the "R" signifying redundant. The Catalyst 3750 series creates Supervisor-like redundancy by interconnecting multiple switches to form one logical switching entity. Although Supervisor redundancy has been available since day one on the Catalyst 6000/6500 platforms, the amount of time it takes to failover from the active to the standby supervisor varies depending on the high-availability mode that is configured.

The general rule of thumb for supervisors is to implement redundancy whenever the devices that are attaching to the switch are single connected. For example, a small organization with only a single core switch connecting two other distribution or access switches should implement dual supervisors in the core switch to eliminate a single point of failure. Environments that implement switch redundancy at the distribution and core layers can implement only a single supervisor and rely on failover between switches instead of supervisors. Administrators often implement redundant supervisors or redundant switching solutions, such as the Catalyst 3750 series in the access layer, to avoid a single point of failure.

Catalyst 6500 Supervisor High Availability (Hybrid)

A look at the mechanisms behind Supervisor failover begins with the Catalyst 6500 series. A wide range of Supervisor failover techniques have been used on the Catalyst 6500 series since its introduction. With the introduction of Catalyst OS 5.4(1), a dual Supervisor Catalyst 6500 supports a high-availability mode that synchronizes the supervisor configuration, operating system, and stateful protocol redundancy. The Catalyst 6500 Series can support up to two Supervisor engines in slots 1 and 2 only. One is the active Supervisor engine and the other is the standby Supervisor engine. The active Supervisor engine is the first one to go online and can be confirmed by the "Active" light emitting diode (LED) on the Supervisor engine or by typing the **show module** command from the Supervisor console. Both Supervisor engines must be the same hardware models for redundancy to operate correctly. This means that if a PFC and MSFC are on a Supervisor IA in slot 1, a PFC and MSFC must be also on a Supervisor Engine IA in slot 2, or if a Supervisor Engine II is in slot 1, a Supervisor Engine II must also be in slot 2. If an active supervisor is taken offline, restarted, or fails, the standby supervisor takes control of the system.

Because high availability was not available until Catalyst OS 5.4(1), it is not enabled by default, but should be enabled whenever supported by compatible software and hardware configurations.

High availability includes stateful protocol redundancy and image versioning. High availability must be enabled via the command line for these features to operate, as shown in Example 11-4.

Example 11-4 *Enabling High Availability*

```
SW1> (enable) set system highavailability enable
System high availability enabled.
```

Many Layer 3 and Layer 4 protocols or features are programmed into the application-specific integrated circuits (ASICs) of the PFC, PFC2, or PFC3 on board the Supervisor engine. Examples include access lists (router and VLAN-based), forwarding tables (MLS cache and CEF tables), IP Phone power and status information, and quality of service (QoS) settings. These protocols are maintained in the protocol database and will continue to be switched in hardware when a Supervisor engine failover occurs.

Stateful Supervisor switchover reduces the time it takes to failover from the active to the standby supervisor to less than 1 second with a Supervisor IA or Supervisor II, and less than 3 seconds with a Supervisor 720. Synchronizing many of the Layer 2, Layer 3, and Layer 4 protocols between the active and standby Supervisor engines makes this possible. In a high-availability configuration, the protocol state database is maintained on each Supervisor engine for all protocols and features requiring high-availability support. Should the active supervisor fail, the standby supervisor becomes active and starts the protocols from the protocol database. Protocol state synchronization is how a redundant Supervisor system can maintain stateful protocol redundancy and achieve a less than 3-second failover.

The protocol state database, illustrated in Figure 11-12, is a repository of up-to-date protocol state information generated by the active supervisor and stored by the standby supervisor. The database contains specific system information including module and port states, VLAN information, nonvolatile RAM (NVRAM) configurations, and various protocol specific data. Both Supervisor engines run a synchronizing operation to allow for transfer of this data. When a database entry is updated on the active Supervisor engine, the synchronizing operation places the update in a first-in, first-out (FIFO) queue. This queue is scheduled to empty periodically for transfer to the standby supervisor. The transfer is a background process and, as such, the update interval varies depending on the number of other active processes in the system. The update interval ranges from 1 to 5 seconds with 2 seconds being an approximate average. The standby Supervisor engine's synchronizing process receives these asynchronous updates and enters them into the protocol state database on the standby Supervisor engine. When the system starts or when a second Supervisor engine is hot-inserted, a global synchronization takes place between the protocol databases to ensure all protocol states are up to date.

Figure 11-12 *Supervisor Protocol Database*

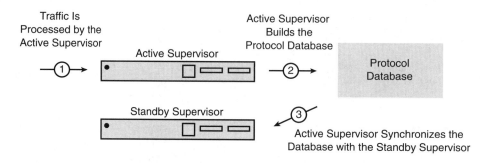

Not all protocols can be synchronized and not all are compatible with the high-availability feature. A feature is considered supported if the state of the feature is synchronized between the active and standby supervisors in the protocol database. A feature is considered compatible if the feature can be used but is not synchronized in the protocol database. A compatible feature must restart when a Supervisor failover occurs. An incompatible feature is simply not supported when high availability is enabled. Table 11-1 lists high-availability support for various features in Catalyst OS.

Table 11-1   *High-Availability Feature Support*

Supported Features	Compatible Features	Incompatible Features
Common Open Policy Service (COPS)	Accelerated Server Load Balancing (ASLB)	Dynamic VLANs
Dynamic Trunk Protocol	Cisco Discovery Protocol (CDP)	Generic VLAN Registration Protocol (GVRP)
Cisco Express Forwarding (CEF) and adjacency tables	GARP Multicast Registration Protocol (GMRP)	Protocol filtering
Private VLANs	Internet Group Management Protocol (IGMP) snooping	
Router access control lists (ACLs)	Remote Monitoring (RMON)	
Multilayer switching (MLS)	Resource Reservation Protocol (RSVP)	
Port Aggregation Protocol/ Link Aggregation Protocol (PAgP/LACP)	Simple Network Management Protocol (SNMP)	
QoS ACLs and policers	Telnet sessions	

Table 11-1   *High-Availability Feature Support (Continued)*

Supported Features	Compatible Features	Incompatible Features
Switched Port Analyzer (SPAN)	VTP pruning	
STP	Uplinkfast	
Trunking		
UniDirectional Link Detection (UDLD) protocol		
VLAN ACLs		
VLAN Trunking Protocol (VTP)		
Port Security		
802.1X		

For a current list of the features that are supported with the high-availability feature, see the "Configuring Redundancy" chapter of the Cisco Catalyst 6500 Series Software User Guide at Cisco.com.

MSFC High Availability

Because a supervisor reset or failover also resets the MSFC routing engine, various methods were developed to provide high availability to a supervisor with a MSFC, MSFC2, or MSFC3.

Although the Catalyst OS high-availability feature maintains the protocol state between redundant Supervisor engines, a dual MSFC configuration offers high availability via either Dual Router Mode or Single Router Mode. As with the Catalyst OS high-availability feature, Cisco recommends configuring high availability for the MSFCs. Single Router Mode was introduced in Catalyst OS 6.3(1) and IOS 12.1(8)E and is the preferred high-availability mode to configure if the supervisors are running at least those code levels.

Dual Router Mode

Dual Router Mode (DRM) represents the original MSFC high-availability option for dual Supervisor engines with MSFCs. In dual router mode, both MSFCs are active routers on the network. Although both MSFCs are active and can be configured independently, they are not to be used as independent routers. In reality, both MSFCs must have nearly identical configurations to function properly. The importance of requirement in DRM cannot be overstated. Configuration parameters such as interfaces, access lists, policy routing, and so on must be configured exactly the same on both MSFCs. Parameters that cannot be duplicated on a network such as IP addresses and HSRP settings are the only parameters that are configured differently on each MSFC.

The first MSFC to go online is considered the designated router, and the second MSFC is considered the nondesignated router. The MSFC is responsible for programming certain functions of the ASIC hardware on the PFC. In a Supervisor Engine IA system, both the designated router and the nondesignated router are able to program Layer 3 entries into the PFC Netflow table for routing functions. With the Supervisor IIs, only the designated router programs the Layer 3 entries in the PFC2 Cisco Express Forwarding (CEF) table. For both Supervisor Engines IA and II, all router ACLs and multicast shortcuts are programmed from the designated router. If the MSFCs in DRM have different configurations, the forwarding ASICs will be programmed incorrectly, resulting in an unsupported and unreliable configuration.

Failover in DRM relies upon HSRP, which allows the two MSFCs to maintain internal communication and react to an MSFC failover. HSRP on the dual MSFCs is configured in the same way as any two independent routers. Because both MSFCs have independent routing tables, little routing protocol convergence is necessary in the event of an MSFC failure. Using DRM and tuned HSRP timers, MSFC failover can be configured to occur in less than 3 seconds for LAN interfaces, matching the Layer 3 failover of the MSFC with Supervisor engine failover time.

MSFC Configuration Synchronization

Up until the introduction of MSFC Cisco IOS 12.1(3a)E4, MSFC configurations had to be manually synchronized. With 12.1(3a)E4 and later, an MSFC redundancy feature called config-sync is available to simplify the configuration process of dual MSFCs. The config-sync feature does exactly what the name implies; synchronize configuration of dual MSFCs. Both the startup and running configurations between the designated (primary) and nondesignated (secondary) MSFCs are synchronized. When a **write memory** or **copy running-config startup-config** command is issued on the designated MSFC, the startup configurations in NVRAM of both MSFCs are updated. Example 11-5 shows the commands needed to enable MSFC high availability with config-sync.

Example 11-5 *Enabling High Availability and config-sync*

```
SW1 (config)# redundancy
SW1 (config-r)# high-availability
SW1 (config-r-ha)# config-sync
```

When config-sync is used, configuration of the designated MSFC and nondesignated MSFC is done through the command line of the designated MSFC. Configuration of the nondesignated MSFC is accomplished by using the **alt** parameter. Use of the alt parameter is the only way to configure the nondesignated MSFC while config-sync is enabled. Example 11-6 demonstrates configuring the nondesignated MSFC.

Example 11-6 *Configuring the Nondesignated MSFC*

```
SW1 (config-if)# ip address 172.16.197.1 255.255.255.0 alt ip address 172.16.197.2
   255.255.255.0
SW1 (config-if)# standby 10 priority 105 alt standby 10 priority 100
```

The portion of the command listed before the **alt** keyword applies to the MSFC in slot 1, and the portion of the command listed after the **alt** keyword applies to the MSFC in slot 2. The config-sync feature is only supported for general IP or IPX configurations; configuration parameters for AppleTalk and DECnet do not have **alt** keyword options.

In DRM, the Optical Service Module (OSM) or Port Adapters of a FlexWAN module are managed by only the designated MSFC. Prior to enabling the config-sync feature, the WAN interfaces do not show up in the nondesignated MSFC configuration and are not configurable on the nondesignated MSFC. DRM represents the first option for MSFC redundancy. Although this solution is successful at providing stateful Layer 3 failover between MSFCs, it also introduces some complexity into switch administration. The requirement for exact configuration parameters on both MSFCs has been a complicated point for many administrators. As a result of the complexity DRM introduced, a high-availability feature called Single Router Mode was developed.

Single Router Mode

Single Router Mode (SRM) provides a single active MSFC, while placing the secondary MSFC in a standby mode not unlike the standby mode of the secondary supervisor. SRM is now the recommended high-availability configuration for Catalyst 6000/6500 series switches with MSFCs operating in hybrid mode. The minimum software requirements for SRM are Catalyst OS 6.3(1) and Cisco IOS 12.1(8)E2 for the MSFC. SRM improves upon DRM by eliminating the need to configure a nearly identical secondary MSFC, resulting in a simpler configuration process for the administrator because only a single command set is entered from one command line into the active MSFC. (See Example 11-7.)

Example 11-7 *Configuring SRM*

```
SW1#config t
Enter configuration commands, one per line.  End with CNTL/Z.
SW1 (config)# redundancy
SW1 (config-r)# high-availability
SW1 (config-r-ha)# single-router-mode
```

SRM Operation

In SRM, only the designated router is visible to the network at any given time. The non-designated router is started and maintains exactly the same configuration as the designated router (the configurations are automatically synchronized when SRM is active). In this mode, the nondesignated router interfaces are kept in a line-down state and are not visible to the network. Routing protocol processes are also created on the nondesignated router, but they do not send or receive updates from the network because all interfaces are down. This is verified from the Catalyst OS command in Example 11-8. Note that both the Supervisor engine and the MSFC in slot 2 are listed as standby.

Example 11-8 *Verifying Standby Status with SRM*

```
SW1> (enable) show module
Mod Slot Ports Module-Type              Model Sub Status
--- ---- ----- ----------------------- ------------------- --- --------
1 1 2 1000BaseX Supervisor WS-X6K-SUP2-2GE yes ok
15 1 1 Multilayer Switch Feature WS-F6K-MSFC2 no ok
2 2 2 1000BaseX Supervisor WS-X6K-SUP2-2GE yes standby
16 2 1 Multilayer Switch Feature WS-F6K-MSFC2 no standby
```

If the designated router fails in an SRM configuration, the nondesignated MSFC changes state from nondesignated to designated. The new designated router changes its interface state to link up and begins to build its routing table. It follows that the control plane failover time will be proportional to the routing protocol configuration and complexity. However, Layer 3 forwarding entries exist in the PFC, which are used to forward routed traffic in the hardware path. The high-availability functions of Catalyst OS are used to maintain this forwarding information after a failover, allowing minimal impact to Layer 3 traffic while the Layer 3 routing protocols converge. After the MSFC builds its routing table, the entries in the PFC are updated.

A transition timer feature for SRM on the Supervisor II/PFC2 was introduced in Catalyst OS 12.1(11b)E. This timer configures the time that the new designated router will wait before downloading any new hardware CEF entries to the PFC2. Because of differences in routing convergence times, the default of 120 seconds might not be long enough to allow for complete routing table convergence before programming the PFC2 hardware.

The same IP and Media Access Control (MAC) addresses are used for the designated router, whether or not the MSFC is the designated router. The MSFC chosen as the designated router will communicate its default MAC address to the MSFC that is the nondesignated router. All subsequent interfaces created on the nondesignated router use this MAC address, unless the administrator explicitly configures a different MAC address. On bootup, the two MSFCs perform a "handshake" process, which takes about a minute, before entering SRM mode. It is important to remember to not make configuration changes on the nondesignated router during the handshake process, as shown in Example 11-9.

Example 11-9 *Verifying SRM Redundancy*

```
SW1# show redundancy
Designated Router: 1 Non-designated Router: 2
Redundancy Status: designated
Config Sync AdminStatus : enabled
Config Sync RuntimeStatus: enabled
Single Router Mode AdminStatus : enabled
Single Router Mode RuntimeStatus: enabled
Single Router Mode transition timer : 120 seconds
```

NOTE   For more details about configuring SRM, see section "MSFC Redundancy-Single Router Mode Redundancy" in the Catalyst OS configuration guide at Cisco.com.

Because the Supervisor and MSFC configurations are synchronized as an inherent part of SRM, all Optical Services Modules (OSMs) and FlexWAN WAN modules are supported with redundant Supervisor engines or MSFCs configured for SRM. In failover scenarios, the new designated router takes over ownership of the WAN interfaces as soon as that MSFC becomes the designated router. With SRM enabled, no manual configuration is necessary on the WAN interfaces to support an MSFC failover.

Catalyst 6500 Supervisor High Availability (Native)

Implementing Catalyst native software versus hybrid software has various pros and cons; one disadvantage with native configurations has been the failover time in a high-availability configuration. Although high-availability failover times in hybrid configurations can vary between 1 and 3 seconds, up until very recently, the best failover times in a native configuration have averaged around 30 seconds. Native IOS now supports Stateful Switchover plus Non-Stop Forwarding (SSO + NSF), enabling failover speeds in line with hybrid failover times. In all native IOS high-availability configurations, the redundant supervisor and MSFC are not visible to the network. This section looks at the evolution of router redundancy options beginning with the first, Route Processor Redundancy.

Route Processor Redundancy

Route Processor Redundancy (RPR) was the first high-availability feature offered in a native IOS configuration for the Catalyst 6500 series, enabling an average failover time of approximately 2 minutes. The 2-minute failover time in RPR mode is due to the lack of a completely booted redundant supervisor, and the requirement for line cards to be reset during the failover to the redundant supervisor. As in the hybrid configuration, the supervisor that boots first becomes the active supervisor, while the redundant supervisor is partially booted but not all subsystems (MSFC and PFC) are operational. RPR requires both supervisors to be the same model. Even though the redundant supervisor is not operational, the GigabitEthernet ports on the supervisor are active.

Route Processor Redundancy Plus

Route Processor Redundancy plus (RPR+) improves upon RPR failover times by fully initializing and configuring the redundant supervisor, and eliminating the need to reset each line card during failover. These improvements provide an average failover time of approximately 30 seconds. RPR+ also allows for Online Insertion and Removal (OIR) of Supervisor modules. RPR+ requires both supervisors to be the same model and run the same software version. Example 11-10 shows the commands necessary to configure either RPR or RPR+.

Example 11-10 *Configuring RPR or RPR+*

```
SW1#config t
Enter configuration commands, one per line.  End with CNTL/Z.
SW1(config)#redundancy
SW1(config-red)#mode ?
    rpr          Route Processor Redundancy
    rpr-plus     Route Processor Redundancy Plus
```

Single Router Mode with Layer 2 Stateful Switch Over

Single Router Mode with Stateful Switchover (SRM + SSO) was introduced in 12.2(17b)SXA, and provides a 1 to 3 second failover between supervisors. One goal of the 12.1(17b)SXA release was to create feature parity for stateful failover between native and hybrid Catalyst software. While RPR and RPR+ will operate with a Supervisor 1A or Supervisor II, SRM + SSO requires a Supervisor 720. With SRM + SSO, Layer 2 states are synchronized between the PFC3s on the active and standby supervisors, and packet forwarding for hardware switched packets continues while Layer 3 protocols do not maintain state on the MSFC3 and must restart. Example 11-11 shows the configuration of SRM + SSO.

Example 11-11 *Configuring SRM with SSO*

```
SW1# config t
Enter configuration commands, one per line.  End with CNTL/Z.
SW1(config)# redundancy
SW1(config-red)# mode sso
```

Catalyst 6500 Switch Fabric Redundancy

In addition to redundant supervisors for the Catalyst 6500, redundant switch fabrics in the form of the SFM or SFM2 may be installed. The Supervisor 720 includes an integrated switch fabric, and as a result, fabric redundancy is provided by redundant installing Supervisor 720s. Unlike with redundant Supervisor 720s, implementing switch fabric redundancy with the SFMs or SFM2s requires no configuration. Switch Fabric modules (SFMs) can be installed in only specific slots depending on the chassis. The SFM in the upper slot will always function as the primary module and the lower slot will always be secondary during normal operation. If the primary is reset, the secondary will take over operation.

Catalyst 4500 Redundancy

Supervisor redundancy on the Catalyst 4500 was introduced with the 4507R chassis, and requires dual Supervisor II+, Supervisor IV, or Supervisor V cards to enable redundancy. As of the writing of this book, the Catalyst 4500 series supports only the features of RPR. No configuration is required to enable RPR; it is enabled by default whenever redundant supervisors are installed. Failover times average around 90 seconds from active to standby supervisor. Unlike the early Catalyst 6500 redundancy modes, no manual config-sync is necessary on the 4500. When a standby supervisor first comes online, its configuration is synchronized to the active supervisor. An optional **auto-synch** command can be enabled so that changes made to the startup configuration on the active supervisor are automatically synchronized to the standby supervisor.

Catalyst 3750 Redundancy

The Catalyst 3750 switching platform is capable of high availability by design, given the stackable architecture. You can stack and interconnect up to nine switches in a self-healing ring. Failover on the 3750 series is less than 1 second for Layer 2 traffic, and Layer 3 failover takes between 3 and 5 seconds. In a Catalyst 3750 stacked configuration, one switch becomes the stack master based on a well-defined selection process. The selection process can be influenced manually by configuring the mastership priority parameter.

The following rules have been defined to determine which unit within a stack is chosen as the master. When adding switches or merging stacks, the master will be chosen based on the following rules in the order specified. If the first rule does not apply, the second rule is tried, and so on, until an applicable rule is found to select the master:

1 The stack (or switch) whose master has the higher user-configurable mastership priority.

2 The stack (or switch) whose master is not using the default configuration.

3 The stack (or switch) whose master has the higher hardware/software priority (based on switch hardware version and/or software version).

4 The stack (or switch) whose master has the longest uptime.

5 The stack (or switch) whose master has the lowest MAC address.

When removing or partitioning stacks, the master will be

1   The switch that is already master.

2   The switch that has the higher user-configurable mastership priority.

3   The switch that has the higher hardware/software priority.

4   The switch that has the lowest switch number.

Much like an active supervisor in a redundant 6500 Supervisor configuration, it is the stack master's responsibility to build the Layer 3 Forwarding Information Base (FIB) and propagate it to stack members. The stack master propagates its configuration to the entire stack, and all switches will use the same bridge-ID derived from the master's MAC-address block. The stack master has control of the console and the entire stack has single VLAN database and same VTP mode. The stack appears as single entity in Cisco Discovery Protocol (CDP), with the stack master controlling the neighbor table.

Summary

This chapter introduced the concept of basic network design "building blocks" and follows that concept by building out a typical campus design using the three-tiered core, distribution, and access layer design model. Traffic flows and redundancy options are explored by examining link redundancy, and by examining supervisor and switch fabric redundancy options on each major switching platform. Chapter 12, "Troubleshooting the LAN Switching Configuration," examines techniques used to troubleshoot an existing Catalyst switching network.

This chapter covers the following topics:

- Checking software versions
- Checking hardware components
- Understanding port errors
- Using syslog
- Using trace
- Local Switched Port Analyzer
- Remote Switched Port Analyzer
- Cisco online resources

Troubleshooting the LAN Switching Configuration

The primary objective of this chapter is to introduce some useful commands and techniques to help with troubleshooting a Catalyst switch. Some of the more common approaches in troubleshooting a Catalyst switch are examining the software version, checking the hardware to ensure that the device is functioning correctly and within specifications, running various commands to pinpoint the network problem, and, if all else fails, using a analyzer, such as a sniffer, to examine the packets seen on the network.

The commands provided in this chapter can help quickly rule out common issues such as bad cables and faulty ports and line modules. This chapter also addresses issues with software that might have caveats that affect the features configured on the Catalyst switch. Software features can affect the hardware configuration as well, causing the hardware to not function correctly or worst yet, reboot or crash.

This chapter examines software issues first and then progresses toward hardware problems and port errors seen on Catalyst switches. The importance of syslog and trace outputs will be discussed as well. Sometimes, it is difficult to exactly figure out what the problem is on the network because the commands provide limited functionality. In these cases, a sniffer device, which captures packets from the network, can be used to see exactly what is happening on the network.

The outline of this chapter should be used as a template when troubleshooting Catalyst switches. You should follow specific steps rather than jumping from one area to another. Examine the software and then the hardware, look for port errors, see what the syslog and trace messages say, and, finally, use a port analyzer when necessary.

Checking Software Versions

One of the most important steps in troubleshooting a Catalyst switch is to determine the software that it is running. The software version provides a wealth of information in many troubleshooting cases:

- Check whether the switch code is General Deployment (GD). GD code is preferred because it provides greater stability. Only bug fixes are integrated in GD codes; no new features are added, which translates to fewer bugs introduced. Typically, customers run non-GD code when they require a new feature that is not available on the GD code.

- Check how old the software is. It is not unusual to see an enterprise customer running a 5-year-old code. This is not acceptable because of bug fixes and possible security holes in some of these codes. After a code goes End of Engineering (EOE), no new changes can be made to the code, and the customer is forced to upgrade. Therefore, it is best to be proactive and ensure the network switches are running reasonably up-to-date codes.

- Network security holes found in the code can make the device or network vulnerable to attack. It is vital to ensure that the code does not have any security holes. For instance, a couple of years ago, a telnet buffer leak vulnerability would eventually cause a switch to crash because the switch would run out of memory. In a Denial of Service (DoS) attack, this vulnerability could affect the whole network. It is, therefore, important to know what code the switch is running and examine all security vulnerabilities published by Cisco against the code.

- Software also provides information about the capability of the feature. Say for the example the feature in question is UniDirectional Link Detection (UDLD). Normal UDLD was first introduced in Catalyst OS 5.1(1). However, UDLD Aggressive mode was introduced in Catalyst OS 5.4(3). Having this knowledge can help direct the decision process on what code level the switch needs to be in.

- Examining the software version provides information about potential or relevant bugs associated with the feature or hardware. Take the UDLD example again. There might be more UDLD bugs in Catalyst OS 5.5(1) than Catalyst OS 5.5(4) because UDLD was first introduced in Catalyst OS 5.5(1). Software might also have some bugs that affect the hardware, such as causing the hardware to reset or crash. Knowing what those bugs are can help the customer move away from those affected codes.

Use either the **show module** or **show version** command to display the current code level for the Catalyst switch. The output in Example 12-1 is from a Catalyst 6506 with Supervisor 1A, which is currently running Catalyst OS 7.6(3a) on the Supervisor and IOS 12.1(8b)e15 on the Multilayer Switch Feature Card (MSFC). The output also shows information on the uptime and the memory capacity on the switch.

Example 12-1 *Switch Software Information*

```
Switch2 (enable) show version
WS-C6506 Software, Version NmpSW: 7.6(3a)
Copyright (c) 1995-2003 by Cisco Systems
NMP S/W compiled on Sep 24 2003, 18:13:40
System Bootstrap Version: 5.3(1)
System Boot Image File is 'bootflash:cat6000-supk8.7-6-3a.bin'
System Configuration register is 0x2102
Hardware Version: 2.0  Model: WS-C6506  Serial #: TBA04081025
PS1  Module: WS-CAC-1000W    Serial #: SON03500044
Mod Port Model                Serial #      Versions
--- ---- -------------------- ------------- -------------------------------------
1    2   WS-X6K-SUP1A-2GE     SAD04310JC3 Hw : 3.4
                                          Fw : 5.3(1)
                                          Fw1: 5.4(2)
                                          Sw : 7.6(3a)
                                          Sw1: 7.6(3a)
         WS-X6K-SUP1A-2GE     SAD04310JC3 Hw : 3.4
                                          Sw :
3    48  WS-X6248-RJ-45       SAD03408164 Hw : 1.1
                                          Fw : 4.2(0.24)VAI78
                                          Sw : 7.6(3a)
15   1   WS-F6K-MSFC          SAD04281ARM Hw : 2.1
                                          Fw : 12.1(8b)E15
                                          Sw : 12.1(8b)E15
         DRAM                   FLASH                NVRAM
Module Total   Used    Free    Total   Used    Free     Total Used  Free
------ ------- ------- ------- ------- ------- -------  ----- ----- -----
1       65408K  47749K  17659K  16384K  10877K   5507K   512K  282K  230K
Uptime is 19 days, 17 hours, 15 minutes
```

To ensure that the Switch2 is not hitting any major bugs or security vulnerabilities, as shown in Example 12-1, the engineer needs to search the Catalyst OS and MSFC IOS code release notes on the Cisco website. This process can seem tedious, but it is crucial. The release notes also provide information such as feature additions and enhancements.

Checking Hardware Components

After verifying that no issues can be found in software, check the hardware modules to ensure proper functioning. A physical check of the hardware can be helpful in situations where the hardware has failed. Sometimes, a faulty module may still show its LED indicator as green even though the switch software does not see the device; such inconsistency can help pinpoint the problem. It is very difficult to rely on physically checking devices because the switches are spread across the network. In most cases, the **show module** command is used to check the status of all the linecards in the Catalyst chassis. The status column displays whether the card is functioning, as shown in Example 12-2. If it is not, the status will indicate faulty. In older software versions, the Supervisor will show faulty if there is only one power supply in the chassis.

Example 12-2 *Modules Currently Installed on the Switch*

```
Switch2 (enable) show module
Mod Slot Ports Module-Type            Model              Sub Status
--- ---- ----- ---------------------- ------------------ --- --------
1   1    2     1000BaseX Supervisor   WS-X6K-SUP1A-2GE   yes ok
15  1    1     Multilayer Switch Feature WS-F6K-MSFC     no  ok
3   3    48    10/100BaseTX Ethernet  WS-X6248-RJ-45     no  ok
Mod Module-Name          Serial-Num
--- -------------------- -----------
1                        SAD04310JC3
15                       SAD04281ARM
3                        SAD03408164
Mod MAC-Address(es)                              Hw    Fw         Sw
--- ---------------------------------------- ------ ---------- ----------------
1   00-01-64-71-d9-6a to 00-01-64-71-d9-6b 3.4    5.3(1)     7.6(3a)
    00-01-64-71-d9-68 to 00-01-64-71-d9-69
    00-01-63-29-bc-00 to 00-01-63-29-bf-ff
15  00-30-b6-3e-53-8c to 00-30-b6-3e-53-cb 2.1    12.1(8b)E1 12.1(8b)E15
3   00-30-b6-d1-5d-e8 to 00-30-b6-d1-5e-17 1.1    4.2(0.24)V 7.6(3a)
Mod Sub-Type               Sub-Model           Sub-Serial  Sub-Hw Sub-Sw
--- ---------------------- ------------------- ----------- ------ ------
1   L3 Switching Engine    WS-F6K-PFC          SAD04170HC1 1.1
```

If a problem exists with the module, the **show test** command provides post-diagnostic information on the module in question. Example 12-3 shows the results for module 3. The 48 ports associated with module 3 all have passed the post-diagnostic test that was performed by the switch. In situations were a port becomes faulty, a failed status will show under the appropriate port.

Example 12-3 *Checking Test Results for Module 3*

```
Switch2 (enable) show test 3
Diagnostic mode: minimal   (mode at next reset: complete)

Module 3 : 48-port 10/100BaseTX Ethernet
Line Card Firmware Status for Module 3 : PASS
Port Status :
  Ports 1  2  3  4  5  6  7  8  9  10 11 12 13 14 15 16 17 18 19 20 21 22 23 24
  -----------------------------------------------------------------------------
        .  .  .  .  .  .  .  .  .  .  .  .  .  .  .  .  .  .  .  .  .  .  .  .
       25 26 27 28 29 30 31 32 33 34 35 36 37 38 39 40 41 42 43 44 45 46 47 48
  -----------------------------------------------------------------------------
        .  .  .  .  .  .  .  .  .  .  .  .  .  .  .  .  .  .  .  .  .  .  .  .
Line Card Diag Status for Module 3  (. = Pass, F = Fail, N = N/A)
```

Example 12-3 *Checking Test Results for Module 3 (Continued)*

```
Loopback Status [Reported by Module 1] :
  Ports 1  2  3  4  5  6  7  8  9  10 11 12 13 14 15 16 17 18 19 20 21 22 23 24
  ----------------------------------------------------------------------------
        .  .  .  .  .  .  .  .  .  .  .  .  .  .  .  .  .  .  .  .  .  .  .  .

  Ports 25 26 27 28 29 30 31 32 33 34 35 36 37 38 39 40 41 42 43 44 45 46 47 48
  ----------------------------------------------------------------------------
        .  .  .  .  .  .  .  .  .  .  .  .  .  .  .  .  .  .  .  .  .  .  .  .

InlineRewrite Status :
        InlineRewrite Test skipped as Minimal diagnostics selected
```

The Test feature has three modes as listed in the output from Example 12-4. By default, the switch does minimal diagnostics on each of the modules.

Example 12-4 *Diagnostic Options*

```
Switch2 (enable) set test diaglevel ?
  complete                Complete diagnostics
  minimal                 Minimal diagnostics
  bypass                  Bypass diagnostics
```

Sometimes, hardware goes faulty because of environmental issues such as lack of power to the switch, fan flow problems, and so on. The **show environment all** command outputs information on how many power supplies currently are on the chassis and the amount of amps the cards are drawing. It also provides information on the temperature of the modules in the chassis. All in all, this command can be very helpful, especially when deploying these devices in new data centers or closets. Example 12-5 shows the output from the **show environment all** command.

Example 12-5 *Switch Environmental Levels*

```
Switch2 (enable) show environment all
Environmental Status (. = Pass, F = Fail, U = Unknown, N = Not Present)
  PS1: .      PS2: N      PS1 Fan: .      PS2 Fan: N
  Chassis-Ser-EEPROM: .     Fan: .
  Clock(A/B): A       Clock A: .      Clock B: .
  VTT1: .     VTT2: .     VTT3: .
                    Intake          Exhaust         Device 1        Device 2
  Slot            Temperature     Temperature     Temperature     Temperature
  -------------- --------------- --------------- --------------- ---------------
  1               23C(50C,65C)    34C(60C,75C)    26C             34C
  3               26C(50C,65C)    28C(60C,75C)    29C             34C
  1 (Switch-Eng) 24C(50C,65C)    29C(60C,75C)    N/A             N/A
  1 (MSFC)        29C(50C,65C)    34C(60C,75C)    N/A             N/A
```

continues

Example 12-5 *Switch Environmental Levels (Continued)*

```
Chassis Modules
--------------------
VTT1: 24C(85C,100C)
VTT2: 24C(85C,100C)
VTT3: 25C(85C,100C)
PS1 Capacity: 852.60 Watts (20.30 Amps @42V)
PS2 Capacity: none
PS Configuration : PS1 and PS2 in Redundant Configuration.
Total Power Available: 852.60 Watts (20.30 Amps @42V)
Total Power Available for Line Card Usage: 852.60 Watts (20.30 Amps @42V)
Total Power Drawn From the System: 390.18 Watts ( 9.29 Amps @42V)
Remaining Power in the System: 462.42 Watts (11.01 Amps @42V)
Configured Default Inline Power allocation per port: 7.00 Watts (0.16 Amps @42V)
Slot power Requirement/Usage :
Slot Card Type          PowerRequested PowerAllocated CardStatus
                        Watts   A @42V Watts   A @42V
---- ------------------ ------- ------ ------- ------ ----------
1    WS-X6K-SUP1A-2GE   138.60   3.30  138.60   3.30  ok
2                         0.00   0.00  138.60   3.30  none
3    WS-X6248-RJ-45     112.98   2.69  112.98   2.69  ok
Slot Inline Power Requirement/Usage :
Slot CardType           Total Allocated   Max H/W Supported   Max H/W Supported
                        To Module (Watts) Per Module (Watts) Per Port (Watts)
```

The next commands provide further proof if there is anything wrong with the hardware, software, and the traffic that is being handled by the switch. Most of these commands are self-explanatory. The commands mentioned in this book help form a basic template of what to look at first when troubleshooting Catalyst switches.

When verifying the functionality of the hardware, **show process cpu** is another helpful command that shows the current load on the Supervisor CPU and also displays what process has invoked the CPU for how long and percentage utilized. If CPU load is above 85 percent for a extended period of time, check if the switch and the network are stable.

The **show scp** (serial line communication) command provides information about communication issues between the line card and the Supervisor module. This is a hidden command. The output in Example 12-6 shows some of the options that are currently available on a Catalyst 6500 switch using SCP. Typically, the **show scp** command is used when a module has disappeared, reloaded, or crashed. You can also use the **show scp** command to check the reliability of communication between redundant Supervisors on the same Catalyst switch. If, for example, a standby Supervisor has disappeared, check the **show scp** command to see if the active Supervisor lost communication with the standby Supervisor.

Example 12-6 *show scp Command Output*

```
Switch2 (enable) show scp
Show scp commands:
- - - - - - - - - - - - - - - - - - - - - - - - - - - - - - - - - - - - - - - - - - - - - - - - - - - - - - - - - - - - - - - - -
show scp failcnt              Show SCP fail count
show scp mc                   Show SCP Multicast groups and their members
show scp memory               Show SCP memory contents
show scp module               Show SCP module based statistics
show scp process              Show SCP process based statistics
show scp registration         Show SCP registration table
show scp traceinfo            Show SCP trace
show scp statistics           Show SCP statistics
```

The **show top** command can be used to analyze data collected for each port by the switch. Example 12-7 shows the type of data gathered by the **show top** command. In a situation where excessive traffic is seen on the network, it might be helpful to find the user responsible for the high volume of traffic. The **show top** command can also be used in situations where users complain about applications not working correctly or slow network response time by examining packet errors, overflow, and utilization, as shown in Example 12-7.

Example 12-7 *The show top Options*

```
Switch2 (enable) show top ?
  <N>                 Number of physical ports (default 20)
  util                Sort the report based on utilization
  bytes               Sort the report based on tx/rx bytes
  pkts                Sort the report based on tx/rx packets
  bcst                Sort the report based on tx/rx broadcast packets
  mcst                Sort the report based on tx/rx multicast packets
  errors              Sort the report based on rx errors
  overflow            Sort the report based on overflow
  interval            Show Topn report in an interval
  all                 Show all port type
  eth                 Show ethernet port type
  10e                 Show 10 ethernet port type
  fe                  Show fast ethernet port type
  ge                  Show gigabit ethernet port type
  10ge                Show 10 gigabit ethernet port type
  background          Running TOPN task in background
  report              Show report for TOPN
```

The **show system** command displays the switch backplane utilization and its peak. It also indicates if Coredump, a log file generated when the switch crashes, has been enabled on the switch. In most circumstances, switch backplane utilization should not be higher than 7 percent. If it is higher, a closer examination of the network and the switch is required. A common source of high backplane utilization has been spanning tree. Make sure that there is no spanning-tree loop occurring in the network.

The next section looks at some of the more common problems seen on Catalyst switches, starting with Supervisor missing, MSFC missing, and specific port issues.

Supervisor Missing

One of the more frustrating troubleshooting events is when a Supervisor disappears from the chassis. It is usually the standby Supervisor. To fix the problem, you must have console access to the Catalyst switch. Typically, a bad configuration is involved; for example, the boot variable field may have an incorrect software filename. As a result, the Supervisor is in ROMMON mode. To help mitigate boot issues, first do a **dir bootflash** to see what Catalyst OS software is available on the box and then select and boot the file using the **boot bootflash** command.

A supervisor can also be forced into ROMMON mode if the Catalyst OS image is corrupted. Two solutions can be implemented to fix this problem:

- Load the desired image on a PCMCIA card from a different switch and then place the PCMCIA card on the bad supervisor. Next, attempt to boot the image using the **boot disk** command.

- Move the Supervisor to a working Catalyst switch and let it synchronize with that switch's supervisor.

Software caveats in rare situations can also cause a Supervisor to disappear from the chassis. A quick search through available Catalyst OS caveats can help determine potential switching problems.

Like any other hardware product, sometimes the device breaks down. A quick check of the light emitting diodes (LEDs) provides the status of the module. If no LED lights, the Supervisor more than likely is faulty. Table 12-1 shows LED states and their meaning.

Table 12-1   *Supervisor LED*

LED	Color/State	Description
STATUS	Green	All diagnostics pass. The module is operational (normal initialization sequence).
	Orange	The module is booting or running diagnostics (normal initialization sequence). An overtemperature condition has occurred. (A minor temperature threshold has been exceeded during environmental monitoring.)
	Red	The diagnostic test failed. The module is not operational because a fault occurred during the initialization sequence. An overtemperature condition has occurred. (A major temperature threshold has been exceeded during environmental monitoring.)

Table 12-1   *Supervisor LED (Continued)*

LED	Color/State	Description
SYSTEM[1]	Green	All chassis environmental monitors are reporting OK.
	Orange	The power supply has failed or the power supply fan has failed. Incompatible power supplies are installed. The redundant clock has failed.
	Red	Two VTT modules fail or the VTT module temperature major threshold has been exceeded.[2] The temperature of the Supervisor engine major threshold has been exceeded.
ACTIVE	Green	The Supervisor engine is operational and active.
	Orange	The Supervisor engine is in standby mode.
PWR MGMT[3]	Green	Sufficient power is available for all modules.
	Orange	Sufficient power is not available for all modules.
SWITCH LOAD		If the switch is operational, the switch load meter indicates (as an approximate percentage) the current traffic load over the backplane.
PCMCIA		The PCMCIA LED is lit when no Flash PC card is in the slot, and it goes off when you insert a Flash PC card.
LINK	Green	The port is operational.
	Orange	The link has been disabled by software.
	Flashing orange	The link is bad and has been disabled because of a hardware failure.
Off		No signal is detected.

[1]   The SYSTEM and PWR MGMT LED indications on a redundant Supervisor engine are synchronized to the active Supervisor engine.

[2]   VTT = voltage termination module. The VTT module terminates signals on the Catalyst switching bus.

[3]   If no redundant Supervisor engine is installed and there is a VTT module minor or major overtemperature condition, the system shuts down.

The **show test** command, as mentioned earlier in the "Checking Hardware Components" section, will also provide information about the status of the hardware. A failed status appears if the Supervisor is faulty, as shown in Example 12-8.

Example 12-8 *Supervisor Failure*

```
Module 1
  Earl VI Status :
        NewLearnTest:            F
        IndexLearnTest:          F
        DontForwardTest:         U
        DontLearnTest:           U
        ConditionalLearnTest:    F
        BadBpduTest:             U
        TrapTest:                U
        MatchTest:               U
        PortSpanTest:            U
        CaptureTest:             U
        ProtocolMatchTest:       U
        ChannelTest:             F
        IpFibScTest:             F
        IpxFibScTest:            F
        L3DontScTest:            F
        L3Capture2Test:          F
        L3VlanMetTest:           F
        AclPermitTest:           F
        AclDenyTest:             .
        InbandEditTest:          F
        RWEngineSpanTest:        F
        ForwardingEngineTest:    F

Loopback Status [Reported by Module 1] :
  Ports 1  2
  -----------
        F  F
```

MSFC Missing

The same logic and reasoning that was used in troubleshooting Supervisor modules applies here as well. The first thing to do when the MSFC disappears is to console into it. The **switch console** command, running Catalyst OS software, allows the console screen to switch from the Supervisor to the local MSFC. In other words, if you are consoled in Supervisor module 1, you can console to MSFC 15, but not MSFC 16, which is on Supervisor module 2. Execute **Ctrl^C^C^C** to switch back to the Supervisor. The following steps outline how to recover an MSFC missing from the chassis:

Step 1   Switch from the Supervisor console to the MSFC console:

```
Switch1 (enable) switch console
Trying Router-15...
Connected to Router-15.
Type ^C^C^C to switch back...
rommon 8 >
```

Step 2   Check what IOS images are currently available on the bootflash:

```
rommon 3 > dir bootflash:
        File size          Checksum    File name
    1688336 bytes (0x19c310)   0x786a3e5f   c6msfc2-boot-mz.121-8b.E11
   12278476 bytes (0xbb5acc)   0x91074cd4   c6msfc2-jsv-mz.121-8b.E11
```

Step 3   After selecting which IOS image to use, use the **boot bootflash** command to load the image on the MSFC:

```
rommon 4 > boot bootflash:c6msfc2-jsv-mz.121-8b.E11
```

Use the **show module** command to verify that the MSFC does, in fact, appear in the chassis.

Understanding Port Errors

Typically, at the port level, you are interested in Layer 1 and Layer 2 errors. Some of the common errors are bad cable, alignment issues, frame check sequence (FCS), and collisions seen on the port. Example 12-9 shows the output from the **show port** command.

Example 12-9 shows excessive collisions seen on port 10/3. Recall from Chapter 1, "LAN Switching Foundation Technologies," excessive collisions are associated with too much traffic on the segment or too many hosts contenting to access the segment.

Example 12-9 *Examining Port Fields*

```
Switch1 (enable) show port 10/3
* = Configured MAC Address
Port  Send FlowControl   Receive FlowControl   RxPause    TxPause
      admin    oper      admin     oper
----- -------- --------  --------- ---------  ---------- ----------
10/3  off      off       off       off         0          0
Port  Status      Channel              Admin Ch
                  Mode                 Group Id
----- ----------  -------------------- ----- -----
10/3  connected   auto silent           620   0
Port  Status      ErrDisable Reason    Port ErrDisableTimeout  Action on Timeout
----  ----------  -------------------- ----------------------- -----------------
10/3  connected                      -  Enable                  No Change
Port  Align-Err  FCS-Err    Xmit-Err   Rcv-Err    UnderSize
----- ---------- ---------- ---------- ---------- ---------
10/3         11          0          0          0         6
Port  Single-Col Multi-Coll Late-Coll  Excess-Col Carri-Sen Runts     Giants
----- ---------- ---------- ---------- ---------- ---------- --------- ---------
10/3     218713     197092          0     401867          0        27         0
```

The following define the more important fields associated with the **show port** command:

- **Alignment Errors**—Frames received that do not end with an even number of octets. Frame also has a bad cyclic redundancy check (CRC). Misconfiguration is generally the culprit. Ensure that adjacent connected devices have the same duplex setting configuration.

- **FCS Errors**—Bad CRC on the frame packet transmitted/received. These packets are dropped by the switch at the port level.

- **Xmit Errors**—Internal transmit buff is full.

- **RCV Errors**—Internal receive buff is full.

- **Single Collisions**—The number of times the transmitting port had one collision before successfully transmitting the frame on the wire. Single collisions are part of normal operation in a half-duplex environment because of carrier sense multiple access collision detect (CSMA/CD) rule.

- **Multiple Collisions**—The number of times the transmitting port had more than one collision before successfully transmitting the frame on the wire. Multiple collisions do occur if the medium is busy enough.

- **Late Collisions**—Usually indicative of the cable exceeding IEEE specifications. Cascading hubs can also cause the length of the collision domain to increase above specification. A Time Delay Reflectometer (TDR) can be used to detect cable fault and whether the cable is within the IEEE standard. Other factors that cause late collisions include mismatched duplex settings and bad transceivers.

- **Excessive Collisions**—The number of frames that are dropped because the transmitting port saw 16 collisions in a row. This should not occur and can be attributed to possibly a design flaw that is exacerbating an already congested link.

- **Runts**—Frames smaller than 64 bytes with a bad frame check sequence (FCS). Bad cabling or inconsistent duplex setting usually cause runts.

- **Giants**—Frames greater than 1518 with a bad FCS. Investigate NIC issues on the port.

Using Syslog Messages

Syslog messages provide a wealth of information as to the possible root cause of the outage by generating, for the most part, meaningful messages such as the reload of module or shielded twisted-pair (STP) root change, and so on. Cisco switches can be configured for various syslog levels on a per-protocol basis or globally for all protocols. For example, it is generally accepted to have spanning-tree syslog level set at 6, meaning the switch will display syslog messages that fall in the range of 0–6. The number of syslog messages generated is directly proportional to the syslog level. A syslog of level 7 generates a lot more syslog messages than a syslog of level 6, and so on. Therefore, syslog level 7 is primarily for troubleshooting where the switch logs all messages that are generated by the feature/hardware in question:

- 0—emergencies
- 1—alerts
- 2—critical
- 3—errors
- 4—warnings
- 5—notifications
- 6—informational
- 7—debugging

The size of the buffer dictates how big the storage room will be for syslog messages on the switch. When the buffer fills up, the old messages will be removed to make room for the new log messages. If the buffer is too small, it is possible to lose relevant unread logs on the switch. To protect against this scenario, syslog buffers are typically set to 1024 and the log messages are also forwarded to a server for storage. Example 12-10 illustrates a standard configuration. The switch is configured to forward syslog level 0–6 messages to server, IP address of 10.1.1.1.

Example 12-10 *Configuring Logging on the Switch*

```
Switch1(enable)set logging server enable
Switch1(enable)set logging server 10.1.1.1
Switch1(enable)set logging level spantree 6 default
Switch1(enable)set logging server severity 6
```

Using Trace

Trace on a switch is equivalent to enabling debugging on a router. It is, however, a resource drain that can potentially crash a switch. In rare situations where syslog messages, protocol analyzers, and pursuing other avenues for potential explanation for the behavior have been exhausted, trace is used. Trace is a hidden command, and, therefore, care is required if it is going to be enabled. The following command shows trace configured for VLAN Trunking Protocol (VTP) at level 4. The higher the level, the more information will be displayed by the switch. The range of levels is from 0, disabled, to 15:

```
Switch1(enable)set trace vtp 4
```

Local Switched Port Analyzer

Switched Port Analyzer (SPAN) allows for a protocol analyzer such as a sniffer to passively inspect traffic generated by a VLAN(s) or specific source port(s). SPAN is flexible enough that the source can be a single port or multiple ports, or VLAN traffic copied to a user-defined SPAN destination port. For example, any traffic that is received or transmitted by ports 10/3-5 is also forwarded to port 10/1. (See Example 12-11.) The source and destination port must be on the same switch for SPAN, also known as *Local SPAN*.

Example 12-11 *Monitoring Multiple Ports*

```
Switch1 (enable) set span 10/3-5 10/1
Destination       : Port 10/1
Admin Source      : Port 10/3-5
!List of all ports that are monitored
Oper Source       : Port 10/3
!List of Admin ports that are currently active on the network
Direction         : transmit/receive
!Incoming/Outgoing traffic on monitored ports that are sent to destination port
Incoming Packets: disabled
!By default normal traffic is disabled on the destination port. If enabled, it does
not support spanning tree for the vlan the port is associated with- Be careful with
enabling this command. Option first became available in 4.2 OS
Learning          : enabled
!MAC address learning is enabled for incoming packets. The option was introduced in
5.3 OS for Catalyst 6500)
Multicast         : enabled
Filter            : -
!filter option is only available with Catalyst 4000 and 6000 family
Status            : active
```

Example 12-12 illustrates monitoring a VLAN rather than a specific port. Notice all the ports that are associated with the VLAN are part of the Admin Source list.

Example 12-12 *Monitoring VLAN 3*

```
Switch1 (enable) set span 3 10/1
Destination       : Port 10/1
Admin Source      : VLAN 3
Oper Source       : Port 10/24,10/47,15/1
Direction         : transmit/receive
!SPAN can be configured to allow only transmit, receive, or both
Incoming Packets: disabled
Learning          : enabled
Multicast         : enabled
Filter            : -
Status            : active
```

Only traffic from VLAN 3 coming from ports 10/3-5 is copied to port 10/1. (See Example 12-13.) If the filter option was not enabled, all other VLAN traffic from the trunk port would also get copied to a SPAN destination port.

Example 12-13 *SPAN Filtering Enabled*

```
Switch1 (enable) set span 10/3-5 10/1 filter 3
Destination       : Port 10/1
Admin Source      : Port 10/3-5
Oper Source       : Port 10/3
Direction         : transmit/receive
Incoming Packets: disabled
Learning          : enabled
Multicast         : enabled
Filter            : 3
Status            : active
```

However, if the goal is to receive traffic from multiple VLANs and retain their associated VLAN tags, the destination port must be configured for trunking. All traffic from trunk 1/2 is also copied to 10/1, as shown in Example 12-14.

Example 12-14 *Monitoring a Trunk*

```
Switch1 (enable) set trunk 10/1 isl
Port(s) 10/1 trunk type set to isl.
Switch1 (enable) set trunk 10/1 desirable
Port(s) 10/1 trunk mode set to desirable.
Switch1 (enable) set span 1/2 10/1
```

The Create option allows for multiple SPAN sessions to be created, as shown in Example 12-15. All traffic from port 1/2 is copied on port 10/1. Furthermore, all traffic from 10/2 is copied on port 10/11 as well.

Example 12-15 *Using the Create Option*

```
Switch1 (enable) set span 1/2 10/1
Switch1 (enable) set span 10/2 10/11 create
```

Remote Switched Port Analyzer

Unlike Local SPAN, Remote SPAN (RSPAN) allows for the SPAN destination port to be anywhere on the Layer 2 network. This can potentially help save time because the network engineer does not have to worry about placing the sniffer on the same switch as the source. In fact, multiple destination ports can be configured. A Catalyst 6500 can support up to 24 RSPAN destination ports. Sniffers can be strategically placed so that they are readily available if needed. A special VLAN is created for RSPAN to carry the copied source traffic to the destination port. The traffic in RSPAN VLAN is flooded because learning of MAC address is disabled. RSPAN VLAN does not generate bridge protocol data units (BPDUs) on the network.

A source switch is where the monitored ports are located. A source switch can only support one RSPAN VLAN. The steps outline has two switches connected back to back using Inter-Switch Link (ISL) trunking. (See Figure 12-1.)

Figure 12-1 *Original Setup of a Router Connected to a Switch*

Switch1 has a source host, and Switch2 has a RSPAN destination port defined, as follows:

Step 1   Define the VLAN used for RSPAN on the appropriate switches. Here, VLAN 4 is used:

```
Switch1 (enable) set vlan 4 rspan
!Cannot use an existing vlan, create a vlan that is currently not used
Switch2 (enable) set vlan 4 rspan
```

Step 2   Configure source port, 10/3, for RSPAN on Switch1:

```
Switch1 (enable) set rspan source 10/3 4
Rspan Type        : Source
Destination       : -
Rspan Vlan        : 4
Admin Source      : Port 10/3
Oper Source       : Port 10/3
Direction         : transmit/receive
Incoming Packets: -
Learning          : -
Multicast         : enabled
Filter            : -
Status            : active
```

Step 3   Associate a destination port, 3/1, for RSPAN VLAN 4 on Switch2:

```
Switch2 (enable) set rspan destination 3/1 4
Rspan Type        : Destination
Destination       : Port 3/1
Rspan Vlan        : 4
Admin Source      : -
```

```
Oper Source      : -
Direction        : -
Incoming Packets: disabled
Learning         : enabled
Multicast        : -
Filter           : -
Status           : active
```

Any subsequent traffic generated or received on port 10/1 on Switch1 will be copied and forwarded to the sniffer on port 3/1 on Switch2.

Table 12-2 shows when the SPAN/RSPAN features became available in Catalyst OS.

Table 12-2   *SPAN Features and Associated Software Release*

Feature	Catalyst 4000	Catalyst 5000	Catalyst 6000
Inpkts enable/disable option	4.4	4.2	5.1
Multiple sessions, ports in different VLANs	5.1	5.1	5.1
Sc0 option	X	5.1	5.1
Multicast enable/disable option	X	5.1	5.1
Learning enable/disable option	5.2	5.2	5.3
RSPAN	6.3	X	5.3

Table 12-3 illustrates the number of SPAN sessions that can be configured on the appropriate platform.

Table 12-3   *SPAN/RSPAN Session Based on Hardware*

Feature	Catalyst 4000 Range of Switches	Catalyst 5000 Range of Switches	Catalyst 6000 Range of Switches
Rx or both SPAN sessions	5	1	2
Tx SPAN sessions	5	4	4
Rx, Tx, or both RSPAN source sessions	5	Not Supported	1
RSPAN destination	5	Not Supported	24
Total Sessions	5	5	30

Cisco Online Resources

Field alert and Cisco Product Security Advisories and Notices (PSIRT) are two popular methods that Cisco uses to announce software caveats, hardware problems, and security vulnerabilities. Both field alerts and PSIRT web pages can be found on the Cisco website (Cisco.com) by using search words field alert and PSIRTs, respectively.

Field alerts are released to the public by Cisco in the hopes of increasing the customers' awareness of potential software/hardware issues. The field alerts typically have detailed information about the nature of the problem and possible workarounds. If there was a bad batch of hardware sold, Cisco typically offers serial number ranges and guidelines on upgrade policy. It is critical for network engineers to be vigilant for field alerts released by Cisco to ensure minimum risk on the production network.

PSRIT is a group within Cisco that is in charge of releasing security vulnerabilities that affect Cisco software/hardware. In recent years, because of sophistication of attacks such as various worms, Code Red and Nachi, it is recommended that you frequent this site.

Summary

This chapter introduced troubleshooting fundamentals. You first examined potential software issues. The software provides details about possible caveats, security vulnerabilities, and other known issues that can help expedite the troubleshooting process.

The second issue addressed was hardware problems. Catalyst switch commands such as **show module** and **show test** were cited to pinpoint hardware failure. Other commands were also cited to address specific Catalyst switching issues. Troubleshooting guidelines were provided to deal with issues such as Supervisor or an MSFC missing from the chassis.

The discussion turned to port errors seen on the network. Some of the more common fields within the **show port** command were discussed.

The importance of syslog and trace feature were examined. Both syslog and trace commands, in most cases, provide meaningful information about the errors seen by the switch. After you understand the root cause of the problem, you can take steps to resolve the issue.

If command-line syntax, syslog, and trace cannot provide further detail about the nature of the network problem, the SPAN and RSPAN features can be used to examine the actual packets on the network.

Finally, this chapter cited the importance behind field alerts and PSIRTs.

Catalyst 6500 Series Software Conversion

Many users are converting Catalyst 6000/6500s from hybrid to native in an attempt to standardize on one interface throughout their organization. Assuming all the software features and modules in the switch running hybrid are supported in a native configuration, a conversion from hybrid to native requires loading new software and converting the switch configuration to the native syntax. Although an automated tool exists for converting from hybrid to native, the process of converting from native to hybrid is a manual one. This appendix covers the automated tool and manual processes for conversion.

Automated Conversion Tools

The configuration conversion tool is available as a link from the Software Center page on cisco.com. This tool allows users to paste in the configuration of a switch running Catalyst OS and see the resulting command equivalents under native IOS. In addition to pasting in the configuration in the supplied window, users may also upload configuration files for conversion.

After the configuration is converted from hybrid to native syntax, native software must be loaded into the Catalyst. As a last step, the proper changes to boot commands must be made pointing to the native software. This can be accomplished by one of two ways:

- Software conversion tool available on cisco.com

- Manual process

The software conversion tool is available as a link from the Software Center page on cisco.com. The software conversion tool is a JAVA-based application that relies on multiple scripts to convert a switch running hybrid to a native configuration. Figure A-1 shows the main configuration screen of the software conversion tool.

Figure A-1 *Software Conversion Tool*

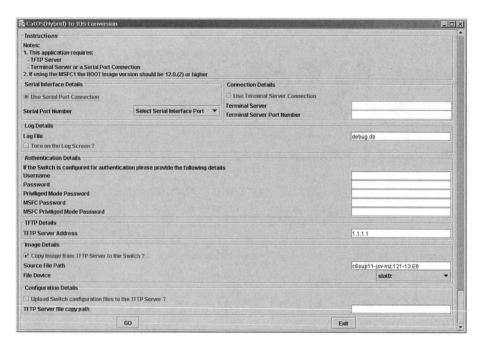

The software conversion tool has a few requirements and limitations. You must understand the preconversion instructions that follow before using the automated tool:

Step 1 Verify that an MSFC is installed.

Step 2 Verify that the Trivial File Transfer Protocol (TFTP) server is reachable from the Supervisor.

Step 3 Verify that the TFTP server is reachable from the MSFC.

Step 4 Verify that the c6sup## image is on the TFTP server.

Step 5 Ensure that enough room is available on the device (slot0: or sup-bootflash:) for the image being copied.

Step 6 If the configurations are going to be copied to the TFTP server, and the TFTP server is a UNIX machine, make sure to "touch" the files and "chmod" the permissions so that they are writable.

Step 7 The configuration files for both the Supervisor and the MSFC are backed up as

SupConfig.cfg—Default Supervisor config filename

RConfig.cfg—Default MSFC config filename

NOTE   The automated software conversion tool and the manual conversion process do not work with dual Supervisors. Switches with dual supervisors must be converted one Supervisor at a time. The secondary Supervisor should be physically ejected while the primary is converted. After the primary is converted to native, it should be ejected, and the secondary should be converted using the same process.

Manual Conversion from Hybrid to Native

The manual process for converting from hybrid to native using a Supervisor II with an MSFC2 is outlined in the following steps. This process can be used with other Catalyst 6000/6500 Supervisor/MSFC combinations using the appropriate software versions for each. Always check the Catalyst 6000/6500 Series Release Notes for memory and ROMMON requirements.

Step 1   Establish a console connection to the Supervisor. It is a good idea to log the console session to a file. This enables the output to be captured as a record of the session and it can be compared against the steps in this process if any issues arise. For example, in Windows Hyperterm, the menu option for logging a console session is **Transfer > Capture Text**. Other terminal emulation programs may have different procedures for capturing text.

Step 2   The switch must be reconfigured after converting to Cisco IOS because the configuration is lost during the conversion process. At this point, it is recommended to back up the Catalyst OS configuration from the Supervisor and the Cisco IOS configuration from the MSFC2. These files can serve as a reference after the conversion or as a backup should it be necessary to convert back to hybrid. Issue the **copy config tftp** command on the Supervisor and the MSFC2 to back up the configurations.

Step 3   Native IOS cannot run on a Catalyst 6000/6500 without a PFC and a MSFC. Issue the **show module** command to confirm that the PFC or PFC2 and the MSFC2 are installed in the switch:

```
SW1 (enable) show module
Mod Slot Ports Module-Type              Model              Sub Status
--- ---- ----- ------------------------ ------------------ --- --------
1   1    2     1000BaseX Supervisor     WS-X6K-S2U-MSFC2   yes ok
15  1    1     Multilayer Switch Feature WS-F6K-MSFC2      no  ok
3   3    48    10/100BaseTX Ethernet    WS-X6548-RJ-45     no  ok
5   5    0     Switch Fabric Module 2   WS-X6500-SFM2      no  ok
Mod Module-Name          Serial-Num
--- -------------------- -----------
1                        SAD060302XM
15                       SAD060102KP
3                        SAL0701B2S0
5                        SAD061506MD
```

```
Mod MAC-Address(es)                               Hw    Fw            Sw
--- -------------------------------------- ------ ---------- -------------
----
 1  00-01-c9-da-ee-d2 to 00-01-c9-da-ee-d3 3.5   7.1(1)        8.1(1)
    00-01-c9-da-ee-d0 to 00-01-c9-da-ee-d1
    00-04-9b-bd-c0-00 to 00-04-9b-bd-c3-ff
15  00-08-7c-a1-cf-80 to 00-08-7c-a1-cf-bf 1.3   12.1(19)E1  12.1(19)E1a
 3  00-09-11-f3-88-48 to 00-09-11-f3-88-77 5.1   6.3(1)        8.1(1)
 5  00-01-00-02-00-03                       1.2   6.1(3)        8.1(1)
Mod Sub-Type               Sub-Model        Sub-Serial  Sub-Hw Sub-Sw
--- ---------------------- ---------------- ----------- ------ ------
 1  L3 Switching Engine II WS-F6K-PFC2      SAD054104B3 3.0
SW1 (enable)
```

Step 4   Make sure the Cisco IOS (native) image is available on the Supervisor bootflash or on the PCMCIA card in slot0. Newer versions of Cisco IOS have outgrown the capacity of bootflash on some Supervisors. The proper location for the Cisco IOS (native) image depends on the Supervisor flash device capacity and image size.

Use the directory command to verify the location of the Cisco IOS (native) image:

```
SW1> (enable) dir bootflash:
-#- -length- -----date/time------ name
  1  8040396 Oct 30 2003 23:17:13 cat6000-sup2k8.8-1-1.bin
23941044 bytes available (8040524 bytes used)
SW1> (enable)
SW1> (enable) dir slot0:
-#- -length- -----date/time------ name
  1 19769600 Oct 31 2003 00:39:30 c6sup22-js-mz.121-19.E1a
5002880 bytes available (19769728 bytes used)
SW1> (enable)
```

If the native image (c6sup*) is missing from either bootflash: or slot0:, download it using the procedure described in Step 5. If the image is present, go to Step 6.

Step 5   (Optional) This step is needed if Step 4 determined the Cisco IOS (native) image (c6sup*) is missing from either bootflash: or slot0:.

Space can be freed up as necessary on the flash devices by using the **delete bootflash:** or **slot0:** *filename* command (which deletes the file) followed by the **squeeze bootflash:** or **slot0:** command (which erases all deleted files from the device).

Use the **copy tftp bootflash:** or **copy tftp slot0:** command to download the image to either Switch Processor bootflash or to the PCMCIA card in slot0:

```
SW1> (enable) copy tftp slot0:
IP address or name of remote host []? 10.1.1.2
```

```
Name of file to copy from []? c6sup22-js-mz.121-19.E1a
24772480 bytes available on device slot0, proceed (y/n) [n]? y
CCCCCCCCCCCCCCCCCCCCCCCCCCCCCCCCCCCCCCCCCCCCCCCCCCCCCCCCCCCCCCCCCCCCCCC
CCCCCCCCCCCCCCCCCCCCCCCCCCCCCCCCCCCCCCCCCCCCCCCCCCCCCCCCCCCCCCCCCCCCCCC
CCCCCCCCCCCCCCCCCCCCCCCCCCCCCCCCCCCCCCCCCCCCCCCCCCCCCCCCCCCCCCCCCCCCCCC
CCCCCCCCCCCCCCCCCCCCCCCCCCCCCCCCCCCCCCCCC
File has been copied successfully.
SW1> (enable)
SW1> (enable) dir slot0:
-#- -length- -----date/time------ name
   1 19769600 Oct 31 2003 21:37:39 c6sup22-js-mz.121-19.E1a
5002880 bytes available (19769728 bytes used)
SW1> (enable)
```

Step 6 Access the MSFC by issuing either the **switch console** or the **session module** command:

```
SW1> (enable) switch console
Trying Router-15...
Connected to Router-15.
Type ^C^C^C to switch back...
SW1-MSFC2>
SW1-MSFC2>enable
SW1-MSFC2#
```

Step 7 Issue the **dir bootflash:** command to verify that the MSFC2 boot image (c6msfc2-boot) is present on the MSFC bootflash. A boot image is not required for the MSFC2, however, it is recommended. A boot image is a much smaller, scaled-down version of the system image that makes it possible to perform a TFTP image transfer in the event the main system image is corrupted or lost. If you choose to use an MSFC2 boot image, you must store it in the MSFC bootflash:

```
SW1-MSFC2#dir bootflash:
Directory of bootflash:/
    1  -rw-     1820676   Aug 20 2003 18:13:11  c6msfc2-boot-mz.121-19.E1a
15204352 bytes total (13383548 bytes free)
```

If the c6msfc2-boot image is missing from the MSFC bootflash, download it using the procedure described in Step 8. If the image is present, go to Step 9.

Step 8 (Optional) This step is needed if the c6msfc2-boot image is missing from the MSFC bootflash.

Space can be freed up as necessary on the MSFC bootflash by using the **delete bootflash:** *filename* command (which deletes the file) followed by the **squeeze bootflash:** command (which erases all deleted files from the device).

Use the **copy tftp bootflash:** command to download the image to MSFC bootflash:

```
SW1-MSFC2#copy tftp bootflash:
Address or name of remote host []? 10.1.1.2
Source filename []? c6msfc2-boot-mz.121-19.E1a
Destination filename [c6msfc2-boot-mz.121-19.E1a]?
Accessing tftp://10.1.1.2/c6msfc2-boot-mz.121-19.E1a...
Loading c6msfc2-boot-mz.121-19.E1a from 10.1.1.2 (via Vlan1): !!!!!!!!!!!!!
!!!!!!!!!!!!!!!!!!!!!!!!!!!!!!!!!!!!!!!!!!!!!!!!!!!!!!!!!!!!!!!!!!!!!!!!!!!!!
!!!!!!!!!!!!!!!!!!!!!!!!!!!!!!!!!!!!!!!!!!!!!!!!!!!!!!!!!!!!!!!!!!!!!!!!!!!!!
!!!!!!!!!!!!!!!!!!!!!!!!!!!!!!!!!!!!!!!!!!!!!!!!!!!!!!!!!!!!!!!!!!!!!!!!!!!!!
!!!!!!!!!!!!!!!!!!!!!!!!!!!!!!!!!!!!!!!!!!!!!!!!!!!!!!!!!!!!!!!!!!!!!!!!!!!!!
!!!!!!!!!!!!!!!!!!!!!!!!
[OK - 1820676 bytes]
1820676 bytes copied in 18.800 secs (96844 bytes/sec)
Verifying compressed IOS image checksum...
Verified compressed IOS image checksum for bootflash:/c6msfc2-boot-mz.121-
  19.E1a

SW1-MSFC2#dir bootflash:
Directory of bootflash:/
    1  -rw-     1820676   Nov 01 2003 00:37:41   c6msfc2-boot-mz.121-19.E1a
15204352 bytes total (13383548 bytes free)
SW1-MSFC2#
```

Step 9   Verify that the BOOTLDR variable statement is set pointing to the c6msfc2-boot image in MSFC bootflash and the configuration register is set to 0x2102, which disables the BREAK key and tells the MSFC2 to autoboot. Issue the **show bootvar** command to check the BOOTLDR variable and configuration register settings.

A BOOTLDR variable statement is not required for the MSFC2, but is recommended and will be used in this procedure:

```
SW1-MSFC2#show boot
BOOT variable = sup-slot0:c6msfc2-jsv-mz.121-19.E1a,1
CONFIG_FILE variable =
BOOTLDR variable = bootflash:c6msfc2-boot-mz.121-19.E1a
Configuration register is 0x2102
SW1-MSFC2#
```

If the BOOTLDR variable statement or the configuration register is not set correctly, go to Step 10 to change them. If both of these settings are correct, go to Step 11.

Step 10   (Optional) This step is required only if Step 9 determined that the BOOTLDR variable statement or the configuration register were not set correctly. Issue the following commands to set the BOOTLDR variable statement and/or change the configuration register setting:

```
SW1-MSFC2#dir bootflash:
Directory of bootflash:/
    1  -rw-     1820676   Nov 01 2003 00:37:41   c6msfc2-boot-mz.121-19.E1a
15204352 bytes total (13383548 bytes free)
SW1-MSFC2#
```

```
SW1-MSFC2#configure terminal
Enter configuration commands, one per line.  End with CNTL/Z.
SW1-MSFC2(config)#boot bootldr bootflash:c6msfc2-boot-mz.121-19.E1a
SW1-MSFC2(config)#end
SW1-MSFC2#
SW1-MSFC2#configure terminal
Enter configuration commands, one per line.  End with CNTL/Z.
SW1-MSFC2(config)#config-register 0x2102
SW1-MSFC2(config)#end
SW1-MSFC2#

SW1-MSFC2#write mem
Building configuration...
[OK]
```

Software defects in some versions of Cisco IOS prevent the **copy run start** command from properly saving the config-register value, so the **write mem** command is used.

```
SW1-MSFC2#show boot
BOOT variable = sup-slot0:c6msfc2-jsv-mz.121-19.E1a
CONFIG_FILE variable =
BOOTLDR variable = bootflash:c6msfc2-boot-mz.121-19.E1a
Configuration register is 0x2102
SW1-MSFC2#
```

Step 11 Go back to the Supervisor by typing **Ctrl-C** three times on the MSFC.

If the MSFC was accessed by issuing the **session module** command, type **exit** instead of Ctrl-C to go back to the Supervisor:

```
SW1-MSFC2#^C
SW1-MSFC2#^C
SW1-MSFC2#^C
SW1> (enable)
```

Step 12 After you are back on the Supervisor, change the configuration register setting on the Supervisor so that the switch does not boot the Catalyst OS image and goes to ROMMON:

```
SW1> (enable) set boot config-register 0x0
Configuration register is 0x0
ignore-config: disabled
auto-config: non-recurring, overwrite, sync disabled
console baud: 9600
boot: the ROM monitor
SW1> (enable)

SW1> (enable) show boot
BOOT variable = bootflash:cat6000-sup2k8.8-1-1.bin,1
CONFIG_FILE variable = bootflash:switch.cfg
Configuration register is 0x0
ignore-config: disabled
auto-config: non-recurring, overwrite, sync disabled
console baud: 9600
boot: the ROM monitor
SW1> (enable)
```

Step 13 Reset the switch so that it goes into ROMMON:

```
SW1> (enable) reset
This command will reset the system.
Do you want to continue (y/n) [n]? y
2003 Nov 01 03:44:12 %SYS-5-SYS_RESET:System reset from Console//
Powering OFF all existing linecards
2003 Nov 01 03:44:12 %ETHC-5-PORTFROMSTP:Port 3/1 left bridge port 3/1
System Bootstrap, Version 7.1(1)
Copyright (c) 1994-2001 by cisco Systems, Inc.
c6k_sup2 processor with 262144 Kbytes of main memory
rommon 1 >
```

Step 14 Issue the **set** command at the ROMMON prompt to check the environment variables. Notice that the switch is currently set to boot into the
Catalyst OS image:

```
rommon 1 > set
PS1=rommon ! >
BOOTLDR=
SLOTCACHE=cards;
RET_2_RTS=22:35:52 UTC Thu Oct 30 2003
RET_2_RUTC=1067553353
?=0
BOOT=bootflash:cat6000-sup2k8.8-1-1.bin,1
CONFIG_FILE=bootflash:switch.cfg
rommon 2 >
```

The CONFIG_FILE environment variable is not used by the Cisco IOS
(native) software, and might cause a problem. This can easily be avoided
here by removing either bootflash:switch.cfg or slot0:switch.cfg from the
environment settings. To do this, issue the following commands:

```
rommon 2 > CONFIG_FILE=
rommon 3 > sync
rommon 4 > reset
System Bootstrap, Version 7.1(1)
Copyright (c) 1994-2001 by cisco Systems, Inc.
c6k_sup2 processor with 262144 Kbytes of main memory
rommon 1 >
```

Step 15 Now boot the switch using the Cisco IOS (native) image. First issue the
dir bootflash: or **dir slot0:** command depending on which device is
storing the Cisco IOS (native) image. Then issue the **boot bootflash:** or
slot0:*filename* command to start the bootup sequence:

```
rommon 1 > dir slot0:
         File size          Checksum    File name
  19769600 bytes (0x12da900)  0x4dbcb14a   c6sup22-js-mz.121-19.E1a

rommon 2 > boot slot0:c6sup22-js-mz.121-19.E1a
Self decompressing the image : ######################################
####################################################################
####################################################################
####################################################################

System Bootstrap, Version 12.1(4r)E, RELEASE SOFTWARE (fc1)
Copyright (c) 2000 by cisco Systems, Inc.
```

```
Cat6k-MSFC2 platform with 262144 Kbytes of main memory
Download Start
!!!!!!!!!!!!!!!!!!!!!!!!!!!!!!!!!!!!!!!!!!!!!!!!!!!!!!!!!!!!!!!!!!!!!!!!!!!
!!!!!!!!!!!!!!!!!!!!!!!!!!!!!!!!!!!!!!!!!!!!!!!!!!!!!!!!!!!!!!!!!!!!!!!!!!!
!!!!!!!!!!!!!!!!!!!!!!!!!!!!!!!!!!!!!!!!!!!!!!!!!!!!!!!!!!!!!!!!!!!!!!!!!!!
!!!!!!!!!!!!!!!!!!!!!!!!!!!!!!!!!!!!!!!!!!!!!!!!!!!!!!!!!!!!!!!!!!!!!!!!!!!
!!!!!!!!!!!!!!!!!!!!!!!!!!!!!!!!!!!!!!!!!!!!!!!!!!!!!!!!!!!!!!!!!!!!!!!!!!!
!!!!!!!!!!!!!!!!!!!!!!!!!!!!!!!!!!!!!!!!!!!!!!!!!!!!!!!!!!!!!!!
Download Completed! Booting the image.
Self decompressing the image : ########################################
#########################################################################
#########################################################################
#########################################################################
#########################################################################
#########################################################################
Cisco Internetwork Operating System Software
IOS (tm) c6sup2_rp Software (c6sup2_rp-JS-M), Version 12.1(19)E1a, EARLY
  DEPLOYM
ENT RELEASE SOFTWARE (fc2)
TAC Support: http://www.cisco.com/tac
Copyright (c) 1986-2003 by cisco Systems, Inc.
Compiled Tue 05-Aug-03 22:27 by hqluong
Image text-base: 0x40008C00, data-base: 0x41B0C000
cisco WS-C6506 (R7000) processor (revision 2.0) with 227328K/34816K bytes
  of memory.
Processor board ID TBA04510556
R7000 CPU at 300Mhz, Implementation 39, Rev 2.1, 256KB L2, 1024KB L3 Cache
Last reset from power-on
Bridging software.
X.25 software, Version 3.0.0.
SuperLAT software (copyright 1990 by Meridian Technology Corp).
TN3270 Emulation software.
1 Virtual Ethernet/IEEE 802.3  interface(s)
48 FastEthernet/IEEE 802.3 interface(s)
2 Gigabit Ethernet/IEEE 802.3 interface(s)
381K bytes of non-volatile configuration memory.
16384K bytes of Flash internal SIMM (Sector size 512K).
Press RETURN to get started!
SW1-MSFC2>
```

Step 16 At this point, the Cisco IOS (native) image has successfully booted, but the Supervisor flash devices are still formatted with the previous Catalyst OS (hybrid) algorithm. This means that Cisco IOS (native) software will not be able to correctly write to sup-bootflash: or slot0:. These flash devices will need to be reformatted and the images replaced on them.

Use the **format** command to format both the Supervisor bootflash and slot0 flash devices:

```
SW1-MSFC2>enable
SW1-MSFC2#format sup-bootflash:
Format operation may take a while. Continue? [confirm]
Format operation will destroy all data in "sup-bootflash:".  Continue?
  [confirm]

Format of sup-bootflash complete
SW1-MSFC2#

SW1-MSFC2#format slot0:
Format operation may take a while. Continue? [confirm]
```

```
Format operation will destroy all data in "slot0:".  Continue? [confirm]
Enter volume ID (up to 64 chars)[default slot0]:
Format of slot0 complete
SW1-MSFC2#
```

Step 17 Formatting the Supervisor flash devices in the previous step has erased
all data on these devices including the Cisco IOS (native) image used to
boot the Supervisor. The Cisco IOS (native) image (c6sup*) will need to
be copied over again.

Remember that the configuration has been lost during the conversion. An
IP address and possibly static or dynamic routing will need to be
configured to establish connectivity to the TFTP server again. Make sure
pings are successful to the TFTP server from the switch.

Use the **copy tftp** command to copy the Cisco IOS (native) image to
either the sup-bootflash: or slot0: flash device:

```
SW1-MSFC2#copy tftp slot0:
Address or name of remote host []? 10.1.1.2
Source filename []? c6sup22-js-mz.121-19.E1a
Destination filename [c6sup22-js-mz.121-19.E1a]?
Accessing tftp://10.1.1.2/c6sup22-js-mz.121-19.E1a...
Loading c6sup22-js-mz.121-19.E1a from 10.1.1.2 (via FastEthernet3/1): !!!!!
!!!!!!!!!!!!!!!!!!!!!!!!!!!!!!!!!!!!!!!!!!!!!!!!!!!!!!!!!!!!!!!!!!!!!!!!!!!!!!
!!!!!!!!!!!!!!!!!!!!!!!!!!!!!!!!!!!!!!!!!!!!!!!!!!!!!!!!!!!!!!!!!!!!!!!!!!!!!!
!!!!!!!!!!!!!!!!!!!!!!!!!!!!!!!!!!!!!!!!!!!!!!!!!!!!!!!!!!!!!!!!!!!!!!!!!!!!!!
!!!!!!!!!!!!!!!!!!!!!!!!!!!!!!!!!!!!!!!!!!!!!!!!!!!!!!!!!!!!!!!!!!!!!!!!!!!!!!
!!!!!!!!!!!!!!!!!!!
[OK - 19769600 bytes]
19769600 bytes copied in 290.032 secs (68164 bytes/sec)
Verifying compressed IOS image checksum...
Verified compressed IOS image checksum for slot0:/c6sup22-js-mz.121-19.E1a
SW1-MSFC2#
```

Step 18 Now set the boot variable to boot from the Cisco IOS (native) image in
sup-bootflash: or slot0:

```
SW1-MSFC2#show boot
BOOT variable = sup-slot0:c6msfc2-jsv-mz.121-19.E1a
CONFIG_FILE variable =
BOOTLDR variable = bootflash:c6msfc2-boot-mz.121-19.E1a
Configuration register is 0x2102
Standby is not up.
SW1-MSFC2#

SW1-MSFC2#configure terminal
Enter configuration commands, one per line.  End with CNTL/Z.
SW1-MSFC2(config)#boot system flash slot0:c6sup22-js-mz.121-19.E1a
SW1-MSFC2(config)#

SW1-MSFC2#write memory
Building configuration...
[OK]
SW1-MSFC2#
```

Step 19 Before reloading, change the config-register of the Switch Processor
from 0x0 to 0x2102. Otherwise, upon reload the router will end up in the
Supervisor ROMMON. Issue the **show bootvar** command again:

```
SW1-MSFC2#show boot
BOOT variable = slot0:c6sup22-js-mz.121-19.E1a,1
CONFIG_FILE variable does not exist
BOOTLDR variable does not exist
Configuration register is 0x2102
```

Viewing the preceding output, it seems that all the variables are set and
you should be able to boot the switch automatically. However, at this
point, if you reload the router you will end up in the Supervisor
ROMMON. This is because the configuration register value for the
Supervisor (set in Step 12) is still 0x0. You can verify this statement by
issuing the **remote command switch show boot** command, which will
display current environment variable settings on the Supervisor.

In Cisco IOS (native) releases earlier than 12.1(5c)EX, the command
format is remote command:

```
SW1-MSFC2#remote command switch show boot
BOOT variable = slot0:c6sup22-js-mz.121-19.E1a,1
CONFIG_FILE variable =
BOOTLDR variable =
Configuration register is 0x0
```

Issue the following set of commands on the Router (RP) to change the
configuration register settings on the Supervisor:

```
SW1-MSFC2#configure terminal
Enter configuration commands, one per line.  End with CNTL/Z.
SW1-MSFC2(config)#config-register 0x2102
SW1-MSFC2(config)#end

SW1-MSFC2#write memory
Building configuration...
[OK]

SW1-MSFC2#remote command switch show boot
BOOT variable = slot0:c6sup22-js-mz.121-19.E1a,1
CONFIG_FILE variable =
BOOTLDR variable =
Configuration register is 0x0 (will be 0x2102 at next reload)
```

Step 20 The final step is to reload the switch:

```
SW1-MSFC2#reload
Proceed with reload? [confirm]
```

Manual Conversion from Native to Hybrid

Although an automated tool exists for converting both the configuration commands and software from hybrid to native, Cisco does not offer automated tools to convert from native to hybrid. Users can be challenged with converting from native to hybrid when integrating equipment from other companies or locations, or when receiving a new Supervisor card already running native, when the organization has decided to run hybrid as the standard. For example, the Supervisor 720 initially shipped with only native IOS support, and only later did hybrid software solutions become available. Some users chose to convert from native to hybrid after the new software became available.

The manual process for converting from native to hybrid using a Supervisor 720 with an MSFC3 is outlined in the following steps. This process can be used with other Catalyst 6000/6500 Supervisor/MSFC combinations using the appropriate software versions for each. Always check the Catalyst 6000/6500 Series Release Notes for memory and ROMMON requirements:

Step 1   Establish a console connection to the Supervisor. It is a good idea to log the console session to a file. This enables the output to be captured as a record of the session and it can be compared against the steps in this process if any issues arise. For example, in Windows Hyperterm, the menu option for logging a console session is **Transfer > Capture Text**. Other terminal emulation programs might have different procedures for capturing text.

Step 2   The switch must be reconfigured after converting to Catalyst OS because the configuration is lost during the conversion process. At this point, it is recommended to back up the configuration. This file can serve as a reference after the conversion or as a backup should you decide to convert back to native. Issue the **copy config tftp** command to back up the configuration.

Step 3   Make sure that the MSFC3 (c6msfc3*) hybrid IOS software image is on the MSFC bootflash:

```
SW1-MSFC3#dir bootflash:
Directory of bootflash:/

    1  -rw-    16050204   Aug 18 2003 12:10:51   c6msfc3-jsv-mz.122-14.SX2
    2  -rw-      649603   Aug 18 2003 13:29:29   c6msfc3-rm2.srec.122-14r.S9

65536000 bytes total (48835936 bytes free)
SW1-MSFC3#
```

If the MSFC hybrid IOS image is not in the MSFC bootflash, go to Step 4. If the MSFC hybrid IOS image is on bootflash, go to Step 5.

Step 4   (Optional) This step is necessary if Step 4 determined the required MSFC hybrid IOS image (c6msfc3*) was missing from the MSFC bootflash.

Space can be freed if necessary on the MSFC bootflash with the **delete bootflash:**<*filename*> command (which deletes the file) followed by the **squeeze bootflash:** command (which erases all deleted files from the device).

Download the MSFC hybrid IOS image into the MSFC bootflash:

```
SW1-MSFC3#copy tftp bootflash:
Address or name of remote host []? 10.1.1.2
Source filename []? c6msfc3-jsv-mz.122-14.SX2
Destination filename [c6msfc3-jsv-mz.122-14.SX2]?
Accessing tftp://10.1.1.2/c6msfc3-jsv-mz.122-14.SX2...
Loading c6msfc3-jsv-mz.122-14.SX2 from 10.1.1.2 (via FastEthernet1/1): !!!
!!!!!!!!!!!!!!!!!!!!!!!!!!!!!!!!!!!!!!!!!!!!!!!!!!!!!!!!!!!!!!!!!!!!!!!!!!!!!!!
!!!!!!!!!!!!!!!!!!!!!!!!!!!!!!!!!!!!!!!!!!!!!!!!!!!!!!!!!!!!!!!!!!!!!!!!!!!!!!!
!!!!!!!!!!!
[OK - 16050204 bytes]

16050204 bytes copied in 159.488 secs (100636 bytes/sec)
Verifying compressed IOS image checksum...
Verified compressed IOS image checksum for bootflash:/c6msfc3-jsv-mz.122-
   14.SX2
SW1-MSFC3#
SW1-MSFC3#dir bootflash:
Directory of bootflash:/

    1  -rw-    16050204    Aug 18 2003 14:10:03   c6msfc3-jsv-mz.122-14.SX2
    2  -rw-      649603    Aug 18 2003 13:29:29   c6msfc3-rm2.srec.122-14r.S9

65536000 bytes total (48835936 bytes free)
SW1-MSFC3#
```

Step 5   Make sure you are running the minimum ROMMON version required for the conversion.

Unlike Supervisor II with MSFC2, no boot image is required on the Supervisor Engine 720 for the MSFC3. The basic functionality to boot the MSFC3 is embedded in ROMMON (including TFTP capability). When converting the Supervisor Engine 720 from Cisco IOS (native) to Catalyst OS on the Supervisor and Cisco IOS on the MSFC (hybrid), a minimum version of ROMMON is required. The required minimum ROMMON version is 12.2(14r)S9.

Issue the **show version** command to verify the ROMMON version:

```
SW1-MSFC3#show version
Cisco Internetwork Operating System Software
IOS (tm) s72033_rp Software (s72033_rp-PSV-M), Version 12.2(14)SX1, EARLY
   DEPLOY
MENT RELEASE SOFTWARE (fc1)
TAC Support: http://www.cisco.com/tac
Copyright (c) 1986-2003 by cisco Systems, Inc.
Compiled Tue 27-May-03 19:24 by ccai
Image text-base: 0x40008C10, data-base: 0x41ACE000
```

```
ROM: System Bootstrap, Version 12.2(14r)S8, RELEASE SOFTWARE (fc1)
```

If the minimum version of ROMMON is not installed, go to Step 6. If the minimum or later version is installed, go to Step 7.

Step 6   (Optional) This step is necessary if Step 5 determined that the required minimum version 12.2(14r)S9 or later version of ROMMON software is not installed.

Download the file c6msfc3-rm2.srec.122-14r.S* from the Cisco IOS Software ROMMON section of the Software Center into the MSFC bootflash:

```
SW1-MSFC3#copy tftp bootflash:
Address or name of remote host []? 10.1.1.2
Source filename []? c6msfc3-rm2.srec.122-14r.S9
Destination filename [c6msfc3-rm2.srec.122-14r.S9]?
Accessing tftp://10.1.1.2/c6msfc3-rm2.srec.122-14r.S9...
Loading c6msfc3-rm2.srec.122-14r.S9 from 10.1.1.2 (via FastEthernet1/1): !!
!!!!!!!!!!!!!!!!!!!!!!!!!!!!!!!!!!!!!!!!!!!!!!!!!!!!!!!!!!!!!!!!!!!!!!!!!!!!!
!!!!!!!!!!!!!!!!!!!!!!!!!!!!!!!!!!!!!!!!!!!!!!!!!
[OK - 649603 bytes]

SW1-MSFC3#dir bootflash:
Directory of bootflash:/

    1  -rw-    16050204    Aug 18 2003 12:10:51   c6msfc3-jsv-mz.122-14.SX2
    2  -rw-      649603    Aug 18 2003 13:29:29   c6msfc3-rm2.srec.122-14r.S9

65536000 bytes total (48835936 bytes free)
SW1-MSFC3#
```

The actual ROMMON upgrade procedure will be performed later. For now, continue to Step 7.

Step 7   Make sure the Catalyst OS image (cat6000-sup720*) is on either the Supervisor bootflash (sup-bootflash:) or on a compact flash card (disk0: or disk1:):

```
SW1-MSFC3#dir sup-bootflash:
Directory of sup-bootflash:/

    2  -rw-    32983632    Aug 16 2003 19:44:42   s72033-psv-mz.122-14.SX1.bin

65536000 bytes total (18912432 bytes free)
SW1-MSFC3#
SW1-MSFC3#dir disk0:

Directory of disk0:/

    1  -rw-    13389508    Aug 16 2003 20:36:40   cat6000-sup720k8.8-1-1.bin
128626688 bytes total (115236864 bytes free)
```

If the Catalyst OS image is not on either sup-bootflash: or on disk0: or disk1:, go to Step 8. If the Catalyst OS image is installed, go to Step 9.

Step 8 (Optional) This step is necessary if the Supervisor 720 Catalyst OS
image is not on either the Supervisor bootflash (sup-bootflash:) or on the
compact flash card (disk0: or disk1:).

The compact flash might need to be formatted if it has never been used
before or was formatted using the hybrid algorithm. To format compact
flash on a Supervisor 720, use the **format disk0:** and/or the **format disk
1:** command. You can also free up space as necessary on the flash devices
using the **delete sup-bootflash:** or **delete disk0:** or **disk1:***filename*
command (which deletes the file) followed by the **squeeze sup-
bootflash:** or **squeeze disk0:** or **disk1:** command (which erases all
deleted files from the device).

Use the **copy tftp sup-bootflash:**, **copy tftp disk0:**, or **disk1:** command
to download the image to either the Supervisor bootflash or to one of the
flash cards:

```
SW1-MSFC3#copy tftp disk0:
Address or name of remote host []? 10.1.1.2
Source filename []? cat6000-sup720k8.8-1-1.bin
Destination filename [cat6000-sup720k8.8-1-1.bin]?
Accessing tftp://10.1.1.2/cat6000-sup720k8.8-1-1.bin...
Loading cat6000-sup720k8.8-1-1.bin from 10.1.1.2 (via FastEthernet1/1): !!
!!!!!!!!!!!!!!!!!!!!!!!!!!!!!!!!!!!!!!!!!!!!!!!!!!!!!!!!!!!!!!!!!!!!!!!!!!!!!!
!!!!!!!!!!!!!!!!!!!!!!!!!!!!!!!!!!!!!!!!!!!!!!!!!!!!!!!!!!!!!!!!!!!!!!!!!!!!!!
!!!!!!!!!!!!!!!!!!!!!!!!!!!!!!!!!!!!!!!!!!!!!!!!!!!
[OK - 13389508 bytes]

13389508 bytes copied in 103.044 secs (129940 bytes/sec)
Verifying compressed IOS image checksum...
Verified compressed IOS image checksum for disk0:/cat6000-sup720k8.8-1-
  1.bin
SW1-MSFC3#

SW1-MSFC3#dir disk0:
Directory of disk0:/

    1  -rw-     13389508    Aug 18 2003 15:17:36  cat6000-sup720k8.8-1-1.bin

128626688 bytes total (115236864 bytes free)
SW1-MSFC3#
```

Step 9 Change the configuration register setting to put the switch into
ROMMON on the next reload:

```
SW1-MSFC3#configure terminal
Enter configuration commands, one per line.  End with CNTL/Z.
SW1-MSFC3(config)#config-register 0x0
SW1-MSFC3(config)#end
SW1-MSFC3#
```

Use the **show boot** command to verify the new config-register setting:

```
SW1-MSFC3#show boot
BOOT variable = sup-bootflash:s72033-psv-mz.122-14.SX1.bin,1
CONFIG_FILE variable does not exist
```

```
BOOTLDR variable does not exist
Configuration register is 0x2102 (will be 0x0 at next reload)

Standby is not up.
SW1-MSFC3#
```

Step 10 Reload the router:

```
SW1-MSFC3#reload

System configuration has been modified. Save? [yes/no]: no
Proceed with reload? [confirm]

02:04:30: %SYS-5-RELOAD: Reload requested by console.
02:04:33: %OIR-SP-6-CONSOLE: Changing console ownership to switch processor

02:04:35: %SYS-SP-5-RELOAD: Reload requested
02:04:36: %OIR-SP-6-CONSOLE: Changing console ownership to switch processor

***
*** --- SHUTDOWN NOW ---
***

System Bootstrap, Version 7.7(1)
Copyright (c) 1994-2003 by cisco Systems, Inc.
Cat6k-Sup720/SP processor with 524288 Kbytes of main memory
rommon 1>
```

Step 11 From the Supervisor ROMMON prompt, verify the Catalyst OS image is
on either the Supervisor bootflash (sup-bootflash:) or on one of the
compact flash devices:

```
rommon 1 > dir disk0:
Directory of disk0:

2      13389508   -rw-     cat6000-sup720k8.8-1-1.bin
```

Step 12 Issue the **boot** command to start the bootup sequence for the Catalyst OS
image:

```
rommon 2 > boot disk0:cat6000-sup720k8.8-1-1.bin

Self decompressing the image : #######################################
#######################################################################
#######################################################################
#######################################################################
#######################################################################
#######################################################################
#######################################################################
#######################################################################
#######################################################################
#######################################################################
#######################################################################
######################################### [OK]

System Power On Diagnostics
DRAM Size ........................512 MB
Testing DRAM .....................Passed
Verifying Text Segment ...........Passed
NVRAM Size .......................2048 KB
```

```
Level2 Cache ......................Present
Level3 Cache ......................Present
System Power On Diagnostics Complete

Currently running ROMMON from S (Gold) region
Boot image: disk0:cat6000-sup720k8.8-1-1.bin

Firmware compiled 29-Jun-03 19:12 by integ Build [100]

Running System Diagnostics from this Supervisor (Module 5)
This may take several minutes....please wait

IP address for Catalyst not configured
DHCP/BOOTP will commence after the ports are online
Ports are coming online ...

2003 Aug 18 15:49:58 %SYS-4-NVLOG:initBootNvram:Bootarea checksum failed:
   0x4665
(0x44AA)

Cisco Systems Console

Console>
```

Step 13 From the Supervisor's console prompt, check the status of the MSFC by issuing the **show module** command:

```
Console> (enable) show module
Mod Slot Ports Module-Type               Model            Sub Status
--- ---- ----- ------------------------  ---------------- --- --------
1   1    48    10/100BaseTX Ethernet     WS-X6548-RJ-45   no  ok
5   5    2     1000BaseX Supervisor      WS-SUP720-BASE   yes ok

Mod Module-Name           Serial-Num
--- --------------------- -----------
1                         SAL06489DVD
5                         SAD07170009

Mod MAC-Address(es)                          Hw     Fw         Sw
--- ---------------------------------------- ------ ---------- -----------
1   00-09-11-f2-f3-a8 to 00-09-11-f2-f3-d7 5.1    6.3(1)     8.1(1)
5   00-0c-ce-63-da-fe to 00-0c-ce-63-da-ff 2.1    7.7(1)     8.1(1)
    00-0c-ce-63-da-fc to 00-0c-ce-63-da-ff
    00-0c-86-a0-10-00 to 00-0c-86-a0-13-ff

Mod Sub-Type              Sub-Model           Sub-Serial  Sub-Hw Sub-Sw
--- --------------------- ------------------- ----------- ------ ------
5   L3 Switching Engine III WS-F6K-PFC3A      SAD071501AB 1.1
Console> (enable)
```

Notice that the MSFC3 in slot 15 is not shown in the preceding output because the MSFC3 (RP) is still in ROMMON mode.

Step 14 Access the MSFC with the **switch console** command.

If the session 15 command is used at this point, it will result in the following error:

```
Console> (enable) session 15
Module 15 is not installed.
Console> (enable) switch console
Trying Router-15...
```

```
Connected to Router-15.
Type ^C^C^C to switch back...
rommon 1 >
```

If Step 6 determined the required minimum 12.2(14r)S9 or later version of ROMMON software was not installed, go to Step 15. If the required minimum ROMMON version is installed, go to Step 16.

Step 15 (Optional) This step is required if the required 12.2(14r)S9 or later version of ROMMON software is not installed.

Nonvolatile random-access memory (NVRAM) must be reformatted for Catalyst OS (hybrid) mode before upgrading the ROMMON version. Issue the **nvram_erase** command from ROMMON privileged mode:

```
rommon 2 > priv
```

Privileged mode grants access to the full set of monitor commands. Be aware that some commands will allow you to destroy the configuration and/or system images and could render the switch unbootable:

```
rommon 3 > nvram_erase
Enter in hex the start address [0xbe020000]: be000000
Enter in hex the test size or length in bytes [0x100]: 200000
rommon 4 > reset
```

Step 16 Verify the MSFC runtime image (c6msfc3*) is present on the MSFC bootflash with the **dir bootflash** command and use the **boot** command to boot this image:

```
rommon 2 > dir bootflash:
         File size           Checksum    File name
  16050204 bytes (0xf4e81c)  0x4221810c  c6msfc3-jsv-mz.122-14.SX2
    649603 bytes (0x9e983)   0x64867cc   c6msfc3-rm2.srec.122-14r.S9
rommon 3 > boot bootflash:c6msfc3-jsv-mz.122-14.SX2
Self decompressing the image : ####################################
############################################################################
 [OK]

                 Restricted Rights Legend

Use, duplication, or disclosure by the Government is
subject to restrictions as set forth in subparagraph
(c) of the Commercial Computer Software - Restricted
Rights clause at FAR sec. 52.227-19 and subparagraph
(c) (1) (ii) of the Rights in Technical Data and Computer
Software clause at DFARS sec. 252.227-7013.

          Cisco Systems, Inc.
          170 West Tasman Drive
          San Jose, California 95134-1706

Cisco Internetwork Operating System Software
IOS (tm) MSFC3 Software (C6MSFC3-JSV-M), Version 12.2(14)SX2, EARLY
  DEPLOYMENT RELEASE SOFTWARE (fc1)
TAC Support: http://www.cisco.com/tac
Copyright (c) 1986-2003 by cisco Systems, Inc.
Compiled Mon 30-Jun-03 14:12 by cmong
```

```
Image text-base: 0x40008C10, data-base: 0x41D16000

flashfs[1]: 2 files, 1 directories
flashfs[1]: 0 orphaned files, 0 orphaned directories
flashfs[1]: Total bytes: 1792000
flashfs[1]: Bytes used: 2048
flashfs[1]: Bytes available: 1789952
flashfs[1]: flashfs fsck took 2 seconds.
flashfs[1]: Initialization complete.cisco MSFC3 (R7000) processor with
  458752K/6
5536K bytes of memory.
Processor board ID
SR71000 CPU at 600Mhz, Implementation 0x504, Rev 1.2, 512KB L2 Cache
Last reset from power-on
Bridging software.
X.25 software, Version 3.0.0.
SuperLAT software (copyright 1990 by Meridian Technology Corp).
TN3270 Emulation software.
512K bytes of non-volatile configuration memory.
8192K bytes of packet buffer memory.

65536K bytes of Flash internal SIMM (Sector size 512K).
Logging of %SNMP-3-AUTHFAIL is enabled

Press RETURN to get started!
Console>
```

If the required version 12.2(14r)S9 or later version of ROMMON software is not installed, go to Step 17. If you have the required minimum or later ROMMON version, go to Step 18.

Step 17 (Optional) This step is necessary if the required version 12.2(14r)S9 or later version of ROMMON software is not installed.

Do not issue the **write memory** or **copy startup-config** commands before completing the ROMMON upgrade procedure.

Issue the **show rom-monitor slot** *x* **rp** command to view the output of MSFC's ROMMON before the upgrade:

```
Console>enable
Console#show rom-monitor slot 5 rp
Region F1: INVALID
Region F2: INVALID
Currently running ROMMON from S (Gold) region
```

Issue the **upgrade rom-monitor slot** *x* **rp file** <*flash device:filename*> command to upgrade the version of MSFC's ROMMON:

```
Console#upgrade rom-monitor slot 5 rp file bootflash:c6msfc3-
  rm2.srec.122-14r.S9

01:31:59: ROMMON image upgrade in progress
01:31:59: Erasing flash
Console#
01:32:02: Programming flash
01:32:04: Verifying new image
01:32:04: ROMMON image upgrade complete
 The card must be reset for this to take effect
Console#
```

Now issue the **reload** command to reset the MSFC and complete the ROMMON upgrade. The MSFC will try to boot the first image in bootflash: If this fails, verify the MSFC runtime image (c6msfc3*) is present on the MSFC bootflash with the **dir bootflash:** command and use the **boot** command to boot this image:

```
rommon 2 > dir bootflash:
         File size          Checksum    File name
   16050204 bytes (0xf4e81c)   0x4221810c   c6msfc3-jsv-mz.122-14.SX2
     649603 bytes (0x9e983)    0x64867cc    c6msfc3-rm2.srec.122-14r.S9
rommon 3 > boot bootflash:c6msfc3-jsv-mz.122-14.SX2
Self decompressing the image : ########################################
########################################################################
[OK]
Console>
```

Issue the **show rom-monitor slot** *x* **rp** command to view the output of RP ROMMON after the upgrade and reload:

```
Console>enable
Console#show rom-monitor slot 5 rp
Region F1: APPROVED, preferred
Region F2: INVALID
Currently running ROMMON from F1 region
```

Step 18 Set the boot variables for both the Supervisor and MSFC to autoboot. Because the MSFC was the last to be configured, alter the MSFC variables first:

```
!Set the boot variable to boot the MSFC image.
Console#configure terminal
Enter configuration commands, one per line. End with CNTL/Z.
Console(config)#boot system flash bootflash:c6msfc3-jsv-mz.122-14.SX2
Console(config)#
!Change the config-register back to its normal setting.
Console(config)#config-register 0x2102
Console(config)#end
Console#

Console#write memory
Building configuration...
[OK]
Console#
!Verify the new boot parameters.
Console#show boot
BOOT variable = bootflash:c6msfc3-jsv-mz.122-14.SX2,1
CONFIG_FILE variable does not exist
BOOTLDR variable does not exist
Configuration register is 0x0 (will be 0x2102 at next reload)
Console#
```

The BOOTLDR variable is not necessary, as the bootloader functionality is contained within ROMMON.

Step 19 The MSFC3 is now up and running properly and is ready for configuration. However, a few things need to be done on the Supervisor. Go back to the Supervisor by typing **Ctl-C** three times on the MSFC:

```
Console#^C
Console#^C
Console#^C
Console>
```

Step 20 If the Supervisor's bootflash: or the compact flash (disk0: or disk1:) was formatted while running Cisco IOS (native), Catalyst OS will not be able to write to the Supervisor bootflash: or onto the compact flash devices successfully, and will only be able to read from them. These flash devices will need to be reformatted and the images replaced on them:

```
Console> (enable) format bootflash:

All sectors will be erased, proceed (y/n) [n]? y
Enter volume id (up to 31 characters):

Formatting sector 1
Format device bootflash completed
Console> (enable)

Console> (enable) format disk0:
All sectors will be erased, proceed (y/n) [n]? y
Enter volume id (up to 31 characters):

Format: Drive communication & 1st Sector Write OK...
Writing Monlib
sectors.............................................................
..............................................
Monlib write complete

Format: All system sectors written. OK...

Format: Total sectors in formatted partition: 251616
Format: Total bytes in formatted partition: 128827392
Format: Operation completed successfully.
Console> (enable)
```

Step 21 Formatting the Supervisor flash devices in the previous step has erased all data on these devices including the Catalyst OS image used to boot the Supervisor. The Catalyst OS image (cat6000-sup720) will need to be copied over again.

Remember that the configuration has been lost during the conversion. An IP address on the sc0 interface and possibly a default route will need to be configured to establish connectivity to the TFTP server again. Make sure pings are successful to the TFTP server from the switch:

```
Console> (enable) copy tftp bootflash:
IP address or name of remote host []? 10.1.1.2
Name of file to copy from []? cat6000-sup720k8.8-1-1.bin
```

```
65535872 bytes available on device bootflash, proceed (y/n) [n]? y
CCCCCCCCCCCCCCCCCCCCCCCCCCCCCCCCCCCCCCCCCCCCCCCCCCCCCCCCCCCCCCCCCCCCCC
CCCCCCCCCCCCCCCCCCCCCCCCCCCCCCCCCCCCCCCCCCCCCCCCCCCCCCCCCCCCCCCCCCCCCC
CCCCCCCCCCCCCCCCCCCCCCCCCCCCCCCCCCCCCCCCCCCCCCCCCCCCCCCCCCCCCCCCCCCCCC
CCCCCCCCCCCCCCCCCCCCCCCCCCCCCCCCCCCCCCCCCCCCCCCCCCCCCCCCCCCCCCCCCCCCCC
CCCCCCCCCCCCCCCCCCCCCCCCCCCCCCCCCCCCCCCCCCCCCCCCCCCCCCCCCCCCCCCCCCCCCC
CCCCCCCC
File has been copied successfully.
Console> (enable)
Console> (enable) dir bootflash:
-#- -length- -----date/time------ name
  1 13389508 Aug 18 2003 16:54:11 cat6000-sup720k8.8-1-1.bin
52146364 bytes available (13389636 bytes used)
Console> (enable)
```

Step 22 Next, set the boot variables and the configuration register value on the Supervisor so that the switch can autoboot successfully. Issue the following commands to set the boot variables and the configuration register values:

```
Console> (enable) show boot
BOOT variable = bootflash:,1;
CONFIG_FILE variable = bootflash:switch.cfg

Configuration register is 0x10f
ignore-config: disabled
auto-config: non-recurring, overwrite, sync disabled
console baud: 9600
boot: image specified by the boot system commands

Console> (enable)
Console> (enable) clear boot system all
BOOT variable =
Console> (enable)

Console> (enable) set boot config-register 0x2102
Configuration register is 0x2102
ignore-config: disabled
auto-config: non-recurring, overwrite, sync disabled
console baud: 9600
boot: image specified by the boot system commands
Console> (enable)

Console> (enable) dir bootflash:
-#- -length- -----date/time------ name
  1 13389508 Aug 18 2003 16:54:11 cat6000-sup720k8.8-1-1.bin

52146364 bytes available (13389636 bytes used)
Console> (enable)


Console> (enable) set boot system flash bootflash:cat6000-sup720k8.8-1-
  1.bin
BOOT variable = bootflash:cat6000-sup720k8.8-1-1.bin,1
Console> (enable)

Console> (enable) show boot
BOOT variable = bootflash:cat6000-sup720k8.8-1-1.bin,1
CONFIG_FILE variable = bootflash:switch.cfg

Configuration register is 0x2102
ignore-config: disabled
```

```
auto-config: non-recurring, overwrite, sync disabled
console baud: 9600
boot: image specified by the boot system commands

Console> (enable)
```

Step 23 Reset the switch:

```
Console> (enable) reset
This command will reset the system.
Do you want to continue (y/n) [n]? y
2003 Aug 18 17:20:43 %SYS-5-SYS_RESET:System reset from Console//
Powering OFF all existing linecards
```

After the switch has booted back up, use the **show version** command on the Supervisor to verify the correct version of Catalyst OS is running.

Session to the MSFC and use the **show version** command to verify the correct version of Cisco IOS for the MSFC is running. That is all there is to converting from native back to hybrid.

Summary

The automated and manual options for converting a Catalyst 6500 series switch from hybrid software to native software and back again can change as new tools and processes are developed by Cisco. Refer to Cisco.com for the latest tools and conversion procedures available.

INDEX

Symbols

F

G-H

Learning is serious business.   **Invest wisely.**

Cisco Press

CISCO CERTIFICATION SELF-STUDY
#1 BEST-SELLING TITLES FROM CCNA® TO CCIE®

Look for Cisco Press Certification Self-Study resources at your favorite bookseller

Learn the test topics with **Self-Study Guides**

Gain hands-on experience with **Practical Studies** books

Prepare for the exam with **Exam Certification Guides**

Practice testing skills and build confidence with **Flash Cards and Exam Practice Packs**

Visit **www.ciscopress.com/series** to learn more about the Certification Self-Study product family and associated series.

Learning is serious business.
Invest wisely.

ciscopress.com

DISCUSS
NETWORKING PRODUCTS AND TECHNOLOGIES WITH CISCO EXPERTS AND NETWORKING PROFESSIONALS WORLDWIDE

**VISIT NETWORKING PROFESSIONALS
A CISCO ONLINE COMMUNITY
WWW.CISCO.COM/GO/DISCUSS**

THIS IS THE POWER OF THE NETWORK. now.

CISCO SYSTEMS

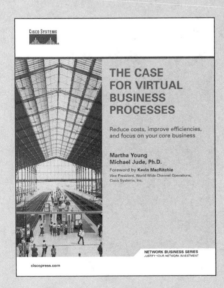

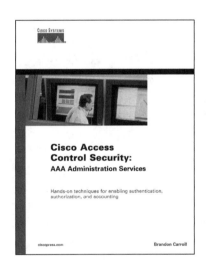

Cisco Press

Learning is serious business.

Invest wisely.

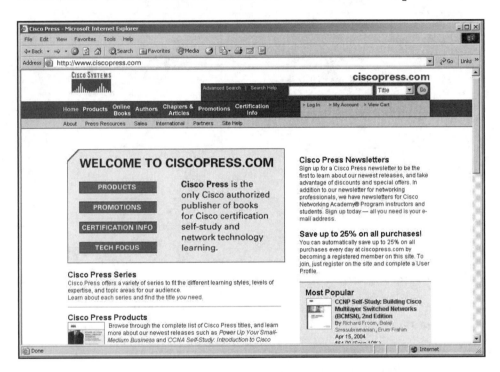
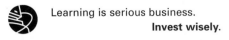

CISCO SYSTEMS

Cisco Press

3 STEPS TO LEARNING

STEP 1

First-Step

STEP 2

Fundamentals

STEP 3

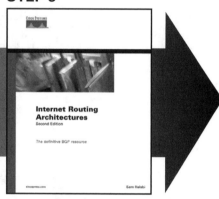

**Networking
Technology Guides**

STEP 1 **First-Step**—Benefit from easy-to-grasp explanations.
No experience required!

STEP 2 **Fundamentals**—Understand the purpose, application,
and management of technology.

STEP 3 **Networking Technology Guides**—Gain the knowledge
to master the challenge of the network.

NETWORK BUSINESS SERIES

The Network Business series helps professionals tackle the
business issues surrounding the network. Whether you are a
seasoned IT professional or a business manager with minimal
technical expertise, this series will help you understand the
business case for technologies.

Justify Your Network Investment.

Look for Cisco Press titles at your favorite bookseller today.

Visit **www.ciscopress.com/series** for details on each of these book series.

SEARCH THOUSANDS OF BOOKS FROM LEADING PUBLISHERS

Safari® Bookshelf is a searchable electronic reference library for IT professionals that features more than 2,000 titles from technical publishers, including Cisco Press.

With Safari Bookshelf you can

- **Search** the full text of thousands of technical books, including more than 70 Cisco Press titles from authors such as Wendell Odom, Jeff Doyle, Bill Parkhurst, Sam Halabi, and Karl Solie.

- **Read** the books on My Bookshelf from cover to cover, or just flip to the information you need.

- **Browse** books by category to research any technical topic.

- **Download** chapters for printing and viewing offline.

With a customized library, you'll have access to your books when and where you need them—and all you need is a user name and password.

TRY SAFARI BOOKSHELF FREE FOR 14 DAYS!

You can sign up to get a 10-slot Bookshelf free for the first 14 days.
Visit **http://safari.ciscopress.com** to register.